RANCH
VACATIONS

Gene Kilgore's
RANCH VACATIONS

SECOND EDITION

The Complete Guide to Guest and Resort,
Fly-Fishing, and Cross-Country Skiing Ranches

John Muir Publications
Santa Fe, New Mexico

The information in this book is subject to change without notice. We strongly recommend that you call ahead to verify the information presented here before making final plans or reservations. All ranches are included without charge to them. The ranches that have photographs have paid a fee to help defray the cost of publication.

John Muir Publications, P.O. Box 613, Santa Fe, NM 87504

© 1989, 1991 by Eugene Kilgore
Cover © 1989, 1991 by John Muir Publications
All rights reserved. Published in 1989
Printed in the United States of America

Second edition. Third printing April 1993

Library of Congress Cataloging-in-Publication Data
Kilgore, Eugene, 1953-
 Ranch vacations : the complete guide to guest and resort, fly-fishing, and cross-country skiing ranches / Gene Kilgore. —2nd ed.
  p. cm.
 Rev. ed of: Eugene Kilgore's ranch vacations.
 ISBN 0-945465-90-4
  1. Resorts—United States—Guide-books. 2. Resorts—Canada. Western—Guide-books. 3. Ranches—United States—Guide-books. 4. Ranches—Canada, Western—Guide-books. I. Kilgore, Eugene, 1953-   . Eugene Kilgore's ranch vacations. II. Title.
TX907.2.K55 1991
917.3—dc20   91-2844
                                                    CIP

Typeface: Berkeley Oldstyle
Typesetter: Copygraphics, Inc.
Printer: Banta Company

Distributed to the book trade by
W. W. Norton & Company, Inc.
New York, New York

Cover photo by Boyd Norton
Back cover photo by Bob Brown

Dedicated with love and grateful thanks
to my father, Eugene, my mother, Mimi,
and my sister, Bee

"Thousands of tired, nerve-shaken, over-civilized people are beginning to find out that going to the mountains is going home; that wilderness is a necessity; and that mountain parks and reservations are useful, not only as fountains of lumber and irrigation rivers, but as fountains of life."

—John Muir

"From the forest and wilderness come the tonics and barks which brace mankind."

—Henry David Thoreau

"All America lies at the end of the wilderness road, and our past is not a dead past, but still lives in us. Our forefathers had civilization inside themselves, the wild outside. We live in the civilization they created, but within us the wilderness still lingers. What they dreamed, we live, and what they lived, we dream."

—T. K. Whipple

"Our world in steel and speed is sometimes a trap in which we become enslaved as we chase after the materialism of life. Thus, we have a tendency to forget that which we too often take for granted . . . Nature's wondrous beauty."

—Bruce Harvey,
Queenstown, New Zealand

"You can get in a car to see what man has created, but you have to get on a horse to see what God has made."

—Charlie Russell

"The Earth does not belong to man, man belongs to the Earth. All things are connected like blood which unites us all. Man did not weave the web of life, he is merely a strand in it. Whatever he does to the web, he does to himself."

—Chief Sealth (Seattle),
Dwamish Indian Tribe

Contents

Foreword

The old West, the new West, and ranch vacations are alive and better than ever. When Eugene Kilgore asked me to write the foreword to his guide, he was aware that I had spent many summers with my family at a great old ranch in Montana. He also knew that I have traveled the world and have always savored artistic and intellectual enrichment as well as the peace and solitude of the great outdoors.

The ranch vacation phenomenon took root back in the late 1800s and today, once again, is taking North America by storm. Fashion and trends change from year to year, but the West, the old, easygoing West, with its beauty, grace, rugged charm, and downright friendly hospitality, has not. People from all walks of life from around the world are rediscovering this marvelous way of life.

Perhaps the best way for me to express the tremendous joy and heartfelt excitement of a ranch vacation is for me to recount my personal experiences at one of the oldest and most acclaimed ranches in North America.

The tall man in the black hat and the flapping bat-wing chaps came toward me, his spurs ching-chinging. He crouched down to my five-year-old size. "Ya ready, pardner?" said wrangler Jack Morgan. I nodded, scared but eager. I lifted my little cowboy boot into the palms of his hands and he boosted me up higher and higher into the saddle, and there I was, on top of Snowball, the whitest, fattest, gentlest horse on the Lazy K Bar ranch.

That was some sixty-two years ago, and I can still feel the heat of the leather of the saddle, smell the sage from the field behind the corrals, and see Jack's grinning face above the red kerchief around his neck. I can still remember the thrill of being high on a horse, alone for the first time, and how the horsehair hackamore reins were prickly between my fingers.

Two years ago I had a similar, but quite different, sensation when I watched a young wrangler boost my five-year-old grandson up onto a horse in the same corral, at the same ranch, and saw the same thrilled look on his face that I had on mine six decades ago. Of course, the horse didn't look as big as mine had, but it was just as white and fat, and when I asked the wrangler the horse's name, I almost knew his answer. Snowball.

I feel sorry for kids who have never had a ranch experience. I was lucky because both my parents and grandfathers were from Montana. They were childhood friends of the Van Cleves, who started one of the country's first guest ranches in the 1920s. It is located in a spectacularly beautiful canyon in Montana's Crazy Mountains, above the little town of Big Timber, and has been a working cattle and horse ranch since 1880. My family first went to the Lazy K Bar a year or so after it began hosting guests and then went back every summer after that for years.

I kept the tradition going with my children, and they are doing the same with theirs. It is the best of all possible worlds for families. I don't ride anymore, but the fishing is great, and while my wife neither rides nor fishes, she loves the hiking, the cookouts, the clean, pine-scented air, and the peace.

Our ranch, as we call it, happens to be rustic and unfancy and almost exactly the way it was when I was a boy. And like the dozens of other families who return year after year, and generation after generation, that's just the way we prefer it.

But these days, there are all sorts of variations on the old traditional guest ranching theme— from outback, fly-in ranches to ranch resorts and everything in between. Ranch vacations are the best do-everything vacation I can think of. Families, corporations, single parents, avid sportsmen and sportswomen, even those who are handicapped, will have the time of their lives. Like my entire family, once you have tried it, you're hooked for life. And the best part of all: you will never regret it.

That's why this book is so needed and welcome. Everyone from individuals and families to corporations and the entire travel industry should have a copy of this definitive guide. Eugene Kilgore is the leading authority on ranch vacations. He has cowboyed in Wyoming, broken horses in Montana, learned about the hotel business in Colorado, and traveled extensively throughout North America to put this exciting guide together. Eugene is a man who is dedicated to preserving the West. He cares about this land of ours and its people, and it shows.

Ranch Vacations is more than a guide. It is a book that will put you in touch with a unique, North American tradition.

With the same zest and enthusiasm of Frederic Remington, Charlie Russell, and Louis L'Amour, Eugene Kilgore has recaptured the West in all its glory.

March 1991   Barnaby Conrad

Preface

This guide will open your eyes to a world of unforgettable pleasure, wholesome fun, and natural beauty. It will put you in touch with beautiful properties in North America as well as the top Western museums around the country and annual Western events in the United States and Canada. After you have taken this guide home and wandered through it, I guarantee that you will pause, wondering how something so unbelievably special has been kept such a secret.

Ranch vacations today offer more than horseback riding and cattle drives. In fact, you don't even have to like horses or horseback riding. On a ranch vacation, you can indulge in gourmet dining, tennis, swimming, white-water rafting, natural history seminars, helicopter fishing, massage, and more. And everyone from grandparents to children to singles to the handicapped can find a ranch vacation to suit them. Ranches offer facilities to professional groups, corporations, schools, and churches for seminars, retreats, and workshops. And they can provide beautiful settings for family reunions, weddings, and honeymoons.

I began researching this guidebook in 1979, while I was working as a cowboy for one of the largest cattle operations in the country, Miller Land and Livestock, which is about seventy-five miles south of Jackson Hole, Wyoming. I undertook this exciting project to share with people around the world a truly magnificent way of life.

Today, more than ever, people are seeking relief from the ever-increasing stresses of our fast-paced world. There is no better way for families and individuals to unwind, recharge batteries, gain perspective, reconfirm values, spend time with family members, meet interesting people from around the world, and, most of all, experience the natural beauty and tranquillity of the outdoors than on a ranch vacation. As we approach the year 2000, I believe there will be a reawakening to our great North American wilderness heritage.

John Naisbitt, author of the best-selling book, *Megatrends*, puts it this way: "To counter a world going mad with technology, man will seek high touch environments to counter the hard edges of technology." What he seems to be saying is that the more advanced we become technologically, the more we crave the simpler pleasures of life. Nature, home-cooked meals, kindness, and hospitality are just a few things that we and our loved ones want, for ourselves and for each other. The vacations described in this book offer all of the above and so much more.

This guide is not the last word, nor is it a history of ranch vacations. It is merely a friendly vehicle to put you in touch with a wonderful, unique group of people who offer an incredible experience. Some call it a way of life; all say it is a vacation devoid of stress, filled with pleasure, and enjoyed by both the young and the young at heart.

Should you not find your favorite property or ranch listed in this guide, please let me know. Chances are, though, your favorite was given the opportunity to be listed. A number of ranches declined to be included.

Ranch vacations offer the greatest year-round vacation opportunity in the world today. Ride on!

Second Edition Thoughts

Since the first edition of the book was released in December 1989, I have been overwhelmed with the interest it has generated. I have had the opportunity to travel around the United States and western Canada, to Germany, to London for the World Travel Market, and to speak on behalf of the American Embassy in Switzerland. I was asked by American Express to be their consultant and to contribute to their American Express Guest Ranch Roundup newsletter and map that went out to over five million card members. In addition, television's "PM Magazine" asked me to coordinate and help them produce a five-part ranch vacation series that was filmed in Jackson Hole, Wyoming. Everywhere I travel, families, individuals, journalists, editors, producers, and bookstore buyers all light up with enthusiastic interest at the incredible vacation opportunities presented by the book.

Traveling around the United States, Canada, and Europe this past year gave me a chance to meet new people, the opportunity to listen and share ideas (I was in Germany during the reunification), the time to think and reflect. People in all these countries seem to be asking themselves the same questions: "Why are we (the human race) going so fast?" "How do we counterbalance a technology-driven world?" The question I heard most was, "How does one counter the stress level that is growing at an alarming rate?" It is alarming to me how technology is so rapidly changing the workplace. What is the remedy for stress? Why are we going so fast?

It is little wonder that so many are reaching back to simpler, less pressurized, and happier times when the pace was slower and things were less complicated and when the word "family" really meant something of precious value. It is not surprising to me at all that so many individuals and families are embracing ranch vacations and that environmental awareness is at an all-time high. Ranch vacations give us all an opportunity to slow down, to share quality family time together, and to ease the stress from the tension of technology.

Ranch vacations today offer more than just a way of life. They offer a glimpse of what nature has so wondrously bestowed upon us. Exposure to nature's wilderness is the best remedy to counter stress and the fast-paced world in which we live. If we are to preserve nature and the delicate balance that exists, we ought to heed the call of the wild. Hopefully we can teach each other, and most of all, our children, that our mountains, parks, forests, and rivers are treasures that must be preserved and protected. They are indeed, as John Muir wrote, "fountains of life."

Finally, I would like to share with you something I heard several years ago at the World Affairs Council in San Francisco when one of our astronauts was talking about space. He said, "When I looked out of my space capsule down at our planet, there were no fences and no boundaries. I saw just one world. It was a sight to behold." Few of us will have the opportunity in our lifetimes to travel into space and see what this man and others have seen. We can, though, imagine what he saw out his space capsule window and think about "one" world, a united planet. Let us all work together for a better world; for peace and understanding, for conservation and the preservation of our natural resources.

Dude and guest ranching is more than a vacation; it is a spirit, a tradition of Western hospitality, warmth, honesty, family, and natural beauty. It is, indeed, a ministry that touches lives and helps to make this a better world in which to live.

Acknowledgments

First and foremost, my heartfelt thanks goes out to my parents, whose inspiration and dedication made this dream come true. Thanks go to my partner and sister, Bee, who has been my traveling companion, editor, navigator, chief critic, and, above all, my best friend throughout. In addition, she has spent hours preparing and coordinating the entire Appendix of the book. I would also like to thank all the ranch owners and managers who have made this book possible. For their help, support, and encouragement, I am most grateful.

I wish to thank Barnaby Conrad—a brilliant writer and artist; a man who has traveled the world and who has a sensitivity for life, art, people, and the great outdoors.

I would also like to thank three gentlemen who have shared their expertise and insights into the worlds of fly-fishing and cross-country skiing: Leigh Perkins, president of the world-renowned Orvis Company, and Vern Bressler, both of whom helped me tremendously with the fly-fishing section; and Jonathan Wiesel, a partner in Nordic Group International and a nationally recognized authority on cross-country skiing, who helped me establish the criteria for the cross-country skiing section and opened my eyes to this exciting winter sport. I also thank Sharon Peterson who cheerfully helped with hours of word processing and translated my written word into print, kept me on my toes, and was always two steps ahead of me. My thanks also go to Wright Catlow, Mark and Amy Grubbs, and Pete and Pat Hillman, as well as the Colorado Dude and Guest Ranch Association and the Dude Ranchers' Association.

I am ever so grateful to my friend Bill Westheimer, one of the world's leading photographers. Since I began work on this in 1980, Bill has given me vast encouragement, support, and advice. I thank Bill Close, Jim Barnett, Carl Livingston, Jules Power, Alan Rosenberg, Albert and Barbara Simms, and Harry Snyder, for their guidance and wisdom, and Paul Alley, Jean Berg, Gabriele Boiselle, Herbert Cerwin, Ray Dryer, Paul In Den Eicken, Ginna Frantz, Eckhard and Edith Helmholz, Joe Kordsmeier, Elvy Peck, Doug and Karla Peterson, Lela Rolontz, and Bob Stack for all their help. I would like to pay special tribute to Dick and Pat Alexander, Bob Bates, Eva Baumer, Mort Beebe, Carl and Ann Berntsen, Melanie Brannan, Barnaby Conrad III, Werner Conrad, Carol Decker, Amy Doelling, Margarita Dryer, Lucinda Dyer, Betsy Farrell, Jon Fletcher, Arthur Frommer, Stan and Fran Galli, Trev Garcia, Bill Graham, Ted and Sherry Guzzi, Walter Hagan, Chris Heffelfinger, Kevin and Lucinda Homan, Patty Jontow, Paula Kline, Rich Lorius, Mary Martin, John McKinnon, Jim and Gayle Murphy, Jim and Helen Nassikas, Lil Nevans, Blanche Pastorino, Bob and Pat Pohl and the entire Pohl family, Dorothy Power, Francis Rich, Cheryl Romano, Elio Sarti, Davyann Schalnat, Eleanor Snyder, Bjorn and Joanne Solberg, Maureen Sweeney, Erik and Lailee Van Dillen, DeWayne Williams, Cal Winslow, Jeff Winslow, the entire Winslow family, and Betty Woolsey.

Unfortunately, limited space prevents including all those who have, over the years, offered their assistance, support, and friendship. I would like to express heartfelt thanks to all of them.

To the many others who have helped, particularly all the federal and state tourism departments, local agencies, and information bureaus, I extend my sincere appreciation. Finally, I am grateful to all those at John Muir Publications for their faith and to the good Lord for his strength and guidance.

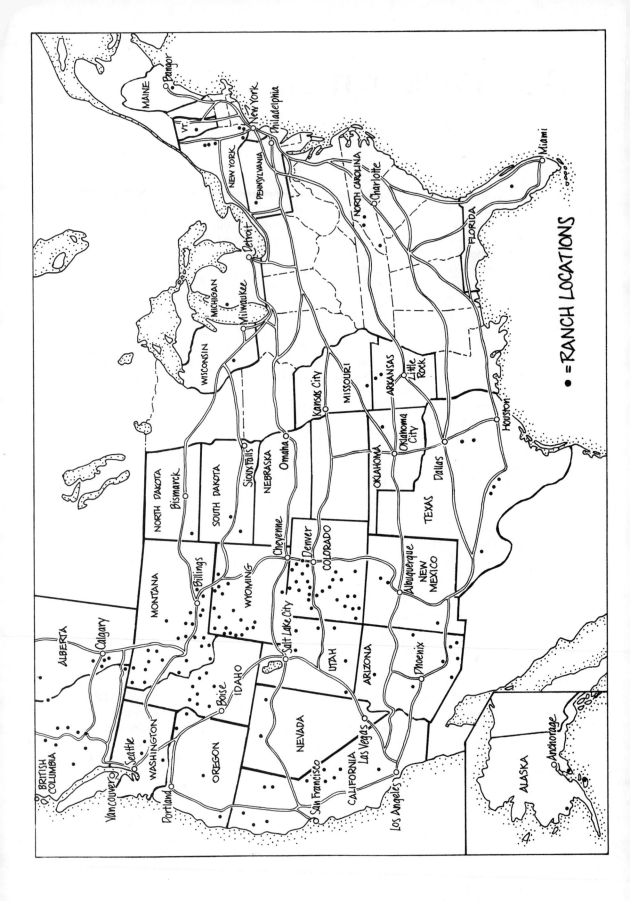

● = RANCH LOCATIONS

Introduction

The Wild West, cowboys, Indians, horses, and cattle have long intrigued the rest of the world. The West's rugged independence, wide open spaces, and rough-and-tumble life-style fascinate us. Every year, millions of Americans, Canadians, and visitors from around the world experience this unique way of life.

One of the most remarkable things about a ranch vacation is the lasting impression it makes, especially on children. Take a boy and a girl to the beach for a week and ask them ten years later the name of it; they will have forgotten. Take them to a ranch, and they will remember its name and the name of their horse for the rest of their lives.

The history of ranch vacations can be traced to the days of Theodore Roosevelt's Rough Riders in the late nineteenth century. As the story goes, the Eaton Brothers—Howard, Willis, and Alden—established a hay and horse ranch near Medora, North Dakota, in 1879. Soon, friends from the East headed West by train to be a part of the Eatons' new and exciting life. Before they knew it, the Eatons were baby-sitting these big-city dudes, taking them out to help with the chores and cattle. The more the dudes did, and the dirtier they became, the happier they were.

Word spread to more of the three-piece-suited, high-heeled tenderfeet, who came out and fell in love with the rugged simplicity of the West and all it gave them. In those days, visitors came not for a week but for months at a time. One guest was so at home on the range that he asked Howard Eaton if he could pay room and board in order to stay on. This exchange of money gave birth to an industry.

The Eaton brothers realized the potential in dude ranching and hosting visitors with varying backgrounds and interests. In 1904, they moved their operation from the flatlands of North Dakota to the mountains of Wolf, Wyoming. Today, the Eaton Ranch is better than ever, run by third and fourth generations of the family.

Soon, other ranchers got into the act. In 1926, the Dude Ranchers' Association held its first meeting. This association is more active today than ever. In 1934, a group of Colorado ranches formed their own Colorado Dude & Guest Ranch Association. In 1989, British Columbian ranches started the British Columbia Guest Ranch Association. All three groups (not to mention all the first-rate fly-fishing, cross-country skiing, hunting, and outfitting organizations) are dedicated to preserving and maintaining high standards in the guest ranching industry.

In general, the underlying theme to today's ranch vacation is the horse. Most of the properties included in this guide provide a variety of riding opportunities—from beginner to advanced riders. Every ranch property is different, however, expressing the personality of the terrain as well as that of the host or owner. Riders and nonriders alike enjoy these vacations.

Today, while most of the properties are preserving the old West, many are keeping up with the present by offering modern amenities and services. Besides horseback riding programs, many offer swimming, mountain climbing, fishing, hiking, rodeos, tennis, skeet shooting, hayrides, llama trekking, and ballooning. Many realize the importance and enjoyment of learning and have incorporated naturalist talks and art and photography workshops.

A ranch vacation also enables parents to vacation with their children. Both learn an appreciation for animals and nature. In addition, on a ranch vacation, people from all walks of life and of all ages can interact socially, intellectually, and artistically in a marvelously wholesome, intimate, and unique atmosphere.

Accommodations range from very rustic cabins (even sleeping under the stars) to plush, modern suites. Some have natural hot-spring pools, golf, and tennis; others feature whirlpool spas, saunas, exercise equipment, and even massage.

Ranches that take guests include guest ranches, resort ranches, working cattle ranches, fly-fishing ranches, hunting ranches, and cross-country skiing ranches. They can be found throughout the United States and Canada and in some other countries. Most are in the western United States (Colorado, Wyoming, Montana, Idaho, California, and Oregon), the Southwest (Arizona and New Mexico), the South (Florida, North Carolina), Texas, and New York State. In Canada, the majority are in the provinces of British Columbia and Alberta.

Ranches in the Southwest or Southeast will have different weather and landscape from those in the Northwest. Native ranch customs, architecture, equipment, and clothes will vary, too. If you want to see adobe buildings and mesquite and enjoy arid, warm temperatures, there is a property in this guide for you. If the sawtoothed Rocky Mountains are your thing, you can experience that, too. Each region offers different attractions and activities. While the location and climate vary, one thing remains the same—down-home hospitality.

On Being a Good Dude
The term "dude" goes way back. Lawrence B. Smith, in his book *Dude Ranches and Ponies*, wrote, "Dude was applied to an outsider, city person, or tenderfoot; one who came from another element of society and locality; in short, a stranger as far as the West and its ways were concerned. As dude was applied to a male, so the word dudeen later was made to fit the female, and the business of catering to them was called dude ranching."

If you feel uncomfortable being referred to as a "dude," you might like to know that President Theodore Roosevelt was one of the first men to receive this name. It could be said that everyone is a dude when traveling in unfamiliar territory. Most ranchers and guests would agree that the key ingredients to being a great dude are a love and respect for nature, a willingness to listen and learn, patience, and understanding. One rancher summed it up by saying, "The perfect dude is one who sees beauty, savors nature's peace and quiet, has compassion for his or her fellowman, and has an understanding for what the host of the ranch must contend with each day to make the ranch holiday seem effortless."

The perfect dude takes it easy the first two days at the ranch and works slowly into the program. "Unwind, relax, don't push too hard too fast," said one rancher to a young options broker from Wall Street. He added, "Remember, you will be able to come back year after year for the rest of your life." Most of all, the ability to relax and have fun is essential to being the perfect dude.

Selecting a Ranch
The ranches included in this guide offer a wide range of choices. The most challenging part of your vacation will be selecting where you want to go and what ranch to choose. As rates are in constant fluctuation, we have chosen to use the following daily rate code:

$= $100
$$ = $100-$150
$$$ = $150-$250
$$$$ = $250 and up

For the most part, rates listed are American Plan with meals, lodging, and activities included. There are ranches that offer Modified American Plan and European Plan rates, and they have been noted. When you are confirming your reservation, it is recommended that you verify what the rates are and what exactly they include. The symbol • preceding the rate code indicates that the ranch offers travel agent commissions.

I recommend that you first turn to the color photographs at the center of the guide. Here you will quickly get a feel for some of the beautiful properties listed. After you have looked these over carefully, making notes along the way, mosey through the rest of the guide. If you have special interests, turn to the back to find a listing of special activities. After you have selected a few ranches, write or telephone those you are interested in. Ask for a brochure.

Questions to Ask

While a brochure will answer many questions for you, here are a few questions to ask when you are making your reservation.

Besides state and local taxes, what do your rates not include? (Rates do not always include gratuities or all activities.)

Children must be what age to ride? Is child care provided? (Insurance regulations may not allow very young children to ride alone.)

Is there a minimum length of stay? (At some ranches you may stay just overnight, others have minimum stay requirements.)

Are there special rates for families, children, seniors, and corporations?

Are there off-season rates?

Does the ranch provide equipment (fishing poles, tennis rackets, etc.)?

Will the ranch cater to special diets? (Some will do vegetarian, low salt, and low cholesterol menus.)

Will the ranch provide guest references? (Usually never a problem. Most guests would love to share their experiences with you.)

Will you send a clothing/equipment list? (Usually standard procedure.)

Should we buy a fishing license before we arrive?

What will the weather be like?

Can we buy sundry items at the ranch? (Not all ranches have stores on the premises.)

Do you provide airport, train, or bus pickup? (Many ranches are happy to pick you up. There is often a nominal charge, however.)

Do you recommend rental cars? (In most instances, you will not want to leave the ranch you have selected. However, you may decide you want flexibility and independence.)

Are laundry facilities available? (Many ranches have laundry facilities; some will even do your laundry.)

Is liquor provided? (Most ranches would like you to bring your own wine or liquor. If desired, you can pick these up on your way, or the ranch will pick them up for you with advance notice. Some ranches offer wine and beer, and a number have fully licensed bars.)

Are any foreign languages spoken?

Are pets allowed?

Do you get the same horse all week?

Can you saddle your own horse?

Do the owners take part in the riding program?

What is the altitude of the ranch?

Are there wheelchair facilities?

Is smoking permitted?

Getting There

Whatever method of transportation you choose, it is a good idea to check with the ranch that you have selected before you make travel plans. The hosts will advise you about roads, major commercial airports, and private airstrips. Should you fly or take the train, your hosts will tell you whether they will be able to meet you.

Your vacation will be greatly enhanced if you make travel plans early. Give yourself plenty of time driving or between flights. A missed plane, lost baggage, or driving all night is not a good way to begin your vacation.

Definitions

British Columbia Guest Ranch Association (BCGRA): An association of Canadian ranches in the province of British Columbia, formed in 1989 to market ranch vacations throughout Canada and the United States. The association works closely with the British Columbia Department of Tourism.

Colorado Dude and Guest Ranch Association (CDGRA): An association founded in 1934, made up solely of Colorado ranch and ranch resort properties and dedicated to marketing and maintaining excellence in the Colorado guest ranch industry. Members meet annually.

Cross-Country Skiing Ranch: A ranch that offers a full cross-country ski package. Trails are normally groomed with specialized, professional equipment. Instruction, guide service, and equipment are available.

Day Ranch: A ranch or ranch setting (Western town) that offers travelers the opportunity to visit and enjoy the spirit of the Old West without providing overnight accommodations. Often there are horseback rides and full meal service available.

Dude: Any individual who is not in his or her natural environment. A business or pleasure traveler who is in another state or even a foreign country. Basically, a dude = you and me.

Dude/Guest Ranch: Usually a family owned and operated ranch with the primary objective of offering its guests a Western experience. Horseback riding is usually the main activity; hiking, fishing, and swimming are often included.

Dude Ranchers' Association (DRA): An association of Western ranchers, founded in 1926, dedicated to maintaining the quality and high standards of Western hospitality established by early ranches. Elected board members meet regularly with an annual general session. Each DRA ranch included in this guide has been designated as such.

Fly-Fishing Ranch: A facility usually surrounded by great natural beauty and offering an extensive fly-fishing program with instruction and guides. Some ranches have an on-premises tackle shop.

Hideaway Report: A privately published newletter dedicated to the discovery of peaceful vacations and executive retreats for the sophisticated traveler. Author's Note: This monthly newsletter is highly esteemed by experts in the travel industry. All those properties that have been written up by *Hideaway Report* are so noted under "Awards."

Gymkhana: A series of games or events on horseback.

Hunting Lodge: A facility that specializes in seasonal big game or bird hunting. Many of these lodges offer activities for non-hunting family members. Some provide full-service hunting and support facilities. Many have father-son programs.

Orvis Endorsed: Several years ago, Orvis, the internationally known fly-fishing company, realized there was a need to check out and endorse top-notch fishing lodges with first-rate guides. Today, Orvis-endorsed lodges are monitored by Orvis personnel. These lodges provide full and complete fly-fishing guide service. Each has its own fly-fishing tackle shop. Each Orvis-endorsed lodge in this book has been designated as such.

Pack Trip: An overnight, multiple day, week-long, or month-long trip on horseback. All supplies, including food, tents, and equipment, are carried by horses, mules, or sometimes even by llamas.

Professional Rodeo Cowboys Association (PRCA): An association dedicated to promoting and setting the standards of the professional rodeo industry.

Resort Ranch: A facility that may or may not have a Western theme but does offer horseback riding. Usually the amenities are very upscale, with a range of activities offered. Some offer facilities with massage.

Rodeo: A cowboys' tournament or competition in which men and women compete in an arena involving livestock such as horses, steers, Brahma bulls, and barrel racing.

Wagon Trains: Original or restored covered wagons that transport participants on day or overnight trips so that they can experience the life of pioneers, explorers, and mountain men. (See Appendix for list of companies.)

Wilderness Lodge: In the heart of wilderness areas, these facilities offer a retreat from civilization. Generally, all supplies arrive by plane, boat, horse, or sometimes four-wheel-drive vehicle.

Wrangler: Originally a cowboy who was hired on at a guest ranch to wrangle horses and take dudes out on day and overnight rides. Today, a wrangler may be male or female, a college student or a cowboy. There is no telling what a wrangler's background might be. The important ingredient is that the wrangler is experienced with horses and with dudes.

Guest and Resort Ranches

Kachemak Bay Wilderness Lodge, Alaska

Mike and Diane McBride call on their special talents to enrich your vacation in North America's last great frontier—Alaska. Mike is a member of the prestigious Explorers Club and has more than twenty years of experience in Alaska's wilderness. He is a master guide, naturalist, licensed skipper, and former bush pilot. His wife and partner, Diane, has a background in biology and will help you to understand the natural history of the region. Kachemak Bay Wilderness Lodge is a hideaway in Alaska's wilderness. It is a place for nature lovers, fishermen, photographers, and those seeking the quiet solitude of lush forests and untracked beaches. The lodge is nestled among the towering spruce of China Poot Bay. It commands a spectacular view of the surrounding mountain peaks, sea, seabird rookeries, and seal herds on sand bars. Kachemak Bay lies at the end of the famous Kenai Peninsula, one hundred air miles southwest of Anchorage, and is accessible only by seaplane or boat. You will see why so many world photographers come. Here the sea is at your feet and the forest at your back.

Address: P.O. Box 956 K, China Poot Bay, Homer, Alaska 99603
Telephone: (907) 235-8910
Airport: Homer
Location: 7 air miles east of Homer
Memberships: Explorers Club, Interpretive Naturalists, Audubon Society
Awards: Listed in *America's Best 100* as "America's best wilderness lodge," *Hideaway Report*
Medical: Homer South Peninsula Hospital, 15 miles; emergency helicopter service
Conference: 12
Guest Capacity: 12
Accommodations: Each of the four log cabins has its own wood-burning stove, electricity, homemade quilts, bathroom, and porch. The main lodge has a wonderful stone fireplace. Private outdoor hot tub and sod-roofed Finnish sauna are about fifty feet from the lodge.

Rates: $$$$. American Plan. Half-price for children; rates may vary for Chenik Camp (bear-viewing camp) and Mountain Lake Loon Song Camp for canoeing and hiking. Rates include float plane transportation.
Credit Cards: None. Personal checks accepted.
Season: May to mid-December; open Thanksgiving
Activities: The lodge is a naturalist's and fisherman's haven. Observe and photograph moose, bears, sea otters, whales, and bald eagles. Dig for mussels and clams (29-foot tides offer great tide pooling), fish for trout, salmon, and halibut. Hikers will enjoy abundant wildflowers, caves, and alpine meadows. Canoeing and kayaking.
Children's Programs: Individualized program. Baby-sitting available.
Dining: Master chef; fresh seafood from the bay including Dungeness crab daily. Fine wine and beer served. Bring your own liquor.
Entertainment: Weekly natural history slide program, piano, guitar, accordion-playing host.
Summary: Without question, Mike and Diane McBride run one of the premiere wilderness lodges in the world. Besides a tremendous emphasis on personal service, both, along with their staff (all of whom have a special interest in and knowledge of the environment), offer a superb naturalist program. Mike is a member of the Explorers Club and is a master guide. Interpretive naturalists, photography workshops, and brown bear photography camp to see the world's largest concentration of brown bears—up to sixty at a time.

Northland Ranch Resort, Alaska

With 45,000 acres, Northland Ranch is right in the middle of some of Alaska's best fishing and hunting. On Kodiak Island, fifty-five minutes by air southwest of Anchorage, the ranch was purchased in 1964 by Omar Stratman and is still an operating cattle ranch with horses and buffalo. Omar runs the ranch with his young wife and their son, Cody. With 11 guest rooms, a comfortable lounge, and restaurant, guests experience a ranch atmosphere and enjoy the excitement of Alaska, too. Besides excellent fishing opportunities, guests can hunt deer, duck, fox, and bear, or enjoy one of 80 ranch quarter horses. After a full day of outdoor activity, guests enjoy country ranch beef, fresh vegetables, and fresh baked breads. In the evenings, guests relax at the Cedar Log Bar in front of the rock fireplace, swapping stories of the day. Many stay up late to see a brilliant Alaskan sunset.

Address: P.O. Box 2376K, Kodiak, Alaska 99615
Telephone: (907) 486-5578
Airport: Kodiak Airport, 24 miles
Location: 30 miles south of Kodiak at Chiniak-Pasagshak Y. (Both of these go through the ranch.)
Memberships: National Buffalo Association, Alaska Farmers and Stock Growers, Scotch Highland Breeders Association, Kodiak Chamber of Commerce, Kodiak Island Convention and Visitors Bureau, Alaska Visitors Association, Kodiak Soil and Water Conservation Service
Medical: Kodiak Island Hospital, 35 miles
Conference: No
Guest Capacity: 24
Accommodations: The Stratmans provide 11 clean, carpeted guest rooms, all in their two-story lodge. Some have private baths, others share baths. There is also a hunting cabin 18 miles away, accessible by horse only. The lodge will provide freezer space for all the fish you catch on Northland Ranch. The ranch is also the Stratmans' home.
Rates: $-$$$. American Plan packages. Includes round-trip transfers between the ferry or airport in Kodiak to the ranch and riding. Daily à la carte room rates, as well as family rates. Children's and group rates available.
Credit Cards: Visa, MasterCard, American Express
Season: Year-round. Open by reservation only Thanksgiving, Christmas, and Easter.
Activities: Superb fishing for all five species of Pacific salmon, particularly silver salmon. Dolly Varden and rainbow trout are in the streams and lakes. Avid fishermen should bring their own equipment. Pick up your license in Kodiak. Horseback riding across valleys and hills that give breathtaking views of the ranch. You may see on various rides the Pacific Ocean, several salmon streams, beaches, mountains (4,000 feet), and even buffalo. Two-hour and all-day trail rides and three-day pack trips, wildlife watching, including whales in May and October. Photography, beach combing, or just relaxing.
Children's Programs: None. Children are the responsibility of parents.
Dining: The ranch serves its own beef and buffalo and will cook your fresh catch. Casual restaurant, order from menu. Delicious country meals and desserts. Everything is fresh. There is a full bar, and the restaurant is open to the public. Be sure to ask Meldonna about her doughnut story.
Entertainment: Tractor hay wagon rides, rodeos in August. The art of conversation thrives at the Cedar Log Bar. July 4th outdoor buffalo barbecues.
Summary: Forty-five-thousand-acre cattle, buffalo, and horse ranch. Ocean and mountain scenery, yearly outdoor play "Cry of Wild Ram," salmon cannery, fishing fleet in harbor. Some Spanish spoken. Best for independent travelers who do not like schedules but enjoy nature and a rural country atmosphere. Most guests tell the Stratmans what they want to do, and they work it out together. Most guests stay 4 to 7 nights.

Circle Z Ranch, Arizona

Authentic Western Ranch, Member–Dude Ranchers' Association

The Circle Z Ranch nestles in a mountain valley at 4,000 feet surrounded by steep canyons, desert cactus, and dramatic hills. Unique to the ranch is a wonderful creek they call "Sonoita" which runs year-round and is bordered by 200-year-old cottonwood trees. This was Apache country in the early days, and relics of the Spanish conquistadors are still found. Hollywood has been here, too, filming *Red River* and *Broken Lance*, to name a few. The Circle Z is romantic with its adobe buildings reflecting the Spanish influence and early West simplicity. A guest ranch since the late 20s, it is owned by Lucia Nash and run by Don and Doris Simmons, friendly enough to be old friends. Excellent horses and a great variety of trails coupled with delicious food and warm hospitality bring guests back year after year. Bird-watchers, or "birders," flock to the Circle Z to see some of the rarest species in the United States, such as the rose-throated becard and the thick-billed kingbird. Whether it's horses, birds, or just the comfortable pleasures of dude ranch life, you'll appreciate them all at the Circle Z.

Address: P.O. Box 194, Dept. K, Patagonia, Arizona 85624
Telephone: (602) 287-2091
Airport: Tucson. Private planes at Nogales International, 8 miles away.
Train: Amtrak in Tucson
Location: 60 miles south of Tucson, off Highway 82, 15 miles north of Mexican border, and 4 miles southwest of the old town of Patagonia.
Memberships: Dude Ranchers' Association
Medical: Holy Cross Hospital, 15 miles
Guest Capacity: 40
Accommodations: There are 7 cottages and 27 rooms with private baths and showers, many with Mexican tile, a variety of bed sizes, and colorful rugs on wooden floors. Electric blankets are available. The accommodations are comfortable and attractive. All rooms, suites, and cottages have individually controlled heat and outside entrances onto porches or patios. Laundry facilities are available.
Rates: • $-$$. American Plan. Weekend and off-season rates available.
Credit Cards: None. Personal checks accepted.
Season: November to mid-May
Activities: There are 70 horses, and riding is the main activity. The rest, as Don Simmons puts it, "is very low-key." Riding instruction, hiking, swimming in an outdoor heated pool, an all-weather tennis court, as well as a pistol, rifle, and shotgun range. Guns and ammunition, as well a certified instructor, are provided. Fishing and golf nearby.
Children's Programs: Children's cantina with jukebox and pool table. Children ride together with wrangler.
Dining: Meals are served in the dining room or on the patio of the main lodge, affording a sweeping view of the valley below. An adobe cantina is nearby; BYOB. Children dine earlier in own dining room.
Entertainment: Mostly rest and relaxation but occasional country music. Ranch has player piano with 100 tunes.
Summary: Riding is the main thing here. Great for people who enjoy nature and don't miss telephones and televisions. Unstructured other than riding and meals. Most guests enjoy the "do what you like" spirit. Bird-watcher's paradise. Nearby attractions include mining and ghost towns, Spanish mission, and adjacent Nature Conservancy preserve. Spanish spoken.

See color photos, page 211

Elkhorn Ranch, Arizona

Authentic Western Ranch, Member–Dude Ranchers'
Association

At 3,700 feet, the Elkhorn Ranch sits in a secluded mesquite-covered valley, surrounded by the picturesque Baboquivari Mountain Range, with canyons, rolling hills, and the open desert to the east. The ranch is small and informal, well out of the city, and with activities centering on the outdoors. It's a lovely part of the Southwest in all its variety. This is a riding ranch, and the Miller family, also known for their other beautiful sister guest ranch in Montana, has been operating this ranch since 1945. Run now by third-generation family, the Elkhorn offers unexcelled riding and relaxed living for 32 guests. The ranch spirit encourages family group fun with lots of time to be alone if so desired. The cabins and ranch buildings are designed in Spanish architectural style. With 10,000 acres and 100 horses, unlimited riding and hiking are assured. The less adventurous can relax by the pool or sun, write, or study outside each cabin. Bring your camera and binoculars as the birds of Arizona are numerous.

Address: Sasabe Star Route 97 K, Tucson, Arizona 85736
Telephone: (602) 822-1040
Airport: Tucson
Location: 50 miles southwest of Tucson, off Route 286
Memberships: Dude Ranchers' Association
Medical: St. Mary's Hospital in Tucson, 50 miles
Guest Capacity: 32
Accommodations: Guests enjoy 19 southwestern-style cabins that vary from one to two bedrooms, some with sitting rooms, all with private baths. Electrical heat as well as open fireplaces. Tiled and cement floors with Mexican throw rugs, some original art.
Rates: $-$$. American Plan. Children's rates available.
Credit Cards: None. Personal checks or traveler's checks accepted.
Season: Mid-November through April

Activities: Some of the best riding in the country. With more than 100 horses, all levels of riding with guides are provided on desert or mountain trails. Rides like Lions' Hotel, Carlotta's Bath, and Mine Canyon are just a few of the favorites. Moonlight rides offered. Surfaced tennis court and kidney-shaped 50-foot heated swimming pool. Shuffleboard, table tennis, horseshoe pitching, and a pistol/rifle range (bring your own guns) are offered, as well as bird-watching and hiking.
Children's Programs: Kiddie wrangler. No special program. No baby-sitting, but nannies are welcome.
Dining: Bonfire dinners. Delicious home-cooked meals served buffet-style in the long house or on the patio. Beer and wine available.
Entertainment: Rest and relaxation. Stargazing, bridge. You are pretty much on your own.
Summary: One of the nicest families in the business. Superb desert and mountain riding program. Excellent ranch-raised horses. Arizona-Sonora Living Desert Museum, Kitt Peak Observatory, the Papago Reservation, and old Spanish missions of San Xavier and Tumacacori.

Flying E Ranch, Arizona

Authentic Western Ranch, Member–Dude Ranchers' Association

George and Vi Wellik discovered the Flying E Ranch from their private plane in April 1949. By 1952, they had become its absentee owners with a resident manager. In 1958, they moved to Wickenburg to manage the ranch themselves. Being guests over those years provided great insights into ranch management and how to keep guests happy. The ranch's guest capacity has increased from sixteen to thirty-two. Today, Vi and her staff get to know all the guests; special service is a trademark of the Flying E. The ranch sits on a mesa at 2,400 feet surrounded by 21,000 acres of high desert hills with endless trails to ride or roam and beautiful desert scenery in every direction. The days are warm, dry, and dust-free, averaging in the mid-70s, and the nights are brisk and starlit. The Flying E is a beautifully kept (the grounds are immaculate) private ranch serving registered guests only.

Address: Box EEE-Dept. K, Wickenburg, Arizona 85358
Telephone: (602) 684-2690; Fax: (602) 684-5304
Airport: Phoenix
Location: 4 miles west of Wickenburg, 50 miles northwest of Phoenix
Memberships: Dude Ranchers' Association
Medical: Wickenburg Community Hospital, 40 miles
Guest Capacity: 32
Accommodations: Rooms are immaculate, comfortable, and delightfully Western. Electrically heated. All rooms have private baths, air-conditioning, and electric blankets.
Rates: $$. American Plan. Children's rates available. Horseback riding is not included.
Credit Cards: None. Cash or personal checks accepted.
Season: November to May
Activities: Very relaxed; do as much or as little as you wish. You will not be programmed every minute. Two-hour morning and two-hour afternoon horseback riding. Instruction available. Breakfast cookouts, lunch rides, and chuck wagon feeds. Shuffleboard, basketball/volleyball, horseshoe pitching, rock hounding, and a lighted tennis court. Swimming in a beautiful solar-heated pool, hot tub, and sauna. Eighteen-hole championship golf course at the Los Caballeros Golf Club three miles away.
Children's Programs: Children are the responsibility of parents; no children's program.
Dining: Hearty and genuinely good food. Cocktail hour with hors d'oeuvres, BYOB.
Entertainment: Occasional "inner ranch" square dancing and "dudeos" (a dudes' rodeo), hay rides, TV, video, and piano in the spacious lounge with fireplace.
Summary: As Vi says, "The Flying E is a spirit." And so it is. All the ranch staff are dedicated to sincere, friendly service. Because of this, most of the families, couples, and singles who come are repeat guests or friends of former guests. Very relaxed atmosphere—you are not programmed every minute. Nearby attractions include the charming Western town of Wickenburg. Excellent golf at championship course nearby.

Grand Canyon Bar Ten Ranch, Arizona

The main lodge at the Bar Ten Ranch is eight miles from the rim of the Grand Canyon. From the modern sandstone brick lodge, one can see in the distance the grandeur of these fabled red cliffs. Since the late 1970s, the Bar Ten has been the launching and returning point for visitors to one of the wonders of the world. The history and excitement of the Grand Canyon and the Colorado River are yours at the Bar Ten Ranch, a 6,000-acre spread with 250 head of cattle. There are no telephones; urgent messages are delivered by two-way radio from town. Tony and Ruby Heaton's guests come from around the country to experience the Colorado River raft trips and helicopter tours of the canyon. The Bar Ten is a wonderful weekend escape offering a unique combination of remoteness and modern comforts.

Address: P.O. Box 1465 K, St. George, Utah 84771
Telephone: (801) 628-4010/(800) 828-9378; Fax: (801) 628-5124
Airport: McCarren, Las Vegas; direct charter flights available; dirt airstrip on ranch
Location: 80 miles south of St. George, Utah, 100 miles east of Las Vegas
Medical: Dixie Medical Center, St. George, Utah; Life Flight helicopter available
Conference: 60
Guest Capacity: 60
Accommodations: For the adventurous, there are several comfortable covered wagons on the hillside behind the main lodge with bathroom facilities nearby. Surrounded by manicured lawns and desert landscape, the two-story Bar Ten lodge has comfortable dormitory-style rooms with bunk beds. The ground level has a gift shop with T-shirts and souvenirs.
Rates: • $-$$. American Plan. Includes everything except airfare and raft trips.
Credit Cards: Visa, MasterCard, American Express
Season: April through September
Activities: The ranch is known for three things: three-, four-, five-, or six-day Colorado River trips; afternoon horseback riding; and scenic morning helicopter tours. In addition, there is volleyball, croquet, hiking, and trap shooting (guns available).
Children's Programs: No specific programs. Children under 10 not advised.
Dining: Country breakfast, chuckwagon sandwich bar, Dutch oven dinners with potatoes, steaks, chicken, biscuits, and corn.
Entertainment: The Heaton gang puts on a terrific patriotic show with singing, clogging, and fiddle playing, country songs with wranglers, and slide shows depicting the evolution of the Bar Ten. Usually the show ends with watermelon and mingling.
Summary: Remote ranch 8 miles from the rim of the Grand Canyon. Most guests spend one night at the ranch and then go on 2-day to 5-day river rafting trips. Scenic helicopter rides, river rafting trips. Video available of the Grand Canyon. Ranch airstrip.

Grapevine Canyon Ranch, Arizona

Authentic Western Ranch, Member–Dude Ranchers' Association

Grapevine Canyon Ranch is in the heart of wide open Apache country at 5,000 feet. This ranch is owned and run by a wonderful couple who know how to combine the best of the Old West with the best in friendly service and true Western hospitality. Gerry and Eve Searle and their staff knock themselves out and do a fine job. Gerry grew up with horses and is a superb cowboy, not to mention a cowboy artist as well. Eve came to the United States from Europe via India, Mexico, and Australia, where she was a commercial pilot and flight instructor. The ranch has been in business since 1984, and already visitors from Germany, Switzerland, Norway, Spain, and Sweden have come to stay. At the Grapevine, experience how the West once was and still is.

Address: P.O. Box 302 K, Pearce, Arizona 85625
Telephone: (602) 826-3185; Fax: (602) 826-3636
Airport: Tucson International
Location: 85 miles southeast of Tucson, off Interstate 10
Memberships: Dude Ranchers' Association
Medical: Benson Hospital, 40 miles
Conference: 25
Guest Capacity: 25
Accommodations: You can select from three modern cabins, two cottages, or several casitas. Each is air cooled. All are quiet and spacious, and most are secluded in groves of Arizona oak, fully carpeted, equipped with full bath, coffee pot, sun deck, and porch. All are individually decorated with a Southwestern touch. Stocked refrigerators in cottages and casitas.
Rates: • $. American Plan. Group rates available.
Credit Cards: Visa, MasterCard, Discover, American Express. Personal checks accepted.
Season: Year-round including Christmas, Thanksgiving, and Easter
Activities: As much as you can or as little as you want. The most popular activity is horseback riding, with half-day and all-day rides. For an additional fee, you can enjoy overnight pack trips and off-ranch riding to historic Fort Bowie and Chiricahua National Monument. Exceptional hiking, beautifully curving swimming pool (heated April to October), dummy steer roping, volleyball, darts, and rec room with pool table and Ping Pong. Golf nearby (7 miles).
Children's Programs: No children under 12 due to insurance restrictions.
Dining: Family-style buffet meals in the simple ranch house dining room. Enjoy roast Cornish game hens, chimichangas, barbecued pork and beef ribs, steaks and roast beef, homemade desserts. Beer and wine available.
Entertainment: Video/TV room with film library, books and magazines, occasional live country music, and cowboy poetry.
Summary: Family and corporate ranch retreat, ghost town excursions, legendary Apache country, bird-watching, historic forts by way of horseback. Some cattle work depending on riding ability. Video available.

See color photos, page 180

Kay El Bar, Arizona

Authentic Western Ranch, Member–Dude Ranchers' Association

Operated by two sisters and their husbands, the Kay El Bar is mostly a riding ranch with lots of friendly Arizona country hospitality. Jan and Jane bought the ranch in 1980 after a lifetime love affair with dude ranches, starting when they were kids in Washington, D.C. This lovely old guest ranch is listed in the National Register of Historic Places. Its warm and friendly adobe buildings are situated on 60 acres, shaded by eucalyptus and salt cedar trees. Since the ranch was established in 1926, there has been an open door policy. Guests don't have to worry about losing room keys; there are none. One word of caution: when you arrive you may be greeted by Trouble, Shamois, and Bear, three fiercely friendly golden retrievers, the unofficial greeters of Kay El Bar.

Address: P.O. Box 2480 K, Wickenburg, Arizona 85358
Telephone: (602) 684-7593
Airport: Phoenix Sky Harbor, 60 miles; private planes, Wickenburg Airport, with a 5,050-foot airstrip, 5 miles
Location: 60 miles northwest of Phoenix off Route 89
Memberships: Dude Ranchers' Association
Medical: Hospital, 5 minutes away
Guest Capacity: 20
Accommodations: The main lodge consists of eight rooms with private baths, each room with hand-painted Monterey furniture, a large living room with 13-foot ceilings, comfortable furniture, a bar, books, and a huge stone fireplace. Homestead House, a two-bedroom, two-bath cottage with living room and fireplace completes the accommodations.
Rates: • $. American Plan. Children's, monthly, and special group rates are available. Two-day stay minimum.
Credit Cards: Visa, MasterCard
Season: Mid-October through April
Activities: Scenic horseback riding through the Bradshaw Mountains with half-day (2 hours) and all-day rides. Heated swimming pool, hiking, bird-watching (over 150 species have been seen), and plenty of wildlife watching, including roadrunners, deer, javelinas, coyotes, and big jackrabbits. Golf at two fine golf courses and tennis nearby.
Children's Programs: Children are the responsibility of parents. Kids under 7 can ride only in the corral. Young children are not encouraged.
Dining: Announced by the dinner bell, excellent family-style meals provide a time to swap stories of the day. American, Mexican, and Chinese cuisine. Food is always good. Honor system at a fully stocked bar.
Entertainment: Card table, board games, lots of Western movies on videotape, large library in main lodge.
Summary: Very cozy, casual atmosphere in a desert environment run by two warm and friendly sisters and their husbands. Singles, couples, and families will feel at home. Historic Registry Ranch, desert Caballeros Museum, Joshua tree forest, old gold mines, and Gold Rush Days each February. Singles are welcome.

Lazy K Bar Guest Ranch, Arizona

Just sixteen miles northwest of Tucson, the Lazy K Bar Guest Ranch nestles against the majestic Tucson Mountains overlooking the Santa Cruz Valley. Owned by Rosemary Blowitz and son, Bill Scott, and managed by Carol Moore, the ranch is run on the "Arizona plan." That is, all facilities and entertainment are included in one nightly rate with a three-night minimum stay. The ranch features a small breeding program for its quarter horses sired by its own registered stallion, Hezasilverbar. The foals provide great enjoyment for children and parents alike. The outdoor swimming pool is heated at a constant 80 degrees, and a nearby Jacuzzi soothes aching muscles at the end of a long day. Guests enjoy the ranch's spacious library with numerous books and can meet before dinner at the ranch's Long Horn Bar for a cocktail (BYOB). While there are no televisions or telephones in the rooms, there is a large screen television in the main lodge. At the Lazy K Bar you will enjoy home cooking, a family atmosphere, and lots of open space.

Address: 8401 N. Scenic Drive, Dept. K, Tucson, Arizona 85743
Telephone: (602) 744-3050 (you may call collect)
Airport: Tucson
Location: 16 miles northwest of Tucson off Silverbell Road. Call ranch for directions.
Memberships: Arizona Hotel and Motel Association
Awards: AAA 2 Diamond
Medical: Northwest Hospital, 10 miles
Conference: 50
Guest Capacity: 75
Accommodations: Twenty-three one- to four-bedroom, modern, single-story adobe cottages. Each has air-conditioning, private baths, carpeting, but no telephone or television. King, queen, and extra-long twin beds. Southwestern motif. Laundry facilities.
Rates: $-$$. American Plan. Rates depend on season and size of cottage. Children's rates available. Minimum three-night stay. Rates do not include trap shooting, riding, or tennis lessons.
Credit Cards: Visa, MasterCard, American Express, Diners Club. Personal checks accepted.
Season: Open September through mid-June
Activities: Horseback riding through desert country, two rides (a slow one and a fast one where horses can lope) twice a day for 1 to 1½ hours. Breakfast and lunch rides. No riding on Sundays. Heated swimming pool, two lighted tennis courts (tennis lessons available), whirlpool, volleyball, horseshoe pitching, trap shooting (guns provided), shuffleboard. Excellent golf in Tucson.
Children's Programs: No special program. Kids under 6 ride in arena. Baby-sitting can be arranged. Kids are the responsibility of their parents.
Dining: Hearty ranch-style meals served in dining area with Mexican tiled floor. On Saturday nights T-bone steaks are mesquite broiled and served under the stars next to the ranch's 10-foot waterfall. Breakfast cooked to order, luncheon buffets, many great Mexican dishes. BYOB.
Entertainment: Team-drawn hayrides, square dancing, Western music, TV room for viewing special programs, rodeos in town.
Summary: Very casual and relaxed resort ranch. Good riding program geared to individual riding ability, and professional tennis instruction available. Ranch store. Old Tucson Desert Museum, San Xavier Mission.

See color photos, page 241

Phantom Ranch, Arizona

If you don't mind a thrilling all-day excursion by mule or on foot down a narrow switchback trail, keep reading. In the early 1920s, Phantom Ranch served as a retreat for the rich and famous. Over the years, the guest book has logged hundreds of entries that sum up the abundant joy experienced at Phantom. Words like "peace," "quiet," and "isolation" are found in entry after entry. Eventually, middle-income Americans discovered the ranch, and now visitors from around the world come on foot or by mule. Phantom offers a glimpse of yesteryear, steeped in stillness and the natural beauty of the Grand Canyon. Phantom Ranch lies at the base of Granite Gorge and is surrounded by high, spring-fed cottonwood trees. The ranch is a welcoming sight after descending the steep 10-mile trail that winds down to it. As in the 1920s, mules pack people, food, supplies, and mail to the ranch. Yes, the mules take everything back out, too. At Phantom you can practice the almost lost art of communication. You may listen and commune with the Lord's greatest creation—nature.

Address: Reservations: Grand Canyon National Park Lodges, P.O. Box 699 K, Grand Canyon, Arizona 86023
Telephone: (602) 638-2401 for reservations; Fax: (602) 638-9247; no telephone at ranch
Airport: Phoenix or Las Vegas with connections to Grand Canyon
Location: 80 miles north of Flagstaff
Medical: Clinic on South Rim, EMT-trained rangers on staff
Guest Capacity: 92
Accommodations: Four dormitories with ten bunk beds each, heated or evaporatively cooled, showers and bathrooms. Beds are made with crisp white sheets, blankets, and pillows. Towels and soap provided. Dorms are segregated by sex. There are eleven private cabins for mule riders, each with a sink and toilet.
Rates: $. Meals are extra.

Credit Cards: Visa, MasterCard, American Express
Season: Year-round
Activities: Six-hour overnight mule rides to ranch and half-day rides to Plateau Point. Hiking, fishing (no equipment or boat provided), Colorado River rafting trips are available with local rafting companies. Camping available with permit.
Children's Program: None
Dining: There are two meal plans: hikers' plan, which is à la carte, and the mule trip plan. All meals are served family-style at set times in the Phantom Ranch dining hall. Breakfasts, sack lunches, and New York steak dinners. Call reservations for details.
Entertainment: Two ranger programs each day discussing the Grand Canyon, geology, wildlife, plants, and history.
Summary: Secluded park ranch at the bottom of the Grand Canyon, mule rides, ranger nature talks. Author's note: While this is a beautiful and tremendous opportunity, people should be in reasonable physical shape, like the outdoors, be willing to endure the elements, that is, the heat, and not be afraid of heights.

Price Canyon Ranch, Arizona

On the northeastern slope of the Chiricahua Mountains at 5,600 feet is Price Canyon Ranch. Since the late 1960s, Scotty and Alice Anderson have been mixing ranching and hospitality on their 19,000-acre working cattle spread just 40 miles from the Mexican border. "We've had guests from around the world except Russia and China," says Scotty. Don't expect anything fancy, though; this is a working ranch. As Scotty explains, "We are not a dude ranch but a working cattle ranch that takes a few paying guests at times." Guests participate in cattle roundups, work with livestock depending on the time of year, and, of course, enjoy plenty of horseback riding. One family has returned nine summers in a row. The terrain is desert mesa, with rolling grasslands, high mountain meadows, and bluffs. Summer temperatures can reach the 90s; winter temperatures can drop into the 30s at night.

Address: P.O. Box 1065 K, Douglas, Arizona 85608
Telephone: (602) 558-2383
Airport: Tucson
Location: 150 miles southeast of Tucson, 42 miles northeast of Douglas
Memberships: Conchise-Graham Cattlemen's Association
Medical: Hospital in Douglas, 42 miles
Guest Capacity: 15-25
Accommodations: Guests are put up in the family bunkhouse, a loft room in the main house, an apartment with kitchen with an adjoining singles' bunkhouse, or the large, cozy people's barn with pool table. Ten RV and trailer hookups available in live oak grove.
Rates: $. American Plan. Children's and group rates available.
Credit Cards: None. Personal checks and traveler's checks accepted.
Season: Year-round including Christmas, Thanksgiving, and Easter
Activities: Daily horseback riding and ranch activities like branding and roundups. Fishing for bass and catfish in pond, solar-heated swimming pool open in summer, pack trips (only if you wish), hiking, cookouts, small jet tub in private room for aching muscles.
Children's Programs: Children are welcome.
Dining: Good home-style ranch cooking.
Entertainment: The main house is always open for guests to watch TV, read, or play board games. Rodeos in town at certain times of the year.
Summary: Pets allowed under supervision. Bring your own horse. English riding on request. Ten RV hookups available. Historical sites, Indian lore, natural well formation, and Mexico just across the border.

Rancho de la Osa Guest Ranch, Arizona

A place where the gracious way of life of the old Southwest is captured and treasured. Established by Franciscan monks in the late 1700s on the border of Mexico, the ranch is one of the last great Spanish haciendas still standing today. Davis, a retired pilot, bought and refurbished the ranch in the early 1980s. Today it is run by his son, Bill, and wife, Cheri. The Spanish settlers called it "Ranch of the She-Bear," and while the ranch offers modern amenities, it has retained its history and its tradition of hospitality. Guests may enjoy a fine string of horses, all bred and trained at the ranch. In addition, visitors may see deer, javelina, coyotes, jackrabbits, and more than 200 species of birds. Rooms and suites are built of adobe. Guests can visit before dinner in the 250-year-old cantina, originally a Spanish/Indian mission. The ranch can accommodate up to sixty people for a sit-down dinner in the 100-year-old hacienda. No golf, tennis, or shuffleboard, just lazy days and quiet nights.

Address: P.O. Box 1 K, Sasabe, Arizona 85633
Telephone: (602) 823-4257
Airport: Tucson International
Location: 66 miles southwest of Tucson
Memberships: Nature Conservancy, Audubon Society
Medical: Tucson Medical Center, 66 miles
Conference: 36
Guest Capacity: 36
Accommodations: There are 18 guest rooms in adobe buildings arranged in a quadrangle. All rooms have fireplaces or wood-burning stoves, modern baths, electric blankets, coffee makers, and ceiling fans.
Rates: • $-$$. American Plan. Special rates for children. Nonriding packages available.
Credit Cards: Visa, MasterCard, American Express
Season: September to late June. Open Thanksgiving, Christmas, and Easter. Tour groups are welcome during summer months.
Activities: Ride the ranch's purebred quarter horses across the desert. Two rides each day, except Sunday, from 1½ to 3 hours. The terrain is rocky, so most rides move carefully. Bird-watching, swimming in the heated pool, whirlpool, lots of peace and quiet.
Children's Programs: Children welcome, but no kiddie wrangler. Children under 7 cannot go on trail rides.
Dining: Meals are served in the beautiful 100-year-old hacienda. Traditional ranch-style recipes, spare ribs, steaks, chicken, and homemade apple pie. Wine served with dinner. Happy hour in the over 250-year-old fully stocked cantina.
Entertainment: Tractor hay-wagon rides, cookouts with country-western singing.
Summary: Lovely old private historic Spanish hacienda run as a great ranch by the Davis family. Very casual and low-key. The 118,000-acre Buenos Aires National Wildlife Refuge borders the ranch property. Nearby attractions include Old Tucson, Sonora Desert Museum, San Xavier Mission. Nogales, Mexico, is almost a stone's throw away. Spanish spoken.

Rancho de los Caballeros, Arizona

Rancho de los Caballeros is one of the premiere ranch resorts in North America. Set amid 20,000 acres of beautiful desert scenery, the ranch has maintained a long tradition of excellence and continues to attract families and individuals who enjoy a host of recreational activities, first-rate personal service, and comfort. In recent years, Los Caballeros has become well known for its 18-hole championship golf course. *Golf Digest* rated it one of the top 75 resort courses in the country! Many do come to play golf. Others come to play tennis, ride horseback in the open desert country, sit by the pool, or just enjoy the relaxing atmosphere and camaraderie. The ranch recently built a superb conference center they call Palo Verde. This center is ideal for small and large groups up to 150 people. Rancho de los Caballeros means "Ranch of the Gentlemen on Horseback." Perhaps what it should really stand for is "excellence." Great people, great resort amenities, and great western fun.

Address: P. O. Box 1148 K, Wickenburg, Arizona 85358
Telephone: (602) 684-5484; Fax: (602) 684-2267
Airport: Phoenix; private planes at Wickenburg Municipal Airport on a 5,050-foot paved runway, fuel available. Call ranch for details.
Location: Four miles southwest of Wickenburg, 56 miles northwest of Phoenix
Memberships: Arizona Hotel and Motel Association, American Cattlemen's Association, Desert Sun Ranchers' Association
Awards: AAA 4 Diamond
Medical: Wickenburg Community Hospital, 4 miles
Conference: 150, 325 (day meetings only); excellent 4,500-square-foot conference center. Ask for conference brochure.
Guest Capacity: 150
Accommodations: Guests enjoy twenty 2- and 4-room air-conditioned Southwestern adobe casitas with private baths, sun patios, and separate entrances. Each room is tastefully decorated in the Southwest style, including hand-

crafted furnishings and Indian rugs.
Rates: • $-$$$. American Plan. Special family, children's, and group rates. Golf and riding packages available. Rates vary depending on season and type of accommodations.
Credit Cards: None
Season: October through May
Activities: The ranch offers slow, medium, and fast riding. Riding instruction on request. Breakfast, lunch, and dinner cookout rides. Four tennis courts with resident tennis pro, swimming, and guided nature walks with information on flora and fauna. Trap and skeet shooting is extra (guns provided). The Los Caballeros Golf Club is rated one of the top 75 resort golf courses in the country. It includes a head pro and several assistants, a driving range, pro shop, locker rooms, golf carts, and rental equipment. Food and beverages available at club grill.
Children's Programs: Optional children's programs for kids ages 5 through 12—riding, swimming, hiking during the day and games in the evening. Baby-sitting is available for younger children. Christmas, Thanksgiving, and holiday programs are popular.
Dining: Reserved individual tables. Menu features four entrées plus daily specials. Luncheon buffets served poolside. Full service bar. Children may eat together or with parents.
Entertainment: Cookouts twice a week, songfests, card and table games, billiards, square dancing, and movies. Bingo games and card tournaments. Occasional cowboy poetry, and sing-alongs.
Summary: One of the great ranch resorts in the country. Championship 18-hole golf course, rated by *Golf Digest* as one of the top 75 resort courses in the country. Golf and tennis pros on staff. Daily horseback riding. Excellent conference facilities for up to 150. Nearby attractions include the town of Wickenburg for shopping, Wickenburg Museum, Vulture Mine, Hassayampa River Preserve (a natural preserve), and the scenic Southwest desert.

Rancho de los Caballeros, Arizona

Rancho de los Caballeros, Arizona

Sprucedale Ranch, Arizona

This is a small working cattle ranch in the White Mountains of eastern Arizona. At 7,500 feet, the ranch is surrounded by forests of ponderosa pine, spruce, and aspen. Owned by the Wiltbank family since 1941, the ranch offers an opportunity to experience life on a cattle ranch and enjoy mountain living in a wholesome, relaxed atmosphere. While many activities are centered on horses, fishing and hiking can be enjoyed as well. In any direction, you will find wildflowers and lots of wildlife. Nothing fancy, just a small old Western ranch run by a great family. There is plenty of hospitality provided by Emer and Esther Wiltbank and their seven children.

Address: P.O. Box 880 K, Eagar, Arizona 85925
Telephone: (602) 333-4984 winter (answering service in summer months). Emergency radio telephone at ranch.
Airport: Phoenix, Arizona, or Albuquerque, New Mexico
Location: 230 miles northeast of Phoenix, 50 miles south of Springerville, 25 miles south of Alpine
Memberships: Arizona Cattle Growers Association
Medical: Springerville Hospital, 45 miles
Guest Capacity: 55
Accommodations: There are 14 one-, two-, and three-bedroom rustic cabins. Each is clean and comfortable, with a wood-burning stove for the cool mountain nights. Twin and double beds, full bathrooms, and quilts made by the family. All electricity is generated at the ranch, so bring only essential electrical items.
Rates: $. American Plan. Children's and off-season rates available. Riding extra.
Credit Cards: None
Season: June to September
Activities: Two-hour rides each morning except Thursdays, when an all-day ride is offered. Branding each week. Guests can work with young horses in corral. Fishing for rainbows and German browns, hiking, watching for elk and deer.
Children's Programs: Kiddie wrangler. Children under 5 ride with parents. Lots of animals—

kittens, several dogs, pigs, and bunnies.
Dining: Three hearty ranch-style meals including ranch-raised beef, soups, salads, casseroles, Esther's famous homemade breads and strawberry, raspberry, and peach jams, and desserts. BYOB.
Entertainment: Weekly gymkhanas, bonfires, square dancing, and weekly slide show of wildflowers. Horse-drawn hayrides.
Summary: Remote, small, family-run cattle ranch. No neighbors, just surrounded by forest. Kids can roam and parents can relax knowing they are completely safe and having a great time. High percentage of return families. Make your reservation early. Ranch may be filled a year in advance. Kids can milk the cows. Apache Indian reservation, Sitgraves National Forest.

Tanque Verde Ranch, Arizona

The Carrillo family founded the Tanque Verde Ranch on a Spanish land grant in the 1880s. It has survived attacks from Mexican bandits and Apache Indians. The U.S. Cavalry, Don Ochoa's mule trains, and even the Butterfield stagecoach have stopped here. In 1928, cattleman James Converse bought the ranch and transformed it from a working cattle ranch to a dude ranch, with massive adobe walls, beamed ceilings, pine log frames, fireplaces, and mesquite wood corrals—all in the Sonoran style. In 1957, the Cote family bought the ranch. In honor of Southwestern tradition and of preserving the desert land and life-style, Bob Cote and his wife, Lesley, provide guests with authentic Western hospitality year-round. They run a first-class operation and have received the prestigious Mobil 4 Star award, as well as being written up in countless magazines and newspapers. Guests come from the United States, Europe, and even Japan. "They love it here," says Cote, "and we love having them." The Cote family's philosophy is simple—provide the very best in friendly professional service in an exciting environment for the entire family. Tanque Verde Ranch is a luxurious oasis and without question one of the country's leading resort ranches.

Address: 14301 E. Speedway—Dept. K, Tucson, Arizona 85748

Telephone: (602) 296-6275; Fax: (602) 721-9426

Airport: Tucson International

Location: 15 miles east of Tucson at the end of East Speedway

Awards: Mobil 4 Star, *Family Circle* magazine Family Resort of the Year Award

Medical: Tucson Medical Center, 15 miles

Conference: 100; 1,000-square-foot conference room, conference director on-site, conference packet available

Guest Capacity: 125

Accommodations: Sixty spacious casitas and patio lodges feature Western decor, private baths, and individually controlled heat and air-conditioning. Each room is decorated with original Southwestern artwork and antiques, down pillows, and Southwestern comforters. Some have adobe-style fireplaces and telephones. Laundry facilities available.

Rates: • $-$$$$. American Plan. Children's rates available. Rates vary depending on season. All activities included.

Credit Cards: Visa, MasterCard, American Express

Season: Year-round

Activities: One hundred fifteen horses; guided daily rides, twice in the morning for up to three hours; breakfast, all-day, and lunch rides; pack trips for beginner and advanced riders; five professional tennis courts with tennis pro; outdoor heated pool; indoor health spa with pool, saunas, whirlpool, exercise room. Fishing for bass in spring-fed ranch lake, hiking, full-time naturalist with guided hikes. Weekly bird banding by licensed professionals. The ranch has banded more than 50,000 birds and 171 species. Golf at two nearby clubs.

Children's Programs: Counselor-supervised programs from November to May; baby-sitting available.

Dining: The Doghouse Saloon for happy hour. Hostess seats you at dinner. Continental and American cuisine featuring Cabrilla Creole and duck à l'orange. Three choices every day or buffet. Enormous salad bar. Weekly cookouts in Cottonwood Grove. Kids can eat with parents or with other children in their own dining room. Wine and beer available at all meals (extra).

Entertainment: Nightly programs include lectures by historians/naturalists. Square dancing.

Summary: Internationally known resort ranch with guests of all ages. Lots of Southwest historical charm and active guest participation. Resident naturalist at ranch and evening lectures on desert wildlife. Delightful ranch gift shop. Nearby attractions include Old Tucson and Arizona-Sonora Desert Museum.

See color photos, page 227

White Stallion Ranch, Arizona

Authentic Western Ranch, Member – Dude Ranchers' Association

Just 17 miles from downtown Tucson, surrounded by rugged desert mountains, is White Stallion Ranch. The True family from Denver, Colorado, bought this quiet and peaceful 3,000-acre ranch in the 1960s. "The only sounds you will hear are those of the desert and the ranch," says Allen True. Guests enjoy Southwest charm and hospitality. One is impressed with the warmth and beauty of the land and the ranch. The ranch features a herd of purebred Texas longhorn cattle and a rodeo each week with team roping, a cutting horse exhibition, and steer wrestling. Many scenes from the television series *High Chaparral* were filmed here. For early risers, there is a breakfast ride with real cowboy coffee. Those less energetic can relax in the cozy living room, read in the large library, or just sit by the pool. Children will enjoy the petting zoo with emus, fallow deer, bighorn sheep, and pygmy goats. Peacocks and guinea hens run free on the ranch, as do roadrunners. White Stallion Ranch is close to civilization and yet so far.

Address: 9251 W. Twin Peaks Road, Dept. K, Tucson, Arizona 85743
Telephone: (602) 297-0252/(800) 782-5546; Fax: (602) 744-2786
Airport: Tucson International
Location: 17 miles northwest of Tucson
Memberships: Dude Ranchers' Association
Awards: Mobil 3 Star
Medical: Northwest Hospital, 11 miles
Conference: 30-75; 1,200 square feet
Guest Capacity: 50
Accommodations: White Spanish-style bungalows with adobe exteriors and a few suites and cabins. Each has a private bath, and most have double beds, rough cedar interiors, and private patios with views through the cactus garden to the mountains. There are no televisions or telephones. Laundry facilities available.
Rates: • $-$$. American Plan. Nightly, weekly, off-season, and children's rates available.
Credit Cards: None. Traveler's checks or personal checks accepted.

Season: October through April. Open Thanksgiving, Christmas, and Easter.
Activities: Riding schedule is posted each day except Sunday. Four rides a day, usually two fast and two slow. If you think you are a fast rider, the ranch has a riding test for you. Breakfast and mountain rides. Nature walks, key-shaped heated pool, shuffleboard, volleyball, basketball, two professional tennis courts, and indoor redwood hot tub. Nature walks. Golf nearby.
Children's Programs: Children are the responsibility of parents. Children under 5 must ride with parents. Petting zoo. Baby-sitting available.
Dining: Breakfast menu-style, lunch buffet, dinner family-style. Wednesday hayrides, desert cookouts, and the Indian Oven are very popular. Happy hour with hors d'oeuvres precedes dinner, when Allen and Cynthia introduce guests and bid farewell to those leaving in the morning.
Entertainment: Mostly guests do their own thing. On request, ranch will organize hayrides or square dancing. Weekend ranch rodeo.
Summary: Lovely Spanish-style ranch close to Tucson but isolated. Part of 100,000-acre game preserve adjacent to Saguaro National Monument. Singles and families welcome. Ranch rodeo, "T-Bone" the longhorn steer, Madera Canyon (bird-watcher's paradise), Living Desert Museum in Tucson, Old Tucson (movie location and Old West park).

White Stallion Ranch, Arizona

White Stallion Ranch, Arizona

The Wickenburg Inn Tennis and Guest Ranch, Arizona

If you can picture yourself riding high in the saddle or perfecting your top spin serve, the Wickenburg Inn is for you. This unique resort combines the informality and spirit of the Old West with the comfort and amenities of today's luxury resorts. This is an activity-oriented resort, where horseback riding, tennis, nature study, and arts and crafts are enjoyed in a magnificent 4,700-acre ranch and desert wildlife setting. A friendly staff and sincere Western hospitality are at their best here. The tennis facilities and programs are outstanding. Riding is also superb, with expert wranglers and vibrant desert scenery. As a desert preserve, the inn has a resident naturalist and an abundance of things to see and observe. Of special interest is the arts and crafts center, where parents and children can sketch, paint, weave, macrame, or make pottery.

Address: P.O. Box P, Drawer K, Wickenburg, Arizona 85358

Telephone: (602) 684-7811/(800) 528-4227; Fax: (602) 684-2981

Airport: Phoenix International, or Wickenburg Airport for private planes, with 5,050-foot paved, lighted runway

Location: 70 miles northwest of Phoenix, 9 miles north of Wickenburg. Ranch will send map.

Memberships: American Hotel and Motel Association, Meeting Planners International

Awards: AAA 3 Diamond, Mobil 3 Star, selected by *Tennis Magazine* as one of the top 50 tennis resorts in the U.S.

Medical: Wickenburg Community Hospital, 9 miles

Conference: 30-75; executive meeting facilities, two meeting rooms with AV equipment

Guest Capacity: 160

Accommodations: *Travel & Leisure* summed it up this way: "The casitas may be the best housing arrangement on any Arizona ranch." Each casita has its own charm and personality. Each comes with a wet bar and a fireplace. Some have private sun decks. Whirlpool spa nearby overlooking ranch. Rooms in the ranch lodge are adjacent to the tennis courts and swimming pool. All rooms have color television and telephone. Self-service laundry facility.

Rates: • $$-$$$. American Plan. Rates vary depending on season. Special rates for children and teens. Group rates available. Tennis clinics available for extra charge.

Credit Cards: Visa, MasterCard. Personal checks accepted.

Season: Year-round

Activities: Riding includes breakfast, moonlight, and sunset rides. Hourly rides are scheduled each day. Riding instruction and gaited horses (Tennessee walkers and Paso Finos) available in season. Tennis on eleven acrylic courts. Clinic with certified instructors and complete pro shop. Heated swimming pool, spa, archery. Golf, gold-panning, and water sports are available nearby; transportation can be arranged. Arts and crafts and nature center.

Children's Programs: Special program with counselors and baby-sitting available during holidays—Christmas, Thanksgiving, and Easter—for an extra charge.

Dining: Continental and Western cuisine from a menu. Licensed bar in lounge.

Entertainment: Holiday "dudeos" in which guests participate. Saturday night cookouts; guests can ride to cookout or take the hay-wagon truck. Western sing-alongs around the camp fire.

Summary: Excellent tennis and horseback riding. Ask about the special brochure on gaited horses. Good for executive retreats. The ranch is on a 4,700-acre wildlife preserve with animals, birds, flowers, trees, and cacti. Full-time naturalist on staff, lots of sightseeing, golf nearby. Desert Caballeros Western Museum, February Gold Rush Days. Close to Sedona and Arizona ghost towns.

Scott Valley Resort and Guest Ranch, Arkansas

Authentic Western Ranch, Member–Dude Ranchers' Association

In the serenity of the Ozarks, amid 214 acres of beautiful meadows, woodlands, rocky cliffs, and spring-fed streams, is the Coopers' white, clean-cut, red-trimmed Scott Valley Guest Ranch. Scott Valley began in 1953. Tom and Kathleen Cooper have shared the joys of their ranch and their down-home hospitality with people from around the country since 1985. Rated as one of the most popular vacation spots in the Ozarks, Scott Valley offers a variety of activities for its guests, including excellent riding for the experienced as well as the novice, on 37 horses. Fishermen will enjoy some of the best fishing on the White (ranked fourth in the world for trout fishing) and North Fork rivers. Both are famous for rainbow and brown trout. You will feel the warm and friendly hospitality that is the secret of the Coopers' success. Children, too, will experience all the treasures of the great outdoors. Guests have been known to say, "It's just like home and being with family."

Address: Box 1447 K, Mountain Home, Arkansas 72653
Telephone: (501) 425-5136
Airport: Springfield, Missouri, Little Rock, Arkansas, or Memphis, Tennessee
Location: 6 miles south of Mountain Home off Highway 5; 156 miles north of Little Rock; 196 miles west of Memphis
Awards: *Family Circle*'s Family Resort of the Year 1990
Memberships: Dude Ranchers' Association
Medical: Baxter County Regional Hospital, 6 miles
Conference: 100; 2 rooms (1,200 square feet), off-season only
Guest Capacity: 65
Accommodations: Each of the twenty-eight one- or two-bedroom, motel-type guest rooms has a full bathroom with tub and shower, air-conditioning, electric heat, and maid service.
Rates: $. American Plan. Children under 3 free. Prefer one-week stay. Weekly family, group,
seniors, and military rates. Rates include horseback riding.
Credit Cards: Visa, MasterCard. Traveler's or personal checks accepted.
Season: Year-round, including Thanksgiving and Easter. Closed Christmas.
Activities: Horseback riding on an hourly basis. Experienced riders should inquire about the spring and fall rides. The Coopers have Tennessee walkers, Missouri fox trotters, and quarter horses. Hiking; swimming in a heated pool that is enclosed during cooler months or in nearby lakes and streams. Ten minutes from world-class fishing on the White River, as well as boating and canoeing. Jet skiing, sailing, and scuba diving available at nearby Lake Norfolk (extra). Table tennis, badminton, tennis, volleyball, and nature and fitness trails. Shuffleboard and nearby 18-hole golf.
Children's Program: Fully equipped playground. Ranch encourages families to interact with their children. Baby-sitting available; children under 7 ride with adults. Lots of animals.
Dining: Down-home, good cookin' including biscuits and gravy, ham, great Mexican fare, corn bread, chicken and dumplings. There are salads for lighter appetites. Special diets catered to. BYOB.
Entertainment: Summer: every evening there is some type of scheduled activity. Cookouts, country-western music show in Bull Shoals (20 miles), hayrides on wagon pulled by tractor. Summer entertainment is geared for families.
Summary: A haven for families to spend quality family time together. Spring and fall months best for adults, singles, and couples (children are in school). Experienced riders should come during these months. Great for off-season bus tours. Bull Shoals and Norfolk Lake, historic Wolf House, Village 1890, Blanchard Springs Caverns, and the Ozark Folk Center. Arkansas is one of the best values you can find for your vacation dollar and is one of the United States' great hidden treasures.

Alisal Guest Ranch, California

This secluded, 10,000-acre ranch is forty miles northwest of Santa Barbara, in the Santa Ynez Valley, near the Danish community of Solvang. Resort elegance in a ranch-country setting is what the Alisal offers, with 30 miles of riding trails, a par 72 championship golf course, a 100-acre lake, and 7 tennis courts. It is also a working cattle ranch with 2,000 head of cattle. Guest rooms are lovely, whitewashed bungalows and garden rooms with fireplaces. Seclusion, sports, excellent food, and pampering are paramount here. While some may wish to visit outside communities, there is really no need to; this year-round ranch has it all. The ranch has been serving many southern California families and movie celebrities since the 1940s. Today, guests come from around the United States and Europe. Deer graze the sycamore- and oak-studded landscape, while guests partake of the many activities or just relax, soaking up California sunshine.

Address: 1054 Alisal Road, Dept. K, Solvang, California 93463

Telephone: (805) 688-6411; Fax: (805) 688-2510

Airport: Santa Barbara Airport with commercial jet service; private planes to Santa Ynez Airport, 3 miles

Location: 40 miles northwest of Santa Barbara

Awards: *Hideaway Report*

Medical: Santa Ynez Hospital, 3 miles

Conference: 200; 5,500-square-foot corporate meeting space

Guest Capacity: 150

Accommodations: Sixty-nine whitewashed cottages and garden rooms scattered around the estate grounds, which feature 100-year-old sycamores. They range from studios with sitting rooms to executive suites, all with fireplaces. All are modern with high ceilings, fireplaces, carpeting. There are no televisions or telephones in the rooms, but pay phones are available. Laundry service available.

Rates: • $$-$$$$. Modified American Plan (lunch not included). A wide variety of seasonal activity packages are available. Ask about the Roundup Vacation Package.

Credit Cards: Visa, MasterCard

Season: Year-round, including Thanksgiving, Christmas, and Easter

Activities: The Alisal's 10,000-acre spread includes 30 miles of riding trails, a 100-acre lake, seven professional tennis courts with professional tennis instruction, an 18-hole championship par 72 golf course, and golf and tennis pro shops. Two-hour trail rides go out twice a day. Riding instruction available. Fishing, boating, wind surfing, swimming in heated pool, and 10-person whirlpool. Volleyball.

Children's Programs: Seasonal, lake barbecues. Summer and holiday arts and crafts program. Baby-sitting available (extra).

Dining: Dinner attire required. Served in ranch dining room, the menu varies daily. Contemporary American cuisine. Excellent wine selection. Summer lunches served poolside. Lunches in the winter served in the main dining room or at golf clubhouse.

Entertainment: The southwestern-decorated Oak Room, with a large stone fireplace and cathedral ceiling, provides nightly dancing, cocktails, and relaxation with live music. There is a large adults-only library for quiet reading. The rec room has a pool table, table tennis, and a large-screen television.

Summary: Superb resort ranch with personalized service, excellent meeting environment, and executive retreat can be booked on an exclusive basis in off-season months. Championship golf course, husband and wife golf tournaments. Nearby Solvang Danish community, twenty-two local wineries, large artist community. Video available on request. Alisal can be booked on an exclusive basis in off-season months.

See color photos, page 238

Alisal Guest Ranch, California

Alisal Guest Ranch, California

Circle Bar B Guest Ranch, California

About twenty-five miles north of Santa Barbara, hidden in the foothills of the Santa Ynez Mountains, is Florence Brown's Circle Bar B Ranch. Cooled by ocean breezes from Refugio State Beach, 3 miles away, this 1,000-acre ranch has played host to guests since Florence opened its doors in 1939. Originally a children's camp, it later became a guest ranch. Today, in addition to accommodating thirty guests (Cary Grant stayed here with his daughter), it offers dinner theater. The ranch's barn has been converted to a 100-seat theater, and each weekend evening from May through mid-December, a semiprofessional group stages musicals and comedy shows for ranch guests and Santa Barbara residents. Whether you are relaxing by the pool, riding one of the ranch's gentle horses, or enjoying the dinner theater, the atmosphere is always informal, friendly, and sincere.

Address: 1800 Refugio Canyon Road, Dept. K, Goleta, California 93117
Telephone: (805) 968-1113
Airport: Santa Barbara Airport in Goleta
Location: 22 miles north of Santa Barbara off Highway 101
Medical: Goleta Hospital, 18 miles
Guest Capacity: 30; Dinner Theater 100
Accommodations: Guests are housed in eight private cabins individually decorated, each with a fireplace and porch. Some have small sleeping lofts. There are also five older ranch rooms with private baths.
Rates: $-$$$. American Plan. Children's rates available. Riding and theater not included. Call for theater rates. Two-night minimum on weekends.
Credit Cards: Visa, MasterCard. Personal checks accepted.
Season: Year-round
Activities: Trail rides take you over the 1,000 acres surrounding the ranch, offering views of the ocean as well as the Channel Islands: 1½ hour minimum rides; 2½ hour rides, and half-day rides (4½ hours) with picnic lunch. Enjoy hiking, ocean fishing, unheated swimming pool, Jacuzzi, golf 12 miles away.
Children's Programs: None. Children are welcome. Children have a good time and make their own fun.
Dining: Hearty ranch cooking, served buffet-style. Tri-tip beef barbecues, chicken, and fish. Special diets catered to with advance notice. BYOB.
Entertainment: Dinner Theater Friday and Saturday nights, May through December.
Summary: Unique dinner theater ranch. Often used as a weekend corporate retreat in winter months. Former President Reagan's ranch is just over the hill. Town of Solvang, wine country, Santa Barbara, Indian caves. Occasional Sunday group brunch and theater matinee.

Coffee Creek Ranch, California

Authentic Western Ranch, Member–Dude Ranchers' Association

In the mid-1970s, Ruth and Mark Hartman sold their house in the San Francisco Bay area and bought a wonderful ranch in northern California. Coffee Creek Ranch, named after the creek that flows through the property, is a 127-acre spread at the base of the majestic Trinity Alps Wilderness Area. At 3,100 feet, Coffee Creek is in a river canyon, surrounded by a mountain wilderness area full of wildlife. The ranch is not far from Trinity Lake and 13 miles from the Trinity Center Airport. A schedule of events is posted daily, and there is always something to do.

Address: HC 2, Box 4940 K, Trinity Center, California 96091
Telephone: (916) 266-3343
Airport: Redding, or Trinity Center Airport (3,000-foot runway)
Train: Amtrak to Redding. Contact ranch concerning Greyhound bus.
Location: 278 miles north of San Francisco, 72 miles northwest of Redding, 45 miles north of Weaverville off Highway 3
Memberships: Dude Ranchers' Association
Medical: Weaverville Hospital (Clinic), 45 miles
Conference: 50
Guest Capacity: 50
Accommodations: All fourteen cabins are completely separate and have carpeting and porches. There are 1- and 2-bedroom cabins, with twin or queen-size beds. Some have fireplaces and pot belly and wood-burning stoves; all have bathrooms with showers and some have bathtub/shower combinations. Laundry facilities available and daily maid service. Satellite TV in main lodge.
Rates: • $$. American Plan. Horseback riding extra by the ride or weekly. Special rates for spring and fall. Senior rates available. One week minimum stay during summer. Two-day minimum stay in spring, fall, and winter.
Credit Cards: American Express, Discover. Personal checks, cash, or traveler's checks.

Season: Year-round, closed periodically between seasons
Activities: Coffee Creek has horses and offers scheduled riding in the summer, including breakfast and moonlight rides. Ask about their riding program in the spring and fall. Picnic and all-day rides and overnight pack trips. No riding on Fridays. Hiking; fishing in stocked pond, Coffee Creek, Trinity Lake, and alpine lakes. Archery, badminton, shuffleboard, volleyball, trap shooting, and rifle range (guns provided). The stocked pond, full of rainbow trout, is also home to ducks and geese. Swimming in heated pool or in Coffee Creek with natural rock slide, and canoeing on the pond. Seasonal hunting of deer and bear. In winter, there is wilderness cross-country skiing, inner-tubing, ice fishing, and ice skating, weather permitting.
Children's Program: Excellent children's program for ages 3-12 includes pony rides, crafts (jewelry making, painting), nature hikes. International counselors. Baby-sitting included during rides for children under 3.
Dining: Three meals a day, all you can eat, family style; fresh fruit, vegetables, and family recipes. Barbecues and steak fries. Ask about their "crazy cake." Beer and wine bar. BYOB, but it must be kept in the cabins (check with office).
Entertainment: Truck-drawn hayrides, bonfires, bingo, talent shows, gymkhanas, live music several times a week by the Coffee Creek band, "The Rattlesnakes," square dancing. Rec room, pool table, table tennis, horseshoes, shuffleboard, and basketball.
Summary: Family-owned and operated with strong emphasis on families. Serious riders should consider spring, early summer, and fall. June and July has the best weather with lots of wildflowers. Trinity Center Western Museum, Trinity County Fair, historical town of Weaverville, and Chinese "Joss House" temple. On Trinity Heritage, a National Scenic Byway. Adults/singles-only weeks. Video available on request. Spanish, Dutch, German spoken. Handicapped facilities.

Drakesbad Guest Ranch, California

Tucked away in the southeast corner of Lassen Volcanic National Park is a century-old guest ranch that is peaceful and quiet, the way it's always been. Forty-seven miles from the park's southwest entrance, Drakesbad is secluded in one of California's most scenic mountain valleys. Surrounded by thousands of acres of forest and oodles of lakes, this rustic ranch—knotty pine lodge rooms with sinks, toilets, and kerosene lanterns—is known for its hot springs that fill the ranch's warm baths and pool. This ranch is for those who like fresh mountain air and quiet surroundings and don't mind not having electricity. One guest commented, "We don't want too many people to know about Drakesbad because we enjoy it so much." There is only one major drawback to this old ranch—its popularity. It gets booked a year in advance. To get on the waiting list, give the office in Red Bluff a call.

Address: Drakesbad Guest Ranch, Lassen Volcanic National Park, Drawer K, end of Warner Valley Road, Chester, California 96020 (summer); 2150 Main Street, Dept. K, Suite 7, Red Bluff, California 96080 (winter)

Telephone: (Summer) Dial operator and ask for Susanville operator in area code 916, then ask for Drakesbad 2. Be patient; this may take a little while. (Winter) (916) 529-1512.

Airport: Redding, Reno, or Sacramento; private planes into Chester Airport, 17 miles

Location: 80 miles southeast of Redding off Highway 36 in Chester; 250 miles northwest of Reno

Medical: Seneca Hospital, Chester, 40 minutes

Guest Capacity: 75

Accommodations: Thirteen cabins and six lodge rooms. All are modest, with creaking wood floors, sinks and toilets, some with showers. Kerosene lamps give an old-time ranch flavor; no electricity; daily housekeeping available; bathhouse for cabins without showers.

Rates: $. American Plan. Discount for stays over seven nights. Horseback riding extra.

Credit Cards: Visa, MasterCard. Personal checks accepted.

Season: Mid-June to early October

Activities: This is not the place for someone who needs something to do every moment of the day. It is leisure oriented and best suited for those who enjoy communing with nature and relaxing. Fishing, riding, hiking, swimming in modern pool heated by thermal volcanic heat. Limited horseback riding is available by reservation.

Children's Programs: None. Parents are responsible for children.

Dining: Breakfast and dinner served in dining room; lunch is buffet or sack lunches. Menu is varied and sometimes unusual when chefs visit from famous resorts. Weekly cookouts of ribs and pork chops, with hamburgers and hot dogs for the kids. Beer and wine service at lunch and dinner.

Entertainment: Star-studded skies and fireside ranger chats.

Summary: Rustic ranch with hot springs and in hydrothermal area. Drakes Lake, Boiling Springs Lake, Lassen Peak, Lassen National Park.

Flying AA Ranch, California

The Flying AA Ranch is in southern Trinity County in the Coast Range mountains. It is particularly popular with private pilots because adjacent to the ranch is a 3,100-foot paved airstrip. Seventy-five percent of the guests fly into the ranch. The ranch has 15,000 acres of its own and sits by more than 100,000 acres of the Six Rivers Forest and National Forest Service land. Though there are no planned activities, there is plenty to do. Owner Larry Brown is a contractor and private pilot who bought the ranch in the 1970s. He has improved the ranch and has entertained actor George Kennedy. Fifteen to twenty flying clubs arrive each year. If you've got wings, set them down at the AA.

Address: Star Route Box 700K, Ruth, California 95526
Telephone: (707) 574-6227
Airport: Sacramento Airport; 3,100-foot paved Ruth County Airport adjacent to ranch. Call for specifics.
Location: 100 miles west of Red Bluff
Memberships: Aircraft Owners and Pilots Association
Medical: Redwood Memorial Hospital, 90 miles
Conference: 100; seminar room 20 feet by 85 feet
Guest Capacity: 100
Accommodations: Guests stay in 26 modest but comfortable motel-type rooms with private baths. No telephone or television. There are also 4 mobile homes and 12 tents on platforms with community bathhouses.
Rates: $. A la carte and American Plan. Children's and family packages available. Horseback riding, trap shooting, and hayrides extra.
Credit Cards: Visa, MasterCard, American Express, Discover, Diners
Season: Mid-April to mid-October
Activities: Daily horseback riding with wranglers through thousands of acres. Instruction available. Swimming in heated pool, hiking, fishing, trap shooting (instructor and guns available), two good tennis courts, volleyball, and mountain-bike rentals available. Seasonal deer hunting. Ruth Lake, 5 miles away, has all water sports—sailing, fishing, swimming, and boating. Photography encouraged.
Children's Programs: Children are the responsibility of their parents. Sitters available. Playground with swings, volleyball, shuffleboard, table tennis.
Dining: The 120-seat licensed dining room is open to the public. Steak and lobster featured. Huge Saturday evening barbecues of ribs and chicken. Families eat together.
Entertainment: Large recreation room with beverage bar, dancing, jukebox, pool table, video games, live music on request, and tractor-drawn hayrides.
Summary: Airstrip adjacent to ranch, Ruth Lake 5 miles away with all water sports. Guests can watch limited cattle ranch activity in the spring and fall. Video available on request.

Greenhorn Creek Ranch, California

Greenhorn Creek Ranch is in the beautiful Feather River country of the Sierras. To many, this part of northern California is a Shangri-la, with its rushing streams, magnificent pine and fir forests, mountain air, and an abundance of wildlife. This 840-acre ranch is surrounded by more than one million acres of Plumas National Forest. Founded in the mid-1960s, the ranch provides outstanding Western vacations for families, many of whom return year after year. Riding is nearly unlimited. Anglers have access to myriad natural and artificial lakes and miles of mountain streams, alive with trout, all within easy driving distance. For golf enthusiasts, there is the Feather River Inn's pine-rimmed course just down the road. Whether you are riding, hiking, golfing, fishing, or just plain relaxing, Greenhorn Creek Ranch offers clear mountain air, meadows of wildflowers, and wholesome family fun.

Address: 2116 Greenhorn Ranch Road, Drawer K, Quincy, California 95971-7010
Telephone: (800) 33-HOWDY/(916) 283-0930 (summer); Fax: (916) 283-4401
Airport: Reno, 70 miles; private airplanes to Gansner Airport, 12 miles
Train: Amtrak to Reno
Location: 70 miles northwest of Reno on Highway 70 off Highway 395; 248 miles north of San Francisco
Medical: Sierra Hospital in Quincy, 12 miles
Guest Capacity: 80
Accommodations: The main lodge is a two-story Western-looking structure with covered balcony and walkways. The second floor has twelve motel-style rooms; the lower level houses the office and lobby. There are sixteen very rustic cabins, usually reserved for families and groups with children. All cabins and lodge rooms have private bathrooms with showers.
Rates: • $. American Plan. Discounts and special rates available to seniors and groups. Off-season rates available.
Credit Cards: Visa, MasterCard

Season: Late March to November
Activities: Activities are offered daily. To some, the number of activities may be a little overwhelming, but you may do as much or as little as you wish. Horseback riding is the main activity; riders can lope horses. Upon arrival, everyone gets a tour of the ranch. Four to six hours of riding are scheduled each day, with instruction available. Swimming in outdoor heated pool. Tennis and golf nearby.
Children's Programs: Kiddie wrangler, kiddie corral, and fishing pond. Separate program for ages 3 to 5 with activities and pony rides. Off-ranch private baby-sitters available on request.
Dining: No choices have to be made; every meal is served family-style. Chuck wagon meals or lawn barbecues. Saturday get-acquainted hour before dinner. Beer and wine served.
Entertainment: Hilarious frog and lizard races, sing-alongs, hay wagon rides, table tennis, pool table, mini ranch rodeos, and square dancing.
Summary: Great place for parents to be on vacation with their children. Rustic ranch in forest of pine trees. Reasonable rates and general ranch discounts. Organized Western fun from breakfast to bedtime. Near Lake Tahoe and Reno.

Highland Ranch, California

Highland Ranch is located in the beautiful Redwood Country of Mendocino County. Secluded and very private, the ranch sits just above the Anderson Valley known for its fine wines and friendly vineyards. Today, Highland Ranch is owned and operated by George Gaines, a world traveler who has had a fascinating international business career. George and his family bought the ranch in the late 1980s and have transformed it into a relaxing, rustic paradise. Here you will find deer and other local wildlife, tall redwood trees, fruit trees, and meadows divided by split rail fences. The wonderful old painted yellow and white ranch house is the meeting spot where guests relax by a crackling fire and savor subtle aromas from the kitchen. Highland Ranch specializes in catering to small corporate/business groups, holiday celebrations, and family reunions. With its proximity to the Mendocino Coast and some of California's finest wineries and towering Redwoods, Highland Ranch is, indeed, unique and very appealing.

Address: P.O. Box 150 K, Philo, California 95466
Telephone: (707) 895-3600; Fax: (707) 895-3702
Airport: San Francisco, 135 miles, and Santa Rosa, 50 miles for commercial flights; Ukiah, 24 miles, for private jets and small planes; Boonville, 7 miles, for small planes only
Location: 125 miles (2½ hours) north of San Francisco, 3 miles northwest of Philo off Highway 128
Medical: Ukiah Community Hospital, 24 miles
Conference Capacity: 12-20. Very quiet 250-square-foot conference room. Audiovisual equipment available.
Guest Capacity: 24
Accommodations: There are eight cabins, most duplex with various sleeping arrangements. Most have fireplaces and sitting areas (a wonderful place to read or write); all have telephones, private baths, porches, electric blankets, good towels, very comfortable mattresses and pillows.
Rates: • $$-$$$. American and European Plans

Credit Cards: None. Master billing preferred for groups.
Season: Year-round
Activities: Do as much or as little as you wish, from wine tasting or whale watching to reading your favorite book. Very individualized program. If you are looking for set schedules and lots of planned activities, this may not the place for you. Wonderful riding on over 100 miles of trails through the towering Redwoods, open meadows, along the ridges overlooking the Anderson Valley or along the Navarro River. Rides are tailored to the individual group with English saddles available. Tennis on two well-surfaced courts, swimming in ranch pool or in several ponds, hiking, fishing, shooting, or simply relaxing in one of four hammocks just outside the main ranch house.
Children's Programs: Children are welcome with a family gathering. No formal programs.
Dining: Delicious food featuring local produce and fresh fish in season is served in the charming country dining room, family-style. Each evening George offers complimentary cocktails and both Anderson Valley and international wines with dinner. Special menus can be planned. The food is scrumptious.
Entertainment: Many enjoy relaxing in a hammock or reading their favorite book. Some tune into the ranch's satellite television. Great local Anderson Valley entertainment.
Summary: Wonderful, small, very private ranch near Anderson Valley wineries and the Mendocino Coast. Superb food and fine wine served. Spectacular redwood groves. Excellent for small corporate/business groups and family gatherings. Lazy Creek, Roederer, Busch, Navarro, Scharffenberger, and other vineyards. Be sure to stop by the Apple Farm for some fresh apple cider. French and Italian spoken. Video available on request.

Howard Creek Ranch, California

In 1867, Howard Creek Ranch covered thousands of acres along California's northern coast. The homesteaders ran sheep and cattle and operated a sawmill, a blacksmith shop, and a dairy. All the buildings were made of virgin redwood milled right on the property. Today, this charming ranch inn is surrounded by bright green lawns and vibrant flowers, offering a simple, wholesome getaway just off the freeway. People come to unwind and enjoy the wilderness, the rustic setting, the dramatic ocean and mountain views. Howard Creek is cheerful, friendly, and countrylike. Charlie and Sally are in the process of restoring the old ranch barn. As in years gone by, the ranch is a cozy nest, close to the sea and mountains with an abundance of wildlife and all the little homey touches that mean someone cares. One guest summed it up, "It's beautiful, quiet, peaceful, and rustic."

Address: P.O. Box 121 K, 40501 North Highway One, Westport, California 95488
Telephone: (707) 964-6725
Airport: San Francisco International
Location: 3 miles north of Westport; 150 miles north of San Francisco
Memberships: Mendocino Coast Innkeepers Association
Awards: Frommer's *The 100 Best Bed and Breakfast Homes in North America*
Medical: Fort Bragg, 18 miles
Conference: 25
Guest Capacity: 12
Accommodations: There are three small cabins (which are by Howard Creek and a meadow) and three rooms in the New England-style white-sided ranch house. All reflect early California character with antiques and fresh flowers. You may listen to the pounding surf or gaze at the stars from skylights and picture windows. Inquire about the boathouse cabin. Some cabins have refrigerators and microwave ovens. All have wood stoves.
Rates: $. European Plan. Winter rates available.
Credit Cards: Visa, MasterCard

Season: Year-round
Activities: Guests enjoy the ambience, the flowers, the very rustic wood-heated hot tub overlooking the ranch, and, most of all, the coastal enchantment. There is also a cold plunge pool, a long sandy beach (a short walk under the overpass), hiking, and nearby horseback riding. To top it off, massage is available.
Children's Programs: By prior arrangement only.
Dining: Only breakfast is served: omelets and Sally's famous fresh blackberry-banana buttermilk hotcakes. When chickens produce, there are fresh ranch eggs. Sally will help you with restaurant selections.
Entertainment: You may sit by the fireplace, read in the library, play a piano, or stroll over the 75-foot swinging bridge.
Summary: Ranch bed and breakfast within walking distance from the beach and ocean. Whale watching, Skunk Train through the redwoods, Mendocino shops, and Fort Bragg. Massage available. Italian, Dutch, and German spoken.

Hunewill Circle H Ranch, California

Authentic Western Ranch, Member–Dude Ranchers' Association

With Lake Tahoe and Yosemite nearby, this old-time family cattle ranch has been taking guests since 1930. The ranch is situated in the lovely Bridgeport Valley in the heart of the Sierras, back-dropped by the sawtooth ridge of mountains that mark the northeastern boundary of Yosemite National Park. It was founded by the great-great-grandparents of the present owners, the Hunewill family. The ranch runs about 2,000 head of cattle over 5,000 acres. Guests can get dirty if they want to help with ranch work. While horseback riding is the main activity, hikers will find miles of trails, and fishermen will be rewarded for the time they spend in nearby streams and lakes with rainbow, Kamloop, German browns, and Eastern brook trout. Camera buffs and artists will have plenty of opportunities to capture nature in her many moods. The Hunewills say, "We who live here love this old ranch and our way of life. We know that your stay will remain in your memory as one of your most pleasant experiences." As Lenore Hunewill says, "Everybody has a great time."

Address: P.O. Box 368 K, Bridgeport, California 93517 (summer); 205 K Hunewill Road, Wellington, Nevada 89444 (winter)
Telephone: (619) 932-7710 (summer); (702) 465-2201 (Mrs. Hunewill) or (702) 465-2325 (Stan and Jan)
Airport: Reno, Nevada; private airplanes, Bridgeport
Location: 115 miles south of Reno, 50 miles north of Mammoth, 5 miles southwest of Bridgeport
Memberships: Dude Ranchers' Association
Medical: Mono General Hospital, 5 miles
Guest Capacity: 40-45
Accommodations: As Bridgeport was one of the early gold mining areas, the ranch buildings have a Victorian flavor. There are twenty-four white cottages in the ranch quadrangle, each with private bath, electric and gas heat, carpeting, and porches. The ranch house is a lovely two-story Victorian, built in 1880 and surrounded by tall poplars. Laundry facilities.
Rates: • $-$$. American Plan. Rates vary depending on accommodation and month. Children's rates available.
Credit Cards: None. Personal checks accepted.
Season: May to late September
Activities: Plenty of horseback riding: breakfast rides, half-day, and all-day lunch rides into the high country. English riding helmets are offered to all guests. Anytime the ranch does cattle work, guests are welcome to join in. Fishing in nearby streams and lakes, nature walks, volleyball, and horseshoes. Tennis five miles away.
Children's Program: "Little Buckaroo" rides (6-11) with kiddie wrangler, resident babysitter.
Dining: Two barbecues each week. All beef is Hunewill grain-fed and carefully aged. All appetites will be satisfied. Wonderful ranch food. Special diets catered to. Don't miss the Hunewill's own mountain spring well water. BYOB.
Entertainment: The Hunewill "Summer House" plays host to square dancing, skit night, impromptu singing, and music.
Summary: One of California's most renowned dude/cattle ranches. Great old California family. Riding is the main activity here. Very casual and low-key. Very Western. Two-day cattle roundup in mid-September. Ghost towns of Bodie, Aurora, and Lundy. Courthouse in Bridgeport. Mono Lake, Virginia City, Lake Tahoe, Yosemite National Park, Reno, watercolor workshops.

See color photos, page 202

M Bar J Guest Ranch, California

Archie and Grace "Bunny" Stockebrand bought the M Bar J Ranch in 1970. Archie, from a Kansas wheat farm, served twenty-seven years in the navy and retired in 1969 as a commander. Grace is from Texas, where she grew up on a farm and became a registered nurse. It was their horse-loving daughter who got them into the exciting guest ranch business. The M Bar J is an old family ranch in the foothills of the Sierra Nevadas, bordering the Sequoia National Forest of central California. On a glacial moraine at 2,700 feet, the ranch has plenty of sunshine. There is a variety of terrain, with hiking and riding to over 6,000 feet. The ranch won't appeal to those seeking "grand luxury" accommodations, but for those who appreciate genuine warmth and hospitality, the M Bar J will provide many happy memories. Some enjoy early spring at the ranch when the hills are green; others love it anytime. One week, there were guests from France, Italy, and Switzerland. Bunny and Archie love people and it shows.

Address: P.O. Box 67 K, Badger, California 93603
Telephone: (209) 337-2513
Airport: Visalia, 40 miles
Location: 200 miles northeast of Los Angeles; 240 miles southeast of San Francisco; 40 miles east of Visalia
Medical: Kaweah Delta Hospital, 35 miles
Conference: 30
Guest Capacity: 30
Accommodations: The nine cabins are well separated, affording privacy. All have excellent beds, modern bathrooms, and electric heaters for cool nights. Two are duplexes, one cinder block, the rest white cedar-batten and boards. All have porches with very comfortable cast-aluminum lounge chairs. Ask Bunny about the deluxe 48-foot mobile home with two bedrooms.
Rates: • $$. American Plan. Children's and group rates available. Weekly stays preferred.
Credit Cards: American Express. Personal checks accepted.

Season: May to October
Activities: Morning and afternoon rides vary, depending on experience of riders. Trails traverse a variety of terrain. Morning and afternoon rides usually with 12-14 guests. Western and English riding available. Hiking in Dry Creek Canyon. Fishing in streams for trout and in the ranch lake for bluegill and bass (cane poles available). Outdoor swimming pool and hot tubs.
Children's Programs: Children are included in all ranch activities and will find plenty to do. Baby-sitting available. Great kids' videos.
Dining: Menus are repeated weekly. Breakfast cookout, quiche, teriyaki flank steak with Caesar salad, roast turkey, prime rib, seasonal baked salmon, salads, vegetarian meals on request. BYOB.
Entertainment: Friday square dancing with talent show, cookouts, videos.
Summary: Great ranch for families. Adjacent cattle ranches and nearby Kings Canyon, Grant Grove, and Giant Forest.

Muir Trail Ranch, California

Since the turn of the century, Muir Trail Ranch has been one of those best-kept secrets. At 7,665 feet, the ranch is the only outpost on the 180-mile John Muir Trail between Mount Whitney and Devil's Postpile National Monument. The ranch experience begins and ends with horseback riding or a hike. After a boat ride across Florence Lake, those who wish to ride will be met by a wrangler for the beautiful 1½- to 2-hour ride to the ranch. In 1990, the ranch began the decade with a new weekly groups-only (15-20) policy. That's not to say an individual or couple could not book the entire ranch for a week. Along with this, guests must supply all their own food, do their own cooking, and bring their own bedding (most bring sleeping bags). On departure, guests must leave the ranch as they found it—spotless. Limited ranch staff are on hand to ensure that all your gear is safely packed in and out, to help you get acquainted, and to maintain the hot springs baths. They are also available for horseback rides/pack trips and to answer questions. This 200-acre ranch is a rustic hideaway in nature's paradise with its own clear mineral-rich and odor-free, two-temperature hot springs (110°F and 99°F).

Address: P.O. Box 176 K, Lakeshore, California 93634 (summer); P.O. Box 269 K, Ahwahnee, California 93602 (winter)
Telephone: No telephones in summer; (209) 966-3195 winter
Airport: Fresno
Location: 100 miles northeast of Fresno off Highway 168
Memberships: National Forest Recreation Association, High Sierra Packers Association-Western Unit
Medical: Fresno hospitals; emergency helicopters available
Guest Capacity: Up to 20
Accommodations: Shelter is in eight log cabins with toilets, wash basins (with cold running water), outdoor fire pits, and electric lights (ranch has a hydroelectric generator). Tent cabins are also available. Many guests like these because they are almost on the south fork of the San Joaquin River. Bring your own sleeping bags or bedding and towels. Hand soap, toilet paper, and cleaning supplies will be provided.
Rates: Weekly minimum ranch rate. Call Adeline Smith (owner) for details. Riding and pack trips extra.
Credit Cards: None. Personal checks accepted.
Season: Mid-June through September
Activities: Beautiful, clear rock pools, hot spring baths with constant running water, nature hikes with some of the best hiking in California, fishing (fly-fishing only on the ranch). Guided horseback rides and overnight pack trips. Fish in glacial lakes, river, and creeks for golden, rainbow, German brown, and brook trout.
Children's Programs: Children should be old enough to enjoy this wilderness experience and the trip into the ranch. They should also be old enough to ride a horse. Those under 6 do not ride.
Dining: You are the chef and are responsible for bringing all your food and beverages. Some groups and families have arranged for their own chefs or caterers who will take care of everything. The kitchen and dining room are fully equipped. Beautiful terrace with wood-burning barbecue, table benches, and buffet-style serving tables. Large walk-in refrigerator and freezer. Automatic ice machine.
Entertainment: Whatever you wish—it's your ranch for the week.
Summary: V.V.S. = very, very special. Rustic wilderness retreat to be rented on a weekly basis by one or more families, groups, or a couple. Accessible by horse or by foot. The Muir Trail Ranch "green sheet" will explain everything, as will owner Adeline Smith when you telephone her.

The Quarter Circle U Rankin Ranch, California

Hidden at 3,500 feet in northern Kern County, among the Tehachapi Mountains, this 30,000-acre cattle ranch has been in business since 1863. Owned and operated by fourth-generation Helen Rankin and her son, Bill, the ranch is secluded and very quiet. Each guest gets plenty of genuine hospitality from the entire Rankin family and staff. Children are welcome and are under the supervision of trained counselors, with an activities program just for them. The ranch has had visitors from around the world. One guest said, "The Rankin ranch is a peaceful oasis." In fact, it is so delightful that many children don't want to leave when their visit is over. The Rankins once wrote, "Please do not leave the ranch without your child." Visitors become friends here, and friends return year after year.

Address: P.O. Box 36 K, Caliente, California 93518
Telephone: (805) 867-2511
Airport: Bakersfield
Location: 42 miles northeast of Bakersfield off Highway 58 via Caliente-Bodfish Road
Memberships: National Cattlemen's Association
Awards: Who's Who in the West; Who's Who in California
Medical: Lake Isabella Hospital, 25 miles
Conference: 36; 1,500-square-foot meeting room
Guest Capacity: 36
Accommodations: There are many wonderful family antiques in the twelve comfortable, wood-paneled duplex cabins named after sites on the ranch. Each cottage has a bath, carpeting, and picture windows. Daily maid service and cribs available.
Rates: • $-$$. American Plan. Children's rates. Rates vary depending on time of year.
Credit Cards: Visa, MasterCard, American Express. Personal checks accepted.
Season: Mid-March through October, open Easter
Activities: Guided horseback rides twice every day except Sunday. Rides generally last about 1

hour. Once a week there is a 3-hour lunch ride. In the fall, if the riders are capable, Bill may take guests on a 5-hour lunch ride to Bull Flat lookout at 6,000 feet. Julia Lake and Walker Basin Creek stream fishing, tennis, archery, volleyball, hiking, horseshoes, Sunday horse-drawn wagon ride into meadow for barbecue. The ranch has a lovely shaded swimming pool area where many guests enjoy swimming in the heated pool, reading, or just plain relaxing. Shuffleboard, table tennis, horseshoes, and volleyball.
Children's Programs: Supervised seasonal children's programs. Trail rides, excellent crafts program, superb talent shows, swim meets, picnics, and games. Children under 4 may not ride.
Dining: Amid Rankin Ranch cowboy photos, guests enjoy three hearty meals in the spacious high-ceilinged dining room they call the Garden Room. Don't come here to lose weight. BYOB for adult patio party at 5:30 p.m. daily featuring the Rankin Ranch famous guacamole dip and chips.
Entertainment: There is something planned each evening. Square dancing, pool tournaments, hayrides. Rec room for all ages.
Summary: A great family running an old-time family cattle ranch. Come here to relax, recharge, and enjoy wonderful easygoing Western hospitality and kindness. Lots of space, peace, and quiet. The smallness of the ranch and the family atmosphere means you won't get lost in the crowd. Nearby is the gold rush town of Havilah. Spanish spoken.

Spanish Springs Ranch, California

Spanish Springs is an authentic working cattle ranch with 5,000 mother cows and 200 head of horses. Located on 70,000 acres of deeded property surrounded by a million acres of public land, Spanish Springs is comprised of a series of ranches and homesteads scattered over northern California's rugged high desert country and Nevada's spectacular Black Rock Desert. Guests may choose from a wide range of outdoor adventure vacations and authentic western ranch activities suitable for families and singles, beginners and experienced riders.

Address: P.O. Box 70 K, Ravendale, California 96123 (reservations); 1102 Second St., Dept. K, San Rafael, California 94901 (business office)
Telephone: (800) 272-8282 (California); (800) 228-0279 (out of state); (415) 456-8600 (general office); Fax: (415) 456-4073; ranch phone: (916) 234-2050; Fax: (916) 234-2041.
Airport: Reno; Lassen County Airport in Susanville; public airstrip in Ravendale, 6 miles from ranch
Location: 125 miles northwest of Reno, 45 miles northeast of Susanville
Medical: Susanville Hospital, 45 minutes
Conference: 100 overnight, 250 corporate/group day cookouts
Guest Capacity: 65; 100 including all outlying ranches
Accommodations: Accommodations vary depending on the ranch you choose to visit. Spanish Springs headquarters is the most modern of all the ranches and is still growing. Guests stay in one of the newly built log cabins or the deluxe bunkhouse with private rooms and two large bunk rooms. Great for large families or groups. There are also comfortable wood-sided duplex units and Western suites. For the experienced rider/adventurer, the old, refurbished outlying ranches—The Marr, Evans, Horne, Cold Springs Camp, and historic Soldier Meadows—all provide a private, remote Western setting.
Rates: • $$. American Plan. Children's rates and special package/group rates available.
Credit Cards: Visa, MasterCard, American Express
Season: Year-round, including Thanksgiving, Christmas, and Easter
Activities: Summer offers tremendous riding potential, from half-hour lessons and barrel racing in the professional rodeo arena to all-day trail rides. The terrain is varied, as is the riding. Three- to ten-day pack trips. Excellent fishing in ranch-stocked trout ponds. Outdoor heated swimming pool. Skeet shooting (guns provided), archery, horseshoes. Tennis, volleyball, shuffleboard. Seasonal hunting for deer, antelope, pheasant, dove, chukker, duck, geese, and buffalo. In winter, weather permitting, guests enjoy cross-country skiing, horse-drawn sleigh rides, sledding, and ice skating. Working ranch vacations include authentic spring and fall round-ups, brandings, cattle and horse drives. Special annual events include wild horse viewings in the spring, a 5-day Black Rock Desert Trail Ride, and 4th of July Junior Rodeo.
Children's Programs: Flexible children's programs. Baby-sitting available with advance notice.
Dining: Western-style meals are served family-style in the intimate, comfortable dining room. Large outdoor barbecue area will accommodate over 250. Sunday champagne brunch served. Bill of fare includes famous Harris Ranch beef.
Entertainment: Western beer and wine bar in the main lodge. Cowboy sing-alongs, camp fires, hay wagon rides, ranch rodeos in professional arena with bucking stock, roping, penning, cutting horse, and gymkhana competitions.
Summary: Seventy-thousand-acre ranch that encompasses a series of new and older outlying ranches. A wide variety of accommodations and western activities. Excellent for family reunions. Well-stocked western apparel ranch store. Spring horse drives. Authentic spring and fall cattle drives and round-ups. You may see wild horses, antelope, and buffalo. Nearby airstrip. Color brochure, newsletter, and video available on request.

See color photos, page 188

Trinity Mountain Meadow Resort, California

This lovely mountain lodge is in the Trinity Alps Wilderness Area, at 5,072 feet. It is owned by ten California families who have operated it since 1976 with a common dedication and love for the wilderness. Surrounded by spectacular jagged peaks, the lodge site was once a trading post for packers and miners in this historic gold mine district. Today, the lodge offers families a host of activities in this mountain paradise. Each day begins and ends with good food and hospitality. It's a great, rustic family vacation, and you don't have to sleep in a tent or cook!

Address: Coffee Creek Road, Star Route 2, Box 5700 K, Trinity Center, California 96091 (summer); 24225 K Summit Woods Drive, Los Gatos, California 95030 (winter)
Telephone: (916) 462-4677 (summer); (408) 353-1663 (winter)
Airport: Redding Municipal Airport, 90 miles; Trinity Center Airport, 29 miles from ranch, where private planes will be met
Location: 6 hours north of San Francisco off I-5, 2 hours northwest of Redding off Highway 299
Medical: Memorial Hospital in Redding, 90 miles; California Highway Patrol emergency helicopter available
Conference: 40
Guest Capacity: 40
Accommodations: Ten rustic one-room family cabins with baths and heaters, double and king-size beds, and bunk beds for kids. All linens provided. Four very small lodge rooms above dining room with a bath at the end of the hall, each with beautiful mountain views.
Rates: $. American Plan. Children's and teenagers' rates available.
Credit Cards: None. Personal checks or cash accepted.
Season: Late June through August
Activities: The beauty of this area can be enjoyed by everyone from the rugged hiker to the sportsman or sportswoman who enjoys a day in the wilderness followed by a dip in the heated pool.

Spinning and fly-fishing at headwaters of the Salmon River. For the historian who wants to relive the days of the gold miners, there are trails with many relics. There is plenty of fishing and endless subjects for the photographer's lens. Bring your own horse; mountain bikes available.
Children's Programs: Full program, early supervised dinner hour, crafts, hikes, 9 a.m. to 5 p.m. child care available.
Dining: Family-style in the main dining room of the lodge. Nothing fancy, just wholesome, plentiful, and delicious. Weekly Mexican dinners and turkey buffet with all the trimmings. Beer and wine available.
Entertainment: Camp fires, sing-alongs, conversation. People like to talk to each other here. Volleyball on request.
Summary: An excellent family place. Very compatible families gather here. Hiking, fishing, photography seminars. You may bring your own horse. Great for family reunions. Dorleska and Yellow Rose gold mines.

Aspen Canyon Ranch, Colorado

Authentic Western Ranch, Member–Dude Ranchers' Association

In 1987, petroleum engineer Ron Mitchell and his family bought a beautiful ranch that straddles the Williams Fork River in Grand County. The family has transformed this lovely old ranch into the Aspen Canyon Ranch, a new guest facility with old Colorado mountain flavor. Aspen Canyon Ranch works its cattle herd in the heart of some of Colorado's best fishing and hunting, with, of course, miles of mountain trails for horseback riding and hiking. The buildings are on the site of an old settlement up the Williams Fork. Local history includes many fascinating tales of the early settlers, giving the ranch a real connection with the Old West. While the Mitchells offer lots of activities, one of the favorites is savoring the magical lullaby of the Williams Fork River as it runs by the guest cabins.

Address: 13206 County Road 3K, Star Route, Parshall, Colorado 80468
Telephone: (303) 725-3518 (ranch), Fax: (303) 724-3559; (812) 473-8747 (business office), Fax: (812) 473-8748
Airport: Denver; private aircraft to Kremmling Airfield
Train: Amtrak to Granby
Location: 25 miles north of Silverthorne, 90 miles west of Denver road sign
Memberships: Colorado Dude and Guest Ranch Association, Dude Ranchers' Association, Colorado Guides and Outfitters
Medical: Kremmling Hospital, 26 miles
Conference: 24
Guest Capacity: 24
Accommodations: Guests stay in three new four-plex log cabins. Each is on the banks of the Williams Fork River, and all have comfortable accommodations, natural gas fireplaces, flannel comforters, carpeting, freshly baked cookies, refrigerators and coffee makers, porches, and old-fashioned swings. A new one-story main lodge, with a wonderful porch on the river's edge, has recently been completed.
Rates: • $-$$. American Plan. Children's, off-season, group, and hunting rates available. Children under 3 free. Baby-sitting available.
Credit Cards: Visa, MasterCard, American Express
Season: Early May through October. Open for hunting October through mid-November.
Activities: Guests will enjoy walking outside their cabins to cast a line into the Williams Fork River for brook, brown, and rainbow trout. Fishing gear available. Half-day and all-day riding, hiking (ask about the Lake Evelyn picnic hike), pack trips, seasonal hunting, mountain bikes available. Guests can participate in seasonal cattle work. Golf, tennis, and ballooning 30 miles. Ranch gymkhana, calf roping, and barrel racing in professional-size rodeo ring. Rafting on the Colorado River is available each week.
Children's Programs: Peggy Mitchell has a background of twenty-five years in children's television as host of her own show. She brings to the ranch a full activity program, as well as her famous puppets. Children under 12 ride in ring and on simple trail rides. Programs for children 3-12. Children may learn how to rope.
Dining: Hearty ranch cooking served family-style with a gourmet flair. Fresh trout, barbecues, and cookouts. Lunches include soups, salad bar, and sandwich buffet. House specialties: steaks, ribs, chicken, and freshly baked pies and cookies. BYOB.
Entertainment: Sing-alongs, square dancing, tractor hayrides, and weekly rodeos in town with demonstration barrel racing and steer roping. Weekly wildlife and Indian talks.
Summary: Small, very friendly guest ranch. Wonderful cabin amenities. Once they arrive, guests don't want to leave. For those who wish, there are the towns of Breckenridge, Vail, and Keystone for shopping, Rocky Mountain National Park, old mining town of Georgetown.

Aspen Lodge Ranch Resort, Colorado

Nestled within a mountain forest of the 9,000-foot Tahosa Valley, the Aspen Lodge may look rustic on the outside, but it is a plush resort on the inside. This unique combination makes it one of Colorado's premier full-service resort ranches and conference centers. This beautiful facility adds a new dimension to executive conference retreats. Fresh air, spectacular views, and quiet surroundings provide an environment that "charges inner batteries, relieves stress, and makes for a tremendously positive work/vacation opportunity for everyone." The focal point of the Aspen Lodge is the newly constructed conference center. Built of lodgepole pine, this magnificent 33,000-square-foot structure is one of the largest log buildings in Colorado. With access to more than 2,000 acres of wooded mountainside and alpine meadows, the Aspen Lodge Ranch Resort offers both summer and winter activities in rustic elegance.

Address: 6120 Highway 7K, Longs Peak Route, Estes Park, Colorado 80517
Telephone: (303) 586-8133, (800) 332-MTNS (6867) nationwide; Fax: (303) 586-8133, ext. 403
Airport: Denver
Location: 7 miles south of Estes Park, 65 miles northwest of Denver off I-25
Memberships: Colorado Dude and Guest Ranch Association
Award: Mobil 3 Star, AAA 3 Diamond
Medical: Elizabeth Knudson Memorial Hospital, 7 miles
Conference: 150; excellent conference facilities
Guest Capacity: 150
Accommodations: The lodge features several hospitality suites and thirty-six executive guest rooms. Separate from the main lodge are twenty-one multiroom, quiet cabins with porches. The Executive Haus has its own hospitality suite, library, and meeting room. Each is designed in a rustic yet elegant style to ensure a comfortable and pleasurable stay. Some with fireplaces, all carpeted.

Rates: • $-$$. American Plan. Horseback riding and equipment rentals (fishing poles, tennis rackets, mountain bikes) extra. Children's, conference, and group rates available. Check with ranch for special winter rates. No minimum stay.
Credit Cards: Visa, MasterCard, American Express, Diners Club, Discover
Season: Year-round
Activities: Summer programs include an excellent horse plan, with rides for all levels. Various horseback packages available. The average excursion has 12 to 15 riders. Weeklong instructional program for kids and adults. Fishing, hiking, climbing, and heated outdoor pool with whirlpool. Two lighted tennis courts, two racketball courts, health club with weights and exercise room, sauna. River rafting and jeep trips can be arranged. Mountain bikes, volleyball, horseshoes. Eighteen-hole par 70 golf course nearby. Winter brings cross-country skiing, snowmobiling, ice skating, tobogganing, sleigh rides, and downhill skiing in nearby Rocky Mountain National Park.
Children's Programs: Extensive children's program. Baby-sitting available.
Dining: Beautiful Longs Peak is framed through the dining room windows. Excellent cuisine featured in the lodge's Ptarmigan's Restaurant, which offers fine American/Western cuisine—everything from steaks to seafood, trout to wild game such as elk, venison, buffalo, and quail.
Entertainment: Hayrides, square dancing, melodramas, barbecues, movies, weekend entertainers.
Summary: Executive conference facilities. Wheelchair facilities available. Van tours to Rocky Mountain National Park, Enos Mills Museum (named after the founder of Rocky Mountain National Park), and many quaint shops in Estes Park. Video available on request.

Bar Lazy J, Colorado

Authentic Western Ranch, Member–Dude Ranchers'
Association

The Bar Lazy J guest ranch began entertaining guests in 1912, when it was known as the Buckhorn Lodge. It is situated on the Colorado River at an elevation of 7,500 feet, about a half-mile from the little town of Parshall. In 1987, Larry and Barb Harmon bought the ranch. Like many, they had been guests at various dude ranches and fell in love with this wonderful way of life. Along with a wonderful staff, the Harmons serve up plenty of western hospitality. A unique feature of the ranch is the beautiful Gold Medal trout river offering anglers the opportunity to fish right outside their cabin doors for rainbow trout and German browns, using both spinning and fly-fishing gear. Horseback riding is the main activity at the ranch. Small groups of riders have a choice of walking, trotting, or loping rides. Larry and Barb have put together a wonderful children's program, which begins at 8:30 a.m. each day for children ages 3 and older. Parents can relax here knowing that their kids are safe, happy, and having lots of fun. At the Bar Lazy J you can ride, fish, read, or just get downright lazy and listen to the Colorado River sing its song right outside your cabin.

Address: P.O. Box NK, Parshall, Colorado 80468
Telephone: (303) 725-3437
Airport: Denver
Location: 15 miles west of Granby off Highway 40, 100 miles northwest of Denver
Memberships: Dude Ranchers' Association, Colorado Dude and Guest Ranch Association
Medical: Kremmling Hospital, 13 miles
Guest Capacity: 40
Accommodations: Guests stay in fourteen spacious, modern log cabins, accommodating two to eight people each. Each is named after wildflowers or fishing flies. Bathroom and thermostatically controlled heat in each.
Rates: • $. American Plan. Children's and off-season rates available.
Credit Cards: None
Season: June through September
Activities: Each guest receives a rawhide bolo name tag on arrival which helps everyone to get to know each other. Gold medal fishing with fishing clinic, if desired. Horseback riding for all levels of experience. Breakfast rides, half-day rides, and all-day rides through open cattle grazing fields dotted with sage. Slow, medium, and fast rides in small groups. Hiking, outdoor heated swimming pool, shuffleboard, horseshoes, volleyball. River rafting nearby. Hunting October and November.
Children's Programs: "Ranch Fun" is for kids 3 years and older. It can be a full day of supervised ranch activity including horseback riding. The program is flexible and optional. Children's playroom and dining room. Young children may go on trail rides if the wranglers feel they are able to.
Dining: Each meal is a joy, served family-style in a beautiful log dining room. Weekly steak fries, barbecue ribs, and Mexican buffet. Enjoy homemade soup, breads, pies, and cakes. BYOB.
Entertainment: Camp fires, hayrides, staff shows, and square dancing in the rec room barn.
Summary: One of the oldest guest ranches in Colorado located along the Colorado River. Great children's program, which allows parents to be on vacation, too. Riding instruction and fishing clinics. Afternoon drives to Rocky Mountain National Park.

Cherokee Park Ranch, Colorado

Authentic Western Ranch, Member–Dude Ranchers' Association

Cherokee Park Ranch has a fascinating history. Believed to be one of the first guest ranches in Colorado, it was once an old stagecoach stop between Fort Collins and Laramie. Before that, the Cherokee Indians frequently used the area as their camp while on their way to Fort Bridger. The Western character of the ranch has been preserved, and while the old structures have been modernized, they have maintained their historic integrity. This is a wonderful ranch for those who appreciate antiques and memorabilia, as many of the furnishings in the cabins and lodge are from the early ranch days. There are also old wagons around the ranch. Host Hank Kaseoru is a great storyteller and Western history buff. He will tell you all about Colorado's early mountain men and Buffalo Bill Cody's famous Wild West Show—a delightful part of the evening camp fire.

Address: P.O. Box 97K, Livermore, Colorado 80536
Telephone: (303) 493-6522; (800) 628-0949
Airport: Denver Stapleton International
Location: 100 miles northwest of Denver, 40 miles northwest of Fort Collins
Memberships: Dude Ranchers' Association, Colorado Dude and Guest Ranch Association
Medical: Fort Collins, 39 miles
Guest Capacity: 35
Accommodations: Depending on family size, there are a variety of accommodations. There are rooms and suites on the second floor of the lodge and five cabins, some with fireplaces, all with private baths. Daily maid service is provided. The lodge has a large living room with a large stone fireplace.
Rates: • $$. American Plan. Children's rates. Off-season and group rates.
Credit Cards: Visa, MasterCard with 5% service charge
Season: May through September
Activities: The ranch features horseback riding with a variety of trail rides (usually 8 guests per ride, but program can be tailored to individual needs). Individual and group instruction. Overnight pack trips (extra) and a riding arena. Fishing on the Poudre River, which runs through the ranch, and stocked pond (fishing equipment available); beautiful and exciting river rafting. Hiking, informal trap shooting (guns provided), heated pool, hot tub.
Children's Programs: Full children's program. Pony rides for children under 6. You may bring your own baby-sitter—ask ranch for special rates.
Dining: Traditional ranch fare of steak, ribs, pork chops, chicken. Specialties are long beef ribs and Hank's chuck wagon stew.
Entertainment: Cowboy and Western stories, ranch rodeo with riding games, weekly square dance, barrel racing, and pole bending. Truck hayrides with campfire music, hot chocolate, and s'mores.
Summary: Very personalized attention to guests. All-day trips to Rocky Mountain National Park and Estes Park. Some Russian and German spoken.

See color photos, page 221

Colorado Trails Ranch, Colorado

Authentic Western Ranch, Member–Dude Ranchers' Association

Since 1960, Dick and Ginny Elder have been welcoming guests to their home—Colorado Trails Ranch. Their ranch and Western village is complete with trading post where they serve old-fashioned ice cream treats, an opera house, and a parlor furnished with antiques. With great fun and relaxation for families, couples, and singles, Colorado Trails offers Western charm and hospitality high in the beautiful San Juan Mountains, just outside Durango. At 7,500 feet, don't worry about smog. The air is clean and sparkling with the scent of fresh pine. While the ranch offers many activities, it takes great pride in its comprehensive riding program. They offer both English and Western riding instruction with certified riding instructors. Dick and Ginny have gone out of their way to give their ranch a real Western flair. Guests love it and keep coming back. Among them are artists, financiers, surgeons, pilots, lots of families, and several astronauts. Artists and photographers are overwhelmed by the fall colors. At his weekly welcome dinner, Dick tells his guests, "You're guests in our home and that's the way you'll be treated."

Address: P.O. Box 848K, Durango, Colorado 81302
Telephone: (800) 323-DUDE (3833), (303) 247-5055
Airport: La Plata County Airport in Durango
Location: 12 miles northeast of Durango on County Road 240; 150 miles north of Albuquerque, New Mexico
Memberships: Dude Ranchers' Association, Colorado Dude and Guest Ranch Association, American Quarter Horse Association, American Humane Association
Awards: *Family Circle* 1990 Family Resort of the Year
Medical: Mercy Medical Center
Conference: 60; three different set-up rooms, 4,800 square feet; from early September
Guest Capacity: 75 (33 rooms)

Accommodations: Guests can stay in four types of comfortably furnished cabins surrounded by pine trees. All rooms have private bathrooms, carpeting, electric heat, and porches. Guest laundry service is available.
Rates: • $$. American Plan, family rates
Credit Cards: Visa, MasterCard, American Express, Discover
Season: June to September
Activities: One of the best riding programs in the country—both Western and English instruction. Heated swimming pool, whirlpool spa, two tennis courts, fishing in stocked pond or nearby lakes and streams. Archery, rifle and trap shooting (guns provided), hiking, and water skiing on Lake Vallecito. Golf and float trips can be arranged.
Children's Programs: Extensive programs—three children's programs divided into age groups, each with full-time counselors. Baby-sitter available. Game room with pool table and table tennis. Kids' groups usually eat together.
Dining: The dining room overlooks the scenic Shearer Creek Valley and Eagle Ridge. Hearty ranch food and plenty of it. No bar. Drinking permitted in cabins only.
Entertainment: A program every evening: staff show and square dancing, hayrides, cookouts, music show and melodrama in Durango. Adults enjoy the turn-of-the-century parlor.
Summary: Superb Western and English horseback riding. Outstanding children's programs. Caring, personable staff. Wonderful musical entertainment. Adults-only week. The famous narrow-gauge train ride to Silverton (this is loads of fun and really takes you back to the old days), guided tours to Mesa Verde National Park with Indian cliff dwellings.

C Lazy U Ranch, Colorado

The C Lazy U Ranch is a vacation ranch that mixes holiday luxury with old-fashioned informality. Facilities and food are Western, comfortable, and of superb quality. It has received the prestigious Mobil 5 Star and AAA 5 Diamond ratings. This 2,000-acre ranch has it all, from designer soap to therapeutic massage that will soothe your tired muscles and help you to unwind. While very family oriented, the ranch has different programs for children and adults. Families eat breakfast together, then the kids go off to work—to work at having the most fun they have ever experienced. The C Lazy U can accommodate up to 120 and tries to give everyone the full Western experience, with a few not-so-rustic amenities. You will get plenty of attention here year-round, which explains why so many guests return year after year.

Address: Box 379 K, Granby, Colorado 80446
Telephone: (303) 887-3344; Fax: (303) 887-3917
Airport: Denver
Location: 6 miles northwest of Granby, 95 miles west of Denver
Memberships: Colorado Dude and Guest Ranch Association, Cross-Country Ski Association
Awards: Mobil 5 Star, AAA 5 Diamond
Medical: Granby Medical Center
Conference: 70; January and October
Guest Capacity: 120
Accommodations: The accommodations are comfortable and casual. Many cabins have fireplaces and vary from single rooms to family suites. Some have Jacuzzi bathtubs.
Rates: • $$-$$$$. Full American Plan includes everything. Off-season rates available.
Credit Cards: None. Personal checks or cash accepted.
Season: June through September and mid-December to March. Special business group months. September is adults only.
Activities: Summer brings a full riding program with 145 horses. There are fast, medium, and slow rides depending on rider's ability and instructional rides for every level. Morning, after-noon, and weekly picnic rides. Some English riding. Horses are assigned for the week and matched to rider's ability. Two tennis courts, swimming in heated pool, indoor sauna and whirlpool, championship racquetball court, trap and skeet range (guns and ammunition extra), fishing in stocked pond or in nearby streams (guided fishing can be arranged), white water raft trips and golf nearby. Winter activities include old-fashioned Christmas week, with Santa arriving in a sleigh; extensive cross-country touring; ice skating; sleigh rides; sledding. All equipment provided at ranch. Downhill skiing 24 miles away at Winter Park (shuttle provided).
Children's Programs: Extensive children's and teens' program for ages 3-17. Kids' playroom and dining room. Children eat together at lunch and dinner. Families with children under age 3 must bring their own nanny/baby-sitter.
Dining: Guests enjoy happy hour before dinner in the cozy lodge bar—no need to BYOB here. Prime rib, steaks, fresh vegetables, and homemade breads. Special meals on request.
Entertainment: Square dancing, cookouts, camp fires, and sing-alongs. Cowboy singer, staff shows, Western band and weekly "Shodeo"—part show, part rodeo. Pro rodeo in town.
Summary: One of the top year-round guest ranches in the world. Destination ranch resort. September is adults-only month. Spectacular Rocky Mountain National Park nearby. French, German, and Spanish spoken.

See color photos, page 195

C Lazy U Ranch, Colorado

C Lazy U Ranch, Colorado

Coulter Lake Guest Ranch, Colorado

Authentic Western Ranch, Member–Dude Ranchers' Association

Coulter Lake Guest Ranch is nestled in a small mountain valley at 8,100 feet and is 21 miles from the nearest town, Rifle. The ranch has been in operation since 1938 and was purchased in 1981 by Norman and Sue Benzinger. Norman is a retired electronics engineer and Sue a teacher who came from the southern California rat race. Coulter Lake rests on the western slope of the Rockies in the White River National Forest. This is some of Colorado's most spectacular mountain country, which stretches for miles in all directions virtually unchanged since Indian times. Forests of quaking aspen and whistling spruce overlook meadows of wildflowers. At beautiful, spring-fed Coulter Lake, one can enjoy fishing, a brisk swim, sunbathing, or just reading a favorite book. Norman and Sue have kept their ranch small, intimate, and rustic. The hardest decision you'll have to make each day is how many eggs you want for breakfast. Family members of all ages will enjoy this ranch. Many lasting friendships have been made here.

Address: P.O. Box 906 K, Rifle, Colorado 81650
Telephone: (303) 625-1473 (summer); call ranch for Fax information
Airport: Grand Junction, Colorado
Train: Amtrak to Glenwood Springs (very popular)
Location: 21 miles northeast of Rifle off State Highway 325
Memberships: Dude Ranchers' Association, Colorado Dude and Guest Ranch Association, Rifle Area Chamber of Commerce
Medical: Clagett Memorial Hospital, Rifle
Conference: 25 (spring and fall only)
Guest Capacity: 25
Accommodations: Eight cabins stand on the mountainside among the trees; Lakeside and Forrest Haven are by the lake. They vary in size and can sleep from two to eight people. Each has a private bath, some with fireplaces (the original log cabins Lakeside, Hilltop, Woodland), and porches.

Rates: • $. American Plan. Children's rates available. Off-season and group rates.
Credit Cards: American Express. Checks or money orders accepted.
Season: Late May to October, December to late April
Activities: Thirty horses provide a host of riding activities, from short to all-day rides. Mondays and Tuesdays have morning and afternoon rides, Wednesdays and Fridays feature all-day rides. Hamburger twilight rides on Thursdays. Four-wheel-drive trips, fishing in stocked lake or in alpine streams and lakes (some fishing poles at ranch). The famous Coulter Lake boat races take place on Saturdays. The Coulter Lake "navy" consists of rowboats and a raft. Hiking and horseshoes. Eighteen-hole golf, tennis, rafting, and hot springs nearby. Photographers should bring a lot of film! Lots to do but no set schedules. Winter: meals and lodging for snowmobilers and cross-country skiers. Guides, rentals, and instruction can be arranged (extra).
Children's Programs: Baby-sitters are available with advance notice. No set program, but supervised kiddie rides are provided.
Dining: Hearty, family-style meals. Cookouts, including a supper ride to 10,000-foot Coulter Mesa. Everyone enjoys the Saturday buffet and Wednesday steak fry and Friday trout dinner. BYOB.
Entertainment: Sing-alongs, square dancing, weekly slide shows.
Summary: Delightful small family ranch. Remote setting situated right on its own lake—no noise, no telephone. As Sue says, "Off the cutting edge of technology." If you enjoy good people, riding, and nature, give the Benzingers a call.

Deer Valley Ranch, Colorado

Deer Valley Ranch is surrounded by 14,000-foot peaks, Mt. Princeton and Mt. Antero, and backdropped by the Chalk Cliffs. This Christian guest ranch has been in the same family since its founding in 1954. Harold DeWalt and John Woolmington, who now run the ranch, are committed to creating a very special atmosphere for all ages. The ranch places a strong emphasis on the family and does not allow any alcoholic beverages. Their program is extensive, with special ranch activities planned from dawn to late evening.

Address: Drawer K, Nathrop, Colorado 81236
Telephone: (719) 395-2353
Airport: Colorado Springs or Denver; private planes in Buena Vista, 12 miles
Location: 100 miles directly west of Colorado Springs on Highway 162
Memberships: Colorado Dude and Guest Ranch Association
Medical: Buena Vista Medical Clinic, 10 miles; Salida Hospital, 25 miles
Conference: 125 can meet in the two-story, 1,500-square-foot "Centennial Hall" or in two other meeting areas. (Off-season only.)
Guest Capacity: 125
Accommodations: Ten-bedroom guest lodge with Western-decorated living area, attached to main dining rooms. Twenty housekeeping cottages of two, three, or four bedrooms and one or two baths. Fireplaces and spacious decks. The cottages are scattered in the trees around the main lodge and pools and offer much privacy. Cottage names like St. Elmo, Whitehorn, Tincup, and Pitkin reflect the Western mining heritage of the valley. Two hot spring pools and bath house. Meeting and recreation rooms.
Rates: • $-$$. Full American Plan in the ranch lodge and a modified European Plan in the cottages. Meals may be prepared in the cottages, though guests are expected to eat at least one meal each day in the lodge. Children's rates for ages 6-12 and 3-5. Horses are not included but may be rented by the week.

Credit Cards: None. Personal checks accepted.
Season: Year-round
Activities: Full daily program including a complete horseback experience. Instructional riding, trail riding in the San Isabel National Forest, and high country riding above timberline. Tennis court. Free golf privileges at the Collegiate Peaks Golf Course in Buena Vista. Trout fishing in Chalk Creek, the stocked ranch lake, high country lakes, or the Arkansas River. Free fly-fishing instruction and trips to the Fryingpan, Roaring Fork, and South Platte rivers. Two hot spring pools (90°-95°), outdoor hot tub, and indoor whirlpool and sauna. Extensive hiking program. Orienteering program. Whitewater rafting on the nearby Arkansas is extra. Four-wheel drives are available at the ranch for half-day or full-day rental.
Children's Programs: Family vacation ranch with most activities planned for families to be together. Children have their own program 2-6 hours each day, at parent's discretion. Full-time children's director. Special play areas for children, including western town and tepees. Babysitting extra. Game room.
Dining: Three meals daily in ranch dining room overlooking Mt. Antero. Box lunches every day for those who are riding, mountain biking, hiking, or fishing the high country. Special diets accommodated.
Entertainment: Nightly programs. Square dancing on the lodge deck. Slide shows and history talks. Horse-drawn hayrides. Camp fires with western music. Western staff show. Big screen TV and many western videotapes. Sunday morning worship service and evening hymn sing.
Summary: Christian family guest ranch for families, couples, single parents, and singles (will not take unmarried couples), with full program of ranch activities. You determine your own activities and even adjust your expenses by determining how many meals you want in the dining room and what riding you do. A complete family destination vacation. Be sure to get a copy of the ranch cookbook.

Diamond J Guest Ranch, Colorado

The Diamond J is a four-season getaway high in the Colorado Rockies. At 8,300 feet, the ranch is at the western base of the Continental Divide, surrounded by the White River National Forest. The ranch has been owned and operated by the Sims family since 1981. Prior to that, it was a hunting and fishing lodge dating back to the early 1920s. The Diamond J offers full summer and winter programs with plenty of activities for all. Cross-country skiing enthusiasts will enjoy some of the best skiing in Colorado. The ranch is an overnight stop on the Tenth Mountain Division Trail between Aspen and Vail. For downhill skiing, four world-class ski areas are just 45 minutes away. Two of the attractions guests find exhilarating are Ruedi Reservoir 4 miles away and the jeep ride to the Continental Divide. At 12,259 feet, the air is wonderfully fresh and the view. . .as far as the eye can see.

Address: 26604 Frying Pan Road, Drawer K, Meredith, Colorado 81642
Telephone: (303) 927-3222
Airport: Aspen via Denver
Location: 45 miles northeast of Aspen, 45 miles east of Glenwood Springs off Highway 82
Memberships: Colorado Dude and Guest Ranch Association, Colorado State Snowmobile Association
Medical: Aspen and Glenwood Springs, 45 minutes
Conference: 50
Guest Capacity: 72
Accommodations: The ranch has a cozy two-story, nine-room lodge and twelve log cabins. Each cabin is decorated in a rustic Western style with fireplaces, stoves, and gas heat. Winter guests stay in the lodge. Laundry facilities available.
Rates: • $. American and European plans. Children's rates available.
Credit Cards: Visa, MasterCard, American Express
Season: All year, including holidays

Activities: Summer program includes horseback riding with instruction if desired, half-day and all-day group trail rides, and pack trips. Children under 8 ride in arena. Fishing in the Frying Pan River (a gold medal stream), which runs through the ranch. White water rafting, four-wheel-drive trips, volleyball, hiking, horseshoes, and tennis on a clay court. Seasonal deer and elk hunting. Whirlpool year-round. Winter brings cross-country skiing. Snowshoeing, downhill skiing, and snowmobile trails nearby. Bring your own cross-country gear.
Children's Programs: Supervised horse program. Baby-sitting available.
Dining: Western home cooking. Barbecued ribs a specialty. Special meals can be prepared. BYOB.
Entertainment: Movies, ranch rodeo, staff shows. Weekly camp fire with marshmallows.
Summary: Year-round, friendly family ranch for families, singles, and honeymoon couples. Victorian town of Aspen, hot springs pool in Glenwood. Town of Marble with nearby quarry.

Don K Ranch, Colorado

The Don K Ranch is in southern Colorado, about thirty miles from Pueblo. From the main road, one takes a 2-mile drive through a canyon with sheer cliffs, which opens to the beautiful ranch valley. The ranch is owned by the Smith family, which hails from Columbia, South Carolina. In the late 1960s, the Smiths began looking for the perfect guest ranch. In 1987, they found it in the Don K. Over the years, the ranch has hosted notables including the ambassador to Uruguay. The Smiths exude Southern hospitality in their Western wonderland. The ranch is surrounded by the San Isabel National Forest. You can ride through meadows, over mountain trails, or through the forest. An abundance of pines surround the buildings. The two-story main lodge is reminiscent of days gone by, with its walkways, lawns, colorful flower boxes, and garden.

Address: 2677 South Siloam Road, Dept. K, Pueblo, Colorado 81005
Telephone: (719) 784-6600. If you can't get through, call (719) 549-0481, the answering service for messages. Fax: (719) 784-6600 (must call if sending Fax)
Airport: Pueblo, Colorado Springs
Location: 30 miles west of Pueblo off Highway 96, 75 miles south of Colorado Springs, 150 miles south of Denver. Call for directions.
Memberships: Colorado Dude and Guest Ranch Association
Medical: Parkview Hospital, 30 miles
Conference: 55
Guest Capacity: 55
Accommodations: The Don K Ranch, the home of Charles Bronson's movie *Mr. Majestyk*, has six upstairs lodge rooms, with names like Mr. Majestyk, War Wagon, and True Grit, and six cabins, with names like Jessie James, Billy the Kid, and Geronimo, and one two-bedroom, two-bath home. All rooms are fully carpeted and have gas and electric heat and wood paneling. Cabins have private baths, while the lodge has large semiprivate baths. The cabins accommodate from 2 to 6 and feature colorful West-

ern and Indian decor. All units offer mountain and forest views. Laundry available.
Rates: • $-$$. American Plan. Children's, family, and off-season rates available.
Credit Cards: Visa, MasterCard, American Express (prefer checks)
Season: Mid-May through October
Activities: Extensive riding program for all levels with instruction, including brunch ride and half-day and all-day rides. Rides are divided into fast or slow. Trail rides go out in groups of ten or less. Overnight campouts. Heated pool, professional tennis court, volleyball, and hot tub. Pasture golf tournament and hiking. White water rafting nearby. Waterskiing at Pueblo Reservoir, 25 miles away.
Children's Programs: Excellent program available for children ages 3 to 5 and 6 to 16. Children 3 to 5 ride under supervision. Children's overnight campout, playground with swings. Kids rodeo, treasure hunts, arts and crafts, and playroom.
Dining: Delicious ranch meals served family-style. Daily fresh breads and pastries. Poolside barbecue cookouts. Optional children's dining table. Drinks and wine available at Bear Head Saloon in lodge.
Entertainment: Square dancing, camp fires, sing-alongs, Western movies, games, staff mystery plays, rodeo awards night, and videos of the guests "in action."
Summary: Wonderful secluded family ranch. Great for family reunions. Nearby attractions include Royal Gorge for white water rafting and scenic trips, Colorado State Fair in August. Air Force Academy, Garden of the Gods, and Pike's Peak.

See color photos, page 190

Drowsy Water Ranch, Colorado

Authentic Western Ranch, Member–Dude Ranchers' Association

This 600-acre ranch is in the beautiful Rocky Mountains bordered by thousands of acres of backcountry and the Arapahoe National Forest. This lovely ranch is wedged in a valley at 8,000 feet and surrounded by shimmering aspen and scented fir. Drowsy Water Ranch is genuine and offers its guests great Colorado hospitality. The comfortable log cabins are scenically situated along Drowsy Water Creek, which meanders through the ranch. The Foshas are hosts and owners of this mountain paradise. Ken and Randy Sue offer an outstanding horse program for experts and beginners and a full program for children. You won't forget their home-cooked meals, whether enjoyed at cookouts, on the trail, or at the main lodge. You'll eat plenty of homemade breads, tasty salads, baked chicken, and sizzling steaks, and you'll sleep like a baby. There is old-fashioned goodness to this ranch. It is without a lot of frills and brings to mind another century when people were less hurried and really cared about each other.

Address: P.O. Box 147K, Granby, Colorado 80446
Telephone: (303) 725-3456
Airport: Denver
Train: Amtrak to Granby, 6 miles
Location: 90 miles west of Denver, 6 miles west of Granby off U.S. 40
Memberships: Dude Ranchers' Association, Colorado Dude and Guest Ranch Association
Medical: Granby Clinic, 6 miles
Conference: 40
Guest Capacity: 60
Accommodations: Guests enjoy comfortable and clean log cabins that are sheltered in stands of aspen and pine overlooking Drowsy Water Creek and the ranch ponds. Cabins have covered porches. The largest is cabin 5 at the north end of the ranch pond. The newly remodeled cabins accommodate from two to nine persons. There are also eight rooms in the main lodge. All have private baths.

Rates: • $-$$. Full American Plan; minimum one-week stay in high season. Family, children's and off-season rates. Pack trips and river rafting extra.
Credit Cards: American Express (prefer cash or personal checks)
Season: June to mid-September
Activities: One hundred fine horses provide all the riding you could possibly want. Ken and Randy Sue raise many of their own paint horses. Fast, slow, and all-day rides to beautiful vistas from 10,500 feet, pack trips, and cookout rides. Riding instruction and advanced horsemanship classes available. River rafting on the Colorado River. Hayrides, fishing (equipment for beginners provided), heated pool, and whirlpool. Golf and tennis nearby. Seasonal hunting for elk and deer.
Children's Programs: Supervised children's program for ages 6 to 13 with daily counseled games and crafts. Special horse program builds confident riders. Children under 5 have a special program that includes horseback riding and games, crafts, and picnic hikes. Weekly kids' gymkhana.
Dining: Lots of home-cooked, hearty meals, salad bar. BYOB in cabins only.
Entertainment: Something different each night. Monday, square dancing; Tuesday, hayride for kids with marshmallow toasting and adults-only dinner; Wednesday, country swing band; Thursday, carnival night; Friday, adults-only hayride; Saturday, staff show. Rodeos in town.
Summary: Family owned and operated guest ranch. Lifelong friendships have been made here. Ranch raises many of its own paint horses. Rocky Mountain National Park, alpine slide in Winter Park.

Drowsy Water Ranch, Colorado

Drowsy Water Ranch, Colorado

Elk Mountain Ranch, Colorado

Authentic Western Ranch, Member–Dude Ranchers' Association

Elk Mountain Ranch, high in the Colorado Rockies at 9,535 feet, is dedicated to excellence in accommodations and hospitality. The ranch is surrounded by a breathtaking panorama of snow-capped peaks, mountain trails, lush aspens, and evergreen forest. Situated ten miles into the beautiful San Isabel National Forest, the ranch has been in operation since 1981. Owners and hosts Susan and LaRue Boyd take great pride in pampering their guests. Elk Mountain is known for its spectacular setting, horseback rides, superb menu, and friendliness. Nature lovers and photographers will love the abundance of deer, elk, antelope, and wildflowers. Everyone will take home fond memories and savor the peacefulness and relaxation. One family remarked, "It was quite simply the best time we've ever had!"

Address: P.O. Box 910K, Buena Vista, Colorado 81211 (summer); 7075 E. Euclid Drive, Box K, Englewood, Colorado 80111 (winter)
Telephone: (719) 395-6313 (summer); (303) 694-2818 (winter)
Airport: Denver
Location: 100 miles southwest of Denver, 70 miles west of Colorado Springs, 20 miles southeast of Buena Vista; ranch will send you a detailed map.
Memberships: Dude Ranchers' Association, Colorado Dude and Guest Ranch Association
Awards: *Hideaway Report*
Medical: Buena Vista Medical Clinic, Salida Hospital
Conference: 25 (early June to late September for less than one week)
Guest Capacity: 35
Accommodations: The main lodge houses the dining room with fireplace, cowboy and mining artifacts, sitting room, library, sun deck, and the upstairs "Elk" guest suite. There are six one- and two-bedroom log cottages with private baths and queen- and king-size beds, as well as the "Pioneer Lodge" with five private rooms and baths, all tastefully furnished. Susan loves flowers and always has a colorful array hanging from cabin porches and on the main deck. The ranch generates its own electricity.
Rates: • $$. American Plan with minimum stay. Children's and off-season rates available.
Credit Cards: Visa, MasterCard, American Express. Personal checks accepted.
Season: June through mid-September
Activities: Horseback riding is wonderful at Elk Mountain with miles of trails and spectacular views of the Collegiate Peaks. Overnight wilderness pack trips and brunch trail rides overlooking Brown's Canyon. White water rafting on the Arkansas River near the ranch. Auto trips to Aspen and Breckenridge, trap shooting (guns provided), trout fishing in two stocked ponds (some loner fishing gear is available at the ranch's trading post), archery, horseshoes, and volleyball.
Children's Programs: Full children's program. Baby-sitting available during the day. Ranch encourages parents to interact with kids.
Dining: Wonderful food—homemade soups, freshly baked breads, and desserts. Evening hors d'oeuvres, BYOB. Weekly barbecues and Saturday candlelight dinners. One guest described it best: "The food is super!" No smoking in dining room.
Entertainment: Old Western and kids' movies, library, chess, backgammon, hayrides, square dances, camp fires. Hammered dulcimer concert.
Summary: Wonderful, remote, small family-run ranch. Delightful hosts and excellent staff. Riding is the main activity. Great for families, couples, and singles who enjoy outdoors and a wilderness setting with all the comforts of home. Occasional cattle branding on neighboring ranch. Great ranch store called the "Trading Post."

See color photos, page 225

Everett Ranch, Colorado

The Everett Ranch was established in the 1880s. This working cattle ranch with 1,000 head has stayed in the family and is now being operated by the third and fourth generations of Everetts. Northeast of Salida, the ranch covers many thousands of acres ranging from desert to alpine meadows, from rocky canyons to open spaces. The Ute Indians used to summer in the high country and come down to the valley in the winter. Over the years, many arrowheads have been found here. In September, the leaves are changing color and the bull elk are bugling. For serious cowboys and cowgirls only—it's the Old West here. You should be in good health and ready for the rough life at cow camp. If you are ready to get away from your fax machine and step back in time, the Everett family will show you how. Guests have come from as far as Germany, France, and Switzerland. If you expect electric blankets, ride on.

Address: 10615 County Road 150K, Salida, Colorado 81201
Telephone: (719) 539-4097
Airport: Denver, 150 miles; Colorado Springs, 100 miles
Location: 20 miles northeast of Salida, 150 miles south of Denver
Memberships: Colorado Outfitters Association
Medical: Salida Hospital, 20 miles
Guest Capacity: 10
Accommodations: Three cow camp cabins, each sleeps four (one double bed and one bunk bed). No electricity, water, or telephone. Outhouse and solar-heated shower nearby. Bring your own bedroll and towels.
Rates: • $. American Plan. Children's rates available under 12.
Credit Cards: None
Season: June to September
Activities: The Everetts provide excellent cow horses, which they try to match to the rider's ability. Lots of cattle work and some basic roping lessons. Float trips can be arranged. Excellent fall hunting for elk and deer.

Children's Programs: Children are welcome but should be old enough to enjoy a full day in the saddle. Recommended for children over eight.
Dining: Wholesome meals are cooked on a wood stove in main cow camp cabin. Dining table seats 15.
Entertainment: Just the stars and Mother Nature. Horseshoe pitching and the famous Everett cow camp "cheat-your-neighbor" card game.
Summary: Real cattle ranch. Abundant wildlife, including elk, mule deer, mountain sheep, coyotes, and antelope. Sixty miles away from the Royal Gorge Bridge, one of the highest suspension bridges in the world. No hookups but will take RVs.

4UR Ranch, Colorado

The ranch property was purchased by wealthy railroad tycoon General William J. Palmer before the turn of the century for its natural hot springs. The present Texas owners bought the 4UR in the early 1970s. Today the ranch is capably managed by Rock Swenson and his wife, Kristen. The same timeless qualities of nature, elegance, history, and hospitality continue to make the 4UR Ranch a delightful experience. The ranch is high in the San Juan Mountains of southwestern Colorado. For its discriminating fly-fishing guests, there is private fishing on 4½ miles of the Rio Grande River and on 8 miles of Goose Creek. There are also the two Lost Lakes at 11,000 feet where brook and native cutthroat trout swim in clear, icy waters. July and August are the ranch's busiest months. September is a favorite for fishermen, and photographers flock here for the fall colors.

Address: P.O. Box 340K, Creede, Colorado 81130
Telephone: (719) 658-2202
Airport: Alamosa airport via Denver; 6,800-foot paved airstrip in Creede, nearby, with hangar facilities for guests
Location: 222 miles southwest of Denver, 60 miles west of Alamosa, 8 miles southeast of Creede off Highway 149
Medical: St. Joseph's Hospital in Del Norte, 40 miles
Conference: 50, June and September
Guest Capacity: 50
Accommodations: Guest facilities consist of three 1950s-vintage cedar shake mini-lodges. Rooms share a common breezeway porch, but each has its own entrance. Numerous rockers are on each porch. All have private baths, thermostatic heating, and daily maid service. Each night beds are turned down. Three family cottages are available at certain times. The main lodge, with its dining and living room, splendid valley views, bar, and game room, is the center stage for evening socializing. Laundry service is available.
Rates: • $$. American Plan. Includes all activities on ranch except jeep trips, trap shooting,

raft trips, and guided hikes. Children's rates available. Children under 4 free. Group and conference rates available. Seven-day minimum stay in July and August.
Credit Cards: Visa, MasterCard, American Express
Season: Early June through September
Activities: Fly-fishing on river and in alpine lakes with instruction available on request. Each evening fishermen roll the dice and select their own half-mile stretch of water for the following morning fishing. Bring your own gear. Some flies available. Breakfast, morning, afternoon, and all-day horseback rides through very scenic country; most rides are walking. Heated swimming pool, log bathhouse with sauna, hot sulfur baths, whirlpool. Exercise and massage room with licensed massage therapist available. Tennis court, hiking, rafting, and jeep trips available. Trap shooting (ranch prefers you bring your own guns).
Children's Programs: Counselor for kids over 6. Junior wrangler program teaches kids about horses. Kids under 6 can ride llamas. Baby-sitting provided with advance notice.
Dining: Fisherman's early continental breakfast followed by regular full-course breakfast. Weekly breakfast ride along the Rio Grande with biscuits and gravy, scrambled eggs and ham, baked apples, and cowboy coffee. Once a week, the ranch features a high noon fish fry along Goose Creek. Gourmet backcountry picnics. Always three hearty ranch meals a day. Full-service bar and wine service available.
Entertainment: Unscheduled children's gymkhana, jeep-pulled hayrides, video movie classics (Westerns and Disney). Evening fly-tying.
Summary: Wonderful guest ranch on scenic Goose Creek, famous for its excellent fly-fishing. Twelve miles of private waters. Select your own schedule. Family oriented during July and August. Mostly adults during September. Hot sulfur pool. Fly-fishing school in June. Old "Doc" buggy and six-seat surrey rides. Historic mining town of Creede.

Fryingpan River Ranch, Colorado

Authentic Western Ranch, Member–Dude Ranchers' Association • Orvis-Endorsed Lodge

Guest ranches began when visitors from other parts of the country came to stay with families in the west. That tradition is alive and well at the Fryingpan River Ranch. In early 1990, after a year-long search, Jim Rea found a ranch with great riding, great fishing, great views, and a great partner, Paula, who helps him share this very special place. This small historic ranch, located at 8,800 feet on the west side of Hagerman Pass and next to Nast Lake, accommodates only a few guests each week who ride, fish, hike, mountain bike, and bask in the warmth of owners and staff who truly enjoy making each guest feel at home. The ranch is the perfect spot for a vacation where some members of the family are avid fly-fishermen and others are more interested in the traditional guest ranch activities. Paula, an extremely talented wildlife artist, leads sketching hikes in fields of wildflowers that bloom in July and August. Personalized service and old-fashioned hospitality are all served in abundance at the Fryingpan River Ranch.

Address: 32042 Fryingpan Road, Drawer K, Meredith, Colorado 81642
Telephone: (303) 927-3570; Fax: (303) 927-3570 (call first)
Airport: Aspen or Denver
Location: 31 miles east of Basalt, Colorado; 1¼ hours northeast of Aspen
Memberships: Colorado Dude and Guest Ranch Association, Dude Ranchers' Association
Awards: Orvis-Endorsed Lodge
Medical: Aspen or Glenwood Springs, 50 miles
Conference: 36
Guest Capacity: 36
Accommodations: Guests stay in six cabins and two 2-bedroom lodge rooms. Each cabin has its own special charm. Some offer views of Nast Lake, while others overlook the Fryingpan River. Two are secluded in the pines away from the main activity of the lodge. Many of the rooms and cabins were redecorated recently with pine and antique furnishings, accented with art collected by Jim and Paula. Each has its own pri-

vate bath and excellent bed. The hot tub overlooks Nast Lake. No smoking in any of the buildings.
Rates: • $$. American Plan. Rates vary depending on the season. Ask about their fishing packages.
Credit Cards: Visa, MasterCard. Personal checks and traveler's checks accepted.
Season: June to mid-October (summer); mid-October to mid-November (hunting); Thanksgiving to April (winter)
Activities: Summer brings a full horse program including instruction, half- and full-day rides, and a breakfast ride once a week. Overnight pack trips are available. Excellent fishing on the Gold Medal waters of the Fryingpan and Roaring Fork rivers. Nast Lake sits less than a hundred yards from the lodge and is full of brook and rainbow trout. Guided hiking and sketching hikes. Mountain biking, trap and rifle shooting along with archery, river rafting, and four-wheel-drive trips are available. The hot tub is always open. Hardy swimmers enjoy Nast Lake. Winter activities include cross-country skiing, snowshoeing, snowmobiling, and excellent winter fishing. The world-famous alpine skiing town of Aspen is 1¼ hours away.
Children's Programs: No formal children's programs. Children are the responsibility of their parents. Paula has two wonderful young children, so your children will be in good company.
Dining: Described by one guest as "recreational eating." The ranch features traditional foods cooked in healthy and creative ways. Wild game is often served along with beef, lamb, pork, chicken, and trout. BYOB.
Entertainment: Well-stocked library, VCR with a selection of videos, and a cozy log lodge.
Summary: You'll find lots of warmth and caring hospitality at this small family ranch located on Nast Lake. Great food and personal service. Good mountain horseback riding. Excellent fly-fishing on Gold Medal rivers. Be sure to talk with Paula about her art. She is a wonderful and very talented artist. Nearby attractions include the famous mountain ski town of Aspen.

See color photos, page 191

The Home Ranch, Colorado

Authentic Western Ranch, Member–Dude Ranchers' Association

As one drives up the gravel road to the ranch and sees the hand-hewn log buildings set among shimmering aspens, two words come to mind—paradise and, maybe better yet, heaven. The beauty of this first-class ranch is overwhelming. The Home Ranch was the long-time dream of co-owner and builder Ken Jones. Ken grew up on horses and got most of his guest ranch experience at the old Valley Ranch, owned originally by Larry Larom, a Princeton graduate, and Winthrop Brooks, of Brooks Brothers fame. While working there he met a guest who shared his enthusiasm. Ken and his partner have created a ranch so special that it boasts the highly coveted Relais and Chateaux Award, along with the AAA Four Diamond award. There is very little this ranch doesn't have for its guests. Best of all, it serves plenty of Old West rustic elegance and hospitality. The *Los Angeles Times* captured the essence when it said, "Here guests commune with a world as fresh as a Rocky Mountain raindrop."

Address: Box 822K, Clark, Colorado 80428
Telephone: (303) 879-1780; Fax: (303) 879-1795
Airport: Steamboat Springs via Denver
Location: 18 miles north of Steamboat Springs
Memberships: Dude Ranchers' Association, Colorado Dude and Guest Ranch Association
Awards: AAA 4 Diamond; Relais and Chateaux
Medical: Steamboat Springs Hospital
Conference: 25
Guest Capacity: 30
Accommodations: Each beautiful log cabin is wonderfully furnished and set in a grove of aspen, ensuring privacy. Each has its own hot tub on a screened deck, great for total relaxation at the end of a day's ride or for warming up after cross-country skiing. There are also rooms in the handsome main lodge.
Rates: • $$-$$$. American Plan. Children's rates available.
Credit Cards: Visa, MasterCard, American Express. Personal checks accepted.

Season: Summer runs Memorial Day through September; winter, Christmas through Easter.
Activities: You are assigned your own horse for the duration of your stay. It's up to you how much you want to ride. Those who are interested will be taught how to saddle and bridle their horses. Ride go out in small groups each day accompanied by a wrangler. Heated swimming pool, fishing and fly casting in stocked pond or in the Elk River, and hiking. Tennis and golf can be arranged nearby. Winter activities include extensive cross-country skiing program with groomed trails, guides, and certified instructors. Sleigh rides and snowshoeing.
Children's Programs: Kiddie wrangler. Complete children's program for ages 3 through teens.
Dining: Excellent, mouth-watering gourmet meals. Special diets catered to. Younger children may eat dinner early.
Entertainment: Home Ranch country blues band. Ranch and Steamboat Springs rodeos, barrel racing. Top local entertainers.
Summary: World-class guest ranch. The town of Steamboat Springs, two photography workshops, Scottish Highland cattle, llamas.

Lake Mancos Ranch, Colorado

Authentic Western Ranch, Member–Dude Ranchers' Association

In the heart of southwestern Colorado's cowboy country, Lake Mancos Ranch is a family-run guest ranch. Since 1956 the Sehnert family has hosted guests from around the country, many of whom return year after year. Lloyd and Kathy and their son Todd believe "American families still want to take a vacation in an atmosphere that isn't reeking of commercialism, with pinball machines and video games." The ranch leaves guests lots of leeway to enjoy all the activities. Many sit on their porches and watch the world go by. At Lake Mancos you can do the things you like, hassle-free. The ranch is above the Mancos Valley at 8,000 feet, on a plateau between the West Mancos River and Chicken Creek, looking out to the La Plata Mountains. One family wrote, "Please know how grateful we are for the most relaxing and refreshing vacation ever." On the cover of their brochure they say, "Easygoin' vacation at its very best." And that's just the way it is.

Address: 42688 CR-N, Dept. K, Mancos, Colorado 81328
Telephone: (303) 533-7900
Airport: Durango via Denver, Phoenix, or Albuquerque
Location: 5 miles north of Mancos, 50 miles west of Durango
Memberships: Dude Ranchers' Association, Colorado Dude and Guest Ranch Association
Medical: Cortez Hospital, 25 miles
Conference: 40
Guest Capacity: 55
Accommodations: There are seventeen bright red guest units: thirteen rooms in cabins of various sizes and four spacious units with private bath in the ranch house for couples and singles. All heated family cabins have comfortable living rooms, bedrooms, bathrooms, private shady porches, king-size beds, refrigerators, and carpeting. Guest laundry available. Daily maid service.
Rates: • $$. American Plan. Nonriding, children's, and off-season rates available.

Credit Cards: Visa, MasterCard. Personal checks accepted.
Season: Early June to October. September is adults only.
Activities: Rides are usually broken up each day into children and adult rides. Adults may ride with children if they like. Several times a week there are family rides. Because of the terrain, it is mostly walk and trot. Guests are assigned their own horse for their stay. Hiking and fishing (rods available for children) in Lake Mancos and nearby ranch stream. Heated pool and hot tub. Four-wheel-drive and wildflower trips. Wednesday is the open day. Many like to raft in Durango, golf in Cortez, or ride the spectacular Durango/Silverton steam train, which was started in 1882.
Children's Programs: Children's program with counselors for children ages 4 and up. Younger children not advised. Movie nights and overnight cookout. Petting zoo and recreation room.
Dining: Home-style cooking and baking. Weekly barbecue creekside at Rendezvous Canyon. Cookies, coffee, and lemonade always plentiful. BYOB.
Entertainment: Fireside chats. Hayrides, cookouts, skits, and awards night.
Summary: Lake Mancos is for families who really enjoy being on vacation together. Very relaxed, time for being alone, sunset walks, and reading. Riding is the main activity. Many singles and couples enjoy the camaraderie of the family ranch. Old Durango and Silverton Railroad, Mesa Verde National Park, Telluride, and Four Corners Monument. McPhea Dam and Dolores River. Adults only in September.

Lane Guest Ranch, Colorado

Lane Guest Ranch is a medium-size ranch that takes a maximum of seventy guests during the summer months. Previously inhabited by Arapaho Indians and later by mountain man Kit Carson, the area is known for its history, its abundance of wildlife, and its spectacular mountain scenery. Since 1954, Lloyd Lane and a staff of forty have received families, couples, and singles from around the country. The ranch sends potential guests plenty of information about the facilities. The motto here is "We aim to please," and their brief poem that captures the spirit of the ranch goes like this: "Your time with us to relax, be at ease, time out from collars, ties, belts and hose. There's no place here for city clothes, leave them home and give them a rest. Slacks are fine, but jeans are best. A jacket, a sweater will fill the bill to ward off the early morning chill. To hike, to ride, to leave cares behind, but remember to bring comfy shoes of any kind. So pack to play, enjoy your stay—there's something doing every day." As one guest put it, "I felt as if I had come home to a warm and cheerful large family." Welcome to the Lane Guest Ranch.

Address: P.O. Box 1766K, Estes Park, Colorado 80517
Telephone: (303) 747-2493
Airport: Denver International
Location: 67 miles northwest of Denver, 12 miles south of Estes Park off Highway 7
Memberships: American Hotel and Motel Association
Medical: Estes Park Hospital, 11 miles
Conference: No
Guest Capacity: 70
Accommodations: Log-sided units accommodate from two to six. Twenty-five units are comfortably furnished with queen-size beds, private baths, patios, hammocks, TV/VCR, stocked refrigerators, and radios. Fifteen units have their own hot tubs. Laundry service provided.
Rates: • $$-$$$. American Plan. Children's, senior, weekly, and honeymoon packages available. No minimum stay required.

Credit Cards: Visa, MasterCard, American Express
Season: June to early September
Activities: Daily ranch activity sign-up sheet, horseback riding in Rocky Mountain and Roosevelt National Forests, overnight pack trips, wine and cheese rides for adults. Guided hikes, wildlife photography trips, fishing trips, riding instruction, four-wheel-drive, heated outdoor pool, hot tub, river rafting. Two tennis courts nearby. Eighteen-hole golf can be arranged. Massage available.
Children's Programs: Counselors, full child care available, kiddie wrangler. Baby-sitting available. Playground with swings and sandbox.
Dining: Mealtimes are flexible. Menu offerings include fresh-squeezed orange juice, salad buffet, charcoal-broiled New York steaks, seafood dinners, broiled and poached salmon, prime rib, selection of California wines and mixed drinks (licensed bar), cappuccino and espresso, poolside cafe, Sunday bar, complimentary house wine and beer.
Entertainment: Music at bar, shuffleboard, volleyball, horseshoes, well-stocked library, chess, table tennis, TV and over 300 video movies, Estes Park rodeos.
Summary: Small and very flexible ranch with high staff/guest ratio. Nearby attractions include Central City, "the richest square mile on earth," gold mines, North St. Vrain Canyon, Estes Park for shopping. Video available on request.

Latigo Ranch, Colorado

Authentic Western Ranch, Member–Dude Ranchers' Association

At 9,000 feet, the air is crisp, the view tremendous, and the hospitality sincere. Nature lovers will enjoy the breathtaking scenery and the abundance of wildflowers and wildlife. Latigo Ranch runs a four-season program, from hayrides in the summer to snowshoeing in the winter. Here you can dine on the fresh Tasmanian trout that you caught earlier in the day, or recount the number of deer and elk that you saw on one of the many splendid hiking trails. Whether you and your family are at the ranch for the Fourth of July or Christmas, you can be sure of one thing—many special memories. If you want to have some interesting conversations, just ask your hosts about their educational backgrounds. It is not uncommon for guests to engage in high-level discussions. Mostly, though, everyone takes in nature's beauty.

Address: P.O. Box 237K, Kremmling, Colorado 80459
Telephone: (303) 724-9009 or (800) 227-9655 out of Colorado; Fax: (303) 724-3449
Airport: Steamboat Springs
Location: 130 miles northwest of Denver, 55 miles southeast of Steamboat Springs
Memberships: Colorado Dude and Guest Ranch Association, Colorado Cross-Country Skiers Association, Dude Ranchers' Association
Awards: AAA 3 Diamond
Medical: Kremmling Memorial Hospital
Conference: 35
Guest Capacity: 35
Accommodations: Guests stay in contemporary log duplexes nestled in the pine forest and one fourplex that overlooks 75 miles of mountain ranges to the Continental Divide. Each is carpeted, with sitting room and fireplace or wood-burning stove.
Rates: • $$. American Plan. Children's rates available. Rates vary depending on the season.
Credit Cards: Visa, MasterCard, American Express
Season: Late May to mid-November (summer); Late November to April (winter)

Activities: Summer offerings include heated swimming pool, fishing in streams and ranch pond, fly-fishing instruction and day fishing trips. Horseback riding with instruction, breakfast and sunset rides, pack trips, special llama trekking program (ask ranch for brochure), hiking, rafting nearby. Hot tub and exercise room with rowing machine. In winter, there's cross-country skiing with instruction, snowshoeing, snowmobiling. The ranch maintains 30 kilometers of trails with set track and 10 kilometers of packed trails.
Children's Programs: Fully supervised program for ages 3 to 13. Arts and crafts center. Kids under 3 do not ride.
Dining: Excellent food both summer and winter. Weekly breakfast, lunch, and dinner cookouts. BYOB.
Entertainment: The three-story "Social Club" is a log-sided entertainment building, where guests enjoy happy hour (BYOB), square dancing, piano, pool room, and library.
Summary: Guest ranch run by two families with very interesting backgrounds. High setting with excellent panoramic views. Photo workshops, special llama trekking program. Jim's geology and wildlife lectures. Be sure to see Jim Yost's movie on Ecuador, *Nomads of the Rain Forest*, a beautiful show that has been on Nova. Fall cattle roundup in late September.

Longs Peak Inn Guest Ranch, Colorado

Longs Peak Inn Guest Ranch, with its white exteriors and dark trim, looks like a beautiful property you would see nestled in the Tyrolian Alps. A natural setting and modern amenities provide all the ingredients for rest, relaxation, and Rocky Mountain comfort. The ranch sits in a valley under one of the most beautiful mountains in Colorado, Longs Peak, the highest mountain in the Rocky Mountain National Park. For many years, guests have enjoyed the genuine hospitality, comfortable accommodations, and lots of activities. Families enjoy this modern ranch that has just enough Western activities to balance the pristine European design. You will find that Bob and Virginia Akins and their daughter, Beth, serve friendly and informal hospitality at their 250-acre ranch. Virginia's Southern upbringing shows. Her warmth and kindness are a wonder.

Address: Longs Peak Inn and Guest Ranch, Longs Peak Route, Box K, Estes Park, Colorado 80517
Telephone: (303) 586-2110; (800) 262-2034
Airport: Denver Stapleton Airport
Train: Union Station in Denver for Amtrak
Location: 75 miles northwest of Denver
Memberships: Colorado Dude and Guest Ranch Association
Awards: AAA 3 Diamond, Mobil 3 Star
Medical: Estes Park Medical Center, 9 miles
Conference: 40, June, late August, and September
Guest Capacity: 80
Accommodations: The ranch offers a variety of modern accommodations. Guest rooms have a country flavor, private baths, carpeting, and gas heat. For those who wish more rustic accommodations, ask about the Grizzly log cabin.
Rates: •$-$$. American Plan. Children's and off-season rates available. Riding not included.
Credit Cards: Visa, MasterCard, American Express
Season: June to mid-September
Activities: Activities are geared to the outdoors. Scenic tours, trout fishing in several stocked ponds, swimming in the heated pool, two hot tubs, horseback riding with an overnight ride available. Lots of great hiking, rafting, or just walking through the wildflowers and aspens. Nearby are 18-hole and 9-hole executive golf courses, tennis, and rafting on the Colorado River.
Children's Programs: Child care for ages 4 to 5, children's program for ages 6 to 12, and teen counselors.
Dining: The Akins are veterans of the restaurant business, so there are many specialties: Rocky Mountain scrambled eggs, New Orleans French doughnuts, fruit and melon salad, cheese fondue, Longs Peak sandwiches, and American regional dishes, fantastic fresh frozen strawberry desserts, French raisin pie, chocolate cake, and lots of baked goodies. All meals are hearty and served in the dining room with floor to ceiling windows looking to Longs Peak on one side and Twin Sisters Mountain on the other. Several entrées are offered at breakfast, lunch, and dinner. Breakfast, steak rides, and barbecue cookouts. Adults enjoy happy hour in the lofty upstairs lounge, where cocktails are served. Cocktails also available at dinner.
Entertainment: Square dancing, bingo, sing-alongs, ice cream socials with homemade ice cream, family games and movies, rodeos and horse shows in Estes Park.
Summary: Family-run resort ranch with personal warmth and hospitality. Great for family reunions. Rocky Mountain National Park, shopping in Estes Park.

North Fork Guest Ranch, Colorado

Authentic Western Ranch, Member–Dude Ranchers' Association

President Eisenhower made the North Fork of the South Platte River famous as he liked to come here to fish and relax. This river happens to run right through North Fork Ranch, a ranch Dean and Karen May have been hosting since 1984. Karen is a registered nurse from Kansas. Dean has a degree in forestry/land surveying and comes from upstate New York. Like many, they moved out west (independently of each other) in the early eighties, fell in love with each other and Colorado, and stayed. North Fork is a 520-acre turn-of-the-century property. The original homestead at the ranch dates back to the 1900s, when the Union Pacific Railroad passed through on its way to the gold mining towns of Fairplay, St. Elmo, and Leadville. In 1930, a gentleman with "deep pockets" by the name of Peterson began building a fortress/stockade estate out of the local native rock, a project that took ten years. This magnificent three-story structure still stands on the side of the hill today and houses guest quarters with elegant raised beam ceilings, field stone fireplaces, Western art, antiques, and collectibles. In the summer months, the flower beds and gardens are filled with color. North Fork Ranch is a ranch for families. Dean and Karen encourage their guests to interact and encourage families to enjoy their vacation time together.

Address: P.O. Box B-K, Shawnee, Colorado 80475
Telephone: (303) 838-9873; (800) 843-7895
Airport: Denver
Location: 50 miles southwest of Denver
Memberships: Colorado Dude and Guest Ranch Association, Dude Ranchers' Association
Medical: Karen May is a registered nurse. Crow Hill Medical Center, 20 miles.
Conference: 20, October through April
Guest Capacity: 38
Accommodations: The main lodge offers 11 rooms, each with private bath. The Homestead cabin offers accommodations for three families of four people; each of the units has two bed-

rooms and a private bath. Stonehenge, the three-story mansion, offers several sleeping arrangements for families. Rooms are carpeted with private baths, king-size beds, children's bunk beds, and daily maid service. Some rooms have fireplaces.
Rates: • $-$$. American Plan. Children's, off-season, and group rates available.
Credit Cards: None
Season: May through September
Activities: Structured weekly program. Experienced wranglers guide groups of 6 to 8 on half-day and all-day rides, champagne brunch rides, and overnight pack trips. A rodeo arena is used for instruction and the weekly guest rodeo. White water rafting on the Arkansas River with certified outfitters. Target and trap shooting (guns and ammunition provided), fishing in the stocked pond or on the North Fork of the South Platte River, which runs through the property. Fishing gear is available. Four-wheel-drive trips. Swimming in heated pool or relaxing in the spa at Stonehenge.
Children's Programs: Dean and Karen feel that the ranch is a place for parents and children to be together. Counselors and baby-sitters are available; however, there is no special kids' program. Petting zoo with lots of farm animals. Child counselor is certified in lifesaving and first aid.
Dining: The ranch takes pride in its food. Enjoy fresh breads, roast beef with bernaise sauce, full turkey dinners, barbecues, steak, and hamburger lunches. Friday candlelight dinner featuring fresh trout or upland duck, quail, or pheasant. Special diets catered to. BYOB.
Entertainment: Square dancing with live caller. Camp fire sing-alongs, evening fishing, and hayrides.
Summary: Located in a beautiful valley along the river. Great small family ranch for families who like to be with their children on vacation. North Fork was included on a "Good Morning America" segment.

See color photos, page 212

Lost Valley Ranch, Colorado

Authentic Western Ranch, Member–Dude Ranchers' Association

In the world of guest ranching, Lost Valley Ranch is right at the top. The qualities that make the Foster family's ranch so unique are their superb staff, excellent accommodations, and fabulous children's/teen program. Everyone at the ranch exudes a caring and enthusiastic spirit. Lost Valley has been in the ranching business for more than one hundred years and under the stewardship of two generations of Fosters for the past thirty years. This year-round cattle and horse ranch is set among tall pines on 40,000 acres of the Pike National Forest. At Lost Valley rugged adventure is combined with fun. Here guests become friends. If attendance and returning guests are any indication, the Fosters are doing everything right. Walt Disney stayed here years ago and said to the Fosters, "If I had this place, I would do all that I could not to change its character." The Fosters took his advice, and the ranch has been one of the best in the business ever since.

Address: Route 2, Box K, Sedalia, Colorado 80135
Telephone: (303) 647-2311, (303) 647-2495; Fax: (303) 647-2315
Airport: Denver or Colorado Springs
Train: Amtrak to Denver
Location: 2 hours southwest of Denver, 1 hour northwest of Colorado Springs, 12 miles southwest of Deckers
Memberships: Dude Ranchers' Association, Colorado Dude and Guest Ranch Association
Awards: AAA 4 Diamond; Mobil 3 Star
Medical: Langstaff-Brown Medical Clinic, 1 hour
Conference: 70, fall and spring only; largest room 1,800 square feet
Guest Capacity: 100
Accommodations: The twenty-four cabin suites are some of the finest in the business. All have fireplaces, refrigerators, covered porches with swings, and amenities such as daily maid service, oversized towels, and a delightful cowboy hat amenities basket. To ensure peace and quiet, the cabins are nicely spaced among the pines and uncluttered with TVs or telephones. Laundry facilities are available.
Rates: • $$-$$$. American Plan. Children's and spring/fall rates available. During summer there is a 7-day minimum stay policy.
Credit Cards: None
Season: February to December
Activities: At Lost Valley, guests learn to be better riders and gain a greater knowledge of Western riding skills. With 150 horses and 200 head of cows and calves, guests are encouraged to participate in ranch and cattle work. Fish in Goose Creek, which runs through the ranch, or drive 20 minutes and wet your fly in the world-famous Cheasman Canyon on the South Platte River. Orvis fishing guides are available. Additional activities/facilities include heated outdoor swimming pool, two whirlpool spas, two plexi-paved tennis courts, trap shooting, and hiking.
Children's Programs: This is one of Lost Valley's strongest attractions. Children are looked after by fully trained staff members. This program provides tremendous fun for children, yet gives parents peace of mind knowing their children are safe and happy. The teens operate within a framework of freedom, friendship, and fun provided by the collegiate staff.
Dining: The Fosters and their staff eat with the guests. This is a wonderful tradition and one that is a real treat. Enjoy roast beef carved to your preference, fresh salads, homemade breads and desserts, wrangler breakfast, evening cookouts and steak fries. Nonsmokers accommodated.
Entertainment: Entertainment is second to none. Lost Valley's staff is exceedingly talented. Enjoy musical entertainment, melodramas with shootouts, square dancing, hay rides, camp fires, and sing-alongs.
Summary: Without question, one of the top guest ranches in North America. Excellent staff and superb children's and teens' programs. Year-round riding, cattle drive, ranch store. A true destination vacation.

See color photos, page 189

Lost Valley Ranch, Colorado

Lost Valley Ranch, Colorado

Peaceful Valley Lodge and Ranch Resort, Colorado

Peaceful Valley Lodge and Ranch Resort is a year-round resort providing genuine hospitality and personal attention in a beautiful alpine setting. The Boehm family has been receiving guests at the Austrian-style ranch since the early 1950s. Near Rocky Mountain National Park and the enchanting St. Vrain Canyon, Peaceful Valley Lodge offers Old World charm coupled with an easygoing Western life-style. During the summer, one can enjoy extensive riding on Arabian and Austrian Lippizaner horses. There is lots of hiking and four-wheel driving in the backcountry, with tours to gold mining camps. The winter months are beautiful and filled with much joy and excitement. Unique to the ranch is a beautiful chapel overlooking Peaceful Valley. This landmark is a tribute to Karl's father. One can worship here on Sunday or share midweek vespers (summer months only). Karl and Mabel have created a year-round resort offering a blend of European charm and American ranch life. With their daughter, Debbie, and son-in-law, Randy, they welcome guests from all over the world.

Address: Star Route, Box 2811K, Lyons, Colorado 80540
Telephone: (303) 747-2881; (800) 95-LODGE (955-6343) for reservations only; Fax: (303) 747-2167
Airport: Denver
Location: 60 miles northwest of Denver
Memberships: Colorado Dude and Guest Ranch Association
Awards: AAA 3 Diamond, Mobil 3 Star
Medical: Longmont Community Hospital, 28 miles
Conference: 80-100 executive, conference center. Extensive conference brochure on request.
Guest Capacity: 130
Accommodations: This beautiful mountain ranch has been designed with Austrian warmth and charm. All ten cabins and thirty-one lodge rooms are spacious and comfortable with living rooms and some with patios. All are informal and cozy, with carpeting, fireplaces, some with hot tubs. Deluxe units have private Jacuzzi-type tubs. Coin-operated laundry machines.
Rates: • $$-$$$. American Plan. Children's, pack trip, and conference rates available. Children under age 3 free (baby-sitting available for fee).
Credit Cards: Visa, MasterCard, American Express, Diners Club
Season: Year-round
Activities: Summer offers extensive riding with indoor arena, overnight pack trips, chuck wagon breakfast rides, and lunch rides to the Continental Divide. Hiking, supper rides, indoor solar-heated swimming pool, Jacuzzi, sauna, tennis, mountain biking (extra), and llama treks. Wintertime transforms Peaceful Valley into a magical wonderland. Cross-country skiing, telemarking, sleigh rides, snowshoeing, ice skating, snow cat tours. Ski equipment can be rented at the ranch; instruction available.
Children's Program: Nursery and supervised children's program in the summer, strong teen program. Children's petting farm with all kinds of baby and small animals.
Dining: Year-round hearty and healthy food. Continental and American cuisine. Beer, wine, and liquor available.
Entertainment: In summer, square dancing, gymkhana, sing-alongs, hayrides, naturalist talks, talent shows, melodrama.
Summary: Wonderful ranch resort with emphasis on personal service, riding, hiking, and communing with the great outdoors. Beautiful alpine chapel and Western gift shop. Visit ghost towns and old mining camps. Van trips to Rocky Mountain National Park (elk, deer, and bighorn sheep can be seen here sometimes, depending on season). Summer video available on request. Fluent German spoken.

See color photos, pages 184-186

Peaceful Valley Lodge and Ranch Resort, Colorado

The Pines Ranch, Colorado

The Pines Ranch has been a guest ranch since the late 1800s, when the first dudes were European visitors. The ranch has seen various owners and today is run by Dean and Casey Rusk. Dean was a cowboy who ran a cattle operation down the road and gave that up to run the Pines Ranch. As Dean said, "I got tired of looking at the back end of cattle. I decided I'd rather look at people." That suited his wife, Casey, just fine, and together with their five kids, Dean and Casey spent three years renovating this lovely old ranch. The Sangre de Cristo mountains stand in full splendor behind the ranch, which is at 8,700 feet. "Guests just can't believe how magnificent these mountains are," says Casey. "We really have a paradise here, with huge views to the valley floor and to distant New Mexico." Deer, elk, turkey, and grouse are some of the wildlife you may see when you visit the Rusks.

Address: P.O. Box 311 K, Westcliffe, Colorado 81252

Telephone: (719) 783-9261

Airport: Pueblo or Colorado Springs

Location: 8 miles northwest of Westcliffe off Highway 69 North, 70 miles west of Pueblo, 95 miles southwest of Colorado Springs

Memberships: Colorado Dude and Guest Ranch Association

Medical: Clinic, 8 miles; Thomas More Hospital, 50 miles

Conference: 40

Guest Capacity: 40

Accommodations: The five wood-sided cabins (one is a two-story duplex) are modern with motel-like rooms, with living rooms, carpeting, separate thermostats, and private baths. There are lots of windows and porches for taking in the views. The completely renovated, circa 1893, shingled main lodge has four second-floor rooms—one with an attached balcony. The lodge is furnished in Victorian antiques and paneled in pine and oak. Laundry facilities are available.

Rates: • $-$$. American Plan. Children's rates available. Baby-sitting included during high season.

Credit Cards: Visa, MasterCard, American Express

Season: May through September

Activities: Fishing in the ranch's three streams and four ponds. Half-day and all-day rides go out daily into the high country. Ten to 15 people per ride, with pack trips into the high country possible. Ranch riding area for riding instruction and rodeo practice. Each week, guests can go on an all-day ride to the three Lakes of the Clouds. No riding on Sundays. Hiking, seasonal hunting, and raft trips can be arranged. Eight-person whirlpool and two saunas.

Children's Programs: Children are looked after during all scheduled adult riding or rafting. Kiddie wrangler. Monday night fishing derby. Two playhouses and video game room. Baby-sitting available.

Dining: PRHC (Pines Ranch Home Cookin')—home-baked, home-cooked, served buffet-style. BYOB.

Entertainment: Square dancing, staff shows, sing-alongs, camp fires, Saturday guest rodeos at the ranch and in town during July. Game room, movies.

Summary: Lots of young families, couples, and singles come to The Pines, as do the young at heart. Wonderful high-country scenery and riding. Ranch at 8,700 feet. Pine Cone General Store. Ranch originally an English settlement. Famous Royal Gorge "Little Grand Canyon" (40 miles away), Buckskin Joe's Western town.

Powderhorn Guest Ranch, Colorado

Authentic Western Ranch, Member–Dude Ranchers'
Association

Powderhorn Guest Ranch is small, secluded, and personal. It is far from the hustle of everyday life and in cool mountain splendor. This ranch is traversed by Cebolla Creek in the Powderhorn Valley and is adjacent to more than a million acres of wilderness and national forest. Don't worry about traffic, city noise, or pollution here; there are none. Probably the only noises you'll hear are kids laughing and the quiet tumbling of Cebolla Creek. Activities are available for all ages and interests. Kids are special and are included in everything that goes on at Powderhorn. Jim and Bonnie Cook, hosts and owners, left the big city of Chicago in the early 1970s to fulfill a long-time dream. They will make you feel a part of their family, and you will meet many interesting friends from all over.

Address: County Highway 27, Drawer K, Powderhorn, Colorado 81243
Telephone: (303) 641-0220
Airport: Gunnison via Denver
Location: 38 miles southwest of Gunnison
Memberships: Dude Ranchers' Association, Colorado Dude and Guest Ranch Association
Medical: Gunnison Valley Hospital
Conference: 35
Guest Capacity: 35
Accommodations: Thirteen individual cabins, some with kitchens, all with refrigerators and front porches large enough to relax on. The cabins have private baths and are carpeted. Daily maid service is provided, with laundry facilities available.
Rates: • $. American Plan. Five-day minimum stay during summer months. Children's and off-season rates available. Kids under 2 stay free.
Credit Cards: American Express. Personal checks and cash accepted.
Season: Early June to mid-September
Activities: Horseback riding is the primary activity at the ranch, with rides scheduled each day except Sunday. Fishermen will enjoy Cebolla Creek, which runs right through the ranch, just steps from the cabins. Rental poles and fishing licenses available at the ranch. Swimming in heated pool, spa, seasonal hunting, hiking, and four-wheel-drive trips. River raft trip is included. Golf and tennis available nearby.
Children's Programs: Kids must be 6 to trail ride. There is a pony for the little ones. Lots for kids to do, including tubing on river. Children's playground with swings and games. Special children's fishing pond. No child care provided.
Dining: Three family-style buffet or ranch-type meals a day. BYOB.
Entertainment: Lots of evening activities including a piano, juke box, pool tables, and table tennis. Rodeos in town and at the ranch. Square dancing; movies (with popcorn) shown throughout the week. Saturday night's "VCR Movie of the Week"—featuring guests' riding performances and ranch activities during the week.
Summary: Very small and friendly, family owned and operated guest ranch. Remote with not a lot of night life. Guests are not programmed every minute. Neighbors are fourth-generation cattle ranchers. Always a nice mix of guests. Old mines and ghost towns, Curecanti National Monument, Blue Mesa Reservoir, and Crested Butte. Video available on request.

Rawah Ranch, Colorado

Authentic Western Ranch, Member–Dude Ranchers' Association

Rawah (pronounced ray-wah) is the Ute Indian word for "wilderness." The ranch sits at the edge of the 76,000-acre Rawah Wilderness Area at 8,400 feet with the Laramie River right at its back door. It is practically surrounded by the Roosevelt National Forest, in some of Colorado's wildest and most beautiful country. Rawah is relaxed and, unlike most ranches, is quite a distance from the closest town. It caters to folks who want to escape the hectic pace of urban life and enjoy nature and wonderful hospitality. Today, Rawah is owned and operated by the wonderful Kunz family, who were guests themselves at dude ranches for over 15 years. They have brought their tremendous love for this way of life and their experiences to Rawah. You can ride, fish, hike, take photographs, pitch a few horseshoes, just loaf, or rock yourself to sleep in one of the rocking chairs on the front porch of the main lodge—it's your vacation. Whatever you decide to do, you're in good hands at Rawah.

Address: Glendevey, Colorado Route, Dept. K, Jelm, Wyoming 82063* (summer). (*Note: The ranch is in Colorado, but mail is collected in Wyoming, where the closest mail drop is located.)
Telephone: (303) 435-5715 (summer)
Airport: Denver, with commuter service to Laramie, Wyoming
Location: 60 miles southwest of Laramie, 75 miles northwest of Fort Collins
Memberships: Dude Ranchers' Association, Colorado Dude and Guest Ranch Association
Medical: Laramie Ivinson Memorial Hospital, emergency helicopter service available
Conference: 32
Guest Capacity: 32
Accommodations: The main lodge is the hub of activity, with two stone fireplaces and a wonderful sitting porch with rocking chairs overlooking Middle Mountain. There are five rooms in the log main lodge and six single or duplex log cabins scattered around the ranch. Each has a fireplace or wood stove, electricity, full bath,

twin and king-size beds. Some have carpeting; others have wood floors.
Rates: • $-$$. American Plan. Children's rates available; special rates for nonriders. Off-season daily rates.
Credit Cards: None. Personal checks, traveler's checks, and cash accepted.
Season: Mid-June through mid-September
Activities: Rawah takes great pride in its horses for novice, intermediate, and experienced riders (ask about the fast meadow rides). Enjoy breakfast rides, mountain trail rides, and arena riding. Weekly half-day horsemanship clinic. Rawah goes out of its way to accommodate guests and their riding preferences. Wild trout fishing on the Laramie River, ¾ mile of which runs through the ranch, the Poudre River nearby, and over 20 high mountain lakes, and the ranch's own stocked fishing pond. Some fishing equipment provided. Of note, each week includes a full afternoon fly-fishing clinic with professional instruction. Hiking, volleyball, lawn sports, and seasonal hunting (deer and elk).
Children's Programs: No children's programs per se. Kids' wrangler. Children under 6 are led around the arena. Fishing pond, swing and slide, and lawn sports. Separate recreation building with table tennis.
Dining: Hearty ranch food. Some Rawah specialties include meats broiled outside over aspen. Everything is home-baked. Special diets are accommodated with advance notice.
Entertainment: Evening sing-alongs, practice roping on "roll-o-roper," cards, checkers, puzzles, and plenty of visiting.
Summary: Great family ranch located on the Laramie River, which flows right behind the main lodge. Lots of riding (you may decide where and when you wish to ride), fly-fishing, and hiking. Bring your own horse if you wish. Abundant flowers, birds, and wildlife—particularly moose. Every party receives a copy of June Wheeler's "Trail Guide," a delightful description of nature and hiking at Rawah. Norwegian spoken.

Rawah Ranch, Colorado

Rawah Ranch, Colorado

San Juan Guest Ranch, Colorado

Authentic Western Ranch, Member–Dude Ranchers' Association

San Juan Guest Ranch is surrounded by more 14,000-foot peaks than any other spot in the United States. The ranch is in southwestern Colorado in the incomparable Uncompahgre Valley, which has been called "the Switzerland of America." It is also just four miles north of quaint, Victorian Ouray, which has been carefully preserved to keep this century-old mining town's special qualities. While the ranch is small, catering to twenty-five guests, it is big in personal service and hospitality. To continue in the Western tradition, San Juan Ranch excels in horseback riding with superbly trained horses. Fall is a wonderful time to visit, as the aspens display a magnificent array of gold before the winter snows. To capture this beauty, Pat MacTiernan and her son, Scott, have created a 35mm photo adventure/workshop for adults only. The course is taught by a professional photographer, and everyone receives hands-on instruction.

Address: 2882 Highway 23, Dept. K, Ridgway, Colorado 81432
Telephone: (800) 331-3015; (303) 626-5360
Airport: Montrose or Telluride via Denver
Train: Ask the MacTiernans about the narrow gauge train to Silverton with free pickup at Silverton
Location: 5 miles north of Ouray, 6 hours southwest of Denver by car
Memberships: Colorado Dude and Guest Ranch Association, Dude Ranchers' Association
Medical: Ouray Clinic, Montrose Hospital, 30 miles; in-house EMT
Conference: 25, off-season only
Guest Capacity: 25
Accommodations: Guests stay in the comfortable two-story "Lodge." It is fully carpeted and very comfortable, with nine individual apartments on both levels. There are two single rooms on the ground floor. Private baths and daily maid service. Queen-size, doubles, and bunk beds. Guests can walk onto common decks with views of the valley from their rooms.

Rates: • $$. American Plan. Children's, off-season, and group rates available. Three-day minimum stay summer and winter.
Credit Cards: Visa, MasterCard, American Express. Personal checks are accepted.
Season: June through September, open Christmas. Off-season for groups.
Activities: Summer brings a full riding program with lessons available in the arena. Weekly half-day and full-day rides and overnight high country pack trip. Jeep trips to ghost towns and abandoned gold mines in the heart of the San Juan Mountains. Fishing in the Uncompahgre River or private stocked ponds. Trap shooting and rifle range (guns available). Hiking, eight-person hot tub, volleyball, horseshoes, surrey rides. Tennis and huge natural hot springs in Ouray. Balloon rides available. Winter offers antique one-horse sleigh rides, snowshoeing, tobogganing, and guided cross-country skiing. Downhill skiing at world-famous Telluride ski area, 45 minutes away.
Children's Programs: A child's paradise with supervised activities including feeding animals and petting zoo. Baby-sitting available.
Dining: Hearty meals served family-style, traditional turkey dinner starts each week, lots of vegetables and salads. Fresh trout served weekly. Weekly cookouts and barbecues. BYOB.
Entertainment: Spectacular multi-image slide show in Ouray. Bonfire with cowboy singing, volleyball games. Shopping in Ouray and Telluride. Nearby team roping demonstrations, local cowboy dance halls.
Summary: Family owned and operated and described as having an intimacy that is contagious. Most guests are either interested in riding or learning how to ride. Spectacular mountain scenery surroundings. Old-fashioned Christmas program with Santa on hand. Great for families, those without families, and single parents. Surrey and sleigh rides, photography workshop, ballooning, Victorian mining town of Ouray, ghost towns, Telluride.

San Juan Guest Ranch, Colorado

San Juan Guest Ranch, Colorado

7W Guest Ranch, Colorado

Authentic Western Ranch, Member–Dude Ranchers' Association

History, hospitality, and the ever-changing splendor of the Rockies await you at the 7W Guest Ranch, one of the oldest guest ranches in Colorado. This 760-acre ranch lies between Vail and Aspen on the border of the White River National Forest. The 7W has developed a variety of family activities geared to each season. Horseback riding is the main feature in the summer. Winter brings the joy of cross-country skiing. Surrounding the 7W is a lot of history and terrific sightseeing in the nearby towns of Vail, Glenwood Springs, and Aspen. Whether you want to sleep under the stars, cast for trout, explore, or just relax, you can do it all here. A warning though—tranquillity at the ranch is broken only by fun, laughter, and enjoyment.

Address: 3412 County Road 151K, Gypsum, Colorado 81637
Telephone: (303) 524-9328
Airport: Eagle, Grand Junction, and Denver
Train: Amtrak to Glenwood Springs, 37 miles east
Location: 30 miles northwest of Eagle off I-70, 60 miles northwest of Vail, 165 miles west of Denver. Pickup service available but extra.
Memberships: Dude Ranchers' Association, Colorado Dude and Guest Ranch Association
Medical: Valley View Hospital, Glenwood Springs, 37 miles
Conference: Groups of up to 15
Guest Capacity: 22
Accommodations: Guests enjoy six log cabins, each with a splendid view of the private, stocked 5-acre ranch lake. Though rustic, each has its own bathroom and a wood burning stove, braided throw rugs, and pitched 10-foot ceilings. Welcome homemade cookies on arrival.
Rates: • $. American Plan. Off-season, children's, and group rates available. Winter rates on request.
Credit Cards: None. Personal checks accepted.
Season: Early June to late September (summer); mid-December to early January (winter)

Activities: Summer brings horseback riding with excellent instruction available. Guest to wrangler ratio is five to one. Morning, afternoon, and all-day rides. No riding on Sundays. Overnight and longer pack trips available. Fishing in stocked lake or in nearby streams and alpine lakes. Serious fishermen should bring their own equipment. Seasonal hunting for deer, elk, cougar, bear. Hiking, float trips on the Colorado River 17 miles away. Challenging mountain croquet course, volleyball, badminton, and horseshoes. Winter activities are cross-country skiing on fully groomed and maintained trails, snowshoeing, snowmobiling. (Must bring your own equipment.)
Children's Programs: No structured program. Children's play area, baby-sitting available. Not recommended for children under age 5.
Dining: Family-style home cooking. Ranch specialties: beef ribs, Mexican fiesta, fresh locally grown apple pie. Weekly steak fry at the old homestead cabin with guests arriving by horseback. BYOB.
Entertainment: Weekly square dancing, country-western singing, cookouts, camp fires under the stars.
Summary: Best for adults and families with older children. Riding and fishing are the main activities. Hot springs at Glenwood, historic tours to Carbondale, Aspen, and Vail.

Sky Corral Ranch, Colorado

Authentic Western Ranch, Member–Dude Ranchers' Association

Sky Corral Ranch is a friendly, family-operated ranch, peacefully removed from hurried city life. This 450-acre ranch is in a scenic valley, surrounded by 780,000 acres of the Roosevelt National Forest. Only thirty guests are received at a time. This small capacity provides a highly personalized atmosphere of fun and relaxation. There is a full activities program for everyone, day and night, highlighted by horseback riding.

Address: 8233 Old Flowers Road, Dept. K, Bellvue, Colorado 80512
Telephone: (303) 484-1362
Airport: Denver or Fort Collins
Location: 89 miles (2 hours) northwest of Denver, 24 miles northwest of Fort Collins
Memberships: Dude Ranchers' Association, Colorado Dude and Guest Ranch Association
Medical: Poudre Valley Hospital, Fort Collins
Conference: 25
Guest Capacity: 30
Accommodations: Guests can choose between six one-, two-, and three-bedroom cabins or six lodge rooms. Each is clean, comfortable, and complete with private baths. Some with fireplaces, most with carpeting. Daily maid service.
Rates: • $. American Plan. Children's rates available. Spring and fall discounts.
Credit Cards: None. Personal or traveler's checks accepted.
Season: Mid-May to October
Activities: Ride on mountain-bred and trail-wise horses. Breakfast rides, half-day 2-hour rides, overnight pack trips. Fishing for rainbow and cutthroat trout in stocked pond or Cache La Poudre River, float trips, hiking, sand volleyball, tennis, swimming in heated pool. Van trips to Rocky Mountain National Park and Estes Park. Whirlpool and sauna.
Children's Programs: Children's program with caring supervision for ages 5-12. Baby-sitting available.
Dining: Hearty family-style meals. Home-cooked meals. Homemade breads, desserts, ice cream, and soups. Several meals on deck. Steak dinner in mountains. Lunch rides.
Entertainment: Sing-alongs and camp fires, recreation hall. Square dancing, ice cream social, movies.
Summary: Small family guest ranch. Nearby attractions include the Cache La Poudre River, a designated wild and scenic river, 8 miles from ranch. Estes Park shopping. Rocky Mountain National Park, Anheuser-Busch tour in Fort Collins.

Skyline Guest Ranch, Colorado

Authentic Western Ranch, Member–Dude Ranchers' Association

When Dave and Sherry Farny bought Skyline Guest Ranch in 1968, their first concern was to preserve the natural beauty so that generations to come could enjoy this magnificent and breathtaking mountain paradise. They succeeded by deeding the property to the great wilderness protector, the Nature Conservancy. Thus, the ambience and tranquillity at Skyline will be savored for years to come. In the southwestern corner of the state, Skyline is nestled in the high meadows and pine-rich peaks of the San Juan Mountains. The crisp air and the crystal-clear mountain water, not to mention the snow-capped 14,000-foot peaks, make this ranch one of the most beautiful. Dave and Sherry have preserved a tradition, a spirit on which guest ranching was founded—honest and friendly hospitality. Privacy and comfort are yours in abundance here. This is one of the best guest ranches in the world.

Address: Box 67K, Telluride, Colorado 81435
Telephone: (303) 728-3757; Fax: (303) 728-5263
Airport: Telluride
Location: 15 minutes from Telluride
Memberships: Dude Ranchers' Association, Colorado Dude and Guest Ranch Association
Medical: Telluride Clinic, 8 miles
Conference: 35
Guest Capacity: 35
Accommodations: Guests stay in ten comfortable lodge rooms or six housekeeping cabins and two apartments in the new log addition. All the rooms have magnificent views, private baths, and excellent beds with down comforters. Awaken in the morning to sweet aromas from Cindy's famous kitchen. Sauna and hot tub are heated year-round. Laundry facilities. No smoking in buildings.
Rates: • $$. American Plan. Rates vary depending upon the season. One week minimum stay, Sunday to Sunday.
Credit Cards: Visa, MasterCard, American Express, Discover. Personal checks preferred, traveler's checks accepted.

Season: June to mid-October (summer); mid-December to April (winter); open Christmas and Easter
Activities: Summer brings a full horse program with instruction for all levels. Pack trips available. Fishing is superb in the ranch's three mountain lakes and nearby streams. Lake swimming, mountain biking, hiking, mountain climbing, backpacking, photography, white water adventures, four-wheel-drive trips. Hot tub and sauna. Massage available. Winter activities are cross-country skiing, snowshoeing, and downhill skiing at Telluride, 3 miles away. Ranch transportation provided.
Children's Programs: No children's program, but kids can participate with parents. Kids under 6 do not ride on trails.
Dining: Out of this world. Cindy's kitchen is world famous. Cindy is one of the Farnys' daughters and a blue ribbon graduate of the Peter Kump's New York City Cooking School and the Ritz Escoffier of Paris. Complimentary beer and wine served with happy hour and dinner.
Entertainment: Singing. Terrific library and cozy main lodge.
Summary: F.F.F. = the Fabulous Farny Family and their spectacular mountain setting. This family will hook you for life. Four-day pack trip for expert horsemen in both June and September. Telluride, filled with museums, galleries, music, and shopping, just 15 minutes away. Spring and fall photo workshops (the ranch has had National Geographic photographers give this course). French and German spoken.

See color photos, page 226

Sweetwater Guest Ranch, Colorado

Authentic Western Ranch, Member–Dude Ranchers' Association

Sweetwater Guest Ranch is an intimate, secluded ranch nestled amid the panoramic vistas of the Flat Tops Wilderness Area. The ranch has a diverse topography, with many different ecosystems that provide the area with a wide variety of wildlife and wildflowers. Sweetwater has a colorful history involving Ute Indians, trappers, gunmen, and gangsters. The ranch property was homesteaded in the late 1800s and the lodge served as a stagecoach stop. The property was purchased by General Frederick Anderson in the early 1960s and is still family owned. Today, John Atwater, a Ph.D environmental chemist, and his wife, Mary, operate the ranch. John grew up in the Adirondacks of New York and first fell in love with Sweetwater twenty years ago. John and Mary chose the ranch life-style to raise their children. The Sweetwater offers a homelike atmosphere, surrounded by tremendous natural beauty and close to beautiful Sweetwater Lake.

Address: 2650 Sweetwater Lake Road, Drawer K, Gypsum, Colorado 81637
Telephone: (303) 524-7949 (summer); (303) 758-9177 (winter)
Airport: Vail or Denver
Train: Amtrak to Glenwood Springs, 33 miles east
Location: 50 miles northwest of Vail, 155 miles west of Denver
Memberships: Dude Ranchers' Association, Colorado Dude and Guest Ranch Association
Medical: Valley View Hospital, Glenwood Springs, 33 miles; staff members are medic first-aid trained.
Conference: Groups of up to 30
Guest Capacity: 30
Accommodations: There are two types of cabins at the ranch—three log cabins that can hold a maximum of six people and two duplex cabins that can hold a maximum of ten people and are ideal for two families who want to go on vacation together. All cabin units have private baths, queen or double beds, and a lounge area (some with fireplaces).

Rates: • $. American Plan. Off-season, children's, and group rates available.
Credit Cards: Visa and MasterCard. Personal checks and traveler's checks accepted.
Season: Late May to early September
Activities: Ranch programs are arranged according to the wishes of the guests. Horse program includes instruction, scenic trail rides, and guest rodeo. Good fly-fishing (equipment and instruction provided) on three miles of private stream will challenge the avid fisherman. Hiking, birding, and canoeing enthusiasts enjoy the many nearby trails and the serenity of Sweetwater Lake. Explore Ute Indian caves. Raft the wild waters of the Colorado. Relax by the pool and hot tub. Additional activities include tennis, campfires, cookouts, and square dancing.
Children's Programs: Optional programs including pony rides, nature hikes, and western arts and crafts, all designed for children between the ages of 3 and 12. Play area for the younger children, and a 2-acre stocked pond and recreation hall for the older ones. Babysitting available.
Dining: Family-style meals are served in the historic lodge. Fresh-baked hearty home cooking. Hors d'oeuvres are served before dinner. BYOB. Twice during the week the ranch has separate seatings for the children and the adults, with complimentary wine for the adults.
Entertainment: Evening games and special events, country swing and square dancing, camp fires, and stargazing.
Summary: Reasonable rates, great for families. Horseback riding in beautiful valley. Good fishing. Nearby Sweetwater Lake for all kinds of lake activities. Day trips to the Glenwood Springs Hot Sulphur Pools, shopping in Vail and Aspen.

Sylvan Dale Ranch, Colorado

The 3,000-acre Sylvan Dale Ranch is located in the Thompson River Valley at 5,325 feet. Maurice Jessup arrived at Sylvan Dale in 1934 from Kansas. In 1946, he bought the ranch and it has been in the Jessup family ever since. Through a lifetime of hopes and dreams solidly based on faith, dedication, and hard work, the Jessups and their two children, Susan and David, have made Sylvan Dale what it is today. Facilities have kept pace with the times, offering newly remodeled accommodations and comfort. Today, Maurice and Tillie's daughter, Susan, manages the ranch along with a crew of friendly and accommodating staff. The ranch has more than fifty head of horses and one hundred beef cattle. Sylvan Dale features 3- and 6-day family vacation packages during the summer months. "Bunk and breakfast" is available year-round. People visit Sylvan Dale for many reasons: business meetings, retreats, family reunions, holiday gatherings, or just to taste basic, down-to-earth, warm, and friendly hospitality. The Jessups put it this way: "Good fun, good food, and good folks."

Address: 2939 N. County Road 31D, Dept. K, Loveland, Colorado 80537
Telephone: (303) 667-3915
Airport: Stapleton International, Denver; limited commercial service to Ft. Collins
Location: 55 miles northwest of Denver, 18 miles east of Estes Park off Highway 34
Memberships: Colorado Dude and Guest Ranch Association
Medical: McKee Medical Center, Loveland, 8 miles
Conference: 50; two conference buildings
Guest Capacity: 60
Accommodations: Individual and family housing in carpeted cabins provides privacy and homey comfort. There are nine cabins and fourteen upper and lower lodge rooms in the Wagon Wheel Barn, a two-story structure with a large fireplace, a stage at one end, and lots of meeting space. No television or telephones.

Rates: • $. American Plan. Three- and six-day packages. Children's and package rates available. Off-season bunk and breakfast package. Riding extra.
Credit Cards: None
Season: Year-round. Full-program dude ranch June through Labor Day.
Activities: Each week guests receive a full riding and activities schedule from which to choose. Escorted daily trail rides, weekly overnight pack trips, rides past Echo Rock, through the Badlands, or to Inspiration Point. Beginner riding instruction. Hiking along the river and up rugged Red Ridge. Fishing from stocked ponds and the Big Thompson River flowing past the ranch lodge. Marked nature trails, two laykold tennis courts, volleyball, basketball, game room, horseshoes, and a heated outdoor pool. Eighteen-hole golf course, 5 miles.
Children's Programs: Supervised activities (daily 11:30 a.m. to 2:00 p.m.), horsemanship, ranch chores, nature hikes, fishing. Baby-sitting available. Children must be at least 7 years old to ride the trails. Younger kids ride in arena.
Dining: Dine in the beautiful antique dining room. Weekly Western-style cookout at the Heart J Grill. All kinds of wonderful home-baked favorites by Mrs. Jessup—cherry pies, cinnamon rolls, and a weekly Thanksgiving feast. Box lunches packed for all-day excursions.
Entertainment: Weekly gymkhanas at the ranch and professional rodeos in town. Recreation room with billiards and table tennis. Square dancing with twilight hayrides.
Summary: Family owned and operated ranch. Great for family reunions. Fourth of July cattle drive, mountain man talk and presentation, nature trail with naturalist, archaeological site on property, hay work throughout the summer. Rocky Mountain National Park, shopping at Ft. Collins. Spanish spoken.

Tall Timber, Colorado

Perched high in the splendor of the San Juan Mountains at 7,500 feet, Tall Timber is a hidden retreat. This Mobil 5 Star, AAA 5 Diamond exclusive hideaway is so secluded that guests arrive by the Silverton, one of the last narrow gauge trains in the United States, or by helicopter. Dennis and Judy Beggrow discovered this remote spot in 1970. Since then, they have, with a lot of time and work, developed this world-class property. Tall Timber is surrounded with history and beauty. The early Ute Indians used the meadows as hunting grounds, and later miners came in search of gold. In recent years the countryside has been used in countless movies, including *Around the World in 80 Days* and *Butch Cassidy and the Sundance Kid*, just to name a couple. No roads, no telephones, no stress, no deadlines. Tall Timber equals seclusion, beauty, and, maybe most of all, a marriage of luxury and nature.

Address: S.S.R. Box 90 K, Durango, Colorado 81301
Telephone: (303) 259-4813 (radio telephone; be patient as there may be lots of static)
Airport: Durango/La Plata; private planes to Animas Air Park with 5,000-foot paved runway
Location: 26 miles north of Durango
Awards: Mobil 5 Star, AAA 5 Diamond
Medical: Mercy Medical Center, Durango; emergency helicopter available
Conference: 24
Guest Capacity: 24
Accommodations: All ten wood-paneled condominium-style units are private and surrounded by quaking aspen. Each year the Beggrows and staff plant more than 25,000 petunias, pansies, and snapdragons. There are eight 1-bedroom and two 2-bedroom suites. Each has its own living room, wet bar, floor-to-ceiling stone fireplace, and balcony. Turn-down service is provided each evening. Furnishings emphasize casual elegance and comfort. The main lodge is a massive three-story structure with a wine cellar, wet bar, lounge, dining room.

Rates: $$$$. American Plan. Four- and seven-day packages, special low season and children's rates available.
Credit Cards: None. Personal checks accepted.
Season: Mid-May through October (summer); mid-December through mid-January (winter)
Activities: In the summer, there is a heated pool (ask one of the staff to tell you how the pool arrived), three outdoor whirlpools (one overlooks the Animas River), sauna; putting green, driving range, 9-hole, par 29 golf course; tennis court; trout fishing; Nautilus fitness room, jogging trail; plenty of hiking; helicopter picnics, hikes, and tours; guided horseback riding to high mountain lakes, Silver Falls (a wonderful seasonal waterfall); morning, picnic, or afternoon rides; riding instruction available at sister property one mile away. The Christmas and New Year's activities are among the special winter events. All suites are decorated with Christmas trees. It's a happy and festive time. While winter is a short season, there is cross-country skiing, ice skating (equipment available), and a daily helicopter shuttle to Purgatory for downhill skiing. Some snowmobiling.
Children's Programs: Well-behaved children welcome. No special program. Tall Timber is great for families who can enjoy the outdoors together.
Dining: Food is not taken lightly. Each table in the dining room has its own picture window. Meals are served from a menu and feature eggs Benedict, grilled salmon, beef Wellington, steak and trout, lots of fresh breads, and pastries. Many vegetables and herbs are fresh from the garden. Dinners are by candlelight with crystal and gold-rimmed china. Picnic lunches will be prepared on request. Stocked bar and wine cellar.
Entertainment: Large library, weekly fireworks with orchestrated music. Summer season only.
Summary: Remote executive wilderness hideaway. Arrive by the exciting and historic Durango-Silverton narrow gauge train or by helicopter.

T-Lazy-7 Guest Ranch, Colorado

T-Lazy-7 Guest Ranch is down the road from some of the most beautiful mountains in the entire world—the Maroon Bells. These awesome, snow-capped peaks rise dramatically toward the sky with their sheer, angular faces. Here you can savor a year-round panorama of color and splendor. This ranch is also close to Aspen, one of the world's most celebrated mountain towns. Lou and her sons, Buck and Rick Deane, own and operate this bohemian ranch. Not to be confused with neighboring Colorado dude ranches, T-Lazy-7 operates on a daily and nightly basis. You can stay here a week, but you can also stay by the day with a two-night minimum. What makes the Deanes' ranch unique is its proximity to Aspen and the Maroon Bells. The price the ranch pays for being in paradise is a road through the ranch property that takes tourists all summer long to the Maroon Bells.

Address: 3129 Maroon Creek Road, Dept. K, Aspen, Colorado 81612
Telephone: (303) 925-7254 for lodging; (303) 925-4614 for horse and snowmobile rental
Airport: Aspen via Denver
Location: 4 miles southeast of Aspen
Medical: Aspen Hospital, 3 miles
Conference: 150
Guest Capacity: 110
Accommodations: There are five lodges and three cabins. A variety of ranch-style rustic accommodations are offered. Guest quarters have no telephone or television. All apartments and cabins have kitchenettes equipped with the essentials. Some with fireplaces and balconies.
Rates: • $. Horseback riding and snowmobiling not included.
Credit Cards: None
Season: Year-round
Activities: Summer programs include guided hourly horseback rides, more than 100 horses (many of which are Tennessee walkers), breakfast rides, Maroon Bells lunch rides, special day rides, matched Belgian team hayrides, pack trips, stocked pond and stream fishing, hiking, pho-

tography, large bell-shaped year-round heated swimming pool, 40-person sauna, and hot tub. Golf and tennis nearby. Winter offers some of the world's most celebrated ski slopes nearby, cross-country skiing, sleigh rides. Guided hourly snowmobiling or tours and lunch trips.
Children's Programs: None. Baby-sitting available. Stocked fishing pond (poles available).
Dining: The ranch does not provide meals on a regular basis. Most guests cook in their cabins, each with a barbecue. Cook your own or go to Aspen for elegant dining.
Entertainment: Midweek Western parties, cookouts and live country-western band. Winter sleigh ride dinner and dancing. Open to public.
Summary: Independent, do-your-own-thing ranch. No structured program. Open to public. Kitchen facilities provided. Unguided summer horseback riding and winter snowmobiling. Tennessee walking horses, Maroon Bells, Maroon Lake, and the famous town of Aspen nearby.

Tumbling River Ranch, Colorado

Authentic Western Ranch, Member–Dude Ranchers' Association

Tumbling River Ranch is the year-round home of Jim and Mary Dale Gordon, two very friendly Texans who serve Southern hospitality high in the Colorado Rockies. At 9,200 feet, the ranch is in Indian country on the banks of Geneva Creek and in the middle of Pike National Forest. This secluded spot is well known for the Ute Indians and trappers who once roamed these parts. The property is divided into an upper ranch (where most of the activities take place), built as a mountain retreat by a former mayor of Denver, and a lower ranch house, the Pueblo, built by Native Americans with carved beams and adobe walls, for the daughter of Adolph Coors. You will find a warm, informal atmosphere here, and plenty of natural ambience and wildlife. Elk, deer, sheep, and mountain goats may be seen. Bear and mountain lions are around; you may have to track them, though. One of the best features at Tumbling River is the children's program. One guest said, "A family can spend its vacation together and still get away from one another." Tumbling River is known, above all, for its superb hospitality and western charm.

Address: P.O. Box 30K, Grant, Colorado 80448
Telephone: (800) 654-8770; (303) 838-5981
Airport: Denver Stapleton International
Location: 4 miles north of Grant, 62 miles southwest of Denver
Memberships: Dude Ranchers' Association, Colorado Dude and Guest Ranch Association
Medical: Denver hospitals
Conference: 40, off-season only
Guest Capacity: 55
Accommodations: Accommodations are in two clusters: the upper ranch and the lower ranch, about a quarter mile apart. Eight cabins (one is bilevel) have names like Indian Hogan, the Frenchman's Cabin, Big Horn, and Tomahawk. Most have fireplaces; twin, queen-size, or bunk beds for kids; and arching ceilings. Some are real log; some log-sided; all the porches have swings, hanging geranium planters, and many bird feeders scattered about. There are also fourteen rooms in the two upper and lower ranch lodges, each with its own fireplace.
Rates: • $$$. American Plan. Children's, off-season, corporate, and group rates available.
Credit Cards: None
Season: Mid-May through September
Activities: The Gordons offer a wide variety of activities: excellent riding with a string of 80 horses, half-day and all-day rides, pack trips, and riding instruction available. Four-wheel-drive, hiking, fly-fishing with instruction in stocked ponds, streams, and mountain lakes, and black powder plus trap shooting (guns and ammunition provided). The heated swimming pool has a full-length cabana with tables and an eight-person hot tub with nearby old-time steam sauna. River rafting available.
Children's Programs: Kiddie wrangler and programs for children 3 years old and up. Separate programs for children 3 to 5, 6 to 11, and teens. Baby-sitting available for kids under 3. Children 5 and under ride with supervision.
Dining: Complimentary coffee served in your cabin each morning. Every day, except Wednesday, there is a cookout. Favorites include apple pancakes with apple cider syrup and luncheon cookouts with homemade soup. Weekly "Gordon's hamburgers" poolside. Two adult candlelight dinners. Entrées include shrimp Dijon, chicken Florentine, and weekly Thanksgiving dinner. Pecan pies and lemon mousse.
Entertainment: Every night there is something different: hayrides, mountain camp fires with hot chocolate, square dancing, ranch rodeos, and talent shows. Old-fashioned farewell hootenanny.
Summary: Excellent family ranch with something for every member of the family. Hosts and staff are tops! Wait until you see the old barn and marvelous old ranch trading post. Nearby attractions include historic narrow gauge train, towns of Georgetown and Fairplay.

See color photos, page 192

Vista Verde Guest and Ski Touring Ranch, Colorado

Authentic Western Ranch, Member–Dude Ranchers' Association

Frank and Winton Brophy, of Westchester County, New York, bought Vista Verde Ranch in 1975 to satisfy their love for space, quarter horses, and nature. An ex-Ford Motor Company executive, Frank traded sophisticated New York for a "special way of life," one that he and Winton have shared with guests from all over the world. Surrounded by 1.3 million acres of national forest, the 600-acre Vista Verde shines year-round. Twenty-five miles northeast of the ski town of Steamboat Springs, Vista Verde has a capacity of 36 guests. Families and singles stay in hand-hewn log cabins. Named after nearby peaks, cabins are built of giant spruce logs. The main lodge, where meals are served, has an antique-filled living room, a library, a game room, and a lounge. At night the lodge is lighted by pewter sconces. Vista Verde is a small, traditional guest ranch offering fine accommodations, excellent food, a wide variety of year-round mountain recreational activities and personalized service.

Address: Box 465K, Steamboat Springs, Colorado 80477
Telephone: (303) 879-3858 or (800) 526-RIDE (7433)
Airport: Year-round commercial airline service to Steamboat Springs via Denver; private jets and commercial service to Yampa Valley Airport in the winter
Location: 25 miles northeast of Steamboat Springs
Memberships: Colorado Dude and Guest Ranch Association, Dude Ranchers' Association, Cross-Country Ski Areas Association
Awards: Mobil 3 Star, AAA 3 Diamond
Medical: Steamboat Springs Hospital
Conference: 25
Guest Capacity: 36
Accommodations: Eight spruce log, one- to three-bedroom cabins with wood stoves, handmade pine and antique furniture, baths, fully carpeted, and decks with mountain views. Some with full kitchens. Down comforters. No telephones or television.

Rates: • $$$. American Plan. Children's and winter rates available. Fly-fishing, balloon rides, and pack trips extra.
Credit Cards: None. Personal checks or traveler's checks accepted.
Season: Summer runs from the end of May to mid-September. Winter season is mid-December to mid-March.
Activities: Summer program includes quality riding with instruction, two rides daily, 5 to 6 in each group, all-day lunch rides each week. Pack trips, hiking, white water rafting, swimming in small lake with beach, gold panning, fishing with a licensed guide who comes to the ranch weekly. Hot air ballooning weekly with a champagne breakfast cookout. Afternoon rock climbing and rappeling with instructor. Sports building with beautiful views of the mountains with twelve-person whirlpool sauna, cold plunge pool, stationary bikes, and rowing machine. A masseuse is available. Winter activities are sleigh rides, tobogganing, ski touring, snowshoeing, and ice climbing with certified instructors. Dog sledding available.
Children's Program: Small farm animals (goats, sheep, ducks, rabbits) and daily egg gathering. Fire engine rides. Child care provided.
Dining: Culinary Institute chefs, American family-style with a touch of gourmet. Wine can be purchased. Wild game (venison, pig on a spit) one night a week. Home-grown vegetables, homemade, just baked everything, hand-cranked ice cream.
Entertainment: Gymkhanas, square dancing, games, hayrides. Music every night, slide shows, weekend rodeos.
Summary: Beautiful guest/working cattle ranch offering a wide range of recreational activities. Sports spa building and small animal farm. Steamboat Springs with a wealth of activities, summer professional rodeo, lots of wildlife. Ballooning, winter ski touring. French, German, and Chinese spoken.

Vista Verde Guest and Ski Touring Ranch, Colorado

Vista Verde Guest and Ski Touring Ranch, Colorado

Waunita Hot Springs Ranch, Colorado

Authentic Western Ranch, Member–Dude Ranchers' Association

Since the early 1960s, the Pringles have been hosting families, couples, and singles looking for an enriching Western experience. Near the Continental Divide at 8,946 feet, Waunita Hot Springs is a place to enjoy beautiful scenery, colorful history, and the naturally soothing waters of the Waunita Hot Springs. The pool is fed by crystal-clear spring water. The ranch is in a secluded valley, surrounded by unspoiled national forest. The ranch has maintained the flavor of the Old West but is modern in all respects. The main lodge has a spacious dining room and lobby. The ranch features non-denominational Sunday services.

Address: 8007 County Road 887, Dept. K, Gunnison, Colorado 81230
Telephone: (303) 641-1266
Airport: Gunnison
Location: 27 miles northeast of Gunnison, 150 miles west of Colorado Springs off Highway 50
Memberships: Dude Ranchers' Association, Colorado Dude and Guest Ranch Association
Awards: AAA 3 Diamond, Mobil 2 Star
Medical: Gunnison, 27 miles
Conference: 25, informal
Guest Capacity: 45
Accommodations: Two lodges are fashioned somewhat like old Western town buildings. Rooms are paneled, carpeted, with private baths, and thermal heating. There are double, queen, and some bunk beds for kids. Laundry facilities available. Recreation center in top floor of new log barn.
Rates: • $-$$. American Plan. Children's rates available. Minimum stay policy. Special winter group rates.
Credit Cards: American Express
Season: June through September; December through March for groups only
Activities: Summer program includes private stream and lake fishing and horseback riding on a variety of trails from flowered meadows to snow-capped mountain ridges, most of which is grouped by age and ability, every day except Sunday. Instruction available. Families may ride together. Favorite rides include the all-day trip to Stella and Granite mountains. Scenic four-wheel-drive trips to Northstar Mine and Alpine Tunnel, swimming in 35- by 90-foot spring-fed 95° pool, river float trips, hayrides, hiking. Winter: Cross-country skiing and ice skating; downhill skiing at nearby Monarch Ski Area.
Children's Programs: Children are welcome and included in most activities. No special program. Special rides and child care available. Children under 5 not advised. Small petting farm with goats and lambs.
Dining: Hearty, wholesome meals served buffet or family-style, featuring homemade soups, breads, and desserts. Fruit, coffee, tea and lemonade always available. No alcohol, please.
Entertainment: Arena games, cookouts, Western music, recreation room with table tennis, pool tables, square dancing. Something special every night—hayrides, Western music show, movies and slides.
Summary: A Christian family owned and operated ranch featuring riding and activities for all ages (5 years and up), at a reasonable price. Located at site of natural hot springs providing thermal heat for buildings and water for pool. Historic, yet modern. Friendly, helpful staff. Ranch emphasis is on families participating in activities together.

Wilderness Trails Ranch, Colorado

Wilderness Trails Ranch offers a vacation package for the whole family and has been sharing its special way of life since the early 1950s. In 1970, Gene and Jan Roberts bought the ranch. Since then, with an excellent staff, mostly enthusiastic college kids from around the country, the ranch has become one of the finest guest facilities in the business. Wilderness Trails is snuggled in the Pine River Valley near beautiful Lake Vallecito. The ranch is in a magnificent setting, with a trout stream that cuts through the property and cattle grazing in meadows. Fine Morgan horses are bred and raised here. These horses, says Gene, "are noted for their good disposition, versatility, and beauty." Wilderness Trails features hayrides and nearby rafting trips and has a wonderful children's and teens' program. Everyone will enjoy "WTR." Children ages 2 to 17 will have the time of their lives.

Address: 776 County Road 300, Drawer K, Durango, Colorado 81301
Telephone: (303) 247-0722; Fax: (303) 247-5212
Airport: Durango via Denver, Albuquerque, or Phoenix
Location: 35 miles north of Durango off U.S. 160
Awards: AAA 3 Diamond, Mobil 3 Star
Memberships: Colorado Dude and Guest Ranch Association
Medical: Durango Hospital, 35 miles; local rescue service
Conference: 40-50 (off-season only)
Guest Capacity: 50
Accommodations: Guests enjoy comfortable 2-, 3-, and 5-bedroom log cabins situated in the trees for maximum privacy and peace. Each has a private bath, and all are cozy with propane heaters. Laundry facilities available.
Rates: • $$. American Plan. Children's and off-season rates available.
Credit Cards: Visa, MasterCard, American Express
Season: June through September
Activities: Half-day and all-day rides, riders divided according to their ability, excellent instruction available, pack trips. Children and adults ride separately. Cowboy boots can be rented. Four-wheel-drive trips, swimming in 72-foot heated lap pool and adjacent whirlpool. Water skiing and other water sports on Lake Vallecito. Sixteen-foot outboard motorboat and mountain bikes available. Plenty of hiking also.
Children's Programs: Very good children's program and kids' rodeo at ranch. Children's activities cabin. Baby-sitting available.
Dining: Children eat separately. Delicious food. Will accommodate any diet and special food requirements.
Entertainment: Saturday night dance—Rodeo Ball. Staff shows, magic shows, rodeos in town, square dancing, camp fire singing, and movies.
Summary: Beautiful setting! Family owned and operated guest ranch. Great hosts and a great staff. Wide variety of activities. Located on river. Seventy-two-foot heated lap pool. Excellent program for ages 2 through 17. Ranch trading post, Morgan horses, cattle roundup late September to early October, old Durango-Silverton train. Trips to Indian country—Mesa Verde. Video available on request.

See color photos, page 222

Wit's End Guest and Resort Ranch, Colorado

Wit's End Guest and Resort Ranch is the creation of Jim and Lynn Custer, a couple with impeccable taste! Wit's End is located in the beautiful Vallecito Valley just off County Road 500. Set amid thousands of aspens and pines, this resort ranch offers its guests a host of activities, all in a setting of luxury, charm, and quality. Wait until you see the beautifully restored two-story main lodge. The craftsmanship and decor is exquisite. The ranch is surrounded by 12,000- to 14,000-foot mountains and looks out over its own Chain O'Lakes and meadows. At Wit's End you can do as much, or as little, as you wish. It is really your vacation. Unlike many guest ranches, Wit's End offers rustic elegance with all the freedoms that you might find at a resort. Ride to the Continental Divide and view all kinds of wildlife, hike, mountain bike, swim, fish, experience the magnificent Durango-Silverton train.

Address: 254 C.R. 500 K, Bayfield, Colorado 81122
Telephone: (303) 884-4113; Fax: Available
Airport: Durango, La Plata Airport
Location: 24 miles northeast of Durango directly off County Rd. 500
Medical: Mercy Medical Center, 24 miles
Conference: 80 (overnight), 150 for the day
Guest Capacity: 80, plus 40 off-ranch
Accommodations: All of the 1-, 2-, 3-, and 4-bedroom log cabins are luxuriously decorated for the most discriminating taste. Knotty pine interiors, native stone fireplaces, queen-size brass beds, custom bed coverings, plush carpets, balloon draperies, French doors, television, telephones, china dishes, attractive kitchens with separate dining areas, and swings on the porches.
Rates: • $$-$$$$. Standard American, Royal American (full ranch package), Modified American (does not include breakfast and lunch), and European plans. Special rates for children, groups, and corporate seminars. Low-season rates available.

Credit Cards: Visa, MasterCard, American Express. Traveler's and personal checks accepted.
Season: Year-round
Activities: Each plan includes unlimited use of pool, tennis, hot tubs, hiking, jogging, and fishing in Vallecito Lake, streams, or Vallecito River. The ranch's own Chain O'Lakes has produced 5-lb. to 10-lb. trout with the average being 2 lbs. Royal American Plan includes meals, riding, bicycling, Durango-Silverton narrow gauge railway, and fly-fishing. Pack trips, river rafting, dinner cruises, sailing, jeep tours, and hunting are available at an additional cost. Winter activities include cross-country skiing, guided snowmobiling, dog sled rides, ice-skating, ice fishing, and sleigh rides. Cross-country skis and ice skates available at the ranch.
Children's Programs: Children are welcome, and child care is available. No special program.
Dining: Two restaurants—breakfast and lunch at "D" Creek Cafe, dinner at the Old Lodge-at-the-Lake Restaurant on ranch property with full bar and gourmet menus.
Entertainment: Beautiful 120-year-old main lodge and Colorado Tavern with cut-glass mirrors from the London World Exposition of 1853. Huge stone fireplace, upstairs library, and game room with a custom antique billiard table. Beautiful antiques everywhere, all set in a structure of hand-hewn beams and original logs. Live entertainment one to seven nights a week depending on the season.
Summary: Luxury ranch resort. Excellent for family reunions and corporate retreats. Also, the romantic atmosphere makes Wit's End an ideal setting for weddings and honeymoons. Get away from it all and do your own thing. Guests plan all their own activities, coordinated by the ranch staff. Wit's End General Store and Cafe. Nearby attractions include Vallecito Lake, Durango-Silverton narrow gauge railway, and Mesa Verde Indian dwellings.

See color photos, pages 197-201

Wit's End Guest and Resort Ranch, Colorado

Wind River Ranch, Colorado

Authentic Western Ranch, Member–Dude Ranchers' Association

Wind River Ranch is in Colorado's high country. At 9,200 feet, the ranch features vistas of beautiful valleys and the rugged peaks of Rocky Mountain National Park. Wind River Ranch is seven miles south of the village of Estes Park. It has been in operation for more than fifty years and in the Irvin family since 1973. The Irvins, originally from Indianapolis, had been guests since 1961. Today, the ranch is run by their son, Rob (formerly a commercial banker in Boulder), and his wife, Jere. The "WRR" has wonderfully preserved the Old West with its rustic setting, antiques, and Indian artifacts. The ranch's fifty-two guests enjoy breathtaking scenery and an unhurried and unstructured pace. Wind River is for the busy executive and his or her family who wants to get away from it all. Be as busy as you want or just sit back with a good book and relax. One guest wrote, "Wind River was our pick because of its beautiful location, smaller size, and wide range of activities."

Address: P.O. Box 3410 K, Estes Park, Colorado 80517
Telephone: (303) 586-4212; (800) 523-4212
Airport: Denver
Location: 7 miles south of Estes Park off Highway 7, 75 miles northwest of Denver
Memberships: Colorado Dude and Guest Ranch Association, Dude Ranchers' Association
Awards: AAA 3 Diamond, Mobil 3 Star
Medical: Estes Park Hospital, seven miles
Conference: 52, early June and early September
Guest Capacity: 52
Accommodations: All of the ten country-decorated cabins and five lodge rooms have modern comforts, including private baths with oversize towels, individually controlled heat, and carpeting. Some have fireplaces or wood-burning stoves. All have a nice country feel. Each has a porch or a patio. There are always hanging baskets with colorful flowers around the main lodge and pool.
Rates: • $-$$. American Plan. Children's rates available. Minimum 3-day stay policy. Horse-

back riding extra on an hourly, daily, or weekly basis.
Credit Cards: Visa, MasterCard
Season: Early June to mid-September
Activities: There is something for everyone to do, including two-hour, half-day, all-day, and breakfast rides. Instruction is available. Hiking on more than 600 miles of trails in the surrounding area. Guided hikes once a week. Swimming in the outdoor heated pool or hot tub. Fishing on and off the property (bring your own equipment). Ranch has its own stocked pond with German and rainbow trout. Tennis, 18-hole golf course, and river rafting available nearby.
Children's Program: Organized program for children ages 4 to 12, all day or mornings and afternoons; children under 6 ride in an arena only. Full fenced-in children's playground.
Dining: Families eat together. BYOB happy hour each evening with your hosts at the main house. Delicious buffets, fine steak dinners, filet mignon, and shrimp scampi. Wind River's famous coffee cake, pastries, cheesecakes, and cherry pies. Patio picnics. Fine wine and beer available.
Entertainment: For those who wish to relax, the ranch has an extensive library in the lovely, rustic, circa 1920 ranch house. Read or play cards in front of the cozy fireplace. Family movies, country-western singing with marshmallow roasts. Evening naturalist talks with slides, movies, bingo, hayrides with Belgian draft horse team.
Summary: Rob and Jere provide a place where busy people can relax. As they say, "It's your vacation." Naturalist guided walks and all-day hikes. Rocky Mountain National Park and 11,200-foot-high Trail Ridge Road. Historic mining town of Central City on the spectacular "peak to peak" highway, now designated as a National Scenic By-Way. Town of Estes Park with many attractions.

Outdoor Resorts River Ranch, Florida

Outdoor Resorts River Ranch is a modern resort community that caters to both RVers and non-RVers who are seeking Western activities as well as recreation more typical of central Florida. River Ranch encompasses more than 1,500 acres of beautifully varied landscape. The roster of activities is long and diverse. The setting is conducive to the recreation that families and retired people traveling in recreational vehicles enjoy. River Ranch Resort, near Lake Wales, was purchased by Outdoor Resorts of America. After an ambitious renovation that included upgrading all facilities, the ranch again opened its doors. The record attendance at this facility can be attributed to comfortable accommodations and a variety of recreational opportunities. The theme of the resort is definitely Western, even though a few water birds are interspersed with barns, stables, a golf course, and a full marina. River Ranch is an RVers' haven that combines Western flavor with a Floridian life-style.

Address: P.O. Box 30030, Dept. K, ORA River Ranch, Florida 33867

Telephone: Nationwide (800) 654-8575; in Florida (800) 282-7935; local (813) 692-1321

Airport: Orlando or Tampa International; private 5,000-foot paved, lighted airstrip at ranch

Location: 24 miles east of Lake Wales on Highway 60, 65 miles south of Orlando

Medical: Lake Wales Hospital, 24 miles; nurse on staff at ranch

Conference: 500; 5,000-square-foot meeting facility

Guest Capacity: 175 units plus over 400 RV sites

Accommodations: Rooms, suites, efficiencies, cottages, and RV sites with full hookups. Call for availability.

Rates: • $, RV rates; $-$$, hotel accommodations. Group rates available. Some activities not included.

Credit Cards: Visa, MasterCard, American Express

Season: Year-round including Thanksgiving, Christmas, and Easter

Activities: There is a recreation director on the property. Special events, holiday programs, escorted horseback rides, four pools, three Jacuzzis, five lighted tennis courts, 9-hole par 36 golf course, miniature golf, horseshoes, lawn bowling, ranch marina where guests can launch their own boats or rent skiffs, fishing, trap and skeet shooting, archery, aerobics, a nicely furnished Mustang Center health spa with saunas, steam rooms, tanning booths, weight room, hair salon, and post office. Exotic game hunting at nearby FX Bar Ranch for deer, wild boar, and quail.

Children's Programs: No program per se. Petting corral with rabbits, sheep, goats, chickens, turkeys, calves; children's playground; hayrides, pony riding. Arts and crafts. Full recreation room with video games. Rental bikes available. Kids can safely run free.

Dining: Ranch Branding Iron Restaurant, Ranch Harbor Bar and Grill, fully stocked country store with deli.

Entertainment: River Ranch Saloon, weekend country-western live entertainment, square dancing, bingo, arts and crafts, card tournaments.

Summary: Appeals to a variety of people—families, seniors, and groups. Laid-back country atmosphere. Resort for RVers and non-RVers. Pets allowed. Ranch airstrip. Western wear and gift shop; professional ranch rodeos; square dancing; live country-western bands; weekly River Ranch newspaper; Cypress Gardens, 35 miles; Walt Disney World Vacation Kingdom, 65 miles; Kennedy Space Center, 100 miles; Bok Tower Gardens with chiming bells. Video available on request.

Allison Ranch, Idaho

In the 1880s, the Allison Ranch was the pioneer homestead of Joe Myers, a miner. Today, Allison Ranch is a private guest facility limited to families and parties of eight people. The Thomases make the ranch available also during the summer months to missionaries home on furlough. The only way into this secluded natural wonder is by small plane or jet boat. There are still some places in the world where roads have not penetrated, and this is one of them. The pilots who fly you in are experienced backcountry commercial pilots. This is a land where the pine-scented air is clear and the only footprints are your own or those of moose, elk, or deer. Allison Ranch, on the Salmon River, is a place where all the trappings of a mechanized world have been kept at bay. Don't expect to find television, automobiles, or telephones—there are none. The only communication with the outside world is by radio, which can be connected to telephone equipment. Otherwise, you and eleven other lucky guests and crew are on your own.

Address: 7259 Cascade Drive, Dept. K, Boise, Idaho 83704
Telephone: (208) 376-5270
Airport: Charter aircraft from Boise or McCall directly to the ranch
Location: 1 hour north of Boise by air, 30 miles south of Elk City on Salmon River
Memberships: Idaho Outfitters and Guides
Medical: No medical facilities nearby; emergency plane or helicopter can be arranged.
Guest Capacity: 12
Accommodations: There are two 2-story hand-hewn log guest cabins—one with three bedrooms overlooking the Salmon River which sleeps up to seven and a two-bedroom ridge unit. Propane lights and wood-burning stoves. Ranch has own hydroelectric plant. Summers are usually pretty warm.
Rates: $. American Plan. Children under 6, no charge. Special missionary packages.
Credit Cards: None. Personal checks accepted.

Season: May to September. October through November for steelhead fishing.
Activities: Enjoy swimming in Idaho's famous Salmon River, which runs right by the ranch, hike to spectacular Myers Creek 100-foot waterfall, and enjoy plenty of fishing on a sandy beach along the Salmon River.
Children's Programs: No special programs. Children are welcome, but kids under 6 are the responsibility of parents. Not recommended for children age 2 and younger.
Dining: Hearty Idaho food, occasional venison and bear. All served family-style. Many meals during the summer are served outside on the deck overlooking the Salmon River Valley. BYOB.
Entertainment: Peace and tranquillity, the melodic Salmon River, and countless birds and wildlife.
Summary: Secluded ranch accessible only by plane or jet boat, in a beautiful wilderness setting located on the Salmon River. Best for families and small family reunions. Great for very small business retreats. One couple even booked the ranch completely for themselves for two weeks. Special arrangements made for missionaries on furloughs. Private airstrip.

Busterback Ranch, Idaho

Authentic Western Ranch, Member–Dude Ranchers'
Association

In just a few short years, Busterback Ranch has developed an international year-round reputation for wonderful down-home friendly hospitality in the magnificent splendor of Idaho's Sawtooth Valley. To the west is the Sawtooth range, and to the east, just beyond several thousand acres of cattle grazing meadows, is the White Cloud Mountain Range. Busterback is just off two-lane Interstate 75. Alone in this open valley, the ranch is both a working cattle ranch (guests do not participate at all in the cattle operation) and an intimate guest ranch. Without question, what makes Busterback unique is its beautiful setting coupled with its proximity to Sun Valley, about 50 minutes away. Above all, though, it is the warm and friendly staff that has given Busterback its fine reputation. General manager Kevin O'Donnell (a Cornell hotel management program graduate), with terrific esprit de corps and pizzazz, his wife, Roberta, and their fine staff really knock themselves out.

Address: Star Route, Drawer K, Ketchum, Idaho 83340
Telephone: (208) 774-2271
Airport: Stanley, 20 miles, for small planes only; Hailey, 54 miles, for commercial planes
Location: 20 miles south of Stanley, 40 miles northwest of Ketchum and Sun Valley
Memberships: Dude Ranchers' Association
Medical: Salmon River Emergency Clinic, 20 miles
Conference: Up to 20; should book entire ranch, off-season only
Guest Capacity: 20
Accommodations: The main lodge has five very cozy country-decorated rooms, two upstairs and three downstairs. Several share bathrooms and all share a wonderful reading/living/quiet room. A stone's throw from the lodge are three small cabins side-by-side, each with a wood stove, double bed, bunk beds, bathroom, and country decorations.
Rates: • $$$. American Plan. Children's rates.
Credit Cards: Visa, MasterCard

Season: Mid-May through September
Activities: Unlimited. You can do just about anything in the Sawtooth Valley or in Ketchum/Sun Valley. The horseback riding is limited. Call the ranch for details on trail rides. A half-dozen mountain bikes can be used by all guests. Hiking, backpacking, canoeing, windsurfing, and swimming in Alturas Lake, which is 15 minutes by car. Fishing in the Salmon River with excellent local guides available. Hot tub and Finnish sauna. Massage available.
Children's Program: Kids are welcome, but there is no program. Baby-sitting available.
Dining: Guests really become a part of the family. Everyone eats in the main kitchen. Everything from quiche and fresh granola at breakfast to rack of lamb and grilled salmon at dinner. Evening cookouts. At happy hour guests enjoy the high-ceilinged Salmon River Bar just off the living room with its stone fireplace. Some will sit out on the large deck and watch the skies glow as the sun sets.
Entertainment: Wine tastings, informative lectures, and swing dancing in Stanley.
Summary: Superb hospitality and delicious cuisine. Set in the beautiful Sawtooth Valley about an hour from the famous ski towns of Ketchum and Sun Valley.

See color photos, page 234

Diamond D Ranch, Idaho

The Diamond D is located in one of Idaho's hidden valleys. Many guests come by car and savor the long and winding gravel road up and over Loon Creek Summit that eventually switches back down into the rugged Salmon River Mountain Valley. This slow but scenic drive is breathtaking and gives everyone a chance to slow down and unwind to the pace that they will enjoy for their week or two, or more, at the ranch. The Diamond D is remote. On all sides it is surrounded by millions of acres of wilderness and plenty of wildlife to go with this magnificent Idaho backcountry. Arriving at the ranch, one feels the same exhilarating feeling the early gold miners must have felt when they exclaimed, "Eureka! We found it!" The Demorest family has been running this wonderful ranch since the 1950s. No telephones, no schedules. Nothing but pure Idaho wilderness and a lot of friendly hospitality. That is just the way it is at the Diamond D. If this strikes your fancy, write or call for their brochure. It is filled with color photographs, and you will see what I mean.

Address: Summer: P.O. Box 1 K, Clayton, Idaho 83227; winter: P.O. Box 36005 K, Grosse Pointe, Michigan 48236
Telephone: Summer: Radio telephone (208) 879-2369 for emergencies only via Challis. The voice answering will probably say "Bob's Aircraft." Note: You may not be able to get through to the ranch. Best to call (313) 821-4975 summer and winter.
Airport: Boise, 45 minutes by charter plane, 5 hours by car. Air charter service available from Boise, Twin Falls, Idaho Falls, and Challis to the 2,800-foot dirt airstrip just 4 miles from the ranch. Private pilots: DO NOT attempt to fly in without contacting the Demorests for specifics.
Location: 75 miles north of Sun Valley off Highway 75. Ranch will send you a map.
Medical: Emergency helicopter service available
Conference: 35; must book entire ranch
Guest Capacity: 35

Accommodations: Three comfortable two-bedroom cabins a short walk from the main lodge and near Loon Creek. One large four-bedroom cabin that sleeps 10. Several one-bedroom suites above the office. Ask about the honeymoon/anniversary suite. Several upstairs lodge rooms. All rooms and cabins have electricity and modern bathroom facilities. Ranch powered by a hydroelectric generator. Guest laundry.
Rates: • $. American Plan. Children's rates available.
Credit Cards: None. Personal checks and cash.
Season: Mid-June through early September
Activities: No schedules, but lots of activities are available each day. Evening and morning sign-up sheets for horseback riding and gold panning (very popular and all supplies are provided). Ask about Rob's Hot Springs and Pinyon Peak (tremendous lookout point at 10,000 feet) rides. The Diamond D offers 2- to 7-day pack trips to hot springs, mountain lakes, and old cattle ranches. Hiking, swimming in modern pool with adjacent hot tub or in ranch's own lake with two row boats and fishing. Volleyball, badminton, and horseshoes on the green lawn in front of the lodge.
Children's Programs: Full supervision can be provided. Most kids under 4 do not ride.
Dining: Wholesome ranch cooking. Special diets will be catered to with advance notice. Birthdays and anniversaries are always special. BYOB.
Entertainment: Campfire sing-alongs. Cards, games, video movies, and fireside conversation in the lodge.
Summary: Lovely remote ranch with all the comforts of home. Area full of western lore, gold mines, and Indian stories. If you drive, you will want to see the old mining town of Custer and the Yankee Fork Gold Dredge. Be sure to ask Linda about her wonderful "Sparkling T-shirts" and crafts program.

See color photos, page 208

Idaho Rocky Mountain Ranch, Idaho

The Sawtooth and White Cloud mountain ranges of central Idaho are some of the most spectacular and least-explored regions of North America. Here lies the beautiful Idaho Rocky Mountain Ranch, overlooking this magnificence. Started in 1930 by Winston Paul, a Frigidaire distributor from New York, the ranch was bought by Edmund Bogert in 1951 and has been run by members of his family since. The ranch is almost exactly as it was, with the original main lodge and log cabins. All the furniture is handmade, with old photographs and animal trophies on the walls. From the front porch of the main lodge, you look out to the jagged, snow-capped peaks of the Sawtooth Mountains. Miles of riding trails meander through the surrounding wilderness. You can climb mountains smelling of pine or hike through green meadows strewn with alpine flowers. At Idaho Rocky Mountain Ranch, you will be surrounded with beauty. Here you can relax your mind and soothe your spirit.

Address: HC 64, Box 9934K, Stanley, Idaho 83278
Telephone: (208) 774-3544
Airport: Boise, 120 miles; Sun Valley (Hailey), 65 miles; private airstrip in Stanley
Location: 50 miles north of Sun Valley
Memberships: Cross-Country Ski Areas Association, National Trust for Historic Preservation
Medical: Medical clinic in Stanley, 9 miles; Moritz Hospital in Sun Valley
Conference: 43
Guest Capacity: 43
Accommodations: Beautifully preserved, 5,000-square-foot hand-hewn log main lodge houses large sitting room, dining room, four rooms with queen-size or twin beds, private baths, and a covered sitting porch extending the length of the lodge and overlooking the Sawtooth Range. Handmade rockers are well used all summer for taking in the views. Nine cozy cabins, each with private baths, stone fireplaces, and comforters. All but one are set up in a duplex arrange-

ment. Winter accommodations include comfortable one- and three-bedroom cabins with wood stoves, private baths, kitchens, and hot spring pool nearby.
Rates: Available on request
Credit Cards: Visa, MasterCard
Season: Late May through September (summer); late November to mid-April (winter). Open Thanksgiving, Christmas, and Easter.
Activities: Summer program includes all-day and half-day horseback rides arranged through outfitter on the lower ranch. You can bring your own horse, instruction available. Pack trips on request, fishing on and off the property, sailboarding on four lakes, twenty-foot by forty-foot hot springs pool (heated in the summer to 100° and in the winter to 105°), volleyball. Float trips through outfitter on Salmon and Payette rivers. Winter programs include informal ranch cross-country skiing. Nearby there are groomed trails with hut-to-hut skiing, alpine skiing, and wildlife viewing.
Children's Programs: None
Dining: The dining room is open in the summer to the public. This is real steak and potato country, with garden-fresh vegetables and sumptuous desserts. Choose from dishes like elk, salmon, Idaho trout, and wild chicken. Wine and beer served. People come from Sun Valley to experience the rustic ambience and culinary delights. Barbecue cookouts once a week.
Entertainment: Library, contemporary and live Western music, wonderful local musicians, sing-alongs, stargazing.
Summary: One of the most beautiful main lodges in the country. Incredible log and iron architecture. Run much like a large bed and breakfast. Most activities are à la carte and off the property. Excellent cuisine. Spectacular views, individualized service, cultural events in Sun Valley area, hot springs-heated pool. Bring your own horse. Spanish spoken.

Indian Creek Ranch, Idaho

This ranch is small and cozy, surrounded by Forest Service land and bordering an Idaho Primitive Area. Here there is no schedule and nothing that you have to do. Indian Creek is secluded and powered with propane. If you need a hair dryer, this is not the place for you. After you have been at the ranch for a while, when the city is behind you, when you are beginning to feel the pine needles under your feet, when you've really relaxed, owners Jack and his daughter Theresa will pick up the pace with activities. With only ten guests at a time, the Briggs can tailor things just for you. Since the mid-1960s, they have created an atmosphere so natural that you can't help but relax and enjoy the things that enhance the spirit, soothe the soul, and rekindle inner strength. They are easygoing Western folks who realize the importance of R&R and are ready to share their hospitality with you. When they say, "Relax up here," they mean it.

Address: HC 64, Box 105 K, Northfork, Idaho 83466
Telephone: (208) 394-2126
Airport: Missoula
Location: 35 miles north of Salmon off Highway 93, 130 miles south of Missoula
Memberships: Idaho Packers and Guides Association
Medical: Salmon Clinic, 35 miles; emergency helicopter service
Guest Capacity: 10
Accommodations: The ranch has a main lodge and four cabins. Each cabin is rustic but comfortable and complete with private bath and shower. No TVs or telephones here.
Rates: $. American Plan. Bed and breakfast rates available.
Credit Cards: None. Personal checks accepted.
Season: April to November
Activities: Lots of mountain country for half-day and all-day rides. Jack plays it by ear. As he says, "It depends on the guests." Fishing on and off the property, hiking, four-wheel-drive trips,

seasonal hunting. Float boat trips can be arranged on the Salmon River.
Children's Programs: Very young children not recommended.
Dining: Prime rib, steaks, chicken, home-baked breads, biscuits, and muffins. BYOB.
Entertainment: Stargazing, nature's solitude.
Summary: Very small ranch. No electricity, powered by propane. Very homey and very low-key. Bed and breakfast or week stays. Trips to the ghost town of Ulysses. Float trips on the Salmon River, Idaho's "River of No Return." Pets allowed.

MacKay Bar Ranch, Idaho

Near the confluence of the main Salmon and the South Fork rivers, deep in Idaho's pristine wilderness, the MacKay Bar Ranch offers unique backcountry vacations adjacent to the 2.2-million-acre River of No Return wilderness area. This ranch is the landing point for some of the world's greatest steelhead fishing. It is secluded, accessible only by jet boat or charter plane, and the ideal setting for group retreats. Private meeting room and cabins, plus a variety of outdoor activities, are designed for individual enjoyment. The ranch was established by explorers who braved Idaho's vast frontier early in this century. There are no televisions, telephones, newspapers, or any distractions other than nature. One can totally relax and enjoy one of Idaho's great hideaways on the banks of the "River of No Return."

Address: 3190 Airport Way, Dept. K, Boise, Idaho 83705

Telephone: For reservations, call (800) 635-5336 (out of state); (208) 344-1881. Radio phones only to ranch.

Airport: Boise. Private ranch airstrip for expert pilots only. Contact ranch for airstrip information.

Location: 1 hour north of Boise by charter plane

Memberships: Idaho Outfitters and Guides Association, White Water Association, Idaho Steelhead and Salmon Unlimited

Medical: McCall Memorial Hospital, 15 minutes by air

Conference: 20

Guest Capacity: 20

Accommodations: Electricity is provided from 7:30 a.m. to 10:30 p.m. The Cougar House down the hill near the river will sleep up to ten in five double rooms adjoining a large meeting/dining/kitchen area. Other private cabins are available. The ranch staff will help you with your laundry.

Rates: • $$$. American Plan. Special steelhead and float trip rates available. Rates for children under 18. Rates do not include charter flights into ranch.

Credit Cards: Visa, MasterCard, American Express

Season: April to November

Activities: Limited riding instruction, but half- and all-day riding and pack trips. Superb spring and fall steelhead fishing, white water float trips on the world-famous Middle Fork and Main Salmon River, charter jet boating, river swimming, and seasonal hunting.

Children's Programs: None. There are not a lot of children here.

Dining: Hearty backcountry food. Homemade breads and pastry. Complimentary Idaho wine served. BYOB. Special diets catered to.

Entertainment: Music sing-alongs, piano in lodge. On request, musical entertainment.

Summary: Most guests come to the MacKay Bar following a white water rafting trip. Very good seasonal steelhead fishing, fall hunting. Ranch airstrip, small trading post with sundry items, area archaeology, Painter Mine, Chinese Terrace gardens. Video available on request.

Shepp Ranch, Idaho

The only way to Shepp Ranch is by jet boat or charter plane service out of Boise. The ranch is in mountainous central Idaho, isolated deep in backcountry 15 miles from the closest road. It is a haven of comfort, healthy meals, good fellowship, and Western traditions. In the roadless wilderness of the Nez Perce Forest, the ranch lies on the north bank of the main Salmon River, at its confluence with Crooked Creek. This spot was homesteaded at the turn of the century by miners Charlie Shepp and Peter Klinkhammer, who built the rustic whip-sawed ranch house still in use today. In 1950, Pete sold the property to Paul Filer, who, with his wife, Marybelle, built a sawmill and new buildings using electricity from the hydropower plant. Fresh spring water comes from a large tank they floated downstream and installed high on a hillside. A sense of history prevails here in the buildings, the orchard, rare hand tools, a fence made of elk horns, antique guns, and horse-drawn farm implements. Paul Resnick, the present owner, purchased the ranch in 1979. It is run by Lynn and Michael Demerse.

Address: P.O. Box 5446K, Boise, Idaho 83705
Telephone: (208) 343-7729 (there is a radio telephone at the ranch)
Airport: Boise
Train: Amtrak to Boise. Contact Jinny regarding transportation to ranch.
Location: 45 miles east of Riggins, Idaho; 200 miles northwest of Boise
Memberships: Idaho Outfitters and Guides Association
Awards: *Hideaway Report*
Medical: McCall Hospital, 100 miles; emergency helicopter service
Guest Capacity: 16
Accommodations: Six rustic individual log cabins with showers, wood-burning stoves, and porches. Each sleeps four comfortably. Of these six, there are two deluxe cabins (the Filer and Shepp cabins), with separate bedrooms. A marvelous hot tub overlooks the Salmon River—

right on the river's edge. A sauna is also available. The ranch has its own generator. Lights out at 11 p.m., although almost everyone is sound asleep by then anyway. The paneled main lodge has a nice fireplace. The walls are decorated with a bearskin rug and hunting trophies. There are also books and a small piano. In the spring and early summer, before it warms up, there is an abundance of wildflowers, wildlife, and many hanging geranium baskets.

Rates: • $$-$$$. American Plan. Charter flight to ranch additional. Children age 13 and under half-price. One-day, weekend, and five-day packages available.
Credit Cards: American Express
Season: March through November
Activities: The Salmon River (Lewis and Clark called it the "River of No Return") is right out the front door. It offers the opportunity for many water sports. Guests enjoy sunbathing on sandy beaches, jet boating, white water rafting, hiking, and exploring. Trail riding on the ranch's sure-footed mules and horses. All riding done at a walk due to the terrain. Trout fishing in the summer and steelhead fishing in the spring and fall. Seasonal big game hunting.
Children's Programs: None. Recommended for ages 6 and older. Children are the responsibility of their parents.
Dining: Family-style meals. Many ranch-grown vegetables. Barbecued steaks and pork chops. Freshly baked breads, hand-cranked ice cream. Special diets with advance notice. BYOB.
Entertainment: Volleyball, horseshoes, archery, and skeet shooting. Very casual.
Summary: Wilderness lodge on Salmon River accessible only by small charter plane or jet boat. No TV or telephones. Warm hospitality. Everybody feels like family. The Salmon River Canyon is one of the deepest river canyons on the North American continent. The "late show" —when the moon comes up and a few million stars shine down. Families or corporations with a minimum of 12 guests may rent the entire ranch.

Stonebraker Ranch, Idaho

Stonebraker Ranch is accessible only by air or forest trail. In Idaho's Chamberlain Basin, it is 140 air miles from Boise. This historic ranch offers wild beauty beyond belief with its hand-hewn log cabins and high mountain lakes and streams in the heart of a vast wilderness. Stonebraker looks much like a mountain hideaway that Billy the Kid might have used way back when. This is one of Idaho's most secluded and really rustic ranches. For those who cherish complete privacy, rustic seclusion, abundant wildlife, forests, and magnificent seasonal wildflowers—Stonebraker is the right choice. To top it off, you are picked up at the dirt airstrip by a mule/horse-drawn wagon for a half-hour trip to the old ranch.

Address: Business office at 3190 Airport Way, Dept. K, Boise, Idaho 83705
Telephone: For reservations, call (800) 635-5336 (out of state only); (208) 344-1881. Radio telephone only at ranch.
Airport: Boise; U.S. Forest Service airstrip on ranch (for experienced pilots only)
Location: 1-hour charter flight time north of Boise
Memberships: Idaho Outfitters and Guides Association, Rocky Mountain Elk Foundation
Medical: McCall Memorial Hospital, 20-minute air-charter ride; life flight helicopter service available
Conference: 10; executive retreat
Guest Capacity: 10
Accommodations: This ranch is so rustic that the old outhouse is about a tenth of a mile walk. The management has updated things somewhat and built a common bathhouse nearby with men's and women's hot water shower and bathroom facilities. There are three original trapper cabins complete with squeaky floors. Each is illuminated by candlelight. No electricity or running water in the cabins. Also available, two tepees and four wall tents. The turn-of-the-century main house, where meals are served, is small and heated with a potbellied stove.
Rates: • $$$. American Plan. Fishing, hunting, and corporate group packages available. Rates do not include air charter to ranch.
Credit Cards: Visa, MasterCard, American Express
Season: June to September
Activities: Half- and all-day trail rides. Slow, nice, and easygoing guided rides, pack trips, and excellent fishing. Seasonal hunting for elk, deer, moose, and bear. Avid fly-fishermen will enjoy the high alpine pack trip (extra). Combination ranch and white water rafting packages on the Middle Fork and main Salmon.
Children's Programs: Special dates set aside for families and children.
Dining: This may be one of the most rustic and secluded ranches in the country, but the food is superb. Complimentary Idaho wines served with dinner.
Entertainment: Most guests like to relax on the old sitting porch at the ranch house and try to take it all in. Music and storytelling from time to time.
Summary: Historic secluded wilderness ranch, wildlife photography, airstrip, mule/horse-drawn buggy ride. Famous Thunder Mountain gold rush area. Video available on request.

Teton Ridge Ranch, Idaho

On the not-so-well-known west side of the Tetons is a paradise they call Teton Ridge Ranch. This luxurious modern-day ranch with splendidly designed log architecture overlooks the distant mighty Grand Tetons, rising some 13,775 feet. While the ranch has only been in operation a few years, it has already hosted people from around the world. Albert Tilt (a retired advertising executive), and his lovely wife, Chris, are your hosts and serve up warm, friendly Idaho hospitality, while you are surrounded by pastoral beauty. If you are looking for lots of scheduled activities, read no further. This is not the ranch for you. Here the pace is slow: you can do as much or as little as you choose. You decide. At Teton Ridge Ranch, you'll relax, unwind, and savor exactly what you came here for. . .away from it all, on the other side of the Tetons.

Address: 200 Valley View Road, Drawer K, Tetonia, Idaho 83452
Telephone: (208) 456-2650; Fax: (208) 456-2218
Airport: Jackson Hole, 45 miles; Idaho Falls, 69 miles; small planes to Driggs Airport, 11 miles (5,200-foot paved and lighted airstrip). Extra charge for airport pickup.
Location: 38 miles west of Jackson, Wyoming; 11 miles northeast of Driggs, Idaho
Medical: Teton Valley Hospital, 12 miles
Conference: 14 overnight, 32 for the day. Excellent for very small corporate retreats.
Guest Capacity: 14
Accommodations: The main 10,000-square-foot log lodge has a spacious living room, lower level dining room, and five suites, each with balconies commanding views of the Teton Range, wood stoves, and large bathrooms with Jacuzzi tubs. A short stroll away is the Cottage, a large two-bedroom home with vaulted ceilings, huge plate glass windows to take in the views, a living room and kitchenette.
Rates: • $$$-$$$$. Low/high season and corporate rates.

Credit Cards: None
Season: Late May through October (summer); Mid-December through March (winter). Note: Christmas at ranch best suited for a family reunion that can book the entire ranch.
Activities: Summer: There is no set program. Horseback riding, hiking, fishing, and plenty of R&R. Pack trips, white water rafting, soaring, guided fly-fishing, sporting clay shooting (the ranch has its own 10-station course) are extra. Ask Albert about the Bechler River Hot Springs horseback ride in Yellowstone. Winter: Most use the ranch as a home base to ski at Grand Targee, about 45 minutes away. Cross-country skiing from lodge on 5 miles of groomed trails. Skis and boots are available.
Children's Programs: None. Well-behaved children only.
Dining: Hearty, home-baked, homegrown cuisine. Garden-fresh vegetables. Weekly horse-drawn hayride cookout. Wine served with dinner. BYOB.
Entertainment: You are on your own.
Summary: Small luxurious corporate retreat. No planned activities. You design your own program. Sporting clay clinic in September. Well-behaved pets allowed, kennel on property. Summer soaring with Eric Soyland at Driggs Airport. Shopping and art galleries in Jackson Hole.

See color photos, page 183

Twin Peaks Ranch, Idaho

Authentic Western Ranch, Member–Dude Ranchers' Association

Twin Peaks Ranch is high in a valley surrounded by the beautiful Lemhi Mountains. At 4,700 feet, this ranch offers peace, serenity, wide open spaces, and warm Idaho hospitality. Twin Peaks is run by the Valvo family. At the ranch, which can accommodate up to thirty people, guests will enjoy wildlife, scenic mountain and valley views, and fishing on the tributaries of the Salmon River, which runs at the foot of the property some two miles away. For would-be fly-fishermen, Frank offers instruction at the ranch pond before you decide to assault the mighty Salmon River or nearby alpine streams. For camera buffs, the fall colors are wonderful, as the ranch is set amid small groves of quaking aspen that turn a shimmering gold as winter approaches.

Address: P.O. Box 951 K, Salmon, Idaho 83467
Telephone: (208) 894-2290
Airport: Missoula, Montana, or Idaho Falls, Idaho, with air shuttle to Salmon (ranch will pick you up for a fee)
Location: 18 miles south of Salmon off Highway 93
Memberships: Dude Ranchers' Association, Idaho Outfitters and Guides Association
Medical: Steele Memorial Hospital, Salmon, 18 miles
Conference: 30
Guest Capacity: 30
Accommodations: There are eleven cabins on the ranch: five singles and six doubles. They vary in size: some are small single cabins, and four are large double cabins, each with twin, double, or queen-size beds and bathrooms with stall showers. Some have tubs. Two rooms are available in the main lodge. All rooms have electric blankets.
Rates: • $-$$. American Plan. Daily and weekly rates. Children's rates available. Call for winter rates.
Credit Cards: Visa, MasterCard, American Express
Season: April through October

Activities: The schedule is very flexible. The Valvos try to accommodate each family's desires. Enjoy a hot tub or swim in the pool overlooking the exquisite mountain valley. Breakfast and all-day rides. Some enjoy riding in the arena. Ask Frank about the overnight hot springs ride into the North Basin at the center of the Lemhi Mountains. Cookouts and steak fries. Pack trips are available. Hiking, fishing, and scenic float and white water trips on the Salmon River can be arranged. Practice roping. Seasonal hunting for game birds, deer, elk, bear, antelope, and cougar.
Children's Programs: Children are well taken care of. Children's activities vary. Kiddie wrangler. Some children may horseback ride with their parents.
Dining: Delicious home-cooked meals served family-style. Weekly steak and homemade chili cookout. Beer and wine available.
Entertainment: Camp fires, sing-alongs, rodeos in town. Arena events.
Summary: Family-operated ranch. The Valvos run a very flexible program, and they try very hard to accommodate each and every guest with his or her desires. Great for families, couples, singles, and even a few honeymooners. Do as much or as little as you please. Hot springs 4 miles from ranch. Kennels provided for hunting dogs.

Timber Ridge Ranch, Idaho

In 1989, Jim and Mona King bought Timber Ridge Ranch with one goal in mind—to provide a place where families could interact together, experience a wilderness setting, all in a Christian environment. Before arriving in Idaho, Mona (who is Austrian) had been in hotel management in Switzerland and she speaks German, Italian, and a little French. Both Jim and Mona recognized that in today's world, families, let alone husbands and wives, have very little opportunity to spend a week of quality time together. So too, they recognized that it is the simple pleasures that ultimately touch hearts and souls and not all the fancy material things. Timber Ridge had been operated as a dude ranch for many years. What has changed since the Kings purchased it has been the Christian atmosphere they have brought, along with their warmth and hospitality. The ranch is situated in a valley, surrounded by large firs and ponderosa pines and grazing meadows. Not far away is Blue Lake where many of the ranch activities take place. Both Jim and Mona will be the first to say that their ranch is not fancy. As they say, "We believe that the Lord has given us this beautiful setting and ranch to share." Chocoholics beware! Mona makes a mean German chocolate cake.

Address: P.O. Box 285 K, Harrison, Idaho 83833
Telephone: (208) 689-3209
Airport: Spokane
Location: 5 miles east of Harrison, 78 miles southeast of Spokane, 1 hour southeast of Coeur d'Alene, Idaho
Memberships: Christian Camping International
Medical: St. Joe Valley Clinic, 45 minutes
Conference: 32; off-season only
Guest Capacity: 32
Accommodations: There are two duplex cabins, one with two rooms, the other with lofts. All have private baths and can sleep from two to six. The lodge has one double room with its own bath. There is also a two-room apartment below the foreman's house which will sleep six.

Rates: • $. American Plan. One-week minimum stay in high season. Three-day minimum stay in low season.
Season: May through September
Activities: Each morning there is a short talk about the day's events. Morning and afternoon rides. Most riding is done at a walk or trot due to the terrain. Families usually ride together. Lake activities include swimming and fishing (you will need an Idaho fishing license). Weekly Lake Coeur d'Alene boat cruises. Lots of hiking, exploring two old gold mines in the area. Soothe your tired muscles at night under the stars in the hot tub.
Children's Programs: No set program. Children are the responsibility of their parents. The Kings have two young children. No baby-sitting available.
Dining: The blessing is said before each meal. Hearty Western American dishes along with many of Mona's European specialties.
Entertainment: Some musically inclined guests enjoy the piano. Horseshoes, singing, or reading. Many just like to plain old visit around the fire in the main lodge or at the campfire.
Summary: Timber Ridge is a small Christian ranch located in the heart of Idaho's beautiful wilderness. Guests of all faiths are welcome. No formal Bible studies, but grace is said at each meal and short Christian talks begin each day's activities. German, Italian, and some French spoken.

Timber Ridge Ranch, Idaho

Timber Ridge Ranch, Idaho

Wapiti Meadow Ranch, Idaho

Authentic Western Ranch, Member–Dude Ranchers' Association

Wapiti Meadow Ranch is one of the great outposts of civilization in the rugged Salmon River Mountains of central Idaho. One of just a handful of private properties in this magnificent National Forest and Wilderness Area, it was originally homesteaded in the days of the great Thunder Mountain gold rush. The lodge was built in 1926 by the Cox family, and it became famous as the Cox Dude Ranch until the mid-1970s. In 1986, Diana Haynes bought the ranch after she experienced the breathtaking beauty of Idaho's backcountry. Today, as before, Wapiti Meadow is surrounded by heavily forested mountains, crystal clear streams, and lush valley meadows, which are home to herds of elk, mule deer, and a fine string of horses and pack mules. What makes Wapiti Meadow special is its rugged seclusion in the heart of Idaho's pristine wilderness coupled with gracious homelike comfort.

Address: H.C. 72 K, Cascade, Idaho 83611
Telephone: (208) 382-4336 (radio telephone)
Airport: Boise. Contact ranch for air charter details.
Location: 130 miles north of Boise, 60 miles east of McCall, 140 miles northwest of Sun Valley
Memberships: Dude Ranchers' Association, Idaho Outfitters and Guides Association
Medical: McCall Hospital, 60 miles; Life Flight helicopter from Boise
Guest Capacity: 15
Accommodations: The main lodge is a fine hand-hewn log structure. In it is Diana's collection of antiques from her days in Virginia and a handsome stone fireplace that takes up to 4-foot logs. There are four newer two-bedroom cabins that are wood sided and stained to match the main lodge and feature large porches, with twin, double or single rooms, a living/dining room, a bath, and a kitchen. Comforters and wool blankets, baseboard electric heaters, and wood-burning stoves keep guests warm on cool summer and winter nights.

Rates: • $$. American Plan. Pack trip and group rates available.
Credit Cards: None
Season: Year-round
Activities: Horseback riding through the Salmon River Mountains to alpine lakes. Two- to five-day pack trips. Extensive backpacking with mules to pack in equipment. Fishing in stocked pond and Johnson Creek at the ranch and high mountain fishing trips. Guided hiking. River rafting available. Cross-country skiing and snowmobiling in-season.
Children's Programs: None
Dining: Gourmet meals with fresh vegetables and exotic desserts like white chocolate cheesecake. The owner's favorite pastime is cooking, and it shows. Special diets can be accommodated.
Entertainment: Relaxing on the main lodge porch, watching the horses and game graze in the meadows, horseshoes, volleyball, camp fires, and hot tub.
Summary: Small family owned and operated ranch. Lots of personal service. Pristine valley setting with lush meadows. Mountain riding instruction, packing and wilderness skills. Historic gold mines, Thunder Mountain Road, Middle Fork of the Salmon River.

Double JJ Ranch, Michigan

The Double JJ Ranch is 25 miles outside Muskegon in west central Michigan. This is one of the few adults-only ranches in the country and has entertained thousands of Midwest singles and couples for almost half a century. It has a wonderful atmosphere, where people over the age of 18 can relax and be themselves. The ranch was started in the 1930s. Since then, it has grown to be a full-service ranch resort. Today, it is owned and operated by Bob and Joan Lipsitz. Since the early 1970s, both have been involved in the outdoor recreation field. The Double JJ accommodates up to 170 adults who can participate in everything from horseback riding to organized sports. Said to be America's friendliest resort for "big kids," the ranch has 1,000 wooded acres set in a natural pine forest. There are hundreds of acres of trails and thousands of acres of the Manistee National Forest. Here the beauty of native Michigan is evident. Move fast or slow, whichever you like. At the Double JJ, you are on your own time.

Address: Box 94 K, Rothbury, Michigan 49452
Telephone: (616) 894-4444
Airport: Muskegon, 25 miles; Grand Rapids International, 45 miles; private airstrip, 4 miles
Location: 25 miles north of Muskegon off U.S. 31, 189 miles east of Chicago, 200 miles west of Detroit
Memberships: Michigan Environmental Association, Michigan Appaloosa Horse Association
Medical: Muskegon General Hospital
Conference: 400; 10,000 square feet of conference space
Guest Capacity: 170
Accommodations: Guests sleep in cabins and lodge rooms with double and single beds, private baths, and showers. All 70 rooms have carpeting and daily housekeeping. Some deluxe accommodations available.
Rates: • $-$$. American Plan. Daily and weekend rates available. Conference and group rates. Holiday packages.
Credit Cards: Visa, MasterCard

Season: Year-round, including Thanksgiving, Christmas, and Easter
Activities: Daily riding with weekly breakfast rides, lessons are available, and groups ride according to experience. All those who claim to be advanced riders are tested first for ability. Rides are typically 1 hour and 45 minutes and go out four times per day. Private lake fishing for bass and pike. Canoeing, outdoor heated swimming pool, twelve-person hot tub spa, two tennis courts, hiking, rifle and archery range, baseball diamond, minigolf, many organized sports. All sports equipment, except fishing poles (fishing licenses are not required), is provided.
Children's Programs: No children allowed.
Dining: Plenty of food served buffet-style. All you can eat. Weekly breakfast and steak rides. BYOB.
Entertainment: Nightly entertainment, including dances with live bands and deejays, musicians, comedians, staff, and game shows. Ranch rodeo each week with contest. Tractor hay wagon rides, game and video room, horseshoes. All-night volleyball. Theme week with costume party.
Summary: Adults-only resort ranch, full group adult activities with director and staff. Health and fitness workshops, motor coach tours welcome. Corporate Management Training, theme weeks, gift shop. Lake Michigan, 6 miles; Silver Lake Sand Dunes, 15 miles; antique shops. Video available on request.

El Rancho Stevens, Michigan

El Rancho Stevens is in northern Michigan, on Dixon Lake, known for its cool, refreshing waters and sandy beaches. This ranch was started by "Doc" and Candy Stevens in 1948. Doc had been an automotive engineer and bought the property with the intent of building a Michigan dude ranch. Today, this ranch/lake resort encompasses about one thousand acres with good lakeside access, well-kept lawns, and open pastures. The Stevenses cater to couples and families with children six years old and up. Those who enjoy water activities and horseback riding will enjoy El Rancho Stevens.

Address: P.O. Box 495 K, Gaylord, Michigan 49735
Telephone: (517) 732-5090
Airport: Traverse City, 70 miles; private planes to Gaylord Airport, 5 miles
Location: 225 miles north of Detroit, 50 miles south of the famous Mackinaw Bridge, 5 miles southeast of Gaylord off McCoy Road
Memberships: West and East Michigan Tourist Association
Medical: Otsego Memorial Hospital, 6 miles
Conference: 100 (Ox Yoke Beach Building)
Guest Capacity: 100
Accommodations: There are two 2-story lodges and two 1-story lodges with thirty motel-style rooms. Each is comfortable, carpeted, with private bath, and double beds. There is one two-bedroom suite with full bath and living room.
Rates: • $. Modified American Plan. Children's, holiday, and off-season rates available.
Credit Cards: Visa, MasterCard
Season: June through September
Activities: Riding and hiking trails wander through the ranch and onto state lands with forested areas. All rides are on a per hour basis and divided into beginner, intermediate, and advanced. Large indoor riding arena. Heated swimming pool. Full lake activities including paddle boats and small sailboats, waterskiing, fishing, and canoeing. Softball, archery, and volleyball. Gaylord is fast becoming the golf capital of northern Michigan, with ten 18-hole golf courses nearby (packages available). Tractor hayrides and cookouts.
Children's Programs: Counselors and daily programs. Special rides for kids 6 years and older. Baby-sitters available.
Dining: Meals from the dining room are ordered from a menu and served on an individual basis. Cookouts and beach barbecues of chicken and ribs are the ranch favorites. Breakfast rides. Licensed cocktail lounge in dining room and the Silver Dollar Saloon at the beach.
Entertainment: Hayrides, country dancing, sing-alongs with marshmallow roasts. Corral capers—guests compete against each other in games like egg and spoon races. Recreation room with video games, table tennis, and pool tables.
Summary: Ranch resort on Dixon Lake. Indoor riding arena (70 feet x 120 feet). Nearby attractions include Mackinaw Island and Bridge, Hartwick Pines State Park.

Wrangler in Wyoming

Wranglers preparing for a pack trip

Turkey Creek Ranch, Missouri

In the Ozark Mountain country of southwestern Missouri, overlooking Bull Shoals Lake, is the Edwards's Turkey Creek Ranch Resort. In 1953, Dick Edwards and his parents bought a run-down farm. Since that time Dick, his wife, Elda, and their children have created a 400-acre working ranch and lake resort. Turkey Creek is an affordable family haven and boasts activities for everyone. The Edwards say, "We have a family place with hills, hollows, trees, and a lake where you can do as little or as much as you like!" The ranch is open most of the year with a special emphasis on family vacations. Early spring and fall are also times for serious fishermen and hunters.

Address: Star Route 3, Box 180 K, Theodosia, Missouri 65761
Telephone: (417) 273-4362
Airport: Springfield, Missouri, 85 miles
Location: 47 miles east of Branson, Missouri; 47 miles northwest of Mountain Home, Arkansas
Memberships: AAA, Missouri Bull Shoals Lake Association, Ozark Mountain Region
Awards: Mobil 2 Star, AAA 3 Diamond
Medical: Mountain Home Hospital, 47 miles
Guest Capacity: 131
Accommodations: There are 24 cabins and motel-type units (most are individual and well spaced from others). They are comfortable with air-conditioning, color TV, daily paper, screened porches. Unit size varies from 4- to 10-person capacity. Deluxe units also have microwave ovens, carpeting, and queen-size beds.
Rates: • $. Meals, riding, sailing, and outboard motorboat rental extra.
Credit Cards: None. Personal checks accepted.
Season: Mid-March to mid-November
Activities: Horseback riding and hiking through the woods and along the lakeshore. Lake activities include canoeing, paddleboating, sailing, waterskiing, and diving (scuba gear available locally). Take a pontoon boat excursion to Bull Shoals Dam (22 miles), or just go to your favorite cove to relax and swim. Bull Shoals Lake has

black, white, and large-mouth bass, crappie, catfish, and the scrappy sunfish. Go after them with well-equipped bass boats or the Bass Buggy pontoon boat. There are also indoor and outdoor pools, whirlpool spa, tennis courts, horseshoes, and shuffleboard. The ranch herd of Simmental-cross beef cattle usually has several baby calves to admire.
Children's Programs: No formal program. Children are part of the family and as such are encouraged to participate in activities with their parents. Children too young to ride on their own (under age 8) may be led on pony rides around the grounds. There is also a playground and wading pool. Baby-sitting available with advance notice.
Dining: Turkey Creek's own Chuckwagon Restaurant offers steaks, a variety of salads and sandwiches, pies, and soft ice cream treats. Special meals (anniversary, birthday, etc.) available with prior arrangement.
Entertainment: 3,000 square feet of recreation rooms include two fireplaces, spa, pool tables, air hockey, video games, board games, shuffleboard, juke box, table tennis, and a piano for sing-alongs.
Summary: Ranch resort on Bull Shoals Lake geared to families vacationing together. Near Silver Dollar City theme park, Shepherd of the Hills Farm and Pageant, White Water Park, Blanchard Springs Caverns, and river canoeing.

Turkey Creek Ranch, Missouri

Turkey Creek Ranch, Missouri

Beartooth Ranch and JLX Outfitters, Montana

Authentic Western Ranch, Member–Dude Ranchers'
Association

Serving guests since 1904, Beartooth Ranch is one of the charter members of the Dude Ranchers' Association. At 5,058 feet, this 160-acre ranch is four miles within the Custer National Forest boundary and adjacent to nearly one million acres of the Absaroka-Beartooth Wilderness Area. As one drives up mineral-rich Stillwater Canyon, Woodbine Falls comes into view, signaling arrival at the ranch. These magnificent falls plummet 1,000 feet before striking the river waters below. In the late 1880s, Beartooth was settled by Byron "Bine" Woods, one of Buffalo Bill Cody's guides. In 1922, he sold it to E. J. "Ed" Ikerman who ran it as a boys' ranch. Soon, parents requested vacations at the ranch, too. In 1956, Jim and Ellen Langston, William G. Mouat, and Col. John C. Mouat bought Beartooth. Today, Jim and Ellen are your hosts at this wonderful historic ranch. Jim is a past president of the Dude Ranchers' Association. Both Ellen and Jim have friends around the world and continue to serve great Montana friendliness and hospitality.

Address: HC 54, Box 350 K, Nye, Montana 59061
Telephone: (406) 328-6194 or (406) 328-6205
Airport: Billings Logan International Airport
Location: 45 miles south of Columbus, 90 miles southwest of Billings
Memberships: Dude Ranchers' Association, Montana Outfitters and Guides Association
Medical: Absaroka Medical Clinic, 30 miles; Stillwater Community Hospital, 45 miles; HELP helicopter from Billings, 90 miles
Conference: Available
Guest Capacity: 30
Accommodations: Twelve log or native rock, heated cabins varying from one to four bedrooms, most with living rooms, some with fireplaces, and all with baths; one two-story lodge with eleven rooms, each with its own bath. Laundry facilities available.
Rates: $. American Plan. Children's and family rates available.

Credit Cards: American Express, MasterCard, Visa
Season: June through Labor Day
Activities: Horseback riding is the main daily activity. Ask Jim and Ellen about their rides to Sioux Charley, Horseman Flat, and Nye Basin. Instruction available. Excellent fly-fishing in the Stillwater River for rainbow, German brown, and brook trout. Fishing licenses available. Pack trips, hiking, swimming in the ranch pond. Horseshoe pitching tournaments, volleyball, softball, badminton, table tennis, billiards, bird-watching, and camp fires.
Children's Programs: Children's supervisors and wranglers arrange treasure hunts on horseback, melodramas, pageants, variety shows, lawn games, crafts, swimming, nature hikes, trail rides. Children usually interact with families.
Dining: Breakfast includes a buffet (juices, fruit, cereal, hot dishes) prepared and served short-order style. A buffet luncheon consists of hot dishes, salad bar, breads, beverages, and desserts. Dinner, served family-style, has five to seven courses, begins at 6:30 p.m., and features Western ranch cooking. At 5:30 p.m. guests gather at the Happy Hour Circle by the chuckwagon. BYOB. Luncheon rides and steak or hamburger barbecues at the riverside picnic area are held several times a week.
Entertainment: Camp fires with Western singing, evenings in the lodge with Western dancing, melodramas, pageants, variety shows.
Summary: Besides the tremendous warmth and hospitality Jim and Ellen give to all their guests, the complete uniqueness of this ranch is its intimate relationship to the fascinating geological formations of this area. A large number of guests each week are professionals in the fields of mining and geology. The Stillwater Complex is a formation where deposits of nickel, copper, chromite, platinum, palladium, silver, gold, and other minerals are studied by geology students from all over the world. Nearby attractions include Memorial Day rodeos, Western Days in Billings in mid-June.

Blue Spruce Lodge and Guest Ranch, Montana

Russ Milleson was injured in an industrial accident in 1974 at the age of 23. Suddenly confined to a wheelchair for life and unable to find places that were wheelchair accessible for hunting, fishing, and other outdoor activities, with the help of his family, he designed and· built the Blue Spruce Lodge. Completed in June 1986, the Blue Spruce Lodge is in the foothills of the Bitterroot Mountains of northwest Montana. Open year-round, the lodge offers a wide variety of recreational activities for all. River raft trips begin in May. Russ also operates a 24-foot pontoon boat on the Noxon Reservoir with sightseeing and fishing trips on Lake Pend Oreille. Fall brings on the hunting season, with a large variety of big game and birds. There is a special program for wheelchair hunters. Cross-country skiing is good December through March, and there are many miles of trails that provide entertainment and challenge. The warm lodge interior features family-style dining, wet bar, and pool table. The cozy wood stove creates a homey environment in a scenic Montana setting.

Address: 451 Marten Creek Road, Dept. K, Trout Creek, Montana 59874
Telephone: (406) 827-4762
Airport: Missoula, Montana, or Spokane, Washington
Location: 25 miles west of Thompson Falls, 140 miles northwest of Missoula, 140 miles northeast of Spokane
Medical: Plains, Montana, 75 miles; Sandpoint Hospital in Idaho, 65 miles; helicopter ambulance from Missoula or Spokane
Conference: Up to 16
Guest Capacity: 16
Accommodations: The two-story main lodge has been designed for wheelchair access and maneuverability. The main floor is serviced by wide entrances and generous porches. There are few obstacles or hindrances. Sleeping accommodations are provided on the second floor, and there is an elevator for convenience. Several of the nine bedrooms have private balconies.

There are five rooms with double beds, two rooms with bunk beds, and a sleeping loft with a double bed. Laundry service is available.
Rates: • $. American Plan. Children's and group rates available.
Credit Cards: Visa, MasterCard, American Express
Season: Year-round
Activities: Week-long programs and activities are tailored to the groups or individuals at the ranch. Trail rides, white water raft trips, and float fishing trips are available for everyone. Even big game and bird hunting are possible for guests in wheelchairs. Winter program includes cross-country skiing, sit skiing for the disabled, sledding, snowmobiling, ice fishing.
Children's Programs: Children go on most outings with parents; baby-sitting available.
Dining: Home-cooked meals served family-style; special diets on request. BYOB.
Entertainment: Fiddle and guitar music around camp fire some evenings.
Summary: A unique, small, family ranch designed and built to give individuals confined to wheelchairs and their families full enjoyment of ranch life and a rustic wilderness experience. Lodge is totally wheelchair accessible, as are most activities.

Boulder River Ranch, Montana

Authentic Western Ranch, Member–Dude Ranchers' Association

Surrounded by the rugged Absaroka Mountains at 5,050 feet, Boulder River Ranch is a neat old ranch on the banks of the beautiful Boulder River. This family owned and operated ranch is on one of the most productive trout streams in North America. Since 1918, the Aller family has played host to families from around the world who return year after year. The Allers take only 30 guests at a time and specialize in superb fishing and horseback riding. Experienced and novice anglers will enjoy tremendous fishing in the cold, crystal clear waters of the Boulder River. Swimmers will love the river's natural pools. Riders savor the beautiful high country and meadow trail rides to abandoned mines, homesteads, and the Indian caves. June is for bird-watchers, with more than seventy species of birds in the area. Deer, elk, and hundreds of wildflowers also abound. Whatever month you choose, you will enjoy every moment with the Allers.

Address: Box 210 K, McLeod, Montana 59052
Telephone: (406) 932-6406
Airport: Billings or Bozeman
Location: 110 miles southwest of Billings, 87 miles southeast of Bozeman, 28 miles south of Big Timber
Memberships: Dude Ranchers' Association
Medical: Sweet Grass Community Hospital, 28 miles
Conference: Up to 25
Guest Capacity: 30
Accommodations: Most of the fifteen individual cabins are arranged in a semicircle around the front lawn; each is comfortable with private baths and daily maid service. Each looks to the Absaroka Mountains across the river. Happy hour at the end of the day brings guests onto the front lawn for tale swapping. It is a nice family arrangement.
Rates: • $. American Plan. Children's and family rates available. Children under age 3, free.
Credit Cards: None. Personal checks and cash accepted.

Season: June to mid-September
Activities: The ranch raises and trains its own quarter horses. Half-day and all-day guided rides. No riding on Sundays. Catch and release fly-fishing. Limited fishing gear available. Hiking and swimming in the river. Seasonal deer and elk hunting.
Children's Programs: Limited children's program. Kiddie wrangler; stocked pond for swimming and fishing. Baby-sitting on request.
Dining: Scrumptious family-style meals. Cookouts. Ranch chef will cook your freshly caught pond trout. Once a week breakfast rides with famous ranch "fry" bread. BYOB.
Entertainment : Most guests like to retreat to the porches of their cabins and reminisce about their experiences of the day. There is no formal entertainment at the ranch.
Summary: Very relaxed, very informal family owned and operated ranch; 90 percent return guests. June and September art workshops. Fly-fishing clinics available on request. Nearby attractions include Yellowstone National Park. Big Timber Professional Rodeo in June, Cowboy Poetry gathering, and world championship pack horse race in August.

C-B Ranch, Montana

Authentic Western Ranch, Member–Dude Ranchers' Association

This small, family-owned cattle ranch is in the famous Madison River Valley. Fly-fishermen know this river for its trophy brown and rainbow trout. The C-B Ranch was established in 1971 by Mrs. Cynthia Boomhower of Palm Beach, Florida, who as a young girl, fell in love with the West and dude ranching. The ranch encompasses 21,000 acres and raises 200 head of Charolais crosses and a small herd of longhorn cattle. At 5,000 feet, the ranch lodge and cabins are situated where Indian Creek comes out of the Madison Range, which rises to 11,000 feet behind the property. You will have a great feeling of Western nostalgia as you pass under the C-B Ranch gate and experience the grandeur of Montana's Big Sky Country.

Address: P.O. Box 604 K, Cameron, Montana 59720
Telephone: (406) 682-4954
Airport: West Yellowstone or Bozeman
Location: 20 miles southeast of Ennis, 60 miles southwest of Bozeman
Memberships: Dude Ranchers' Association
Medical: Ennis Hospital
Guest Capacity: 12-14
Accommodations: Three large double log cabins, each with two double beds and a fold-out couch, with private entrances. All cabins have private baths and open fireplaces or Franklin stoves. Furnished with real Navajo rugs, clip-on reading lights, candles, and fresh flowers. Additional electric heat and air-conditioning (which is seldom needed) in all cabins.
Rates: • $-$$. American Plan.
Credit Cards: None. Personal checks or cash accepted.
Season: Mid-June to early September
Activities: There are no planned activities at the C-B Ranch. Most guests spend their time fishing. However, those who want to ride are assigned their very own horse for the length of their stay. Half-day and full-day rides; lunch rides are available once a week with a wrangler. Fly-fishing on the Madison River or the famous waters of Henry's Fork. The C-B has access to Odell Creek, a private stream noted for its tremendous brown trout. Float trips can be arranged, or just relax and enjoy the day with the family.
Children's Programs: Kiddie wrangler is available.
Dining: All meals are prepared fresh. There is always plenty of food.
Entertainment: The howls of coyotes at night. You may see deer, antelope, coyotes, elk, or moose, and lots of bears (one year the ranch trapped eight bears).
Summary: Small family-owned cattle ranch. Excellent fly-fishing nearby and women's fly-fishing lessons. Nearby attractions include Yellowstone Park, Intercollegiate Rodeo Finals in Bozeman, and rodeos in Ennis.

Circle Bar Guest Ranch, Montana

Authentic Western Ranch, Member–Dude Ranchers' Association

The Circle Bar Ranch is a dude/cattle ranch in northern Montana where the scenery ranges from dry prairie to towering mountains. Host and owner Sarah Hollatz bought the ranch in the early 1980s. While her first love is guest ranching, she is very talented and among other things, has produced children's records. The ranch takes forty guests at a time and is bordered on two sides by the Lewis and Clark National Forest. The ranch encourages full participation in ranch activities or just plain relaxing and savoring the goodness of ranch life. Out by the "old red barn," a guest can sit under the big cottonwood trees and listen to the sounds of the Judith River. Here you can catch rainbow trout that the cook will gladly prepare for you.

Address: P.O. Box K, Utica, Montana 59452
Telephone: (406) 423-5454; Fax: (406) 423-5686
Airport: Great Falls
Location: 90 miles south of Great Falls, 13 miles southwest of Utica near Route 87
Memberships: Dude Ranchers' Association, Montana Outfitters and Guides
Medical: EMT on premises; Lewistown Central Montana Hospital, 50 miles
Conference: 40
Guest Capacity: 40
Accommodations: There are nine one- to four-bedroom log cabins; all have propane or electric heat and private baths. Most cabins have their own fireplace or wood stove. The exquisite new T-shaped lodge has a huge fieldstone fireplace and four additional rooms for guests. All rooms have porches or decks with C. M. Russell Western prints in cabins. A bouquet of fresh wildflowers in each room upon arrival. Laundry facilities.
Rates: $$. American Plan. Conference, winter, hunting, and pack trip rates available on request. Three-day minimum.
Credit Cards: None. Personal checks or cash accepted.
Season: Year-round, including Thanksgiving and Easter

Activities: In summer, riders will enjoy the ranch's fine string of horses. All-day and half-day rides in groups no larger than 8 to 10 persons. Moonlight rides through open meadows and pines once a week. Riding instruction is available. Pack trips with advance notice. Light harness carriage driving with instruction. Fishing on the Judith River, which runs through the ranch. Hiking, volleyball, indoor basketball, horseshoes, heated swimming pool, and hot tub. Fall hunting. In winter, provided there is snow, wilderness cross-country skiing, sleigh rides, ice skating, and snowmobiling are available.
Children's Programs: Parents are responsible for children. Young children ride with supervision.
Dining: All meals served in the lodge. The ranch is proud of the fresh breads and homegrown herbs and vegetables used in preparing the daily meals. Ranch specialties: Caribbean chicken, home-grown steak, fresh rhubarb pies. Sunday barbecue. BYOB.
Entertainment: Team-drawn hayrides, occasional square dances, camp fire sing-alongs. Evening swimming.
Summary: Actual working ranch raising cattle and quarter horses. Flexibility to cater to specific interests. Families, couples, and singles all feel comfortable. Fossil hunting, horse-drawn carriage driving with instruction. Artist workshops. Ask Sarah about the historic 4-day Charlie Russell horseback ride. Branding in May and roundups in June and October. Sapphire and gold mining. Trips to Charles M. Russell Museum. Castle ghost town. Some French spoken.

Elk Canyon Ranch, Montana

John and Kay Eckhardt and the Texas-based Schoellkopf family all shared a dream, a love, and a vision. Together, in 1985, they created a guest ranch masterpiece along the Smith River in central Montana. The Eckhardts have been in the guest ranching business since the early 1960s and have a tremendous following of guests from around the world. From their beautifully laid out brochure to nightly bed turndown service, John and Kay have not forgotten a thing. In addition to their luxurious amenities, they recruit some of the nicest collegiate staff in the business. Numbers may run the world, but people make it. In the world of guest ranching, Elk Canyon Ranch is a "top gun."

Address: Dept. K, White Sulphur Springs, Montana 59645
Telephone: (406) 547-3373; Fax: (406) 547-3719
Airport: Bozeman. Private planes may land at 4,600-foot paved airstrip at White Sulphur Springs, Montana
Location: 30 miles northwest of White Sulphur Springs off Highway 360, 110 miles north of Bozeman
Medical: White Sulphur Springs Hospital; emergency helicopter service available
Conference: 24; off-season only
Guest Capacity: 42
Accommodations: Eight sensational one- to four-bedroom deluxe log cabins among manicured lawns and beside a small manmade creek. The cabins have 15- to 20-foot peaked ceilings and fieldstone fireplaces, pine interiors, large country windows, and sitting areas or living rooms. Each bedroom is carpeted and has its own private bath. All the cabins have front porches. Each cabin also features washer/dryer, private telephones with direct outside lines, baseboard heating, air-conditioning, and old-fashioned overhead fans and brass bathroom fixtures. A few deluxe cabins even have full kitchens (most families never use these, though). One cabin even has a wheelchair-access shower. To top it off, your handmade log bed will be

turned down each night.
Rates: $$$. Full American Plan, children's rates available.
Credit Cards: None
Season: June to early October. Conference groups in the off-season.
Activities: Each guest is assigned a horse for the entire length of stay. Beginners receive full instruction. Experienced riders cover more territory. Rides usually go out in groups of five to seven. Hourly, half-day, and all-day rides, cookouts and breakfast rides to Spring Creek and Songsters Divide. Twenty-five-foot by fifty-foot outdoor heated swimming pool with lifeguard on duty during the day. River rafting on the Smith River with rafting guides and rafts available. Two professional tennis courts; a breathtaking trap and skeet shooting range. Excellent catch and release fly-fishing only. Completely stocked tackle shop at the ranch. There is a stocked meadow pond for those who wish fresh trout at breakfast. Golf carts are available for getting around the ranch.
Children's Programs: Terrific, but nonmandatory, program from 9:00 a.m. to 2:00 p.m. and again from 6:00 p.m. to 9:00 p.m. each day for children ages 4 to 13. Baby-sitting for younger children on a limited basis.
Dining: Full breakfast, lunch buffets, and wonderful salads poolside (weather permitting). Weekly noon and evening cookouts. Children eat with other children and counselors. Dinner entrées include wonderfully prepared beef, fish, lamb, veal, poultry served with fresh vegetables, and California wine.
Entertainment: After dinner, parents reunite with their children. Some go for short walks, others sit on their porches or just drift off to sleep.
Summary: A luxury guest ranch. Outstanding, newly built, superbly run. Excellence in every way. Fully appointed individual cabins with complete amenities. Sundry items available. Museum of the Rockies, Charles M. Russell Museum, and Glacier, Teton, and Yellowstone national parks nearby.

See color photos, page 233

Diamond J Ranch, Montana

Authentic Western Ranch, Member–Dude Ranchers'
Association • Orvis-Endorsed Lodge

In 1959, Peter and Jinny Combs were on their way to Alaska, looking to move from the ever-increasing development of southern California. They stopped at the Diamond J Ranch, and the rest is history. The Diamond J was built in 1930 by Julia Bennett and run as a guest ranch. It was her masterpiece, located in the Madison River Valley, famous for cattle ranching and fly-fishing. The ranch is surrounded by the Lee Metcalf Wilderness Area, and is nestled in a separate canyon at 5,800 feet with Jack Creek running along side. Today the Combses spend winters in Mexico for warmth but return each summer to greet old friends and meet new guests. Tim and Ginger, their son and daughter, are the managers of this small family ranch. Together, they see to it that all thirty-six guests are well looked after. The Combs run a great operation and families return to the Diamond J Ranch, year after year.

Address: P.O. Box 577 K, Ennis, Montana 59729
Telephone: (406) 682-4867; Fax: (406) 682-4106
Airport: Bozeman, commercial; Ennis, 4,800-foot paved air strip 12 miles away for light aircraft
Location: 14 miles east of Ennis off Highway 287, 60 miles south of Bozeman
Memberships: Dude Ranchers' Association
Awards: Orvis-Endorsed Lodge
Medical: Ennis Hospital, 12 miles
Conference: 36 (June and September)
Guest Capacity: 36
Accommodations: The ten log cabins are constructed with lodgepole pine logs. Each has its own rock fireplace, tongue-and-groove hardwood floors, matching furniture, and beds. Each cabin features a few of Julia Bennett's personal big game trophies, a full bath with separate shower stall, and cast iron tub. The bedroom-living rooms feature twin beds, writing desks, and front porches, each with different railing designs. No television or telephones.
Rates: • $$. American Plan. Children's and seasonal rates available. Skeet and trap shooting, sporting clays, pack trips, and guided fly-

fishing are extra. July and August, one-week minimum stay.
Credit Cards: MasterCard
Season: June through September
Activities: Activities can be tailored to individual or family needs, as schedules are flexible. The ranch emphasizes a relaxed, unstructured atmosphere. The Diamond J has great children's horses. Breakfast, half-day, all-day rides. Annual June horse drive for expert riders only. Ask about the Yellowstone National Park ride. Mountain pack trips are possible. Hiking. Excellent fly-fishing, since the ranch is near some of the best blue ribbon streams in Montana, like the Madison, Gallatin, Jefferson, Beaverhead, and Missouri, 70 miles away. Private 2-acre lake with rainbow trout. Full-time guides are available. Indoor tennis, mountain bike trails, heated swimming pool. Float trips arranged. Massage available. Trap and skeet shooting (guns provided), and 10-station sporting clay course.
Children's Programs: Kiddie wrangler and riding instruction. Usually children ride together. Baby-sitter available.
Dining: Meals served family-style in three rooms. At lunch and dinner, children and adults usually eat separately (not mandatory). House specialties: fruit pancakes, tostadas, ham loaf with honey mustard, and steak barbecue. Special diets catered to with advance notice. Cookouts. Prefer no smoking in dining room. A BYOB happy hour.
Entertainment: Square dancing, camp fire, sing-alongs, games, and an excellent library (ranch subscribes to best-seller list).
Summary: Lovely unstructured family owned and operated guest/fly-fishing ranch. Very flexible programs; do as much or as little as you wish. Excellent fly-fishing, horses for children, 10-station sporting clay course, float trips, indoor tennis. June horse drives. Ask about fall spa program. Yellowstone National Park, 70 miles. Museum of the Rockies in Bozeman, 60 miles. Fluent Spanish spoken. Orvis endorsed.

See color photos, page 223

Diamond J Ranch, Montana

Diamond J Ranch, Montana

Elkhorn Ranch, Montana

Authentic Western Ranch, Member–Dude Ranchers' Association

The Elkhorn Ranch is one of the old-time, no-nonsense dude ranches. A ranch steeped in history, it was started in the early 1920s by Ernest and Grace Miller. Located one mile from the northwest corner of Yellowstone Park, Elkhorn is at 7,000 feet in a beautiful valley surrounded by the Gallatin National Forest and the Lee Metcalf Wilderness. They call this the Gallatin Gateway, and for good reason. It is a gateway to incredible natural beauty, mountain scenery, and loads of wildlife. Since the early days, the ranch has been famous for its superb riding program, its dedication to preserving our Western heritage, and to uniting families. Today, as in years gone by, the Elkhorn combines old-fashioned Montana-style hospitality, rustic warmth, and natural beauty. At the Elkhorn Ranch, they still serve up the West that used to be.

Address: 33133 Gallatin Road, Drawer K, Gallatin Gateway, Montana 59730
Telephone: (406) 995-4291
Airport: Bozeman and West Yellowstone
Location: 60 miles south of Bozeman off Highway 191, 30 miles north of the west entrance to Yellowstone Park
Memberships: Dude Ranchers' Association
Medical: Bozeman Deaconess, 60 miles
Conference: 45; June and September only
Guest Capacity: 45
Accommodations: Sixteen original log cabins. Each is set apart from the others and varies in size, sleeping one to six persons. Most have colorful Hudson Bay foot blankets, comforters, some even have squeaky wooden floors. Most have electric heat in the bathrooms and wood stoves in the sitting areas. Limited laundry facilities.
Rates: $$. American Plan. Children's rates available.
Credit Cards: None. Personal checks or traveler's checks.
Season: Mid-June to mid-September
Activities: This is, indeed, a western riding ranch. Beginners will feel just as much at home as do experienced riders. A great emphasis is placed on safety. Riding starts each morning at 10:00. Groups usually go out with 6 to 8 people and two wranglers. All-day rides three times a week. Fishing rides twice a week. Because there is such a diversity of riding, guests will seldom go on the same ride twice. Fly-fishing enthusiasts will enjoy the Madison, Gallatin, and Yellowstone rivers, all blue-ribbon trout streams. Swimming in the ranch spring-fed pond, hiking.
Children's Program: Peanut Butter Mother is with children ages 6 to 12 all day for dining, riding, and activities. Teenager "Jets," as they are called, ride and eat together. Baby-sitting available with advance notice.
Dining: Home-cooked meals served buffet family-style in the big dining room located in central lodge. Children dine at their own table. Weekly breakfast, lunch, and dinner on the trail. BYOB (no liquor in dining room). Guests usually have cocktails in their or other guests' cabins.
Entertainment: Weekly bonfires with singing and marshmallows, square dancing, and speakers on topics of local interest (grizzly bears, wildflowers).
Summary: One of the classic, old-time dude ranches. Emphasis on horseback riding. Excellent fly-fishing on nearby blue-ribbon waters. Longer than week stays encouraged.

G Bar M Ranch, Montana

Authentic Western Ranch, Member–Dude Ranchers'
Association

Sage-covered, rolling foothills of the Bridger Mountains are a part of Brackett Creek Valley, home to the G Bar M guest ranch. The Leffingwell family has operated this no-nonsense 3,200-acre cattle ranch since 1900 and has welcomed guests since the early 1930s. This part of the country was made famous by one of North America's early explorers and mountain men, Jim Bridger. The Leffingwells make no bones about it: "We have no golf, no pool, no tennis, and no structured entertainment." At the G Bar M, you can join in the daily activities that are part of this 100-head cattle/guest ranch or you can enjoy everything at your own pace. Part of the ranch has been designated as a game reserve; no hunting is allowed. George Leffingwell points out to his guests, "We here at the G Bar M think it is important to live in harmony with the land." Eagles, elk, deer, and even hummingbirds frequent the ranch. While most guests come from the United States, many come from Europe, Australia, and other parts of the world.

Address: Box AE, Dept. K, Clyde Park, Montana 59018
Telephone: (406) 686-4423
Airport: Bozeman
Location: 26 miles northeast of Bozeman off State Highway 86
Memberships: Dude Ranchers' Association
Medical: Deaconess Hospital in Bozeman, 26 miles
Conference: No
Guest Capacity: 15
Accommodations: The G Bar M accommodates guests in two cabins, one of which is a large family cabin, both with full bathrooms. Four rooms in the ranch house have private baths, double and twin beds, and are fully carpeted.
Rates: • $. Full American Plan. Rates include everything, including pickup at airport. Children's rates available. Sunday to Sunday minimum stay.
Credit Cards: None. Personal checks accepted.
Season: May through September

Activities: Your horse is matched to your riding ability. Guests may participate in various kinds of cattle work, mostly herding, changing pastures, or ranch chores like checking fences or placing salt licks for the white-faced Herefords. Ranch fishing for rainbow trout in Brackett Creek.
Children's Programs: Children enjoy helping to milk cows and feed the 50 chickens. Children are the responsibility of parents.
Dining: Families, ranch hands, and wranglers all eat together. Eggs and milk, as well as beef and pork, are all ranch fresh. There are two dairy cows milked daily. Mrs. Leffingwell, Sr. (in her seventies), has been cooking for 60 years and is well known for many specialties. Be sure to get a copy of Mrs. Leffingwell's *Sage Brush and Snow Drifts* cookbook.
Entertainment: No organized entertainment. Occasionally, a local family plays old-time Western music—three guitars and a banjo. Once-a-week steak fry.
Summary: Rest and relax at a tranquil old-time Western ranch. "The coffee pot is always on here." Small family cattle ranch, Yellowstone National Park, 90 miles; Museum of the Rockies; Lewis and Clark Caverns. Ask about the family cookbook.

Flathead Lake Lodge, Montana

Authentic Western Ranch, Member–Dude Ranchers' Association

Flathead Lake Lodge is on the shores of the largest freshwater lake in the West, surrounded by 2,000 private acres of riding trails that border national forest. Written up in *Better Homes & Gardens* and *Sunset* magazines (to name a few), as well as being a Mobil 4 Star property, this ranch resort features the best of two worlds. For those who like the water, there are all kinds of lake activities. If you would rather be on horseback than on a pair of water skis or in a sailboat, there are plenty of horses and many scenic trails. In the lake and timber country of northwestern Montana, the lodge is 35 miles from one of nature's greatest wonders—Glacier National Park—and one mile from the tiny "Western" village of Big Fork. Built and developed by Les Averill, a former airline pilot, and his wife, Ginny, the ranch is owned by the Averills' four sons and operated by Doug. What makes Flathead Lake Lodge great, said one guest, is that "the Averills love people and the Western tradition and have friendly personalities that make you feel at home." *Travel & Leisure* rated the ranch as the "best do-everything vacation in Montana."

Address: Box 248 K, Big Fork, Montana 59911
Telephone: (406) 837-4391; Fax: (406) 837-6977
Airport: Kalispell
Train: Whitefish, 25 miles
Location: 1 mile south of Big Fork, 17 miles south of Kalispell
Memberships: Dude Ranchers' Association
Awards: Mobil 4 Star, AAA 4 Diamond
Medical: Big Fork Medical Center, 1 mile
Conference: 120; with 3 meeting rooms, one that can seat 180 convention-style. Conference video available.
Guest Capacity: 120
Accommodations: There are three lodges and twenty 2-and 3-bedroom cottages/cabins set amid the well-kept lawns. The log cabins can sleep four to six people. Built in the 1940s, each cabin is carpeted, has original handmade log furniture and a living room, bathroom, and one, two, or three bedrooms. The lodge rooms overlook the lake. The main lodge is a beauty, with a huge rock fireplace. Everything at the ranch radiates warmth and charm.

Rates: • $$-$$$. American Plan. Children's, corporate, off-season, group, and convention rates available.
Credit Cards: Visa, MasterCard, American Express. Personal checks preferred.
Season: May through September
Activities: Horseback riding, including breakfast, day, and evening rides. Swimming in a heated pool right next to 28-mile-long Flathead Lake. Four plex-pave tennis courts. Extensive lake activities, with a big stretch of lawn and beach. Motorboating, sailing, canoeing, lake cruising, waterskiing, sailboarding. Tremendous fishing for kokanee, Dolly Varden, and cutthroat trout. Hiking. White water rafting and float fishing nearby.
Children's Programs: Nature program with arts and crafts. Complete recreation room and games. Kids' overnight camp-out once a week (ask what kids will need). Kids under 6 ride in stable area.
Dining: Family-style meals with plenty of home-baked bread, pies, and preserves made from fresh mountain huckleberries. Mountain steak fries, barbecues, salmon seafood barbecues, whole roast pigs weekly. Social hour each evening before dinner in the Saddle Sore Saloon.
Entertainment: Camp fires with sing-alongs, western barn dance, guest rodeo once a week with various horse games twice weekly, team roping with local cowboys, canoe and sailboat races.
Summary: Beautiful world-class dude ranch on 28-mile-long by 15-mile-wide Flathead Lake, with full ranch and lake activities. Glacier National Park, midsummer cherry picking. Big Fork Summer Theatre (has featured such musicals as "Oklahoma!" and "Sugar") 1 mile away. Language interpreters available.

See color photos, page 194

Flathead Lake Lodge, Montana

Flathead Lake Lodge, Montana

Hargrave Cattle and Guest Ranch, Montana

Authentic Western Ranch, Member–Dude Ranchers' Association

When the original homesteader retired in the 1960s, he handed the reins of this historic cattle ranch to the Hargraves. The ranch is nestled in a valley shouldered by tall pines, bordered by national forests. The Thompson River flows through its broad green meadows. It's the kind of beauty that gives peace, interrupted occasionally by the cry of a coyote on the crystal evening air or muffled honks of Canada geese in the morning mist. The log buildings date from the 1930s and 1940s, hewn by true craftsmen. You walk amid history in the huge log house barn. Hargrave Ranch is a working cattle operation on 87,000 acres. Leo, Ellen, and local cowboys welcome guests year-round. Guests can thrill at new life as calves are born, join in brandings, drive cattle to the summer range, and ride roundup in fall. You can ride to check fences or simply check out the two miles of private trout stream. For those seeking more adventure, there are pack trips in the proposed Cube Iron Wilderness among alpine lakes, flowers, and wildlife. Your trips are led by your host, Ellen, who always has an eye out for photographic opportunities. The ranch limit of 12 guests means personalized attention.

Address: Thompson River Valley, Dept. K, Marion, Montana 59925
Telephone: (406) 858-2284
Airport: Kalispell, 40 miles
Location: 40 miles west of Kalispell
Memberships: Dude Ranchers' Association, Montana Guides and Outfitters Association, National Cattlemen's Association
Medical: Kalispell Regional Hospital, 40 miles; emergency helicopter service available
Guest Capacity: 12
Accommodations: "The Stable" has a bedroom, loft, fireplace, kitchen, and bath and houses 2 to 6 guests. Rooms for 2 to 6 people in the main ranch house they call "Headquarters." Not far away is "Grandfather's Cabin," a small cabin with twin beds. Bathroom and shower are about 100 feet away. Leo and Ellen provide all

bedding. Ellen likes color and usually has planted red petunias and geraniums.
Rates: • $$. American Plan. Wilderness pack trips additional.
Credit Cards: Visa, MasterCard. Personal checks preferred.
Season: Year-round
Activities: Spring—newborn calves everywhere. Summer—hiking, riding, timber barbecues, overnight camp-outs, four-wheel-drive jeep rides to mountaintop fire lookout, cattle drives, fishing in private stream or nearby lakes, fly-fishing river float trip can be arranged. "Artists of the Mountains" studio tours arranged. Fall—cattle roundups, guided big game hunting. Winter—cross-country skiing, cedar sauna, 1½ hours from good downhill skiing at Big Mountain, Whitefish.
Children's Programs: None; children welcome. Children under 7 do not ride.
Dining: Your hosts enjoy fine food. Ranch-raised beef, local lamb and pork, fresh vegetables, and homemade desserts. Western fare and plenty of it. Happy hours with creative hors d'oeuvres. BYOB.
Entertainment: Weekly rodeo action in Kalispell, local Western saloon, occasional slide show. Mostly visiting with other guests about the day's adventures. Northwest Montana Fair in August.
Summary: Family owned and operated. Leo and Ellen both went on the historic Great Montana Cattle Drive and enjoy sharing this magnificent event with their guests. Working cattle ranch, cattle drives, art and photography workshops. Women's week. Glacier National Park, 60 miles; National Bison Range, 60 miles, Big Mountain Ski Resort, 1½ hours; Big Fork Center for the Performing Arts.

See color photos, page 179

Hargrave Cattle and Guest Ranch, Montana

JJJ Wilderness Ranch, Montana

Authentic Western Ranch, Member–Dude Ranchers' Association

The "Triple J" Ranch is run by the Barker family—Max and Ann and Ernie and Kim. They cater to a very limited number of guests each season. Here in the pure mountain air, the emphasis is on enjoying the great outdoors, unwinding, relaxing and having fun. The ranch lies in a valley at 5,500 feet in the Rocky Mountain Front Range of the Lewis and Clark National Forest, above the beautiful Sun River Canyon and Gibson Lake (7 miles long). The Barkers specialize in family vacations and emphasize riding, hiking, and trout fishing. For the adventuresome and pioneers at heart, Ernie takes pack trips to remote mountain lakes and through pine forests of the famous Bob Marshall Wilderness. The Barkers have hosted people from around the country over the years, including a good number of VIPs. They have a saying, "Let us show you some new horizons." Indeed, they will! Most have left refreshed and renewed, realizing just how special the Barkers are and how very special life can be.

Address: Box 310 K, Augusta, Montana 59410
Telephone: (406) 562-3653
Airport: Great Falls
Location: 80 miles west of Great Falls, 25 miles northwest of Augusta off Sun Canyon Road
Memberships: Dude Ranchers' Association, Professional Wilderness Outfitters Association
Medical: Teton County Hospital in Choteau, 45 miles; Great Falls, 80 miles
Guest Capacity: 20
Accommodations: The ranch has several large, modern, and comfortable cabins. The lodge has a loafing area complete with fireplace, library, and piano.
Rates: $. American Plan. Week-long stays encouraged (Sunday to Sunday). Children's and pack trip rates available.
Credit Cards: American Express. Personal checks accepted.
Season: June through September
Activities: The emphasis is on horseback riding, with optional overnight 7- to 10-day pack trips into the Bob Marshall Wilderness. Nature hikes, special cookouts, and trout fishing in three stocked trout ponds. There is also river and lake fishing. Nontechnical mountain climbing.
Children's Programs: No specific program, but children are welcome. Special attention is given to horsemanship skills. Children are encouraged to learn about the wonders of nature.
Dining: All meals are served family-style. Healthful, low cholesterol meals; wheat and other grains ground for fresh home-baked breads. Vegetables from the garden garnish the meals. Fresh-caught trout served at least once a week.
Entertainment: Campfire sing-alongs and storytelling. Seasonal rodeos in Choteau, Augusta, and Great Falls.
Summary: You will discover new dimensions to life after spending a week or more with the Barkers. The ranch was included in a feature article on Bob Marshall (of Bob Marshall Wilderness fame) in the 1985 issue of *National Geographic*. Max is a graduate forester and gives nature hikes explaining local flora and fauna. Other nearby attractions are Glacier National Park, the Plains Indian Museum, and the Charles Russell Museum in Great Falls.

Klicks' K Bar L Ranch, Montana

Authentic Western Ranch, Member–Dude Ranchers' Association

The K Bar L Ranch is warm, cozy, friendly, and beyond all roads! To get to the ranch, you take a half-hour jet boat ride across Gibson Lake or ride by saddle horse on a scenic mountain trail. The ranch was founded in 1927 by the senior Klicks, and today's owners and hosts, Dick and Nancy, are third generation family. The ranch is in a magnificent setting, almost right on Gibson Lake and near the Bob Marshall Wilderness. The ranch buildings are wonderfully old and weathered. Inside and out they exude comfort. You know that each one has a story to tell you. Indian rugs are on many of the floors. The ranch is like the hub of a huge wheel, with miles of mountain trails leading in every direction. The wilderness area is all scenic fish and game country. One of the highlights at the K Bar L is the natural hot springs pool—great for total relaxation with the stars twinkling overhead at night. A good piece of advice: make your reservations early; others have also discovered "Klicks' West."

Address: Box 287 K, Augusta, Montana 59410
Telephone: (406) 467-2771 (summer); (406) 562-3589 (winter)
Airport: Great Falls
Location: 75 miles west of Great Falls, 35 miles west of Augusta
Memberships: Dude Ranchers' Association
Medical: Great Falls
Conference: 35
Guest Capacity: 35
Accommodations: The main lodge houses the kitchen, dining room, and library in a comfortable fireside setting. There are thirteen cabins, five single, five double, and three triple, each with single and double beds and rustic furnishings including Hudson Bay blankets and Navajo rugs on the floors. Clean, separate cabins provide hot showers and modern toilet facilities. Water is piped to each cabin door, and a wash basin is provided just like in the "good old days" (cabins do not have running water). Laundry facilities available.

Rates: $-$$. American Plan. Six-day minimum stay.
Credit Cards: None. Personal checks accepted.
Season: June to December
Activities: Superb catch and release fly-fishing right at the ranch. Your daily catch of wild rainbow trout will vary from 12 to 20 inches. You can keep 3 fish (under 12 inches) per person per day. Pack trips for the more adventurous are usually planned as loop excursions, leaving the ranch one way and returning another, over trails leading to the Chinese Wall and Continental Divide. Each guest is assigned his or her own saddle horse. Dick is a master guide and in the fall offers superb hunting. Swimming in natural warm water pool or in the crystal clear Sun River.
Children's Program: Children under age 6 not recommended.
Dining: As Nancy Klick says, "Never had a complaint." Good, wholesome food served family-style.
Entertainment: Sing-alongs, volleyball, baseball.
Summary: Remote ranch accessible only by saddle horse or jet boat. Great for adventuresome families and couples. "Western folks" as Nancy says, who like the outdoors and like meeting people from all over. Many come here to fly-fish. Naturally warm swimming pool. Yellowstone and Glacier national parks.

Lakeview Guest Ranch, Montana

Lakeview Ranch is surrounded by Montana's Red Rock Lakes National Wildlife Refuge. This 43,000-acre refuge is one of the most important nesting and wintering areas in North America for the endangered trumpeter swan. At Lakeview, guests can take it all in. Photographers, bird-watchers, anglers, horseback riders, and seasonal hunters will find the Red Rock Lakes area an unforgettable outdoor experience. Informality and hospitality of this unspoiled country are further complemented by a wide range of summer, fall, winter, and spring activities. To perpetuate an appreciation and understanding of the great outdoors, Lakeview offers a professional 30-day guide and outfitters school and a 10-day backcountry horsemanship program. During the winter, the ranch's mountain chalet at the top of the ranch's ski slope is warmed by an open fireplace and looks out over a winter wonderland.

Address: 2905 Harrison Avenue, Dept. K, Butte, Montana 59701 (summer); Monida Star Route, Dept. K, Lima, Montana 59739 (winter)
Telephone: (406) 276-3300 (summer); (406) 494-2585 (winter)
Airport: Idaho Falls and West Yellowstone airports
Location: 45 miles southeast of Lima, 110 miles north of Idaho Falls
Memberships: Montana and Idaho Outfitters and Guides Association
Medical: Dillon Hospital, 85 miles; emergency helicopter service
Conference: 50, off-season only
Guest Capacity: 50
Accommodations: Guests are housed in a variety of accommodations: rustic cabins, dormitories for groups, and private rooms. Some guests like to camp under the stars.
Rates: $. American Plan. Children's rates, combination packages, and fishing pack trips available. Call for information about outfitters and horsemanship school.
Credit Cards: None

Season: June through October (summer), December to March (winter)
Activities: In summer, enjoy all-day and half-day rides, pack trips into primitive and wilderness areas of Montana and Idaho for fishing and photography, seasonal hunting with both bow and arrow and black powder rifle. Fishing in alpine lakes and streams, bird-watching, hiking, four-wheel-drive trips, indoor heated swimming pool, whirlpool, and sauna. In winter, there are 7 kilometers of groomed trails and skating lanes with certified instructors and guides. Cross-country and downhill skiing. Backcountry ski camp, snowshoeing.
Children's Programs: Horsemanship and wildlife education. Kids are the responsibility of parents.
Dining: Home-cooked, hearty family meals. If you like pastries, hold onto your hat. The Rushes used to be in the bakery business.
Entertainment: Recreation room, indoor pool, whirlpool, sauna, and games.
Summary: Small, family-oriented ranch, with summer and winter programs; 43,000-acre Red Rock Lakes National Wildlife Refuge established in 1935 to protect the rare trumpeter swan. Outfitters, horsemanship, and hunting schools.

Laughing Water Ranch, Montana

Authentic Western Ranch, Member–Dude Ranchers' Association

If you are looking for a small, family owned and operated guest ranch where you will actually live with the family in their modern ranch-style home, then you ought to keep reading. Since 1988, Laughing Water Ranch has provided a private and personal ranch experience. Guests here become part of the Mikita family and will enjoy not only great home-cooked meals but friendly Montana-style hospitality. Laughing Water is a 200-acre ranch surrounded by evergreen trees. In fact, at one time this used to be a Christmas tree ranch. As you drive in you will pass the old barn and a lovely meadow, and up on a rise you will see the main ranch house. Surrounded by the Kootenai National Forest, the Mikitas' ranch offers singles, couples, and families a low-key Western experience. Author's note: Be sure to ask the Mikitas about the beautiful Christmas wreaths they make each year and send all over the country during the holiday season. Summer guests receive a complimentary wreath at Christmas. You might also be interested in knowing that Ted Jr. is a commercial pilot and flies regularly to Europe and Asia. Both he and Ted Sr. are licensed "ham" radio operators and communicate all over the world. The ranch's call letters are N7JKF.

Address: P.O. Box 157 K, Deep Creek Road, Fortine, Montana 59918
Telephone: (406) 882-4680
Airport: Kalispell
Location: 50 miles north of Kalispell off Highway 93 near the Canadian border
Memberships: Dude Ranchers' Association
Medical: Hospital in Whitefish, 40 miles
Guest Capacity: 16
Accommodations: Four two-room "suites" in the family's modern, one-story, log-sided, ranch-style house. Each room varies, with comfortable furnishings, full baths, carpeting, and baseboard heating. Family-style dining room and open-beamed living room with parquet floors. Fully equipped recreation room with fireplace. Deck and Jacuzzi off living room.

Rates: • $. American Plan. Children's, family, and off-season rates available.
Season: May through October
Activities: Two guided 2- to 4-hour horseback rides each day. Riding instruction is tailored to individual guests. Riding through scenic mountainous terrain. Loping in arena only. Fishing in two stocked trout ponds. Fishing gear, fly-casting, and off-ranch fishing can be arranged with prior notice. Weekly white water rafting day trips to Glacier National Park and into Canada to see the historic Canadian Mounted Police post.
Children's Programs: Morning activity program with Native American/Western theme the Mikitas call "Kamp Kootenai," which includes corral rides, beaded crafts, nature walks, and Native American food.
Dining: Some of Shirley's guests call her the "best chef north of Yellowstone." Her menus include prime rib, trout fish-fry, huckleberry muffins, and delicious pies. BYOB.
Entertainment: Cowboy singing and storytelling. Ping Pong, pool table, game tables, and a large video library with a tremendous selection of Westerns, musicals, and classics.
Summary: Small, easygoing, very friendly owner-operated guest ranch. Access to Glacier National Park, British Columbia. Be sure to ask the Mikitas about their beautiful Christmas wreaths, which they make each Christmas and send to customers all over the country.

Lazy AC Ranch, Montana

Authentic Western Ranch, Member – Dude Ranchers' Association

The Lazy AC Ranch is the home of Millie and Arlie Craig, who have been in the dude ranching business since the late 1960s, offering a friendly, relaxed ranch program for a maximum of 24 guests. Their ranch encompasses 6,000 acres of frontier landscape that still has echoes of early gold prospecting and the push West by frontier explorers. The Lazy AC is at the foot of the beautiful Grassy Mountains, bordered by Helena National Forest and just fifty miles from Helena, the capital of Montana. Millie and Arlie are proud of their fine string of horses, which provide many hours of relaxed riding in the mountains or open cattle range. Guests at the Lazy AC find that a peaceful atmosphere abounds, whether on horseback viewing the magnificent scenery or sitting by the crackling fire in their own cabin or in the lodge. One can't help but gain a fresh outlook on life after spending a week or more with the Craigs.

Address: P.O. Box 460, Dept. K, Townsend, Montana 59644
Telephone: (406) 547-3402
Airport: Helena
Location: 50 miles southeast of Helena
Memberships: Dude Ranchers' Association
Medical: Townsend Hospital, 24 miles; White Sulphur Springs, 19 miles
Guest Capacity: 24
Accommodations: Four cozy triplex log cabins are scattered among the aspen and pine trees. All have fireplaces, comfortable twin beds, carpeting, porches, and private baths. The main lodge is the hub of activity.
Rates: $. No children's rates.
Credit Cards: None. Personal checks or cash accepted.
Season: Middle of June to after Labor Day
Activities: Relaxed program. The emphasis is horseback riding with all-day and breakfast rides available. Guests also enjoy wonderful fishing in nearby lakes and streams, a heated swimming pool, hiking, and volleyball.

Children's Programs: No formal programs, but children are welcome. Must be age 7 to ride.
Dining: Good, wholesome meals served family-style. Chuck wagon cookouts once or twice a week. Everyone eats together.
Entertainment: Square dancing, table tennis, and pool in recreation room. There is an antique nickelodeon that plays old 78 records that guests dance and sing to. Horseshoe pitching, rodeos in nearby towns in August and September.
Summary: Small family ranch. Relaxed, friendly atmosphere with emphasis on horseback riding. Yellowstone National Park and the town of Helena.

Lazy AC Ranch, Montana

Lazy AC Ranch, Montana

Lazy K Bar Ranch, Montana

Authentic Western Ranch, Member–Dude Ranchers' Association

In southern Montana where the Crazy Mountains pierce blue sky at 11,178 feet, families have returned year after year to one of the oldest and most celebrated guest ranches—the Lazy K Bar. With endless meadows and hundred-mile views, this historic ranch is tucked at the end of an unmarked, winding dirt road. For guests, the appeal is serious riding on registered quarter horses and a chance to experience authentic ranch life. Founded by the Van Cleve family in 1880, the ranch became a founding member of the National Dude Ranchers' Association back in 1926. The ranch is run today by Barbara Van Cleve and her three children. Her late husband, Spike, was a legendary horseman. Chairman of the board of directors of the Cowboy Hall of Fame, Spike was also a gifted writer and story-teller. Regarding horses, he used to say, "If God had meant man to walk, He would have given him four feet." For spectacular Big Sky scenery, unlimited riding on 22,000 acres, and plenty of Old West hospitality, the Lazy K Bar and the Van Cleve family are one of a kind.

Address: P.O. Box 550 K, Big Timber, Montana 59011
Telephone: (406) 537-4404
Airport: Bozeman or Billings; Big Timber Airport will accommodate small private jets
Location: 25 miles northwest of Big Timber off U.S. 191 North, 85 miles northeast of Bozeman, 100 miles west of Billings
Memberships: Dude Ranchers' Association
Medical: Big Timber Hospital and Clinic, 25 miles
Guest Capacity: 45
Accommodations: Nineteen hand-hewn one- to four-bedroom log cabins have rustic but cozy furniture, some with living rooms. All with fireplaces or wood stoves. Two without baths. All with views of the mountains. Wonderful old log main lodge with 1880 Brunswick billiards table. Personal laundry service available; coin operated machines as well.

Rates: • $-$$. American Plan. Rates vary with size and type of cabin and number of occupants. Special rates for children under 6. References required. One week minimum stay.
Credit Cards: None. Personal checks accepted.
Season: Late June through Labor Day
Activities: Unlimited riding through alpine country or open rangeland. Day and overnight rides. Guests may help with cattle and ranch work when there is work to be done. Mountain fishing (kitchen staff will cook your catch), hiking, swimming pool (unheated but refreshing). No organized activities except Saturday night square dancing and Sunday camp fire breakfast.
Children's Programs: Wrangler for children ages 6 to 14. Ranch requires parents to bring a governess for children under 6.
Dining: Milk, cheese, butter, and meat are all fresh from the ranch. Children eat first at dinner. Guests may drink and entertain in their own cabins. Sunday campfire breakfast walk option.
Entertainment: Grand piano, 1880 billiards table, extensive and unusual library, occasional slide shows and talent shows, local rodeos. Nearby Cowboy Poet gathering each August.
Summary: Historic working ranch not open to general public—references required. Ranch store. Trips to Yellowstone Park, ghost towns, Indian reservation, Hutterite colony, Custer Battlefield, Lewis and Clark Caverns. Be sure to ask one of the Van Cleves about *A Day Late and A Dollar Short* and *Forty Years' Gatherin's*, books written by their late father, Spike Van Cleve. Spanish spoken.

Lone Mountain Ranch, Montana

Orvis-Endorsed Lodge

Lone Mountain Ranch is one of the premier, year-round, family-run guest ranches in the country. What makes this ranch so special is that it offers nature enthusiasts from around the world the opportunity to enjoy first-rate guest ranching in the summer, a world-class cross-country skiing program in the winter, and superb fly-fishing. The ranch is in Montana's famous Gallatin Canyon, just down the road from Chet Huntley's Big Sky Ski Resort and Yellowstone National Park. The Schaap family acquired the ranch after a long search for a property with all the attributes of Lone Mountain. Lone Mountain's naturalist program is an increasingly popular ranch activity. Several times each week, staff naturalists lead hikes that give everyone opportunities to learn about Montana's spectacular natural history. Subjects and activities are varied but often include spotting soaring eagles, wildflower identification, geology, learning about old Indian trails, early morning trips to hear bugling elk, or evening stargazing. Whether you are riding, hiking, skiing, fishing, or just daydreaming, Bob and Vivian Schaap and the Lone Mountain crew will show you Montana's best.

Address: P.O. Box 69 K, Big Sky, Montana 59716
Telephone: (406) 995-4644; Fax: (406) 995-4670
Airport: Bozeman
Location: 40 miles south of Bozeman
Memberships: Cross-Country Ski Area Association
Awards: Orvis-Endorsed Lodge
Medical: Bozeman Deaconess Hospital
Conference: 50
Guest Capacity: 70
Accommodations: Twenty-three, well-maintained, fully insulated one- and two-bedroom log cabins sleep up to 9. Each features comfortable beds, electric heat, modern bathrooms with tub/shower, and a rock fireplace or a wood stove. The cabins are close to the clear mountain stream that winds through the property, and all have front porches for relaxing.

Rates: • $$-$$$. American Plan. Children under age 2 stay free. Special rates for white water rafting, guided fishing.
Credit Cards: Visa, MasterCard
Season: June to early October (summer); early December to early April (winter)
Activities: Horses are a way of life at the ranch. Summer guests enjoy daily rides (except Sundays) to the surrounding wilderness with experienced wranglers. Riding instruction and pack trips offered. Exceptional fishing on the Madison, Gallatin, and Yellowstone rivers and the lakes and streams of Yellowstone National Park. All fly-fishing guides are experienced on the local waters and will bring you a variety of fishing opportunities. Half-day and full-day walk/wade trips, drift boat fishing, float tubing, and backcountry horse trips to alpine lakes. Fly-fishing equipment may be rented or purchased at the ranch. Tennis and swimming pool nearby. In winter, the ranch offers a variety of cross-country skiing right from each cabin's front doorstep. Lessons and naturalist guide trips to Yellowstone backcountry. Sleigh rides open to the public. Outdoor whirlpool adjacent to the dining lodge.
Children's Programs: Full program for ages over 6. Limited group baby-sitting.
Dining: Ranch cooking with a gourmet flair in the new dining lodge—nutritious, wholesome, and widely acclaimed. Cookouts, streamside dinners. Special diets catered to. Restaurant open to the public.
Entertainment: Naturalist slide programs and slide lectures. Barbecue sing-alongs. Evening fly-tying demonstrations, dancing to country-western music.
Summary: Excellent, world-class, year-round guest ranch. Fly-fishing with guides and instruction, top cross-country skiing program. Yellowstone National Park, Museum of the Rockies in Bozeman, Lewis and Clark Caverns, Nevada City, Virginia City. Retail shop. Video of winter program available. Orvis-endorsed lodge.

See color photos, page 203

Mountain Sky Guest Ranch, Montana

Authentic Western Ranch, Member–Dude Ranchers' Association

The Mountain Sky goes way back to the early days of dude ranching. Originally it was the famed Ox Yoke Ranch, run by an old Montana family who attracted guests from around the world. Today, under the ownership of Alan and Mary Brutger, the ranch has guests again hailing from around the globe. Alan, who has owned and operated hotels in the past, has tried to blend the competence and service that one customarily expects in a fine hotel with the casualness and sincerity of a Western ranch. Mountain Sky Ranch has recently undergone extensive renovation and has emerged as a premiere AAA 4 Diamond ranch resort. Don't be misled by the word "resort," though. The ranch has retained its Western charm and takes a maximum of 75 guests at a time. It is in the magnificent Paradise Valley, home of the famous Yellowstone River. Just as in the early days, there is great emphasis placed on the family. The wranglers and staff go out of their way to ensure that both young and old are happy and having one of the greatest experiences of their lives. Mountain Sky offers outstanding scenery, clean, fresh air, tranquillity, award-winning accommodations, and fine dining. At this ranch, the "Sky's" the limit.

Address: Box 1128 K, Bozeman, Montana 59715
Telephone: (800) 548-3392, (406) 587-1244; Fax: (406) 587-3977
Airport: Bozeman
Location: 60 miles southeast of Bozeman, 30 miles south of Livingston
Memberships: Dude Ranchers' Association
Awards: AAA 4 Diamond
Medical: Livingston Clinic, 30 miles; Bozeman Deaconess Hospital, 60 miles
Conference: 75
Guest Capacity: 75
Accommodations: There are 25 cabins, some new, with carpeting, modern baths, large picture windows, and sitting rooms that can sleep up to seven. The older, more rustic cabins have been preserved, keeping the Old West charm

with stone fireplaces or wood-burning stoves, pine furniture, and small front decks. All of the cabins have inviting front porches with hanging flower baskets. A bowl of fresh fruit is brought to each cabin daily. Yellowstone City, the newly rebuilt main lodge, radiates warmth and comfort with three stone fireplaces, a hand-hewn trussed ceiling, and braided rugs. It has a lounge, intimate bar, dining room, and for those who are musically inclined, a Yamaha grand piano.
Rates: • $$$. American Plan. Children's rates.
Credit Cards: Visa, MasterCard. Personal checks accepted.
Season: Late May to mid-October.
Activities: Rides go out daily, except Sunday. Riding instruction is available. Swimming in heated pool. Whirlpool and sauna. Guided nature hikes. Tennis on two championship courts. Fishing on the Yellowstone River with guides available. Fishing on the ranch in a stocked trout pond. Big Creek is minutes from your cabin door.
Children's Programs: Children of all ages are well looked after here. Kiddie wrangler, kids' cookouts and meals, hiking, swimming, and fishing. Children can eat separately. Outstanding all-around program.
Dining: The food is wonderful and fresh. Gourmet, five-course dinners Tuesday and Saturday nights, featuring favorites like poached salmon or rack of lamb. Hearty breakfasts; lunch is buffet-style. Poolside barbecues. Children's meals with counselor are available. Special diets catered to.
Entertainment: Evening country-western dancing and folk singing in front of the fire. Light, relaxing music with the twice-weekly gourmet dinners. Saturday ranch "shodeos." Volleyball, billiards. Monday night get-acquainted session with Western dancing. Plenty of spots to curl up in and snooze or read a favorite book.
Summary: World-class ranch. Excellent fly-fishing and children's program. River rafting on the Yellowstone River. Nearby Chico Hot Springs, which is famous for its fine dining and hot springs pool. Yellowstone National Park, 30 miles.

See color photos, page 220

Mountain Sky Guest Ranch, Montana

Mountain Sky Guest Ranch, Montana

Nez Perce Ranch, Montana

In the Bitterroot Mountains in a private setting, the Nez Perce is owned and operated by Bob and Judy Kline. Bob was formerly a corporate pilot, and Judy was raised on a farm in Iowa. The lodge and homes are next to the Selway-Bitterroot Wilderness Area, the largest federally classified wilderness in the continental United States, with millions of acres. In addition, the property is on the historic Nez Perce Trail, with the Nez Perce Fork of the Bitterroot River running through the property. Here, Bob and Judy blend unspoiled nature, comfortable accommodations, and healthy outdoor activities. There are no planned activities. Plenty of fishing, hunting, eating, and relaxing can be found here, along with access to nearby hot springs. If you want to get away from the tensions of modern life and spend time pretty much on your own in this beautiful part of Montana, consider the Nez Perce, a special, do-your-own-thing retreat for the discriminating traveler.

Address: West Fork Route, Dept. K, Darby, Montana 59829 (summer); 19802 North 32nd Street, #8K, Phoenix, Arizona 85024 (winter)
Telephone: (406) 349-2100 (summer); (602) 569-6776 (winter).
Airport: Johnson/Bell Field in Missoula; 4,000-foot paved runway in Hamilton for smaller aircraft
Location: 40 miles south of Hamilton off Highway. 93, 84 miles south of Missoula. Ranch will send detailed directions.
Medical: Hamilton Hospital, 40 miles north; paramedics, 10 miles
Guest Capacity: 18
Accommodations: Three log homes with lofts can sleep up to six. Each has a large family room with fireplace, open beam ceiling, and efficiency kitchen. These homes are completely and comfortably furnished.
Rates: $-$$. The three completely furnished log homes are rented by the week to individuals or families. Meals not included.
Credit Cards: None

Season: June through September
Activities: No planned activities. You are on your own. Fly-fishing in large and small streams, rivers, reservoirs, and high mountain lakes. Miles of horseback riding can be arranged through a local outfitter. Hiking, swimming in area mineral hot springs, bird-watching, wildlife (deer and moose). A photographers' paradise.
Children's Programs: Parents must look after their children. Sitters are available with advance notice.
Dining: Guests may dine in the privacy of their own cabin (most eat breakfast and lunch in their cabin). Dinners are available with Bob and Judy with advance notice. Good Western cooking, homemade bread.
Entertainment: When guests arrive on Saturday, Judy and Bob host an informal evening meal. Relax on your porch, take an evening drive up the valley. Most go fishing in evenings.
Summary: Many couples and families come here to fly-fish, relax, and do their own thing. No set program. Three individual log homes.

Nine Quarter Circle Ranch, Montana

Authentic Western Ranch, Member–Dude Ranchers' Association

Since 1946, from early June to mid-September, the Nine Quarter Circle Ranch has been doing what it does best—dude ranching. High in the Montana Rockies and nestled among lodgepole pines, the Nine Quarter Circle has a 4,000-foot airstrip on the property and raises and trains Appaloosa horses. The ranch is 7 miles from the northwest corner of Yellowstone National Park. One has to drive 5 miles up a winding, scenic, dirt road until the ranch is visible in its secluded valley. Taylor Fork, a fly-fishing river, runs through the ranch, and most of the log structures overlook the green, grassy meadows to the striking mountain peaks in the distance. This lovely ranch is run by Kim and Kelly Kelsey, the son and daughter-in-law of the founders, Howard and Martha Kelsey. As the Kelseys say, "Two things can never change or end, the goodness of nature and man's love for a friend," and you will find both things here.

Address: 5000 Taylor Fork Road, Box K, Gallatin Gateway, Montana 59730
Telephone: (406) 995-4276
Airport: Bozeman or the ranch airstrip. Contact ranch for airstrip fact sheet.
Location: 60 miles south of Bozeman
Memberships: Dude Ranchers' Association
Medical: Bozeman Deaconess Hospital, 60 miles
Conference: 80, off-season only
Guest Capacity: 80
Accommodations: Twenty one- to four-bedroom log cabins with wood stoves and porches. Most of the cabins are named after guests. Cabin furnishings are simple but comfortable; all cabins have private or family baths. The main lodge has one of the largest rock fireplaces you will ever see. The Kelseys have a clever "Medallion" award board for guests who have returned year after year. It's hanging in the dining room. Guest laundry facilities.
Rates: $-$$. American Plan. Children's and off-season rates available. Minimum one-week stay policy.
Credit Cards: None. Personal checks accepted.

Season: Mid-June through mid-September
Activities: Plenty of horses. The ranch raises and trains over 120 Appaloosas. Four or five rides, ranging from kiddie rides to Kelsey Killers "for those who want a real thrill," go out daily. Weekly overnight pack trips, great fly-fishing with a ranch fishing guide. Limited loaner rods and retail fishing shop on ranch. A spring-fed "swimming pool."
Children's Programs: Full program for kids under age 10. Talk to the Kelseys regarding their program for children under 6. Kiddie wrangler for children ages 6-9. Playground and playroom. Weekly kids' picnic.
Dining: Children and teens eat early while parents enjoy happy hour. BYOB. Meals are home cooked and family-style. Weekly barbecues and cookouts.
Entertainment: Live music, square dancing, weekly movies, volleyball, and games on horseback.
Summary: Wonderful family-run ranch for families, many of whom have returned year after year. Appaloosas bred and trained on the ranch. Private airstrip. Ranch store. Yellowstone National Park, Madison Buffalo Jump, and Museum of the Rockies in Bozeman.

Pine Butte Guest Ranch, Montana

Authentic Western Ranch, Member–Dude Ranchers' Association

This is one of only two Nature Conservancy retreats offering lodging. Pine Butte is the former Circle 8 Guest Ranch that was privately owned before the Conservancy took it over in 1978. The ranch is surrounded by wilderness—18,000 acres managed by the Conservancy and an additional one million plus acres in the Bob Marshall Wilderness, one of the largest wilderness expanses in the continental United States. The Pine Butte Swamp, adjacent to the ranch, is one of the largest wetland complexes along the eastern slope of the Rockies. Also, it happens to be one of the last grizzly bear strongholds in the United States. The ranch hosts a variety of nature adventures. Each spring and fall, there are week-long, custom nature tours and workshops led by regional experts. If you need to be constantly entertained, this is not the ranch for you. This is a ranch for those who love to hike and commune with nature. Pine Butte offers one of the best naturalist programs of any guest ranch in North America.

Address: HC 58, Box 34C, Dept. K, Choteau, Montana 59422
Telephone: (406) 466-2158
Airport: Great Falls, 90 miles
Location: 90 miles northwest of Great Falls, 27 miles west of Choteau off Highway 89
Memberships: Dude Ranchers' Association, Nature Conservancy, Audubon Society
Medical: Choteau Clinic, 27 miles
Conference: 25
Guest Capacity: 25
Accommodations: Ten rustic cabins and two lodge rooms. The cabins are set among the aspens, cottonwoods, and firs that line the South Fork of the Teton River. Built of native stone and wood, each cabin is complete with fireplace, private full bath, and hand-made hardwood furniture. The central lodge, with its huge fireplace and homey front porch, provides a perfect spot for guests to gather and get to know each other.
Rates: • $$. American Plan. Children's and off-season rates available. Group rates in spring and fall.
Credit Cards: None
Season: May through September
Activities: A traditional Western guest ranch atmosphere is combined at Pine Butte with an in-depth natural history program available to guests interested in furthering their knowledge of the outdoors. During the summer, a full-time naturalist conducts daily treks that focus on local plants, animals, geology, and paleontology. Enjoy fishing and a heated outdoor swimming pool. Rides go out twice a day with a wrangler and last 2 to 2½ hours. All-day rides, breakfast rides, and steak fry rides go out weekly.
Children's Programs: None. Children under 8 not recommended.
Dining: Family-style meals served in the lodge dining room, featuring healthy food (homemade soups, breads, and pastries) presented with simple grace. Fresh, homegrown vegetables are featured. BYOB.
Entertainment: Weekly square dance, slide shows and lectures three to four evenings. Tour of Egg Mountain dinosaur nesting site with evening lecture/slide show given by a paleontologist from the Museum of the Rockies. Beaver watching.
Summary: Marvelous ranch for those who love to hike and commune with nature. Excellent natural history tours with naturalists and workshops include birding, mammal tracking, nature photography, paleontology, wildflower identification. Ask about the Montana grizzly bear and writers' workshops. Two hours south of Glacier National Park.

Schively Ranch, Montana

Authentic Western Ranch, Member–Dude Ranchers' Association

Ever dream of being a cowboy? At Joe and Iris Bassett's Schively Ranch, you will experience firsthand a real live cattle operation. No more than 12 guests at a time saddle up and help drive cattle. Each year, the spring cattle drive starts the first part of May and continues through mid-June. It begins at the ranch's winter feedlot in Lovell, Wyoming, and ends at their summer pastures in south central Montana on the Crow Indian Reservation, 52 miles north. During this drive, you will cross the Shoshone River, the Big Horn Recreational Area (famous for its wild horse range), and eventually arrive at the foot of the Pryor Mountains. During these drives, Iris and Joe, along with their cowhands, set up cow camps along the trail. You will enjoy chuck wagon meals and bed down in real tepees under the stars. From mid-June until mid-October, nights are spent at the ranch. Daily activities consist of riding to check and care for any sick cattle and to make sure there is plenty of salt and water, in addition to the fencing and other ranch chores that must get done. In October, cattle are driven by horseback from Montana to Lovell. Depending on the time of year, you will experience branding, doctoring, roping, gathering, sorting, weaning, and rotating pastures. You pick the time, the Bassetts will give you one of the greatest experiences of your life. (Author's note: Get in as much horseback riding as you can before you arrive on the cattle drive.)

Address: 1062 Road 15, Dept. K, Lovell, Wyoming 82431
Telephone: (307) 548-6688 (winter); (406) 259-8866 (summer)
Airport: Billings International Airport
Location: 50 miles south of Billings
Memberships: Dude Ranchers' Association, National Cattlemen's Association
Medical: Deaconess Hospital in Billings, 50 miles; Med Evac helicopter available
Guest Capacity: 12
Accommodations: Separate bunkhouse for single men and women; small cabins with electric blankets and electric heat for married couples. Each cabin is close enough that you can hear the creek and directly behind the main house, which has shower and bathroom facilities. Not to worry, you will not be spending much time in the bunkhouse or cabins.
Rates: • $. American Plan. Children's rates vary.
Credit Cards: American Express. Personal checks, money orders, and cash accepted.
Season: May through October
Activities: This is a real ranch, caring for many cattle, and they offer you the opportunity to participate in as much of it as you wish—5 to 6 hours of riding each day when possible.
Children's Programs: No organized children's program, just a vast experience of life on a ranch. Children are welcome but are the responsibility of the parents. Kids should like horses and be good riders. Children under 10 not advised.
Dining: Home-cooked, ranch-type meals served family-style with ranch's own antibiotic-free beef, served summers in the ranch house dining room and spring and fall on the trail. Specialties include real ranch breakfasts, steak, and homemade ice cream.
Entertainment: Sharing the day's experiences around the supper table, a weekly home video with popcorn, a Big Sky heaven full of stars, and a peaceful, well-earned sleep.
Summary: Cattle drives, great horses, wide open spaces (looks like it did 100 years ago), vast cattle experiences. Custer Battlefield National Monument and Yellowtail Dam. (Author's Note: Be in good physical shape and get as much riding in as you can before you arrive.)

Seven Lazy P Ranch, Montana

Authentic Western Ranch, Member–Dude Ranchers' Association

Chuck and Sharon Blixrud's scenic Seven Lazy P Ranch is ideally situated for hiking, fishing, hunting, backpacking, and horseback trips. The Teton River flows through the property. Rocky cliffs in this magnificent canyon have given geophysicists from all over the world an opportunity to study and enjoy this scenic part of Montana. The Seven Lazy P brings out the best in families. It is a place where sitting on the porch is a joy, whether you are looking out to towering Wind Mountain, watching rufous hummingbirds, or simply listening to nature's peace and quiet. Smack dab up against one of the largest wilderness areas in the United States, the Bob Marshall, Seven Lazy P offers great hospitality and plenty of nature.

Address: P.O. Box 178 K, Choteau, Montana 59422
Telephone: (406) 466-2044
Airport: Great Falls, Montana
Location: 80 miles northwest of Great Falls, 100 miles south of Glacier Park, 30 miles west Choteau off Highway 89
Memberships: Dude Ranchers' Association, Professional Wilderness Outfitters Association, Montana Wilderness Association
Medical: Choteau, 30 miles
Conference: 20
Guest Capacity: 20
Accommodations: The ranch has a large main lodge with a huge stone fireplace, lobby, and porch. There are six rustic cabins, one of which is an A-frame with loft. Five have private shower/ baths, and two have fireplaces. Most with twin beds. All are carpeted and have porches. Laundry facilities available.
Rates: $. American Plan. Children under age 8 half price.
Credit Cards: None. Personal checks and cash accepted.
Season: Year-round. Winter, by reservation only.
Activities: In summer, the 50 horses and mules provide a terrific combination for superb riding and pack trips, which are an important part of the Blixrud's program. Chuck has been running pack trips from the ranch since 1959 and knows this spectacular country like the back of his hand. He has shared it with guests from around the world. The "Chinese Wall" pack trip is a fantastic journey to the high alpine country. Some have called this formation North America's "Great Wall of China." Fishing in the Sun River and in alpine lakes; hunting in September and October for elk and deer. There is a whirlpool to soothe tired muscles after a long day of riding. Winter brings wilderness cross-country skiing at ranch (bring your own gear).
Children's Programs: No special programs.
Dining: Hearty ranch cooking. Special diets catered to. Occasional barbecues, shish kebab, steaks.
Entertainment: Library and wildlife movies. Most guests like to visit with each other, go for an evening walk, or drift off to sleep.
Summary: At the Seven Lazy P you will slow down, relax, and enjoy the sounds of nature. There is lots to see and do if you have the eyes and ears to see and hear it. Low-key family owned and operated ranch specializing in scenic mountain pack trips. If you expect to be constantly entertained, this may not be the ranch for you. Many couples and older families. Glacier National Park, C. M. Russell Museum, Egg Mountain Dinosaur Archaeological Site.

63 Ranch, Montana

Authentic Western Ranch, Member–Dude Ranchers' Association

The 63 Ranch is in the land of the Big Sky, 50 miles north of Yellowstone National Park. One of the first dude ranches in the country to be chosen as a National Historic Site, the 63 Ranch is one of the oldest ranches in the business. It is still run by the same family that started it in 1930. At an altitude of 5,600 feet, one breathes the exhilarating mountain air and listens to the soothing sounds of Mission Creek as it tumbles down its rocky course through the ranch on its way to the Yellowstone River. The 63 offers guests an eye-opening view of what the early West was all about. Depending on the time of year, one can join the cattle roundup and branding. The 63 features summer pack trips into the Absaroka-Beartooth Wilderness. There is also plenty of riding, fishing, hiking, and Indian lore. The food is great. Sandra, Bud, their son, Jeff, and Sandra's mother, Jinnie (who founded the ranch with her husband, the late Paul Christensen), know the meaning and spirit of Western hospitality and serve up plenty of it to guests from all over the U.S. and many foreign countries.

Address: Box 979 K, Livingston, Montana 59047
Telephone: (406) 222-0570
Airport: Bozeman, 50 miles; or a small airstrip for private planes, 6 miles
Location: 12 miles southeast of Livingston
Memberships: Dude Ranchers' Association, Montana Outfitters and Guides Association
Awards: National Register of Historic Places
Medical: Livingston Hospital, 20 minutes
Conference: Off-season only, October to June
Guest Capacity: 30
Accommodations: Guests stay in their choice of 8 comfortable 1- to 4-bedroom cabins with wonderful log furniture, all different and unique. All have baths and showers, some are heated with gas, others with electricity or by wood stoves. Double and twin beds. Laundry facilities available.
Rates: • $-$$. American Plan. Rates vary depending on the season.

Credit Cards: None. Personal checks, traveler's checks, cash accepted.
Season: Summer runs mid-June to mid-September. Winter is by special arrangement on a limited basis.
Activities: Sixty horses provide a full riding program. The 63 is known for its great horses and excellent riding. Sidesaddle and Western lessons available. Picnic and barbecue rides. Pack trips into the Gallatin National Forest and Absaroka-Beartooth Wilderness. Blue ribbon fly-fishing (ask Sandra for her "Montana's First Best Place for Fishing" pamphlet), wagon rides, swimming in a pond, hiking, history lesson, and jeep trips. Photography workshops in spring and fall (ask ranch for workshop brochure).
Children's Programs: No formal program. Each week is planned around the particular guests who are at the ranch. Recreation room, baby-sitter available. The ranch will teach 4-year-olds to ride if they want to learn.
Dining: Hearty ranch cooking with plenty of fresh fruits and vegetables. Dining room in the lovely, old, and cozy log lodge with porch cookouts. House specialties are prime rib and full turkey dinners. BYOB.
Entertainment: Square dancing to records each week, rodeos in town, evening float trips, or just peaceful reading.
Summary: Wonderful old-time historic dude ranch with emphasis on riding. Be sure to see their beautiful new brochure. Beautifully rugged and handsomely decorated main lodge. First Montana ranch to be listed in the National Register of Historic Places. Spring and fall photography workshops. Fourth of July rodeo, museums, and 9-hole golf course in Livingston. Video available on request.

Sweet Grass Ranch, Montana

Authentic Western Ranch, Member–Dude Ranchers' Association

"We are not a resort but a family place. We are a working cattle ranch. Guests are welcome to take part in all pleasures of ranch life," say Sweet Grass hosts and owners, Bill and Shelly Carroccia, who radiate warmth and sincere Western hospitality. And so it is. The Sweet Grass Ranch is secluded in the Crazy Mountains 40 miles outside the small town of Big Timber. Cattle and dude ranching have been in the family for five generations. The Carroccias limit the number of guests so that everyone will actually feel like family. As you might expect, families from all over have come to enjoy the 10,000 acres of beautiful foothills and alpine country. Share in the ranch activities if you like, or do your own thing. Life is unstructured. The Sweet Grass Ranch is a place where the whole family can enjoy the great outdoors, the real Old West, and the fabulous Carroccia hospitality.

Address: Melville Route, Box 173 K, Big Timber, Montana 59011 (summer); Melville Route, Box 161 K, Big Timber, Montana 59011 (winter)
Telephone: (406) 537-4477 (summer); (406) 537-4497 (winter)
Airport: Billings
Location: 120 miles northwest of Billings, 40 miles northwest of Big Timber
Memberships: Dude Ranchers' Association, National Register of Historic Places
Medical: Sweet Grass Community Hospital, 40 miles
Conference: No
Guest Capacity: 20
Accommodations: Guests are housed in 9 rustic log cabins (built between 1928 and 1935) or in 4 rooms on the second-floor of the main house. Lots of rustic comfort. Private baths in 4 cabins, bath/shower house for 5 cabins, laundry facilities available. Most have old Navajo rugs. Early photographs of the ranch in the main house, along with a marvelous burl second floor railing and banister.
Rates: • $. American Plan. Children's rates available.

Credit Cards: None. Traveler's checks and personal checks accepted.
Season: Mid-June through Labor Day
Activities: Unlimited trail and open country horseback riding, including bareback riding, moonlight rides, pack trips, monthly cattle round-ups, and riding instruction are available. Fishing in alpine lakes and on the Sweet Grass River, which runs through the ranch. Swimming in the creek.
Children's Programs: No special programs. Children are welcome and are included in all ranch activities. Baby-sitting can be arranged.
Dining: The meals and bread are home cooked and served family-style in the circa 1925 main lodge. Ranch-raised Montana beef, vegetable garden with lots of fresh salads served each day. Weekly dinner ride. Picnic lunches are served on all-day rides and trips. BYOB.
Entertainment: Square dancing, sing-alongs, and moonlight rides. Monthly local rodeos.
Summary: Bill and Shelly are two of the nicest people you'll ever meet. Their rustic ranch serves up plenty of Western spirit and genuine hospitality. Sweet Grass is a riding ranch. No set schedule, do as much or as little as you please. Cattle roundups, trips to Yellowstone National Park, ghost towns, and Indian ceremonies. National Register of Historic Places.

Triple Creek Ranch, Montana

Triple Creek Ranch is an exclusive, mountain hideaway almost at the foot of beautiful Trapper Peak just outside the tiny town of Darby. This modern "diamond in the rough" (adults-only property) was built in 1986 by Homer Tolliver. Years ago, he decided he would one day create a wilderness retreat for those who yearned for nature's wildness but wanted to experience it with luxurious amenities. Triple Creek is managed by Wayne and Judy Kilpatrick, and, together with their wonderful staff, they have created a haven of rest, relaxation, and mountain splendor.

Address: West Fork Stage Route K, Darby, Montana 59829
Telephone: (406) 821-4664; Fax: (406) 821-4666
Airport: Missoula Airport; private planes to Hamilton Airport with 4,200-foot airstrip
Location: 12 miles south of Darby, 74 miles south of Missoula
Awards: *Hideaway Report:* Hideaway of the Year 1988; *Hideaway Report:* One of six U.S. Hideaways of the Decade; *Hideaway Report:* Distinguished Staff and Service Award 1990.
Medical: Marcus Daly Memorial Hospital, Hamilton; emergency helicopter service available.
Conference: 28; 28 singles or 14 couples
Guest Capacity: 28; 14 couples
Accommodations: Plush, spruce log single cabins, deluxe single cabins, poolside suites, and several luxury cabins (with everything). Each is tastefully furnished with wall-to-wall carpets, dressers, breakfast tables, and small kitchenettes. Refrigerators are fully stocked with an array of beverages and there is a full complimentary supply of liquor. For those who wish, there is satellite TV. VCR units are available. In the larger cabin suites, there are massive handcrafted log king-size beds. For the romantic, there are double showers and a private hot tub on the deck which looks out into the forest. Daily housekeeping and laundry service available.
Rates: • $$$-$$$$. American Plan, per night per couple. Single rates available. Not included

are special horseback rides, guided river rafting, guided fishing, or guided winter snowmobiling service.
Credit Cards: Visa, MasterCard, American Express
Season: May through October (summer); December through February (winter). If rented in full, Triple Creek can be available during off-season months.
Activities: For summer, there is an informal program that caters to each couple or individual. Horseback riding, hiking, swimming in the lovely outdoor heated pool. Fishing in the nearby Bitterroot River or in high country lakes, tennis, mountain bike riding, bird and wildlife watching (Wayne has a small herd of buffalo), photography. Serious golfers can drive to the Hamilton 18-hole golf course. White water river rafting on Salmon River and pack trips can be arranged. In winter, Triple Creek comes alive with the spirit of Christmas: hot buttered rum, sleigh rides with bells, and horseback riding in freshly fallen snow. Snowmobiling is one of Triple Creek's specialties, wilderness cross-country skiing (limited instruction available), downhill skiing, 28 miles away. The ranch will tell you what you will need.
Children's Programs: Children under 16 are allowed only when ranch is reserved in total by a family or group.
Dining: All meals are varied and designed to tempt even the most finicky diners. Complimentary wine served. Special diets not a problem. Triple Creek will help you celebrate your birthday or anniversary.
Entertainment: Lovely upstairs bar in the main lodge with occasional live music. Many go for a stroll under the stars or enjoy a glass of fine cognac in the hot tub.
Summary: Luxurious, adults-only mountain-top guest ranch. Superb and friendly staff with personalized service second to none. Quiet, restful atmosphere with gourmet cuisine. Triple Creek may be booked for family reunions and corporate retreats.

West Fork Meadows Ranch, Montana

As a young boy growing up in Germany, Guido Oberdorfer dreamed of America's West—cowboys, cattle, mountain air, and ranch food. He promised himself that he would work very hard for his family's international manufacturing company, and one day he would have a ranch. It took him years to realize that dream, but Guido and his soft-spoken Swiss bride, Hanny (pronounced Honey), have built one of the newest guest ranches in the business and are proudly welcoming guests from around the world. Set in a picturesque valley with a meadow in front and mountains behind, West Fork Meadows Ranch combines American Old West tradition with European style and comfort. The Oberdorfers cater especially to families, individuals, and the ever-growing European market. Their new ranch opens its doors to the world with style, warmth, hospitality, and natural splendor.

Address: Coal Creek Road, Drawer K, Darby, Montana 59828
Telephone: (406) 349-2468; Fax: (406) 349-2031
Airport: Commercial jets to Missoula; 4,000-foot paved runway in Hamilton for small aircraft. Helicopter and airport pickup available.
Location: 93 miles south of Missoula (2-hour drive), 50 miles south of Hamilton, 31 miles southwest of Darby
Medical: Hamilton Hospital, 50 miles
Conference: 30
Guest Capacity: 30
Accommodations: Three brand-new two-bedroom log cabins, each with lofts, separate showers and baths, comfortable living room/sitting area, and fireplace. Wonderful covered balconies overlooking the meadow. Four remodeled one-bedroom cabins behind the main lodge, each with private bath, wood stove, and covered balcony. The newly built 6,000-square-foot log main lodge combines a main level dining/living room with decks with an upstairs "watering hole" and office. Ask Guido to show you his wine cellar.

Rates: • $$-$$$. American and European Plans. Corporate and winter rates available.
Credit Cards: Visa, MasterCard, American Express, Diners Club
Season: Mid-May through mid-March
Activities: Western horseback riding with instruction. Trail rides, all-day picnic rides, and pack trips. Guests are assigned their own horse to use while at the ranch. Guided river rafting, hiking, wildlife viewing (deer, elk, moose), and photography. Fishing in stocked pond, in the West Fork of the Bitterroot River (which runs through the property), in nearby streams and mountain lakes. Boating, swimming, and jet-skiing in Painted Rock Lake, 5 minutes from lodge. Winter: Guido offers alternate weeks of cross-country skiing (you must bring your own equipment) and guided snowmobiling. Shuttle to downhill skiing at Lost Trail Pass, ski-safari (a Swiss specialty). Special Christmas season program.
Children's Programs: No specific program. Well-behaved children welcome to share activities with their families.
Dining: Superb food prepared by American/European-trained chef. Five-course gourmet dinners, menu changes nightly. Wine, beer, and liquor available. Breakfasts and lunches casual. All food is fresh, locally grown, organic produce in season. Breads, pies, cakes, pastries, and Italian ice cream are all made fresh daily. Guido and Hanny are very proud of their deluxe kitchen.
Entertainment: Horseshoes, bottle-shooting contests, European games with Eisstockschiessen (winter German game on ice). Mostly just relaxing and making friends from around the world.
Summary: Beautiful new ranch hosted by Europeans, catering especially to individuals, families, Europeans, and guests from around the world. Fine food and accommodations. German, Swiss, Italian, and English spoken.

See color photos, page 181

West Fork Meadows Ranch, Montana

West Fork Meadows Ranch, Montana

White Tail Ranch, Montana

"You touched my heart and your wilderness captivated my soul," wrote one guest, and so it goes at the White Tail Ranch in Ovando, Montana. Owned and operated by Jack and Karen Hooker, the ranch was built in the late 1950s by "Hobnail" Tom Edwards. Tom explored the backcountry for many years and trained many cowboys in the art of packing mules and horses. White Tail Ranch is a well-established, 1,400-acre ranch specializing in summer wilderness pack trips and big game hunting. Once Jack reported that he and a group of guests silently crept up on a herd of 60 elk feeding in a high mountain meadow. Later that day he came over a high pass, around a corner, and there were grizzlies feeding on huckleberries. Before the day was over, they had seen 9 grizzlies, 5 black bears, a coyote, several mountain goats, eagles, deer, and elk. Well, that is not always the case, but Jack knows the country and how to find the animals if they are there. If you like backcountry horse packing trips, pay a visit to Jack and Karen Hooker's White Tail Ranch.

Address: 663 Cooper Lake Road, Dept. K, Ovando, Montana 59854
Telephone: (406) 793-5666
Airport: Missoula
Location: 65 miles east of Missoula
Memberships: Montana Outfitters and Guides, Professional Wilderness Outfitters Association
Medical: St. Patrick's Hospital, Missoula, 65 miles
Guest Capacity: 10
Accommodations: Wilderness enthusiasts are put up in 9 frame cabins with four set along the creek, before, after, and between pack trips. Most of the time, though, you will be sleeping under the stars in the land of crystal clear lakes, winding streams, rugged peaks, and gorgeous flowering alpine meadows.
Rates: • $$. Group and children's rates available.
Credit Cards: None

Season: Late June through August; hunting season mid-September to November
Activities: Wilderness pack trips and hunting trips on horseback. Most trips begin some distance from the ranch. This is one of the few ranches that has permits to send trips to the four huge wilderness areas that comprise the Bob Marshall Wilderness Complex. Enjoy the pristine wilderness and wildlife, photography, and fishing. Women's healing workshops/retreat pack trips.
Children's Programs: None, but children are welcome. Children under 6 are not recommended.
Dining: Karen cooks excellent down-home high country meals, including mountain chicken chow mein, barbecued chicken, corn on the cob, roast beef, tacos, stew, and steak. Special diets catered to with advance notice.
Entertainment: Jack's high adventure wilderness stories. Primitive fire demonstration.
Summary: The ranch specializes in exciting wilderness pack trips into the Bob Marshall Wilderness Complex. Women's healing workshop (call ranch for details). C. M. Russell Museum, buffalo preserve nearby.

Cottonwood Ranch, Nevada

The Cottonwood Ranch is in great American cattle country on Cottonwood Creek in the O'Neil Basin of Elko County. This working ranch runs 500 head of cows, calves, bulls, and horses over 2,000 acres. In addition, the fourth-generation Smith family leases more than 5,000 acres from the forest service and Bureau of Land Management. Horace Smith, his wife, Renie, and their adult children go out of their way to ensure that each guest is well looked after. With an open-beam guest lodge, the Smith family offers the best in Western hospitality. Cottonwood Ranch specializes in wilderness pack trips, offering sightseeing tours by horseback lasting almost a week. These tours take guests into the isolated and beautiful Jarbidge Wilderness, where one can see dramatic views of mountain peaks, quaking aspen, willows, and meadows filled with sunflowers and lupine. The only sounds you'll hear in this country are those of nature. Keep your eyes open—you may see mule deer, coyotes, and golden eagles. This country offers terrific wilderness trout fishing. Here you'll catch rainbows, German browns, and Dolly Vardens. Photographers should bring a lot of film.

Address: O'Neil Basin, Dept. K, Wells, Nevada 89835
Telephone: (702) 752-3604 (this is a radio telephone and you may have difficulty getting through); (916) 832-4861
Airport: Elko, Nevada, or Twin Falls, Idaho; private airstrip, 7 miles, helicopter shuttles available
Location: 65 miles southwest of Jackpot, 120 miles northwest of Elko, 120 miles south of Twin Falls, 75 miles northwest of Wells
Memberships: Nevada Outfitters and Guides Association
Medical: Twin Falls Hospital, Idaho
Guest Capacity: 20
Accommodations: A comfortable 7-bedroom lodge has 3 rooms with double beds, 4 rooms with twin beds and bunk beds. Bathrooms are both private and shared. Once on the trail, the ranch provides all your gear, except sleeping bags and personal belongings. Check with the ranch for exactly what you need.
Rates: • $-$$. American Plan. Pack trip and children's rates available.
Credit Cards: Visa, MasterCard
Season: June to September
Activities: For many years the Smiths have been known for their high-country pack trips. Recently they have been welcoming guests to participate in their weekly cattle ranch activities. The Smiths and their expert guides will show you some of Nevada's magnificent backcountry. Seasonal cattle drive, trap shooting at ranch, and just relaxing in the outdoor unheated pool. Seasonal big game and bird hunting.
Children's Programs: Children welcome, but check with ranch.
Dining: Hearty, home-cooked meals, BYOB. Cooking under the stars pack trips. Wine served.
Entertainment: Hay wagon rides, cookouts, sing-alongs, cowboy poetry.
Summary: Friendly, family-run working cattle ranch offering full ranch activities and excellent wilderness pack trips. Photography workshops (contact ranch for dates), cowboy poetry. The Jarbidge Wilderness, and Cougar, Matterhorn, and Jumbo peaks. (Author's note: You should be in reasonable physical condition. It would be a good idea to ride as much as you can before you arrive at the ranch.)

The Ponderosa Ranch, Nevada

The Ponderosa Ranch is a day ranch known to millions as home to *Bonanza*, one of the world's most famous television series. Although you cannot stay overnight, you can tour the Cartwright Ranch House and ramble through the streets of this re-created Western town. There are a saloon, general store, church (you can even get married), antique barber shop, photo studio, and much more. View carriages, horse-drawn farm equipment, vintage cars, steamrollers, tractors, and thousands of other pieces of Western memorabilia. There is also lots to do. Take a hay wagon breakfast ride, pet the animals in the petting farm, go through the mystery mine, try the shooting gallery, savor a Hoss burger, and then belly up to the bar in their authentic Western saloon. You can browse through the souvenir shop or go for a hike on trails that take in the spectacular beauty of Lake Tahoe. The Ponderosa Ranch is owned by Bill and Joyce Anderson. Bill and Joyce founded the ranch in 1967, and since the opening, they have worked tirelessly to make it as memorable an attraction as possible for the 250,000 visitors annually. The Ponderosa Ranch is still a family-run operation, with the emphasis on giving the guest good, old-fashioned Western hospitality, and an unforgettable memory.

Address: P.O. Box AP, Drawer K, Incline Village, Nevada 89450
Telephone: (702) 831-0691; Fax: (702) 831-0113
Airport: Reno Canon International, 35 miles
Location: On the north shore of Lake Tahoe in Incline Village, 35 miles southwest of Reno, 20 miles from South Lake Tahoe
Medical: Incline Village, 5 minutes
Conference: 2,000
Guest Capacity: 3,000
Accommodations: None. Six thousand beds available within 5-mile radius.
Rates: • $. Check with ranch for general admission and group rates. Hay wagon breakfast extra.
Credit Cards: Visa, MasterCard, Discovery, American Express
Season: General admission May through October; hay wagon breakfast late May through Labor Day
Activities: There are all kinds of activities at Lake Tahoe and in the surrounding Sierras. Contact the Incline Village/Crystal Bay Convention and Visitors Bureau, 969 Tahoe Boulevard, Incline Village, NV 89451, or call (800) 468-2463 (out of state) or (702) 831-4440 (in Nevada), for further information.
Dining: Daily, all-you-can-eat cowboy breakfast on the hay wagon ride; barbecue lunches including Hoss burger, hot dogs, corn dogs, and deep-pit beef barbecue sandwiches. Special dinner arrangements can be made for large groups.
Entertainment: Shopping, souvenirs, and specialty stores; petting farm with goats, horses, rabbits, pigs, sheep, roosters, donkeys, and mules.
Summary: Famous day ranch where television series *Bonanza* was filmed. Excellent for large groups and tours. Beautiful Lake Tahoe and nearby Reno, Nevada.

The Spur Cross Ranch, Nevada

Long before Nevada became known for its neon lights and one-armed bandits, this far-reaching state had developed quite a reputation in the cattle industry. Still today, many of the country's largest cattle operations are found in the Silver State. While the Spur Cross Ranch is by no means one of Nevada's largest cattle spreads, this 585-acre ranch shares 100 miles of BLM rangeland and offers guests an authentic hands-on cattle ranch experience. Rich in history, this ranch was homesteaded in 1864. Today, the ranch is run by Richard Hubbard, an experienced, easy-going man who loves the cowboy life, the peace and beauty of this wide-open country. Here you will go back in time. No telephone, no television, no stress. Just the call of the wild and the call of calves for their mothers.

Address: P.O. Box 38K, Golconda, Nevada 89414
Telephone: None. Emergency radio telephone on ranch
Airport: Reno, 190 miles; Winnemucca, 36 miles; Elko, 125 miles
Location: 36 miles east of Winnemucca off Interstate 80
Medical: Winnemucca, 36 miles
Guest Capacity: 12
Accommodations: Five-room "station" house with two separate indoor bathrooms with showers or two private cabins with shared bathroom. These accommodations are old-time Western rustic.
Rates: • $. American Plan. Includes three meals and all activities. Free transportation from Winnemucca to the ranch.
Credit Cards: None. Personal checks accepted.
Season: March through November
Activities: At breakfast each morning, "Hubb" will discuss the day's activities. This is a working ranch and you ought to enjoy some ranch work. Daily activities keep the ranch in good working order. Guests should bring their own gloves, jeans, and boots. Included during the week may be cattle work such as branding and herding (on or off a horse). Freshwater, wide-mouth bass fishing is available on the ranch's pond (there are always a few poles at the ranch). Overnight trips to the ranch's cow camp where you will see many species of birds. Four-wheel-drive trips to old mining sites can be scheduled. Seasonal hunting is available by special arrangement.
Children's Programs: None. Children are the responsibility of parents. Not recommended for very young children.
Dining: Traditional ranch-style, sit-down meals including ranch-raised beef, some wild game, and vegetables. Fresh-baked desserts. BYOB.
Entertainment: After-dinner table games, stargazing, and listening to the call of the coyotes. Some guests visit the casinos in Winnemucca.
Summary: A working cattle ranch where you will experience a week or more in a cowboy's life. No set schedules, do as you like. You should enjoy physical work and be in reasonable physical shape. Beautiful, wide open, Nevada landscape.

See color photos, page 239

Bear Mountain Guest Ranch, New Mexico

Bear Mountain Guest Ranch is not the typical dude ranch. Horseback riding is not provided. This is a small ranch for southwestern nature lovers. It is on the north edge of Silver City, once a mining town. Here, a century ago, the streets teemed with miners, freighters, prospectors, and outlaws (boyhood home of Billy the Kid). Parts of Silver City still retain its Victorian elegance, reflecting the prosperous mining years. Bear Mountain is southwestern in architecture and landscape. This 160-acre property sits in the mountains high above the desert. This was once the territory of prehistoric Indians who hunted and fished in the surrounding Gila Wilderness, the nation's first designated wilderness area. These pine-clad mountains are testament to a highly developed civilization with their Gila Cliff Dwellings, a community that was suddenly abandoned centuries ago. Bear Mountain Ranch is hosted and owned by Myra McCormick. Myra loves nature, respects its peace and tranquillity, and cares about people. Her nature program is highly regarded by her guests. One of Myra's most treasured guests was the late actor Steve McQueen. Said Myra, "We just sat in the kitchen and traded stories."

Address: P.O. Box 1163 K, Silver City, New Mexico 88062
Telephone: (505) 538-2538
Airport: Silver City, Grant County Airport
Location: 2.8 miles north of Silver City, 325 miles southwest of Santa Fe, 160 miles northwest of El Paso, Texas
Memberships: Nature Conservancy, National Audubon Society, International Wildlife Wilderness Society
Medical: Gila Regional Medical Center
Conference: 30
Guest Capacity: 40
Accommodations: Built in the traditional southwestern style to provide shady, cool rooms in the summer as well as snug, warm winter quarters, the guest houses are off-white plaster with dark brown trim. They reflect the decor of the 1920s and 1930s but provide modern comforts, electric blankets, modern baths, antique furniture, and twin or double beds. There are guest rooms in the 2-story ranch house, a 5-bedroom house, three 2- and 3-room suites in the ranch house, and two 1-bedroom cottages.
Rates: • $-$$. American Plan. Contact ranch for children's and group rates.
Credit Cards: None
Season: Year-round, including Thanksgiving, Christmas, and Easter
Activities: "The big one is enjoying nature," says Myra. Gila Cliff Dwellings National Monument is enjoyed by everyone. Fishing in nearby lakes and Gila River, bird-watching, wild plant identification, archaeological exploration, and bicycling.
Children's Programs: None. Baby-sitting available.
Dining: The high-windowed dining room is designed to give the best view of an aviary. Nutritious, home-cooked food with home-baked breads. Favorite is enchilada pie. Desserts include peanut butter pie and carrot cake.
Entertainment: "After a full day in the field, most people are happily pooped," says Myra.
Summary: Friendly and very low-key ranch. Bed and breakfast at 6,250 feet. If you need a TV, this is not the place for you. Bring your own horse. Lodge and learn program, workshops (pottery, archaeology, birding), Glenwood Catwalk over White Water Creek, Gila Cliff Dwellings, City of Rock State Park.

The Bishop's Lodge, New Mexico

Nestled in the foothills of the Sangre de Cristo mountains, Bishop's Lodge is a spectacular, sun-drenched resort. This world-class oasis of southwestern hospitality has been under the active stewardship of the Thorpe family for years. In 1917, Denver mining man James R. Thorpe discovered Old Santa Fe. He bought the property and began creating a world-class resort that preserved southwestern ambience, simplicity, and comfort. Today, Bishop's Lodge is one of the great jewels of the Southwest. This Mobil 4 Star property can host up to 160 guests and offers a wide range of activities. It is situated on 1,000 privately owned acres that back up to the Santa Fe National Forest. At 7,000 feet, the high desert scenery bursts with its red sunbaked soil, juniper and native shrubs dotting the hills, fresh desert air, and plenty of sunshine. Service and kindness reign supreme. The informal, relaxed atmosphere at Bishop's Lodge, combined with its proximity to Santa Fe, the cultural center of the Southwest, make it ideal for families and corporations.

Address: Box 2367 K, Santa Fe, New Mexico 87504
Telephone: (505) 9836377; Fax: (505) 989-8739
Airport: Albuquerque
Location: 3 miles north of Santa Fe off Bishop's Lodge Road
Awards: Mobil 4 Star, AAA 3 Diamond
Medical: St. Vincent Hospital in Santa Fe, 5 miles
Conference: 200; 5 conference rooms, executive conference facilities, the largest of which is 1,924 square feet
Guest Capacity: 160
Accommodations: The adobe-style buildings blend comfortably with the ranch property. Rooms are decorated Santa Fe style with southwestern motifs, soft accents, locally sculpted furniture, air-conditioning, and television. Deluxe rooms and suites all have traditional corner fireplaces, open beamed ceilings, and plenty of private patio space. Each room has a selection of southwestern magazines.

Rates: • $$-$$$$. Modified American Plan June through August; $-$$$. European Plan. Rates vary depending on time of year. Horseback riding, tennis, and skeet and trap shooting are extra.
Credit Cards: None
Season: April through January
Activities: Tennis courts with teaching professional and full pro shop, pool complex includes large heated swimming pool with lifeguard, whirlpool, sauna. Stable of fine riding horses with morning and afternoon rides lasting about 1½ hours. Usually slow, scenic rides. Trap and skeet shooting (guns provided), plenty of hiking trails, summer breakfast rides, and tennis tournaments. Golf privileges nearby.
Children's Programs: A summer children's program keeps kids ages 4 to 12 happily occupied and parents free to sightsee and browse in Santa Fe. Limited program for teens. Baby-sitting available on request.
Dining: Bountiful breakfast and luncheon buffets. Dinner is formal, featuring fresh fish and regional specialties; jackets and dresses are requested attire. Daily room service available. Fully licensed bar.
Entertainment: Live guitar, harp, mariachi music in summer months.
Summary: Mobil 4 Star, AAA 3 Diamond Resort Ranch. Conference facilities. Golf nearby. Lovely Archbishop Lamy's Chapel on hill above lodge. Santa Fe, the cultural mecca of the Southwest, including Santa Fe Opera and six museums; Indian pueblos; old mining ghost towns; ancient pueblo ruins; and traditional Spanish mountain villages (Truchas, Chimayo).

The Lodge at Chama, New Mexico

More than ever I have been asked by corporations, boards of directors, incentive meeting planners, and families to identify ranches that offer nothing less than excellence. Welcome to the Lodge at Chama. It is here that men and women come to enjoy privacy amid 32,000 acres of unspoiled mountain and forest scenery. The Lodge at Chama provides first-rate amenities and excellent service—in a word, luxury. Over the years, the Lodge has hosted many leaders in business and industry. Because it takes only twenty-four guests at any one time, guests quickly feel at home. Whether it's a high-level board meeting or plain old rest and relaxation, The Lodge at Chama has what it takes for groups or families who appreciate beauty, kindness, and a host of recreational opportunities. The Lodge at Chama's fine staff go out of their way to tailor everything to the preferences of each group.

Address: Box 127 K, Chama, New Mexico 87520
Telephone: (505) 756-2133; Fax: Available on request
Airport: Albuquerque International; private jets to Pagosa Springs. Call regarding ranch airstrip.
Location: 100 miles north of Santa Fe, 90 miles west of Taos
Awards: *Hideaway Report:* 1986 Fishing/Hunting Lodge of the Year; *Hideaway Report:* 1990 Best Sporting Retreat
Medical: Local clinic; hospital in Espanola; emergency helicopter service available
Conference: 24 in boardroom, 50 for day meetings. Fax, speaker telephones, copy room, overhead projection, flip chart. Ask for conference brochure.
Guest Capacity: 24
Accommodations: Vaulted ceilings, full animal mounts, and views of the Chama Valley overlooking the well-kept lawns are the first thing you see as you enter the 13,500-foot main lodge. Just off the Great Room are 10 rooms, each with private bath and upscale amenities (bathrobes, hair dryers, and oversized towels), and two suites with fireplaces, television, and

vanity baths. All rooms have telephones.
Rates: $$$$. Full American Plan. Special rates for full lodge rental. Winter rates available.
Credit Cards: None
Season: Year-round
Activities: The Lodge will send you a detailed brochure outlining all the activities. During the summer months guests enjoy fishing, hiking, drives through the ranch property to view spectacular vistas and wild game, horseback riding, wildlife photography, and sporting clays. Be sure to ask about the historic steam-powered train ride from Chama to Antonito, Colorado. Limited hunting of elk, deer, buffalo, bear, bobcat, and grouse is offered September to December. Photographers will go through many rolls of film shooting the magnificent fall colors. Winter activities November to March include cross-country skiing (gear, guides and instruction available), some snowmobiling, sleigh rides to view wildlife, snowshoeing, and snow tours.
Children's Programs: None, unless the entire facility has been reserved for private use. Thus, you are assured of an adult atmosphere when you visit The Lodge at Chama.
Dining: Hearty ranch fare. Special requests and diets accommodated. Ask about Chama's delicious northern New Mexico dishes.
Entertainment: Enjoy the spectacular sunsets, take an evening stroll, wide screen TV, relax in front of the fire, in the huge indoor whirlpool and sauna, or read yourself to sleep. Hayrides, picnics, and country/western band available upon special request.
Summary: Excellent for small group/corporate/family retreats. Personalized service, delicious cuisine, and tremendous wilderness recreational activities. Superb fishing and hunting.

See color photos, pages 230-231

Los Pinos Ranch, New Mexico

Los Pinos is "where the road ends and the trail begins." In 1910, a Santa Fe family purchased the property as a family hideaway. One of the daughters fell in love with an Easterner and returned to build this wonderful mountain ranch. Perched 500 feet above the Pecos River, the ranch has been in operation since the late 1920s. In 1964, Bill McSweeney, an architect from New Jersey, bought the property. He and his wife, Alice (who loves cooking, arts and crafts, and singing), and their daughter run their special Los Pinos Ranch. Small, informal, and limited to 16 guests, Los Pinos is in the heart of the Sangre de Cristo Range. It is near the headwaters of the Pecos River at an elevation of 8,500 feet, surrounded by distant peaks rising to 13,000 feet and higher. The average summer temperature is 76 degrees at noon and 40 degrees at night. The quaint and historic cities of Santa Fe and Taos with colonial artists, Indian pueblos, and ruins are all within a few hours of Los Pinos by car over fine roads. Los Pinos is said to be located in "the most interesting fifty-mile square in America."

Address: Route 3, Box 8 K, Tererro, New Mexico 87573 (summer); P.O. Box 24 K, Glorieta, New Mexico 87535 (winter)
Telephone: (505) 757-6213 (summer); (505) 757-6679 (winter)
Airport: Albuquerque
Location: 45 miles northeast of Santa Fe off I-25
Medical: Medical clinic in Pecos, 23 miles
Conference: 16
Guest Capacity: 16
Accommodations: The four original log cabins (three 1-bedroom, one 2-bedroom) are rustic but comfortable. All are heated with wood stoves and have plenty of blankets. Each with private bathroom and shower. The main lodge is old and rustic. The outside screened and glassed-in porch looks out to the magnificent scenery. Inside there are a piano, artifacts, and paintings given to Alice and Bill by their artist friends. Laundry available.
Rates: $. American Plan. Riding is extra.
Credit Cards: None. Personal checks or cash accepted.
Season: Late May to September
Activities: Horseback riding is one of the main activities at Los Pinos. Horses are sure-footed and gentle. All-day and half-day guided rides through dense pine, quaking aspen forests, and meadows. The many sparkling streams with their deep pools and swift riffles and tiny hidden lakes make the upper Pecos region a tempting spot for the trout fisherman. New Mexico fishing license required. Plenty of hiking, bird-watching (owls, quail, wild turkey).
Children's Programs: No children under 6 years of age. Family reunions are an exception. Children are the responsibility of parents.
Dining: "Best Chef West of the Pecos River." Be sure to get Alice's cookbook. Hot breads at breakfast. Lamb, chicken; Italian, Irish, German dishes. BYOB.
Entertainment: A wonderful library of local history and nature references. Evening stars and Mother Nature.
Summary: Wonderful scenery, food, and fellowship. Old Santa Fe Trail, Pecos National Monument. Planned trips to Indian pueblos and Spanish villages. Mountain Folk Festival in June; the Mill and Mine Reunion in July. RV campsites within 2 miles.

Hidden Valley Mountainside Resort, New York

The resort was founded in 1940 and has been owned and operated by the Woodin family since 1965. Hidden Valley blends the old with the new, recapturing the charm of days gone by in a country-style atmosphere, between Lake George and Lake Luzerne in the Adirondacks. Just 3 hours from New York City, Hidden Valley captures the Old West spirit and offers a varied year-round program. Below the rolling Adirondack Mountains of upstate New York, on beautiful Lake Vanare, you will find this lovely Western ranch resort that can accommodate up to 250 guests. With many of the ranch buildings and cabins built of real logs and surrounded by tall, sky-searching pines, you immediately feel akin to the Old West right in New York. Conference groups and families will find the best of the West in the East at Hidden Valley.

Address: Rural Route 2, Box 228 K, Lake Luzerne, New York 12846
Telephone: (518) 696-2431; (800) HIDDENV (443-3368)
Airport: Albany, 60 miles
Train: Amtrak to Fort Edward
Location: 5 miles south of Lake George off Route 9N, 220 miles north of New York City
Memberships: New York State Tourism Association
Medical: Glen Falls Hospital, 15 miles
Conference: 200-250; 8,000-square-foot complete conference center
Guest Capacity: 250
Accommodations: Twelve rustic one- and two-story log lodges house a total of 100 rooms, all with private entrances, baths, air-conditioning, electric heat, color television, and wall-to-wall carpeting. There are 1 or 2 queen-size beds in each room. Ten suites have fireplaces.
Rates: • $-$$. Modified American Plan. Does not include horseback riding. Children's and corporate rates on request.
Credit Cards: Visa, MasterCard, American Express, Diners Club, Discover

Season: Year-round
Activities: In summer, horseback riding with instruction. Rides go out several times a day and are broken down into beginner, intermediate, and advanced. All advanced riders must clear checkpoint. Surrey rides, swimming in Lake Vanare and the modern outdoor and indoor pools, boating, canoeing, fishing, spring and autumn picnics, 18-hole golf at nearby course, tennis on 3 professional lighted courts, badminton, archery, table tennis, bicycling, 2 whirlpools and 2 saunas (most equipment provided). In winter, horseback riding, indoor heated pool, beginner downhill ski hill with double chair lift and snowmaking equipment, cross-country skiing, sleigh rides, ice skating, snowmobiling, whirlpool, and saunas. Rental ski equipment available.
Children's Programs: None. Children are the responsibility of parents. Baby-sitting available.
Dining: Dining in rustic log Frontier Room with vaulted ceilings and fireplaces; excellent buffet, continental dining from menu; breads and pastries freshly baked at ranch. Wine list available. Dining room is open to the public.
Entertainment: Varies throughout season. Always something going on. The air-conditioned lounge serves drinks and provides live entertainment with dancing, beach parties, songfests. Winter skating parties with Irish coffees. Skates provided.
Summary: Family owned and operated ranch resort for families, couples, and singles. Ideal for intermediate and beginner riders. Caters to large groups. Good for corporate and association meetings. Surrey and sleigh rides; from Fourth of July to Labor Day, the weekend Adirondack Championship Rodeo. Nearby attractions: Fort William Henry on Lake George, paddle wheel steamboat on Lake George.

Pinegrove Resort Ranch, New York

You might wonder what a kid from Queens and a June Taylor/ballet dancer have in common. In the case of Dick and Deborah Tarantino, a lot now. The story of Pinegrove Ranch is a love story; a wonderful expression of the love between two people and their common love for beautifully spirited Arabian horses. Pinegrove is nestled in the peaceful, gentle, rolling hills of upstate New York. It is the home of Safire, a four-time international champion Arabian stallion, along with 150 head of ranch-raised and trained Arabian horses. The Tarantinos feel that by breeding their Arabs, they can assure their guests the finest possible riding experience. During a stay at the ranch, you will see foals and young horses being trained, groomed, and shod. You can ride both English and Western. Pinegrove is a year-round family vacation wonderland that serves up Western hospitality. Dick and Debbie started Pinegrove with an indoor pool, tennis courts, and ski slopes and turned it into a ranch resort. Together, the Tarantino family share their way of life and a common love with each other and all those who visit them.

Address: Box K, Kerhonkson, New York 12446
Telephone: (914) 626-7345; (800) 346-4626
Airport: New York, Newark, Newburgh
Train: Poughkeepsie
Location: 100 miles northwest of New York City, 1 miles west of Kerhonkson off Route 209
Memberships: American Hotel and Motel Association, International Arabian Horse Association
Medical: Ellenville Hospital, 6 miles
Conference: Up to 500; 5,000 square feet of meeting space
Guest Capacity: 400
Accommodations: Guests sleep in comfortable, modern rooms with wall-to-wall carpeting, TV, air-conditioning, and private baths. All 125 rooms are in three 2-story lodge buildings that have been connected. There are 1- to 4-bedroom villas, some with fireplaces, all with kitchenettes.
Rates: • $-$$. American Plan. Children ages 3 to 16 half-price; children under 3 free. Single parent, group, and senior discounts.
Credit Cards: Visa, MasterCard, American Express, Discover
Season: Year-round
Activities: In summer, free beginner and advanced riding instruction available. Rides over acres of picturesque rolling hills. Most trails are quite wide. You can go deep into the forest for miles of secluded trails crossing streams and affording distant views. Fishing in stocked lakes, boating, hiking. Free golf nearby. Indoor facilities: tennis, heated swimming pool, miniature golf, boccie ball, archery, basketball, rifle range, sauna, volleyball, paddle and hand ball, table tennis, and shuffleboard. Outdoor Olympic-size pool. In winter, downhill skiing on two slopes, ice skating. Equipment available at ranch. Ranch has own snowmaking equipment.
Children's Program: Children's day camp with arts and crafts. Teen program. Baby-sitting available, including "night patrol."
Dining: Meals are served in the main dining room with a view of the Shawangunk Mountains. Sunday barbecue in season.
Entertainment: Hayrides, night club, and cocktail lounge with live music. Western saloon with swinging doors and popcorn machine. Hitching Post Pool Bar. Game nights with prizes. Weekly Arabian horse show including tricks.
Summary: A rustic and comfortable family-oriented, family owned and operated, full facility resort ranch. All Arabian horses are bred and raised at ranch. Nearby Roosevelt and Vanderbilt mansions, country fairs, wineries, and honey farm. Video available on request. Spanish spoken.

See color photos, page 232

Ridin-Hy Ranch Resort, New York

This is a year-round family resort ranch in the timberlands of Adirondack State Park and along the shores of beautiful spring-fed Sherman Lake. The ranch is owned and operated by Andy and Susan Beadnell and their three sons. Since 1940, when the ranch was started by Susan's father, the property and guest accommodations have grown. Today, the ranch hosts 175 guests who enjoy the privacy of the resort's 800 acres. Most guests come from New York, Connecticut, New Jersey, and Massachusetts. As one happy guest said, "There are not many resorts where you can catch good-sized bass in the morning, trail ride in the afternoon, have a swim before dinner, enjoy an after-dinner drink, and square dance to your heart's content." The lake activities, including fishing, are complemented by a friendly staff and a year-round riding program. Ask the Beadnells about their beautiful fall colors; many love to ride at this time of year.

Address: Box K, Sherman Lake, Warrensburg, New York 12885
Telephone: (518) 494-2742; Fax: (518) 494-7181
Airport: Albany
Location: 65 miles north of Albany, 15 miles north of Lake George off Route 87
Memberships: New York State Hotel Association
Medical: Glens Falls Hospital, 20 miles
Guest Capacity: 175
Accommodations: Rooms range from budget singles to deluxe private cottages. All are clean and comfortable, heated, with private baths, and not far from the main lodge, beach, and pool. The main lodge has a large stone fireplace that provides a warm and cozy atmosphere. It is situated on the lake with views to the Adirondacks.
Rates: • $. American Plan. Summer riding and nonriding rates. Children's rates according to age. Winter rates and various ranch packages offered. Off-season rates.
Credit Cards: Visa, MasterCard, American Express. Personal checks accepted.

Season: Year-round, including Thanksgiving, Christmas, and Easter
Activities: Unlimited horseback riding with picnic lunches on the trail; slow, fast, and intermediate rides. Most rides last about 2 hours. Riding through the scenic Adirondack hills. The fall colors are spectacular. Experienced wranglers will give instruction to beginners. Fishing for trout, pike, and small- and large-mouth bass. Plenty of water sports on Sherman Lake including paddleboats and rowboats. Swimming in lake or heated pool. Archery, 2 tennis courts, and whirlpool. Golf nearby. Full winter program including cross-country skiing, sleigh rides, snowshoeing, ice skating, downhill skiing with instruction, snowmobiling, indoor pool, horseback riding (equipment provided).
Children's Programs: Children's activities director. Organized activities year-round. Babysitting available. Under 7 ride in arena.
Dining: The large country-style dining room looks out over Sherman Lake. Enjoy poolside steak barbecues, weekly smorgasbord dinners featuring ham and turkey roasts. Full weekly menu. Families eat together at assigned tables.
Entertainment: Nightly entertainment with social program year-round. The main lodge has a dance floor, cocktail lounge, TV, card tables, and complete game room. Jackpot rodeo at ranch with professional contestants, midweek minirodeo for guests.
Summary: Run by the Beadnell family for families. One-stop, one-price family vacation. Nearby Lake George, Fort William Henry, Adirondack Museum, Stone Bridge Caves, Gore Mountain gondola.

Roaring Brook Ranch and Tennis Resort, New York

Roaring Brook Ranch and Tennis Resort is one of the country's largest destination ranch resorts. Roaring Brook is fortunate in having an ideal location in the Township of Lake George in New York's Adirondack Mountains. The ranch has been under the continuous stewardship of one family since 1946. This picturesque 500-acre estate specializes in family, group, and corporate activities with accommodations for 300. The high percentage of repeat guests appreciate the all-inclusive vacation package. Although the ranch spirit prevails, tennis and poolside relaxation appeal to many. Roaring Brook has recently added a large conference facility that can seat up to 1,000. The ranch draws most of its guests from metropolitan New York and New England.

Address: P.O. Box K, Lake George, New York 12845
Telephone: (518) 668-5767; Fax: (518) 668-4019
Airport: Albany, 60 miles
Location: 2 miles south of Lake George, 60 miles north of Albany, 200 miles north of New York City
Memberships: New York State Hotel/Motel Association
Awards: Mobil 3 Star, AAA 3 Diamond
Medical: Glen Falls Hospital, 7 miles
Conference: 300; 17,000-square-foot full conference facility. Full audiovisual equipment available.
Guest Capacity: 300
Accommodations: There are 140 motel-style rooms in nine buildings spread out around the property. All rooms have private baths, wall-to-wall carpeting, heat and air-conditioning, color television, and telephones. Most with deck areas. There are several two-room suites available.
Rates: • $-$$. Modified American Plan. Children's, weekend riding, and conference rates available.
Credit Cards: Visa, MasterCard
Season: Mid-May to mid-October; conference year-round

Activities: 1½-hour horseback rides, 5 tennis courts (2 with lights), resident tennis pro, 3 swimming pools (both outdoor and indoor), badminton, archery, hiking, volleyball, table tennis.
Children's Programs: Children's playground and counselor. Summer season only.
Dining: Full-service, licensed, dining room, coffee shop; choose from varied menu.
Entertainment: Two cocktail lounges with musical entertainment. Table tennis, billiards, movies.
Summary: Full-service destination ranch resort. Shoreline cruise on Lake George, Fort William Henry, National Museum of Racing, hot air balloon festival, nearby dinner theater.

Rocking Horse Ranch, New York

Just 90 minutes north of New York City, the Rocking Horse Ranch is one of the largest year-round dude ranches for the entire family. Rocking Horse was started by Bucky and Toolie Turk, two brothers from Manhattan, who bought a small hotel and over the years created their resort ranch, complete with everything from a full riding program, tennis, and swimming in the summer to skiing and sleigh rides in the winter. Since 1958, the Turk family has operated this 500-acre ranch. Most guests come from New York, Pennsylvania, New Jersey, and Connecticut. With no hidden costs, the ranch recognizes that not everyone wants to ride, so there are plenty of options. For those who love Western activity, there are square dances, hayrides, horseshoes, bonfires, marshmallow roasts, and lots of riding supervised by professional wranglers. Kids and parents will find a lot to do together and apart, at an affordable price.

Address: Route 44-55, Dept. K, Highland, New York 12528

Telephone: (914) 691-2927; (800) 647-2624; Fax: (914) 691-6434

Airport: Stewart Airport in Newburgh, John F. Kennedy and La Guardia airports in New York City

Train: Poughkeepsie

Bus: To New Paltz

Location: 75 miles north of New York City

Memberships: New York State Hotel Association

Awards: Mobil 3 Star

Medical: Poughkeepsie Hospital, 6 miles

Conference: 250 in 2,800-square-foot auditorium

Guest Capacity: 400

Accommodations: The ranch has 20 motel-style rooms and 100 rooms in main lodge building with two wings that can sleep up to 6 people each room. All rooms have television, telephone, air-conditioning, carpeting, double and king-size beds, private baths with showers, and daily maid service.

Rates: • $-$$. American Plan and Modified American Plan depending on season. Group rates available. Free child specials (ages 0-16).

Credit Cards: Visa, MasterCard, American Express, Discover

Season: Year-round

Activities: Full-time activity director; over 100 horses give everyone the opportunity for plenty of rides with riding instruction available. Guided trail rides are divided into levels of experience. Several rides, lasting one hour, go out daily. Outdoor and indoor heated pools, two professional tennis courts, waterskiing, canoeing, volleyball, basketball, rifle range, archery, softball, paddleboats, fitness program with aerobics every morning. Winter program includes cross-country skiing, downhill skiing, sleigh rides, ice skating, horseback riding, tobogganing. Equipment and instruction provided for all sports.

Children's Programs: Full program with counselors. Milk and cookies every afternoon. Babysitting available. Day camp for children ages 5 and older.

Dining: Rotating menus, all you can eat, great salad bar, fresh fruit and dessert assortment. Licensed bar and nightclub.

Entertainment: Dances every night, band and disco, magic-comedy stage shows, square dancing, great talent shows, movies on big screen television, backgammon, and cards.

Summary: Year-round destination resort ranch. Ceramics workshop run by Miriam, a retired teacher who travels to the ranch most weekends from Manhattan. Historic Hudson Valley, oldest street in America, Kingston (first capital of New York), Roosevelt's Hyde Park Mansion and Library, West Point Military Academy, 40 miles south. 1990 *Family Circle* resort poll winner. Large outdoor group barbecues for up to 1,000.

Roundup Ranch Resort, New York

Since 1947, Roundup Ranch Resort in the scenic Catskill Mountains of New York State has been a popular vacation and getaway destination for guests from throughout the Northeast. Situated in a mountain hollow with nearly 2,000 acres of forests and fields, Roundup Ranch is the ideal setting for those who long to get in touch with the natural world, yet still enjoy the amenities of a complete resort environment. Horseback riding is the main attraction, with trails winding through ranchlands and adjacent Bear Spring Park. The riding program is instruction oriented, with three riding levels for each trail ride, plus lessons, horsemanship clinics, and popular "Own Your Own Horse" weekends scheduled throughout the year. Roundup also features a 9-hole regulation golf course, tennis court, and a complete activity program. Nightlife centers around the El Gaucho Room dance hall and bar. Winter welcomes guests to enjoy cross-country skiing and horse-drawn sleigh rides as well as horseback riding in the snow. Three hearty meals a day are served family-style. Roundup Ranch is a great ranch for all seasons.

Address: Box HK, Wilson Hollow Road, Downsville, New York 13755
Telephone: (607) 363-7300; Fax: (607) 363-2200
Airport: Broome County Link Field, 50 miles
Bus: Pick up in Roscoe, New York, 15 miles
Location: 130 miles northwest of New York City, 60 miles east of Binghamton
Memberships: American Hotel and Motel Association, New York State Travel and Vacation Association, Associate Member of the Dude Ranchers' Association
Awards: Mobil 2 Star
Medical: Delaware Valley Hospital, 7 miles
Conference: 80; banquet facilities for 200
Guest Capacity: 100
Accommodations: A variety of log cabin and lodge rooms, most with private baths and carpeting. Decorated in a rustic country motif. No telephones or television in guest rooms.

Rates: • $-$$. Full American Plan. Children's and group discount rates available. Rental of golf clubs and carts extra.
Credit Cards: Visa, MasterCard, American Express
Season: Year-round. Open Thanksgiving and Easter. Closed Christmas.
Activities: In summer, the riding program caters to both beginners and experienced riders. Rides go out in groups of 20 four times a day. Rides are divided into riding ability. Some cantering. Riding instruction and picnic rides. Indoor riding arena (75 feet by 200 feet). Swimming in new outdoor freeform heated swimming pool with horseshoe-shaped spa next to it. Also, indoor heated pool and sauna. Nine-hole, par 36 golf course with golf carts and club rentals available on property. Tennis court, volleyball, and game room. Fishing in stocked pond or in Beaverkill and Delaware rivers. In winter, cross-country skiing (rental equipment available), horse-drawn sleigh rides, ice skating, horseback riding, and sledding. Special event weekends, including own your own horse weekend. Complete gift shop at ranch.
Children's Programs: Social director arranges activities for children during day and evening hours. Pony rides for kids under age 6. Trail riding for children begins at age 6. Baby-sitting available.
Dining: Three delicious meals daily including buffets, cookouts, and family-style dining. A second dining facility, the Roundup Restaurant, offers complete dinners including New York sirloin, prime rib, seafood platter, a bar, and desserts. A full-service bar and cocktail lounge adjoin the restaurant.
Entertainment: Live music on weekends featuring country, popular, and square dancing. Also sing-alongs, nature walks, casino nights, softball games, mixers, and movies.
Summary: A year-round family resort with year-round horseback riding, golf, swimming, and winter activities. A warm, casual, natural environment attractive to couples, families, and groups. Roundup is less than a three-hour drive from New York City.

Timberlock, New York

As a young boy, Dick Catlin used to spend his summers with his family at Timberlock. Dick went on to graduate from Middlebury College with a degree in biochemistry. Not long after, he became a navy fighter pilot. But it was at Timberlock, way back in his youth, that a seed was planted. So, when this beautiful Adirondack retreat on Indian Lake came up for sale, Dick and his young bride, Barbara, didn't think twice. They bought it and have been carrying on the great Timberlock tradition since the mid-1960s. As the Catlins say, "Timberlock is unique among today's small resorts. We are informal, rustic, woodsy, one menu American Plan, unprogrammed, relaxed. We are not a luxury place, and we are not for everyone." They may not be for everyone, but over 70 percent of those who discover Timberlock return. In fact, some return year after year, bringing third and fourth generations. If you are looking for a vacation retreat where the pace is slow, the folks are friendly, and life is the way it used to be, give the Catlins a call. Don't wait too long, though. Timberlock books up months in advance. (Note: The Catlins will not confirm your reservation until they are sure you have read their brochure.)

Address: Indian Lake, Dept. K. Sabael, New York 12864 (summer); RR 1, Box 630 K, Woodstock, Vermont 05091 (winter)
Telephone: (518) 648-5494 (summer); (802) 457-1621 (winter)
Airport: Glens Falls, New York, 50 miles; small planes to Lake Pleasant (Piseco)
Bus: Adirondack Trailways leaves via the Port Authority or connects in Albany
Location: 250 miles north of New York City. Brochure gives good directions with map; 10 miles south of Indian Lake on Route 30
Medical: 10 miles to health center with doctor
Guest Capacity: 65
Accommodations: Cabins with and without baths. The only electricity is in the main kitchen. If you cannot live without your hair dryer, Timberlock is not for you. Gas lamps provide light and propane provides hot water. Wood stoves heat cabins when necessary. The Catlin's 24-page brochure is excellent and has a map that locates all the cabins.
Rates: $. American Plan. All-inclusive, except horseback riding and motor boat rentals. Daily, weekly, off-season, group, and senior rates available. Two-day minimum.
Credit Cards: None
Season: Late June to October
Activities: As Dick says, "Everything on the place is on a take it or leave it basis. There are no preplanned programs other than meals. Do what you want when you want." Sleep, read, cool off in the lake, canoe, sail, ride (English or Western) on one of seven horses (except Saturday), water ski, play tennis on clay courts, archery, golf on 9-hole courses 10 miles away. Many enjoy the nature walks and birding.
Children's Programs: Bring your own high school sitter if you want your children to be completely looked after. Ask about the adventure camp for ages 11 to 15.
Dining: Family-style. Eat under the covered porch overlooking the lake. Sunday noon special, full turkey dinner. BYOB in cabins only.
Entertainment: The Catlins attract a wide variety of guests with varied intellectual and musical backgrounds. Evening discussions and music make for rich artistic and educational enrichment.
Summary: The wonderful Catlin family. Timberlock is a rustic lakeside paradise. The 24-page brochure tells you everything you could possibly want to know. Ask about special foliage weekends, Elderhostel, ladies-only hiking trips, adult canoe trips, and the teen camp.

Cataloochee Ranch, North Carolina

In 1939, Tom Alexander, a young forester, began the tradition and spirit of Cataloochee Ranch. A mile high in the Great Smoky Mountains of western North Carolina, Cataloochee (Cherokee for "wave upon wave") is a 1,000-acre spread bordered by almost half a million acres of the Great Smoky Mountains National Park to the north and west. For half a century, the Alexander family has been sharing their Southern warmth and hospitality with old and new guests. This Southern cattle ranch, with its mountaintop location, looks out over the rolling hills of Maggie Valley, providing guests with a ringside seat for the four seasons as they unfold. Cataloochee offers an unhurried Southern-style pace with the Smoky and Blue Ridge mountains as a wonderful backdrop. For those who would rather not ride, the ranch happens to be situated in the middle of western North Carolina's year-round recreational playground. In less than a day's drive, you can see everything from clogging to Appalachian folk art.

Address: Route 1, Box 500 K, Maggie Valley, North Carolina 28751
Telephone: (704) 926-1401, (800) 868-1401; Fax: (704) 926-0737
Airport: Asheville
Location: 35 miles west of Asheville, 150 miles northwest of Charlotte off Interstate 40 and U.S. 19
Memberships: American Forestry Association, Southeast Tourism Society, North Carolina Travel Council, National Recreation Association
Awards: Mobil 3 Star
Medical: Waynesville Hospital, 10 miles
Conference: 50
Guest Capacity: 65
Accommodations: Open fireplaces, handmade quilts, and antiques set the tone for each of the 8 cabins, some with kitchenettes. There is no air-conditioning, as the mile-high elevation brings lots of cool mountain air. Guests enjoy electric heaters, midmorning fires, and warm summer days of about 75 degrees. Silverbell Lodge has 6 units, two of which have full kitchens. The main lodge is the heart of the ranch, with an impressive stone fireplace, bear skins, and chandeliers made from ox yokes. There are a number of rooms on the second floor.
Rates: • $-$$. Modified American Plan. Horseback riding is extra. Children's and low- and high-season rates available.
Credit Cards: Visa, MasterCard, American Express. Personal checks accepted.
Season: Summer, May through October; winter, late December to March
Activities: Summer programs include mostly slow, easygoing horseback riding, but experienced riders can move along; half-day and all-day rides. Each spring the ranch offers week-long backcountry pack trips. Fishing in ranch pond stocked with rainbow trout. Croquet, hiking, twenty-foot heated swim-spa, tennis, four-wheel-drive van tours. Float trips and 6 golf courses nearby. In winter, weather permitting, very casual cross-country skiing; downhill ski area 1 mile away is the main attraction.
Children's Programs: Not recommended for infants or children under 6.
Dining: Weekly outdoor barbecue, fresh garden vegetables (lettuce, broccoli, cabbage, squash, and spinach), fresh homemade jams and jellies, Richard's ribs, mountain trout, fall harvest game feast, including bear, venison, and rabbit.
Entertainment: Nearby regional mountain music, clogging, folk/ballad singer. Horse-drawn wagon rides at ranch.
Summary: Family-oriented ranch with great southern charm. Southeastern scenery, cool climate, hospitality, twice yearly week-long pack trips, Maggie Valley, Cherokee Indian Village, Biltmore House, Mountain Heritage Center, clogging, Blue Ridge Parkway.

See color photos, page 207

Pisgah View Ranch, North Carolina

Pisgah View Ranch has been in the Davis family since the 1700s. Initially, the ranch was a farm and later became a boarding house for local loggers and the well-known traveling dentist, Dr. Lee Davis. The present ranch really began to take shape in 1940, when Chester Cogburn, a distinguished attorney, found he no longer wished to battle away in court. Instead, he decided to play host to people from around the world. Together with his wife, Ruby, he bought out other family members and began today's Pisgah View Ranch. Named appropriately, the ranch is overshadowed by 5,749-foot Pisgah Mountain. Chester definitely had his own style. He began to build cabins each year, designing and building each differently. There is everything from a log cabin to a New England-style white clapboard lodge. When the book on Southern hospitality was written, it may well have been drafted at Pisgah View Ranch. Today, Ruby Cogburn, the ranch's matriarch, and her daughter, Phyllis, welcome their guests, as always, with an outpouring of Southern warmth.

Address: Route 1, Box K, Candler, North Carolina 28715
Telephone: (704) 667-9100
Airport: Asheville, 45 minutes
Location: 15 miles southwest of Asheville, 100 miles west of Charlotte off NC 151
Memberships: National Forest Recreation Association
Medical: Memorial Mission Hospital, 15 miles
Conference: 110
Guest Capacity: 110
Accommodations: There are twenty-three cottages that range in style from log cabin and A-frame to several duplexes, triplexes, and 4-plexes and one 8-plex. Most rooms have two double beds, hardwood floors, all have private baths, heat, air-conditioning. Some with front porches with wooden rockers to pass the time Southern-style. Laundry facilities available.
Rates: $-$$. American Plan. Children under age 7 half-rate. Horseback riding not included.

Credit Cards: None
Season: May to November
Activities: Two thousand acres of hiking and riding trails. Riding caters mostly to beginners and intermediate riders. Four 1-hour rides each day. Many guests enjoy sight-seeing throughout the valley and in nearby towns. Outdoor, heated, L-shaped pool, tennis court. Softball games, shuffleboard, horseshoes.
Children's Programs: Children are the responsibility of their parents. Children under age 8 must ride with adults. Baby-sitting can be arranged. Children under 4 do not ride.
Dining: Next to its fine Southern hospitality, Pisgah is renowned for its Southern cooking. Fresh vegetables come from the garden, including rhubarb, corn, and asparagus. Breakfast includes sawmill gravy and biscuits; light lunches. For dinner, enjoy old favorites like Southern fried chicken, country ham, cornbread dressing, and sweet potato souffle. For dessert—Grandma's apple cake and famous oatmeal and buttermilk pies. The food is so popular, the restaurant is open to the public. Picnic lunches provided. Dieters beware.
Entertainment: Different entertainment every night. Weekly square dancing, clogging, country and bluegrass music with local fiddlers, professional magician.
Summary: Southern meals and hospitality. Nearby Vanderbilts' Biltmore House (much like Hearst's Castle in California), Blue Ridge Parkway, Sliding Rock, Cherokee Indian Reservation, Mount Mitchell, two ranch gift shops. RV campground. The Great Smoky Mountains National Park, lots of outlet shopping.

Snowbird Mountain Lodge, North Carolina

Snowbird caters to two groups—those wanting to relax and look at the mountains and those wanting to hike. Bing Crosby visited here back in the 1940s and savored the peace and ambience. Designed in harmony with the great hardwood forest that surrounds this 100-acre paradise, Snowbird Mountain Lodge is one of America's great hideaways. A haven for naturalists, bird-watchers, botanists, hikers, fishermen, and those who just want peace and quiet. At an elevation of 2,880 feet, this mountain retreat offers privacy, relaxation, and Old World rustic, but elegant, comfort. One will find cathedral ceilings, chestnut logs, native stone, two huge fireplaces, paneling in butternut and cherry woods, and handmade custom furniture in most rooms. Forty-six guests enjoy the marvelous Southern hospitality and intimate informality here. Hosts Eleanor and Jim Burbank go out of their way to ensure a memorable time. For cool weather, magnificent scenery, a relaxing way of life, and, most of all, relief from the traffic noise and heat of the cities, escape to this marvelous mountain lodge. You'll enjoy fantastic views and incredible, serene peace and quiet.

Address: 275 Santeetlah Road, Dept. K, Robbinsville, North Carolina 28771
Telephone: (704) 479-3433
Airport: Charlotte, 250 miles east; Knoxville, 75 miles north; Asheville, 100 miles east
Location: 75 miles south of Knoxville, Tennessee
Memberships: National Parks and Conservation Association, Sierra Club, Natural History Association
Awards: Mobil 2 Star
Medical: Bryson Hospital, 40 miles
Guest Capacity: 46
Accommodations: Sixteen guest rooms in the main lodge are paneled in a variety of native woods with custom-made furniture to match bare floors, steam heat, comfortable beds with reading lamps, and mountain air to induce sound sleep. There are also 7 rooms in two newer sep-arate cottages close to the main lodge. Five of the rooms have private baths, two share a bath.
Rates: $. Full American Plan.
Credit Cards: Visa, MasterCard, American Express. Personal checks, travelers' checks, and cash preferred.
Season: Late April to mid-November
Activities: Hiking and wildflower walks are extremely popular. Families, couples, and singles return year after year just for these. Mountain stream swimming, lake and stream fishing (boats can be rented nearby), shuffleboard, table tennis, croquet, horseshoes, billiards, miniature indoor bowling, old-fashioned skittles, cards, library, white water rafting, and horseback riding nearby, guided wildflower hikes.
Children's Programs: No children under age 12.
Dining: Enjoy French toast, blueberry pancakes, Cornish game hens, fresh pan-fried trout, rib eye steak, prime rib, BYOB.
Entertainment: Sing-alongs, slide shows on wildflowers in late April and early May.
Summary: Quiet, secluded hideaway with views to Snowbird Mountains, spring wildflowers, and bird spotting hikes with prominent experts. Hiking week led by leader in June. Nearby Joyce Kilmer Memorial Forest, logging road in Nantahala Forest, Fontana Dam, Great Smoky Mountains National Park, Cherokee Indian Reservation.

Logging Camp Ranch, North Dakota

Logging Camp Ranch was established in 1884 as a horse trading company. Early on, the ranch property, because of its proximity to the Little Missouri River, became the center from which commerce, settlement, and socializing evolved. Timber products were floated down to the ranch—thus the name Logging Camp. Since 1904, the Hanson family has ranched these parts, running cattle over more than 10,000 acres. John Hanson's ancestors, who settled this part of the country, were stockmen and farmers who came from as far away as the Falkland Islands, wanting to experience firsthand North America's wild West. In 1983, Logging Camp Ranch extended its stewardship and began welcoming paying guests. The ranch is famous for its bow hunting. It also offers an informal eco-naturalist ranch stay for guests who wish to see this part of the country.

Address: HC1 Box 27 K, Bowman, North Dakota 58623
Telephone: (701) 279-5501; (701) 279-5702, bed and breakfast only
Airport: Bismarck, 180 miles
Location: Amidon, 18 miles; 30 miles south of Medora; 180 miles west of Bismark
Memberships: Old West Trails Association
Medical: St. Lukes Hospital in Bowman, 45 miles
Conference: 50; day groups only
Guest Capacity: 30
Accommodations: There are two cabins with electricity and wood-burning stoves but no running water or bathrooms. Two communal lodge/cabins. One sleeps six and the other sleeps twenty bunk bed-style. Both with full bathroom and full kitchen. All accommodations are constructed of native pine.
Rates: • $. American Plan (Ranch Plan), bed and breakfast rates, and three- to five-day ranch packages.
Credit Cards: None
Season: Year-round, including Thanksgiving, Christmas, and Easter

Activities: Most of the nonhunting guests want to commune with nature and relax. Many hike, study the geology, biology, and watch an abundance of wildlife, particularly song and game birds and deer. You will be able to see ranch life firsthand. For the more active, John Hanson will arrange four-wheel-drive trips and horseback riding. Ask John about his three- to five-day packages. Fall bow hunting from September to December, trap shooting. The ranch caters to individuals and small groups.
Children's Programs: No special program.
Dining: Cook your own meals in the communal lodge kitchen. With prior arrangements, the Hansons will provide meals.
Entertainment: Environmental/historical and ecological seminars by local authorities, if arranged in advance with the Hansons.
Summary: Low-key independent ranch atmosphere known for its bow hunting. Good for youth groups, church groups, and families. Diverse ecosystems, rich in history. Theodore Roosevelt National Park, historic HT Ranch, Tepee Buttes, dinosaur at Marmarth. Video available on request.

Allen Ranch, Oklahoma

The Allen Ranch is an 800-acre day and evening ranch open to the public. Fifteen miles south of Tulsa, Allen Ranch is the creation of Ted and Fern Allen. Together with four grown children, the Allens have built a ranch that is the launching pad for a variety of Western experiences. The Allens offer groups, families, and corporations everything from hayrides, public and private rodeos, and breakfast and moonlight horseback rides to Halloween "Trail of Fear" hayrides and a Christmas "Holiday Hayride." The Allens have become famous for their old-fashioned chuckwagon suppers and cowboy music shows which highlight all visits to the ranch. You will experience wonderful cowboy meals followed by musical entertainment by the Allen Ranch Wranglers—lots of singing and yodeling of some of your favorite western tunes. If you are a group or corporate planner wishing to organize a company picnic, barbecue, or western extravaganza, give the Allens a call. The Allen Ranch has lots of entertainment and fun for all. As Ted says, "We feed our guests good and do one heck of a job entertaining them." As you drive in, keep an eye out for the longhorn cattle and buffalo.

Address: 19600 South Memorial, Drawer K, Bixby, Oklahoma 74008
Telephone: (918) 366-3010
Airport: Tulsa International
Location: 15 miles south of Tulsa on Highway 64
Medical: St. Francis Hospital in Tulsa, 11 miles
Conference: Indoor seating for 500, outdoor seating for 5,000
Guest Capacity: 5,000
Accommodations: There are no formal guest facilities—accommodations are under way. Most of the activities are oriented for day guests. RV hookups and some camping permitted.
Rates: Vary with activities. Check with ranch.
Credit Cards: Most major cards accepted.
Season: Year-round (closed Thanksgiving, Christmas, and New Year's)

Activities: The main attractions are the chuckwagon supper and the cowboy music show. Hourly and 3- to 6-hour horseback riding. Breakfast and moonlight rides can be arranged. Horse-drawn hayrides. Carriage and horse-drawn vehicle rentals for weddings, parades, and birthday parties.
Children's Programs: Birthday party packages for all ages. Boy and Girl Scout outings and camp-outs.
Dining: Tremendous Western barbecue feed. As Ted says, "We can feed an army." Steaks, hamburger fries, and hot dog roasts. Be sure to ask the Allens about their famous biscuits. Special meals on request. No liquor is served. Companies and groups usually bring their own if it is desired.
Entertainment: The Allens can arrange just about any kind of western entertainment. Private and public rodeos, cowboy and country bands with dancing. Ask about the donkey ball games and wheelbarrow races.
Summary: Ideal for people (families, groups, companies) looking for a one-day outing with a western theme. Great for parties, small and large. The Allens will customize a Western package to suit you. Ted's son Stanley has his own saddle shop on the ranch and ships custom-made saddles all over the world. Full gift/what-not shop on the ranch where you can buy everything from a cup of coffee to buggy whips and Western art. They even sell wagons!

Western Hills Guest Ranch, Oklahoma

Western Hills Guest Ranch is a 101-room state resort located in Sequoyah State Park in scenic eastern Oklahoma. Not far from Oklahoma's first frontier post, Fort Gibson, and right on 19,000-acre Fort Gibson Lake, this resort property is in the heart of Oklahoma's vacationland. This modern horseshoe-shaped facility specializes in family vacation fun with an emphasis on the Western heritage so unique to Oklahoma. Western Hills is well known in this part of the country for its comfortable accommodations, good hearty food, complimentary recreation, and Western programming, all at affordable family rates. A bonus is the state park, which offers interpretive naturalist programs, a nature center with resident naturalist, and a week-long "cowboy camp" program right at Western Hills. The property was acquired from a private company in 1955 and has been operated by the state ever since. Western Hills operates with the philosophy of a theme destination, friendly service and fair rates. A strong emphasis is placed on history, conservation, safety, and education with activities oriented to children, families, and convention groups.

Address: Box 509 K, Wagoner, Oklahoma 74467
Telephone: (918) 722-2545 (ranch); (800) 654-8240 (nationwide reservation/information service)
Airport: Tulsa International; 2,800-foot lighted airstrip in the park
Location: 8 miles east of Wagoner, 52 miles east of Tulsa
Memberships: Oklahoma Hotel/Motel Association
Awards: AAA 3 Diamond; Mobil 3 Star
Medical: Wagoner Municipal Hospital
Conference: 20-500
Guest Capacity: 450
Accommodations: Two-story lodge with rooms, cabanas, and suites situated around the huge keyhole-shaped outdoor swimming pool. Poolside and lakefront views are available. All are heat-controlled/air-conditioned rooms, with carpeting, television and telephones, full bathrooms with amenities, and daily maid service. Cottages complement the main lodge accommodations and feature carpeting and air-conditioning, and some have kitchenettes.
Rates: • $-$$. American and European Plans. Cowboy camp package, group, corporate, and off-season rates available. Children under 18 stay free in same room with parents.
Credit Cards: Visa, MasterCard, American Express, Discover
Season: Year-round
Activities: Cowboy camp featuring full horse program. Full horse care is taught. Riding is also available on an hourly basis with instruction. Stagecoach and covered wagon rides. Eighteen-hole, par 70 golf course, 2 lighted tennis courts, miniature golf, marina and nature boat tours.
Children's Programs: Depending on time of year, there are swimming lessons, nature hikes, nature programs, arts and crafts, story telling, little wranglers' night out (program for children 5-15 that gives parents time off during parts of the day and evening). Baby-sitting available with advance notice.
Dining: Full-service Calico Crossing restaurant. Specialties include pecan pancakes, smoked ribs, briskets of beef and chicken, fried catfish, and grilled steaks. Poolside lunches and cookouts. Ask about the Oklahoma Meal. Liquor and wine available.
Entertainment: Weekend live entertainment during summer. Black Jack's saloon with juke box. Live country-western music with square dancing. Banjo and fiddle playing.
Summary: Full-service resort on Fort Gibson Lake with Western activities and cowboy camp. Wagoner Indian Territory House Museum, Fort Gibson, Tsa-La-Gi (an accurate reconstruction of a 1600s Cherokee Indian village), Indian Museum in Muskogee, scenic canoe trips on the Illinois River.

See color photos, page 224

Baker's Bar M Ranch, Oregon

Authentic Western Ranch, Member–Dude Ranchers' Association

Since the late 1930s, the Baker family has owned and operated the Bar M Ranch. This 2,500-acre ranch is in the Blue Mountains of northeastern Oregon bordering the North Fork of the Umatilla River Wilderness. Hope and Gene Baker run a traditional guest ranch with emphasis on horseback riding and good family fun. The ranch was a stagecoach stop in the 1800s. An old ledger in the attic shows that Teddy Roosevelt stayed here. You will still find the marks of an old stage road on the hillside above the ranch. The main lodge, built in 1864, is a vital part of the ranch. The notched, weathered logs were hewn while the Civil War raged. There are three special things that bring guests back year after year: the superb riding, excellent food, including baked goods (Gene bakes up to 18 loaves of bread at a time), and the newly remodeled geothermal warm springs pool. The soothing, crystal clear water stays an almost constant 90 degrees, summer and winter. After a long day in the saddle, the pool is heaven. The Bar M is a family operation; when you walk in the front door you may be a stranger, but when you have been there just a day, you feel like part of the family; when you pack up to leave, you can hardly wait to return. The Baker's Bar M is one of the best.

Address: Route 1, Box 263 K, Adams, Oregon 97810
Telephone: (503) 566-3381
Airport: Pendleton, Oregon, and Pasco, Washington
Train: Amtrak to Pendleton (many enjoy the scenic ride)
Location: 31 miles east of Pendleton
Memberships: Dude Ranchers' Association
Medical: Pendleton, 30 miles
Conference: Up to 45 people off-season only
Guest Capacity: 32
Accommodations: Guests stay in the old homestead with four 2-room apartments; the circa 1864 ranch house with 8 rooms in period furnishings (bathrooms down the hall); the 2-bedroom Brookside; or 3-bedroom Lakeside cabins with porches looking to the pine-studded hills. There are queen-size beds in most rooms.
Rates: • $. American Plan. Family and children's rates available.
Credit Cards: None. Cash or personal checks accepted.
Season: May through September; March, April, May, and September for conferences
Activities: No schedules. The emphasis is on family activities and horseback riding. Guests are assigned a horse for the week and are invited to saddle and groom it. Two rides daily plus all-day rides and bareback riding, weekly horseback games. Private riding for proven and trustworthy riders. Fishing in the Umatilla River on ranch, hiking trails, natural 40-by-60-foot warm springs pool, a bird-watchers' paradise.
Children's Programs: No planned activities. Children welcome and may help feed the horses. Children under 6 ride only with parents.
Dining: Marvelous meals with Gene's famous raspberries, homemade bread, and ranch-raised beef and pork. Occasional Mexican fare. Always freshly baked cookies. No preservatives. BYOB.
Entertainment: Square dancing and singing. Nightly games of basketball and volleyball, evening swimming.
Summary: One of the great family owned and operated guest ranches in the Northwest. Gene and Hope Baker are two of the nicest people you'll ever meet. Lots of friendly Oregon hospitality. Warm springs pool, Pendleton Roundup in mid-September. Spanish spoken.

See color photos, page 213

Flying M Ranch, Oregon

It's not called the Flying M for nothing. In Oregon's beautiful northwest corner in the heart of Oregon wine country, the Mitchell family ranch has its own 2,200-foot turf airstrip. Many private pilots and guests savor this grass landing strip, making travel to the ranch so convenient. The heart of the ranch is the hand-hewn log lodge built in 1984. The lodge rests at the edge of a meadow where the North Yamhill River and Hanna Creek join under alder and maple trees cloaked with moss. A bar in the lodge was hand-made from a six-ton Douglas fir log. Some of the lounge tables surrounding the dance floor are made from cross cuts of myrtle, cedar, walnut, and maple. Hanging from the ceiling of the Sawtooth Room is Mitchell surrey, which came from the early homestead. While most guests come from surrounding counties, the Flying M has had visitors from as far away as South Africa and Australia.

Address: 23029 N.W. Flying M Road, Dept. K, Yamhill, Oregon 97148
Telephone: (503) 662-3222; Fax: (503) 662-3202
Airport: Portland International; 2,200-foot turf/gravel airstrip at ranch
Location: 45 miles southwest of Portland off Highway 47
Memberships: Oregon Guides and Packers; Unique Northwest Country Inns
Medical: McMinnville Hospital, 15 miles; Life Flight helicopter available
Conference: 150
Guest Capacity: 150
Accommodations: Eight cabins with kitchens, 24 rooms in the "bunkhouse" motel, and 4 rooms in the line shack. These rooms vary considerably; some have queen-size beds and are painted brown and orange; all have full baths and electric heat (except the cabins). The honeymoon cabin is the most deluxe with fireplace, deck, queen-size bed, two-person indoor bath, whirlpool, television, carpeting, and view overlooking the North Yamhill River.

Rates: $-$$$. Meals and horseback riding extra. Multiple daily rates.
Credit Cards: Visa, MasterCard, American Express, Discover, Diners Club
Season: Year-round, including Thanksgiving and Easter. Closed for Christmas, December 24 and 25.
Activities: Horses rent by the hour. There are overnight trail rides and in July a 3- to 4-day ride to the Oregon coast. Great spring steelhead fishing in the North Yamhill River, lighted black-top tennis court, and pond for swimming. Seasonal hunting elk and deer. In winter, the ranch doesn't get much snow, and there is no specific program. Most people come to enjoy the fine dining, visit wineries, listen to country music, and ride horses.
Children's Programs: The Flying M has a children's horse camp each year.
Dining: Ranch cooking ordered from a menu, homemade desserts, weekly steak fries and cookouts, lots of seafood. Wonderful selection of local wines; mixed drinks available. Dining room seats 180, open to the public. Monthly brunch. Winter dinners at Elk Camp (rain or shine) along the river, including seafood and wild game buffet.
Entertainment: Horse-drawn hayrides, sleigh rides weather permitting. Nightly music.
Summary: Dining open to public, private airstrip, and steelhead fishing. Nearby local wineries, the Gallery Players of Oregon theater company, horse shows in the DeLashmutt Equestrian Center.

The Horse Ranch, Oregon

The Horse Ranch is deep in northeastern Oregon's Eagle Cap Wilderness. This magnificent country contains over 50 lakes and many streams, including the Minam River, which runs along the ranch property. The ranch was started in the early 1930s as a pack station. Since then it has changed hands several times. Today Cal and Betsy Henry run their isolated, rustic ranch accessible only by small plane or horseback. You may not meet them, though, as they run two other pack stations and are on the go all summer and fall. Don't worry though, they always have friendly staff on hand. They have their own 3,000-foot dirt and grass airstrip. The ride into the ranch is 8 miles. Either way you arrive, as you catch a glimpse of the property, you will feel as though you have gone back in time. There are wonderful elements of back-country peace and rustic simplicity. Except for the wind sock and a few planes, you might think you have come upon some old-time cattle rustlers' hideaway.

Address: P.O. Box 26, Dept. K, Joseph, Oregon 97846

Telephone: (503) 432-9171 for reservations; there is only an emergency radio telephone at the ranch. From September to December, don't expect your calls to be returned immediately, but they will be returned.

Airport: 3,000-foot dirt/grass airstrip; charter flights to ranch available; contact ranch for specifics

Location: 260 miles east of Portland, 45 miles southeast of Pendleton off I-5

Memberships: Oregon Outfitters and Guides

Medical: Grand Round Hospital, 18-minute flight

Conference: 20; very low-key and rustic

Guest Capacity: 20

Accommodations: Rustic but comfortable log cabins with tiled floors, by the Minam River. Each has a fireplace and hot shower, single and double beds. These sturdy cabins were built with timbers from the ranch and are lighted by generator and Coleman lanterns. All have covered porches; you can hear and see the river from the cabin.

Rates: • $-$$. American Plan. Children under age 5 free. Children 5 to 8 half-price. Includes transportation in and out by horse. Charter flights to and from the ranch are extra. Group rates available.

Credit Cards: Visa, MasterCard

Season: Mid-May to November

Activities: Cal and Betsy specialize in pack trips, fishing, and hunting trips, but those who would like to just enjoy the peace at the ranch can do so as well. Horses are furnished to guests of all ages, or you can bring your own. Fishing in Minam River or mountain lakes. Combination horseback and float trips on the Snake River in Hell's Canyon are separate from the ranch but can be arranged. Seasonal hunting for elk, deer, bear, cougar, and bighorn sheep. Ask Gil about his drop camps, deluxe hunts, and lodge hunts.

Children's Programs: None. Kids welcome.

Dining: Home cooking, served family-style. BYOB.

Entertainment: You are on your own. Guitar music occasionally.

Summary: Secluded ranch accessible by small plane or 2½-hour horseback ride. Airstrip, pack trips. You can bring your own horse, Chief Joseph Memorial, artists' foundry, Wallowa Lake, Hell's Canyon (deepest gorge in North America).

Rock Springs Guest Ranch, Oregon

Authentic Western Ranch, Member–Dude Ranchers' Association

Just outside Bend, Oregon, in the foothills of the Cascade Mountains, Rock Springs Guest Ranch was founded by the late Donna Gill. A schoolteacher, Donna developed an early love for young people, their parents, and the great outdoors. Her spirit and the tradition she inspired are carried on by her nephew, John Gill, and his wife, Eva. "Our goal is to provide the highest quality vacation experience for each of our guests," says Gill. Rock Springs attracts guests from all over the world. With the snow-capped peaks of the Three Sisters Mountains behind, Rock Springs provides all the trappings of the Old West as well as modern conveniences. The result—Rock Springs Ranch is one of the best guest ranches in the West. The ranch is abundant with natural beauty, radiant with hospitality, cozy with warmth, and as for activities—you name it, they've got it. Rock Springs is also popular for business meetings and retreats during the non-summer months.

Address: 64201 Tyler Road, Box K, Bend, Oregon 97701
Telephone: (503) 382-1957
Airport: Redmond, 13 miles
Location: 9 miles northwest of Bend, 180 miles southeast of Portland
Memberships: Dude Ranchers' Association, Meeting Planners International
Medical: St. Charles Hospital, Bend, 9 miles
Conference: 50; ask for the detailed conference information packet
Guest Capacity: 50
Accommodations: Individual cabins and duplex-triplex units with large suites and bedroom cottages nestled in the ponderosa pines. Rooms are finished in knotty pine, and many are newly remodeled. All cabins have decks and most have fireplaces and refrigerators.
Rates: • $$$. Full American Plan in summer. Modified American Plan Thanksgiving, Christmas, and Memorial Day weekend. Corporate meeting package available.
Credit Cards: Visa, MasterCard, Diners Club, American Express, Discover
Season: Late June through Labor Day; Thanksgiving, Christmas, and Memorial Day. All other times are dedicated to corporate conferences, retreats, and seminars.
Activities: Horseback riding is the ranch's summer specialty. Heated, hourglass-shaped swimming pool, 2 lighted professional tennis courts, stream and lake fishing, hiking, nature walks. Everyone enjoys relaxing in the huge free-form whirlpool with spectacular 15-foot waterfall over volcanic boulders. Golf and white water rafting nearby. Downhill and Nordic skiing at Mount Bachelor. Trapshooting, billiards, table tennis, and volleyball.
Children's Programs: During the summer, children ages 3 to 5 and 6 to 12 have youth counselors to help them enjoy a variety of activities and adventures. Lunch and dinner are available in their own dining room or out on the trail. Counselors on duty from 9:00 a.m. to 1:00 p.m. and again from 5:30 p.m. to 9:00 p.m. Children under 6 do not take trail rides. Special infant and nanny rates available.
Dining: All meals are served buffet-style, offering a wide variety of cuisine. Entrées of prime rib and fresh Northwest seafood. Special dietary preferences are always accommodated. Hors d'oeuvres precede the evening meal. Fresh fruit, homemade cookies, and beverages always available in the dining room. Domestic and imported wines and beer available.
Entertainment: Tractor-drawn hayrides, nightly volleyball (staff against the guests), pool table, table tennis, and a variety of game tables and games.
Summary: One of the premiere guest resorts in North America for families and children. Excellent also for corporate and business groups. Superb corporate meeting ranch offering exclusive use of all facilities for each group. Mount Bachelor ski area. Lava Lands Visitors Center, Newberry Crater, High Desert Museum (wildlife and cultural museum).

See color photos, page 210

Flying W Ranch, Pennsylvania

Near the remote northern town of Tionesta is the Weller family's 500-acre Flying W Ranch, home of the Allegheny Mountain Annual Championship Rodeo. Each year, this professional rodeo attracts over 15,000 visitors and professional cowboys from around the country. In 1965, the Flying W ran Hereford cattle. Today, this working ranch, surrounded by a half million acres of the Allegheny National Forest, offers secluded peace, hay fields, and rolling hills to individuals as well as groups. Unique to the Flying W is its "à la carte" riding program, which includes horse camping and a bring-your-own-horse program. Each summer, children enjoy the Western riding camp for beginner to intermediate riders. At the Flying W, one can ride for an hour, stay for a weekend, spend a week, or enjoy the ranch's own professional rodeo in July.

Address: Star Route 2, Box 150 K, Tionesta, Pennsylvania 16353 (summer)
Telephone: (814) 463-7663; Fax: (814) 463-5003
Airport: Pittsburgh
Location: 150 miles north of Pittsburgh, 40 miles south of Warren, 14 miles northeast of Tionesta
Memberships: International Professional Rodeo Association
Medical: Titusville Hospital, 30 miles
Conference: 90
Guest Capacity: 100
Accommodations: Sleeping arrangements vary greatly. The campground has RV hookups, bathhouse with showers, and coin-operated laundry. There are three heated bunkhouses with bathhouse nearby. Each sleeps sixteen. One duplex cabin and one 3-bedroom, one-bath lodge with full kitchen and fireplace.
Rates: • $-$$. Package rates available for adults and children. Most activities are à la carte.
Credit Cards: Visa, MasterCard
Season: April through mid-December. Late December through March by reservation only.

Activities: More than a half dozen riding opportunities, from hourly rides with instruction to overnight trips through the Allegheny National Forest. All trail riding done at a walk. You may bring your own horse (stall rental extra). Outdoor unheated pool, canoeing at Tionesta Creek and Allegheny River. Hiking on the North Country Hiking Trail, fishing and seasonal hunting for bear, white-tailed deer, turkey, and small game.
Children's Programs: Youth (9-16) camp program summer months only. Contact ranch for specifics.
Dining: Restaurant open to the public. Eat in the "Trails End" dining room. Pennsylvania ranch cooking, including chicken and biscuit dinners, steaks, prime rib, stuffed pork chops, cod, and haddock. Snack bar and ice cream parlor.
Entertainment: Live country-western music most weekends, tractor hayrides, game room with pool table, electric games.
Summary: Family-run ranch. Great for families, scouts, and church groups. Bring your own horse program, RV hookups. On-site professional Allegheny Mountain Championship Rodeo in July, American Indian powwow, adults-only getaway weekend, Western tack and gift shop. Local attractions include Sawmill Museum, Music Museum in Franklin, Blair Company Clothing Outlet.

Triple R Ranch, South Dakota

Authentic Western Ranch, Member–Dude Ranchers' Association

The Triple R Ranch occupies the site of an old mining town and is only 8 miles from Mount Rushmore. In the heart of the 27,000-acre Norbeck Wildlife Preserve and surrounded by Black Hills National Forest, the ranch is only 2 miles from the 10,000-acre Black Elk Wilderness, the only wilderness area in the Black Hills. The Triple R's mile-high elevation assures cool evenings to enjoy pine-scented air, a star-speckled sky, peace and quiet. The ranch offers an eye-opening look into the Old West of South Dakota. Names like Wild Bill Hickok, Calamity Jane, General Custer and General Crook, along with Indian Chiefs Crazy Horse and Sitting Bull, are synonymous with the Wild West, and their names still linger in the ghost towns and gulches. Considered Indian Territory until 1876, the Black Hills were opened for settlement during the gold rush. In 1967, Jack and Cherrylee Bradt moved to South Dakota from nearby Nebraska. Since 1977, they have been receiving guests. Their love for the unique beauty of the Black Hills is evident, as they extend their warmth and hospitality to you at Triple R. One professor and his wife wrote from Wisconsin, "We've traveled all over the world and you are the best hosts we've ever had."

Address: Highway 16A, Box 124 K, Keystone, South Dakota 57751
Telephone: (605) 666-4605; (800) 843-1300, ext. 3600 (evenings only)
Airport: Rapid City
Location: 28 miles southwest of Rapid City off Highway 16A
Memberships: Dude Ranchers' Association
Medical: Rapid City Regional Hospital, 28 miles
Guest Capacity: 15
Accommodations: Carpeted, air-conditioned, wood-sided, flattop simple cabins, with small refrigerators for snacks. Each cabin is comfortably decorated in an individual manner. Some have air-conditioning. New guests will find a bowl of fruit on their table and fresh-smelling air-dried sheets on their beds.
Rates: • $$. American Plan.
Credit Cards: Visa, MasterCard, American Express, Diners Club. Personal checks and cash accepted.
Season: Late May through early September
Activities: Horseback riding tailored to the guests' requests. Small guest capacity allows personalized activities. Rides to old mines and ghost towns. Half-day, all-day, and breakfast rides. This is rugged country. Most riding is done at a walk. Fishing for trout in Lakota Lake and Iron Creek, adjacent to the ranch. Some fishing equipment available for rent or sale in general store, but it is recommended that you bring your own. Solar heated swimming pool, horse-drawn wagon rides. Hiking trails abound.
Children's Programs: No children's program. Ranch activities are suited to children 7 years and older.
Dining: Delicious home-cooked meals, family-style. Ranch specialties are barbecued ribs and South Dakota steaks. Meals are served in a "sit down, pass around, down-home" manner. Special meals are provided on request for light eaters. All meals are hearty and wholesome.
Entertainment: Recreation and dining hall in Rendezvous Lodge. Cowboy chuck wagon supper and musical show near Rapid City, Mount Rushmore lighting ceremony.
Summary: Tremendous hospitality. Both the Norbeck Wildlife Preserve and the Black Elk Wilderness Area are abundant with wildlife and vegetation. One will see the scenic beauty created by nature, while riding trails blazed by Indians, gold miners, and frontiersmen. Mount Rushmore lighting ceremony, buffalo herds in Custer State Park, historic town of Deadwood now with legalized gambling, and other area attractions.

Western Dakota Ranch Vacations, South Dakota

When the farm and ranch economy became depressed in the mid-1980s, Lavon and Dorothy Shearer put their heads together. Since they enjoyed people and always seemed to have someone visiting, they decided to open their 15,000-acre ranch and their way of life to fellow Americans and guests from around the world. Lavon, a Texan, and Dorothy, from the Badlands, have been in the ranching business since the early 1950s. The Shearers run a bed and breakfast and offer a wide range of Western activities for a handful of guests. The ranch is along the Cheyenne River, with alfalfa fields on the bottom lands and cedar tree canyons extending up to grass-covered, rolling prairies. The area is rugged enough for good deer hunting and yet protected for the 800 Angus, registered Texas longhorns, and cross-bred cattle. Lavon and Dorothy serve a low-key real ranch vacation—nothing fancy, just lots of downhome goodness. As outfitters for movies and commercials, Kevin Costner rode with them on the ranch in search of locations for the movie *Dances with Wolves*. Several of their wagons, teams, and drivers were used—one son is a driver in this movie. Another son did a television commercial for Winchester ammunition.

Address: HCR 1, Dept. K, Wall, South Dakota 57790
Telephone: (605) 279-2198
Airport: Rapid City Airport; 3,500-foot lighted paved airstrip in Wall, 9 miles
Location: 1 hour east of Rapid City, 10 minutes north of Wall
Memberships: Stock Growers Association; American Quarter Horse Association; Old West Trails Association; Black Hills, Badlands and Lakes Association; Old West Trails Association
Medical: Rapid City Regional Hospital, 60 miles; Wall clinic, 9 miles
Conference: 75 for chuck wagon cookouts
Guest Capacity: 20 comfortably
Accommodations: "People sleep here, there, and everywhere," says Dorothy. The Shearers'

split-level home provides comfortable lodging. Some rooms have private baths and patio entrances in a sunken garden or one large deck looking across the plains. The ranch also has a rustic cabin with a wood stove, outdoor plumbing, and candlelight; a bunkhouse with modern conveniences; a tepee; and a sheepherders' wagon in a cedar canyon away from everything.
Rates: • $. Bed and breakfast. Family and weekly rates available. Horseback riding, wagon rides, and hunting extra.
Credit Cards: None. Personal and traveler's checks accepted.
Season: Year-round
Activities: Guests who stay three days or more can do as little or as much as they desire. Lavon and Dorothy go out of their way to make you a part of their ranch. They do prefer that all riders are good to experienced. Inexperienced riders will not be able to ride. With 90 horses to choose from, guests may help with cattle work or ride a leisurely 15 miles to the Shearers' son's ranch. Fish for catfish in the Cheyenne River running through the property or ponds stocked with bass, hike or hunt fossils. This ranch is well known for trophy deer, antelope, turkey, prairie dog, and coyote hunting.
Children's Programs: No specific program. Children are welcome.
Dining: Dorothy cooks great meals, including her famous sourdough pancakes. Regular chuck wagon suppers are prepared over an open fire along the river for small or large groups. You will really feel like you are on the range.
Entertainment: People talk in this part of the country. The Shearers have time to listen and share. Large recreation room with trampoline, wagon rides and chuck wagon dinners.
Summary: Overnight bed and breakfast or weekly ranch vacation. Wagon train trips (10 person minimum), guided bow and trophy deer hunts, famous 1880 desperado trek with shoot-out, and Labor Day weekend Western artist ride, ranch antiques, Indian and homemade crafts.

Dixie Dude Ranch, Texas

Five generations of the same family have operated this nostalgic working ranch since 1901. The ranch was founded by Rose Crowell and run by her grandson, Clay Conoly, and his wife, Diane. A dude ranch since 1937, the Dixie Dude captures the authentic Old West. Over 700 acres make up the setting for scenic horseback rides through the Texas hill country. Hearty Texas cuisine is served daily in the family-style dining room, occasionally on the range, or poolside. Dixie Dude is a great place for rest and relaxation or taking part in daily planned activities. No one remains a stranger long. Folks gather in the Round-Up Room, play games, dance, or just get acquainted by the fireplace. Guests return year after year for the family atmosphere, delicious food, and scenic rides.

Address: P.O. Box 548K, Bandera, Texas 78003
Telephone: (512) 796-4481; Fax: (512) 796-3067
Airport: San Antonio International; Flying L Ranch in Bandera for private airplanes
Location: 9 miles southwest of Bandera
Memberships: Texas Travel Industry Association
Medical: Sid Peterson Hospital, Kerrville, 34 miles
Conference: 50
Guest Capacity: 70
Accommodations: Guests stay in comfortable motel-like rooms in the main lodge and in individual rustic and modern duplex log and stone cabins. Many are of early Texas architecture. All complete with air-conditioning, vented heat, and television but no telephone. Mostly double beds, all with private baths and tiled floors.
Rates: • $. American Plan. Children's, weekly, and group rates available.
Credit Cards: Visa, MasterCard, American Express
Season: Year-round
Activities: In the summer, there are two supervised morning and afternoon rides daily. This is rocky hill country, so most riding is done at a walk. Outdoor pool, hayrides, bonfires, cookouts, river tubing in Medina River in Bandera, hiking, volleyball, table tennis, horseshoe pitching, tetherball. Winter program is the same as summer, weather permitting. Seasonal hunting for white-tailed deer and turkeys. Bandera Gun Club for skeet shooting. Shotguns can be rented.
Children's Programs: Riding instruction and baby-sitting available but extra. Children under 6 ride with adult or parent. Shallow children's pool.
Dining: Family-style and buffet. Texas ranch-style meals served, briskets and pork rib barbecues, and famous fried chicken dinners. Weekly breakfast rides. Hamburgers and hot dogs at poolside.
Entertainment: Old ranch truck hayrides through hill country. Dancing, bonfires, and sing-alongs with guitar-playing cowboys. Weekly rodeos in Bandera and cowboy trick roping exhibition.
Summary: Old-time Western stock ranch turned guest ranch with lots of Old West charm. 100-year-old barn, Range War Cemetery, and the surrounding Texas hill country. Nearby Frontier Times Museum, Cowboy Artists of America Museum, Sea World of Texas, and Bandera Downs thoroughbred racing. Opryland USA in San Antonio. Fluent Spanish spoken.

Flying L Ranch, Texas

The Flying L guest ranch is in Bandera, which some call the Cowboy Capital of the World. This 542-acre "country club" ranch is a guest ranch with resort-style facilities. Here you will sample Old Texas and enjoy modern comforts. They don't spare any good ol' Texas hospitality, either. The ranch is in the Hill Country of Texas, known for winter green grass, limestone cliffs, and scrub brush. The Flying L continues a wonderful tradition of treating each guest as a star. Parents with strollers and older couples who enjoy walking like the paved roads and sprawling lawns. The countryside is flat, and people can get around easily. One guest said, "Your facility is modern and relaxed. What will bring us back is the staff." When they say, "Y'all come back," people do!

Address: HCR 1 Box 32K, Bandera, Texas 78003
Telephone: (512) 796-3001; (800) 292-5134; Fax: (512) 796-8455
Airport: San Antonio International; paved, lighted, 3,250-foot airstrip on property
Location: 1 hour northwest of San Antonio, 1 mile south of Bandera
Memberships: Texas Tourism Council, Meeting Planners International
Awards: AAA 3 Diamond
Medical: Sid Peterson Hospital, 25 minutes
Conference: 110; 2,500-square-foot conference center; audiovisual equipment available.
Guest Capacity: 120
Accommodations: Among the private homes scattered around the property, there are 38 guest houses that accommodate 76 people, double occupancy. All are comfortable and spacious suites with color TV, small refrigerators, microwaves, and air-conditioners. All have living, dining, and bedroom areas. There are golf and ranch view suites. Villa suites are the most basic. Ranch view and villa units come in pairs—small and large—and are great for families.
Rates: • $-$$. Full American Plan including golf. Children's rates available. Senior, military, and AAA discount.

Credit Cards: Visa, MasterCard, American Express
Season: Year-round
Activities: A 20-horse stable provides hourly guided rides. Up to seven rides go out a day (you are only guaranteed one ride a day). Swimming in the Texas-size pool, with hot tub, or tubing in San Julian Creek (very popular). Fishing in nearby Medina Lake for bass, perch, and catfish. Year-round 18-hole/par 72 golf course with carts and golf clubhouse (cart rental extra). Two lighted tennis courts. Horseshoes, shuffleboard, volleyball, table tennis, water volleyball, and basketball. All equipment provided.
Children's Programs: Full children's program during summer and holidays. Supervised activities such as pony rides, story telling, fishing, and trek to dinosaur tracks.
Dining: Weekly Texas-style barbecues with barbecued beef brisket and chicken, coleslaw, potato salad, corn on the cob, beans, and homemade bread. Weekly Mexican fiestas with fajitas, tamales, enchiladas, tacos, refried beans, guacamole, tortillas, and authentic Mexican desserts. All meals are theme oriented and served buffet-style. Fully licensed Branding Iron Saloon.
Entertainment: Following dinner, there is theme entertainment: Italian night with pasta and poker chips. Mexican night with fiesta music and traditional barbecues. Hayrides and sing-alongs at San Julian Creek. Square dancing, Wild West shows, with trick roping, and gunslinging.
Summary: Texas-style resort ranch with 18-hole golf course and, private airstrip. Pari-mutuel horse racing, rodeos, unique shopping, antiquing, cowboy and Western museums, and many charming historical buildings. The Alamo, Sea World, and the San Antonio Zoo nearby. Video available on request.

Garrett Creek Ranch, Texas

Garrett Creek Ranch is, without a doubt, one of the premiere executive conference ranches in the country. Veteran meeting planner Leslie Schultz came up with the idea after years of conference work. Her goal was to create an environment where executives and business groups could meet away from city life—one that would lend itself to creative thinking and would foster positive intellectual interaction with the very best in professional service and amenities. She did it! Today the ranch hosts groups from around the country, with most of the business coming from the Dallas/Ft. Worth areas. Just off the foyer is a wall that is filled with letters of praise from company heads and meeting planners. Make no mistakes, this is a ranch exclusively for business and professional groups. The information that the ranch sends to prospective groups is extremely thorough and well thought out. Included is a detailed planning guide, description of facilities, price and billing information, and a well-illustrated color brochure. Perhaps the ranch motto says it best: "Paradise is closer than you think."

Address: Route 2, Box 235K, Drawer K, Paradise, Texas 76073
Telephone: (817) 433-2055 (Ranch); (214) 680-8679 (Sales)
Airport: Dallas/Ft. Worth International
Location: 45 miles northwest of Dallas/Ft. Worth
Memberships: International Association of Conference Centers, Meeting Planners International
Medical: First-aid-trained staff; Bridgeport Hospital, 20 miles; emergency helicopter available
Conference: 80
Guest Capacity: 80
Conference Accommodations: The ranch tries to book one large group or several small groups at a time. It has been designed to provide a wide range of meeting formats. There are 6 conference rooms seating 25 to 80 comfortably. Standard audiovisual equipment and comfortable padded, swivel-reclining meeting chairs.

Guest Accommodations: Six clustered log cabins with 4 to 6 rooms per cabin, with covered porches and rocking chairs. Each is decorated individually with high ceilings, hardwood floors, business telephones, and color TV. Adjacent is the newly constructed "Old West Town" with 16 rooms and a parlor. The total number of guest rooms on the ranch is 42.
Rates: • $$-$$$. Full American Plan, complete meeting package
Credit Cards: Visa, MasterCard, American Express. Master billing preferred.
Season: Year-round
Activities: Swimming, jogging, 4-station par course, ropes course, horseback riding, volleyball, basketball, bicycles, and two paddle tennis courts.
Children's Programs: None
Dining: Delicious food and a variety of menus. Breakfast and lunch buffets and sit-down dinners. Ask about the special menus which include South of the Border Mexican Fiesta, Spaghetti Western, Paradise Luau, Cattle Baron's Spread, and Bunkhouse Spread. Full bar.
Entertainment: Ranch will arrange any entertainment you desire. Theme nights, campfires, and cowboy singers.
Summary: One of the premiere conference ranches in the United States. Designed by a meeting planner for business and professional groups. Executive ropes course. Be sure to get a copy of the *Garrett Ranch Cookbook* and a packet of their ranch wildflower seeds.

Lazy Hills Guest Ranch, Texas

In 1958, Bob and Carol Steinruck were in Venezuela. Bob, who is from Pennsylvania, was working for Gulf Oil. Most of their colleagues at Gulf were Texans. Through the grapevine, they heard that Lazy Hills Guest Ranch was for sale. In 1959, they mustered enough money to buy it. Today, Lazy Hills is run by the Steinruck family: Bob, Carol, and their three married children. This 750-acre ranch is in the Texas hill country, surrounded by oaks and sycamores. The ranch, very family oriented, is a children's haven, with lots of riding, always under the supervision of a wrangler. Lazy Hills is not far from the LBJ Ranch and National Park. Summer temperatures reach into the mid-90s with a slight breeze. The countryside is tranquil, the pace slow. Listen to nature's peace, watch deer or an occasional armadillo. Lazy Hills is a great family holiday!

Address: Box K, Ingram, Texas 78025
Telephone: (512) 367-5600
Airport: San Antonio International
Location: 70 miles northwest of San Antonio, 105 miles southwest of Austin
Memberships: Texas Hill Country Tourism Association
Awards: Mobil 2 Star
Medical: Sid Peterson Memorial Hospital, Kerrville, 10 miles
Conference: 100-150
Guest Capacity: 100
Accommodations: Lazy Hills' accommodations consist of 26 spacious, air-conditioned guest rooms, each with light blue jean bedspreads, twin or queen beds, some with bunk beds and fireplaces, all with showers. Most sleep 4 easily, some 6. Room also available in ranch house.
Rates: • $. American Plan. Corporate and group rates available.
Credit Cards: Visa, MasterCard
Season: Year-round, including Thanksgiving, Christmas, and Easter
Activities: Informal. Over 30 miles of wooded hiking and horseback riding trails with four excellent guided trail rides daily. Experienced riders may find the riding a bit tame, but the scenery and wildlife more than compensate. First-rate wranglers carefully supervise children. Olympic-size swimming pool, children's wading pool, hot tub, two lighted tennis courts, archery, fishing for bass and catfish, volleyball, basketball, shuffleboard, table tennis, hayrides, seasonal hunting.
Children's Programs: Scheduled activities during the summer, plenty to keep children busy, playground with tree house, sandbar, merry-go-round. Baby-sitting.
Dining: Family-style or buffet, hearty Texas meals, chicken-fried steak with mashed potatoes and cream gravy, biscuits, beef brisket, sausage and chicken barbecue, weekly Mexican dinners, Mary's Texas meatloaf, cookouts. Pecan pie, buttermilk pie, chocolate-pumpkin cake. BYOB.
Entertainment: Bonfires with s'mores, Crider's Rodeo on Guadalupe River, hay wagon rides pulled by Belgian draft horses or tractor, sing-alongs.
Summary: Family owned and operated. Ideal for small groups and family reunions. RV hookups available. Group barbecues. Off-season bed and breakfast. Nearby Cowboy Artists Museum of America, Kerrville, Fredericksburg (Little Europe U.S.A.), LBJ Ranch and National Park. Spanish spoken.

Mayan Dude Ranch, Texas

The Mayan Dude Ranch is along the Medina River in the heart of Texas hill country near the town of Bandera. At the Mayan Dude Ranch, the whole staff cooperates to see that guests are introduced to activities and horseback riding. This ranch delivers warmth, hospitality, and relaxation; it has been doing so since the early 1950s. Judy and Don Hicks and their children (all 12) quickly make you feel like family. Guests come mostly from Texas, though some have come from Japan and England. Summers are on the warm side. Winters are short and mild. From little buckaroos to older cowpokes—there is something for everyone. They say at the ranch, "Go wild! Go cowboy! Go Mayan!" Some of the guests have been known to say, "Go peacocks." (The Hicks have a few that parade around.)

Address: P.O. Box 577 K, Bandera, Texas 78003-0577
Telephone: (512) 796-3312 or 796-3036; Fax: (512) 796-8205
Airport: San Antonio
Location: 47 miles northwest of San Antonio, 260 miles south of Dallas
Memberships: Discover Texas Association
Awards: Texas Governor's Award for Hospitality 1985
Medical: Bandera Clinic, Kerrville Hospital, 24 miles
Conference: 140 classroom-style in 1,150-square-foot conference facility; audiovisual equipment available.
Guest Capacity: 145
Accommodations: Twenty-nine Texas rock air-conditioned cottages, carpeted and decorated with many handmade furnishings. Six cottages with fireplaces nestle under old cedar trees. There are two 2-story lodges with carpeted motel rooms and handmade Western furniture. All rooms have private baths and color televisions but no telephone. Laundry facilities available.
Rates: • $. American Plan. Children's and weekly rates available.

Credit Cards: Visa, MasterCard, Diners Club, Discover, American Express
Season: Year-round
Activities: One-hour morning and afternoon trail rides, 25 guests per ride with two wranglers. The cool, clear Medina River offers swimming, tubing, and fishing for catfish, perch, and bass (cane fishing poles available). Unheated swimming pool, 2 tennis courts, and a nearby fitness center with Nautilus weight machines; 18-hole golf nearby. The Hicks will send you their activity chart filled with lots of information.
Children's Programs: Summer season only. Children's arts and crafts, games and outings, varied and well-planned program. Twice a week children eat separately. Children under 6 ride in corral.
Dining: The Mayan Cocktail Lounge features happy time from 6:00 to 7:00 p.m. Steak fries, barbecues, and cookouts along the river. Theme nights including Indian night, Mexican fiesta, weekly musical nights. Lunches may be served poolside.
Entertainment: Planned entertainment each night, Western dancing at ranch "ghost town," truck and horse-drawn hayrides to cowboy breakfasts. Entertainment in the bar. Your children are supervised in the summer months.
Summary: Run by a large Texas family for families. Be sure to ask for a copy of the Mayan Ranch newspaper "The Mayan Ranch Express." Frontier Times Museum in Bandera; Cowboy Artists Museum in Kerrville, 24 miles; former President Johnson's ranch, 60 miles; the Mexican border, 3 hours; Sea World, 45 minutes.

Prude Ranch, Texas

The Prude Ranch was established as a cattle ranch in the late 1800s. Over the years, the Prude family became involved in the "people business." Since the late 1920s, guests and cattle ranching have been the main concerns of six generations of the Prude family. The Prudes specialize in tour groups, retreats, family reunions, and business workshops; they also welcome individuals and families all year long. This ranch is recognized throughout West Texas as a fun place for the entire family. Guests enjoy open range riding and many other activities. There are 50 horses and 100 head of cattle on over 3,000 acres. Many guests visit the ranch in their RVs and the Prudes have 42 hookups. From single parents to business groups of 250, the Prudes make guests feel at home Texas-style with their warm, gracious, and sincere hospitality. As the Prudes say, "We are one mile high in elevation and a damn good place to spend any vacation."

Address: Box 1431K, Fort Davis, Texas 79734
Telephone: (915) 426-3202, (800) 458-6232; Fax: (915) 426-3502
Airport: El Paso or Midland; private plane to Marfa Municipal Airport, 25 miles
Location: 6 miles west of Fort Davis off Highway 17 North, 210 miles east of El Paso, 150 miles west of Midland
Memberships: Discover Texas Association
Medical: Big Bend Memorial Hospital, 25 miles; EMT, 5 minutes
Conference: 250; 4,000 square feet
Guest Capacity: 250
Accommodations: Guests stay in batten and board ranch-style cottages with 35 spacious bedrooms. Single, double, and king-size beds, carpeting and Mexican tile, private bathrooms, and private porches. There are an additional 15 family cabins. There are several bunkhouses for singles, youths, and tour groups, with 10 to 20 bunk beds per room. Multiple baths and single stall showers.

Rates: • $-$$. Rates depend on group and individual packages. Ask ranch for specifics. Riding may be extra depending on package selected.
Credit Cards: Visa, MasterCard, American Express
Season: Year-round, including Thanksgiving, Christmas, and Easter
Activities: Activities are planned according to the size and interest of the group. Sign-up sheet in main lodge for guests to fill out daily. Four rides a day, all-day luncheon rides with advance notice. Families ride together. Two lighted tennis courts, large indoor/outdoor heated pool. Float trips on Rio Grande and 18-hole golf nearby can be arranged. Guests will see working ranch activities.
Children's Programs: Summer ranch camp for kids 7 to 16 mid-July to early August. Babysitting available.
Dining: Cafeteria-style suitable for large groups. Homegrown bacon, ham, and sausage. Chuck wagon dinners with pepper steak, squash, green beans, and chili beans. Mexican dishes, chicken, turkey, catfish, and white cod.
Entertainment: Team-drawn hayrides, sing-alongs, country-western dancing with fiddler and caller. Stargazing at world-famous McDonald Observatory. Mysterious Marfa lights.
Summary: Specializing in large groups, corporate, family, and foreign/domestic tour buses. Elderhostel supersite, art school. RV hookups. Carlsbad Caverns and Big Bend National Park. Side trips to Mexico, Chihuahua Desert Research Project. Video available on request.

See color photos, page 209

Silver Spur Dude Ranch, Texas

Authentic Western Ranch, Member–Dude Ranchers' Association

Tom Winchell, or "Texas Tom" as he likes to be called, and his wife, Debbie, are the proprietors of Silver Spur Dude Ranch, about 10 miles south of the cowboy town of Bandera. Tom used to vacation in the Bandera area, and finally the urge to buy a piece of land and build a ranch became so great that he did just that. The Silver Spur consists of 275 acres surrounded by hill country. The ranch caters to large day groups, business retreats, seminars, family reunions, weddings, and school outings. Tom loves Texas and likes to do everything in cowboy/Texas style. Everything here is bigger than ever.

Address: P.O. Box 1657K, Bandera, Texas 78003
Telephone: (512) 796-3639
Airport: San Antonio
Location: 40 miles northwest of San Antonio, 10 miles south of Bandera off Highway 10-77
Memberships: Dude Ranchers' Association
Medical: Sid Peterson Hospital, Kerrville, 32 miles
Conference: 20
Guest Capacity: 20
Accommodations: There are 3 duplex stone cabins with names like "Wyatt Earp" and "The Dalton Gang." There are also 6 single guest rooms in the three-story main ranch house of native limestone. Double and king-size beds, private baths, color television, air-conditioning, heating, carpeting, wood paneling, and front porches.
Rates: • $. American Plan. Children's and group rates available.
Credit Cards: Visa, MasterCard, American Express, Discover
Season: Year-round
Activities: With 275 acres on the ranch and 5,000 acres adjoining, there are plenty of trails. Horseback riding is the main activity, tailored to the ability of the rider. Each guest is offered 3 hours of riding a day on Tennessee walkers, fox-trotters, and quarter horses. Many rides go out in groups of up to 20, but Tom will divide things up if need be. Experienced riders are allowed to let their horses run. Swimming in the junior Olympic-size pool. River floating in Bandera, hiking, fishing in the Hill Country State Natural Area or in Bandera on the Medina River, horseshoe pitching, volleyball, wildlife watching (white-tailed deer, armadillos, and jackrabbits).

Children's Programs: No special program. Child care available with advance notice.
Dining: Cookout breakfasts. Ranch meals served family-style in the huge native stone dining room with vaulted ceiling which seats 125. Huge cowboy breakfasts with eggs, biscuits and gravy, and pancakes. Afternoon and evening meals feature rib-eye steak cookouts and Texas barbecues with brisket of beef and German link sausage. Warning: This is not the ranch for dieters. BYOB.
Entertainment: Hay wagons pulled by a "cowboy Cadillac" (Tom says, "That's cowboy for pickup truck"), campfire cookouts, cowboy dancing, and occasional live Western bands, Arkie Blue's Silver Dollar Bar in Bandera.
Summary: Colorful "Texas Tom," one of the best guest ranches in Texas for experienced riders. Old Chisholm Trail, Comanche and Apache Indian grounds, Frontier Museum, Hill Country State Park, Bandera Downs racetrack.

Texas Lil's Diamond A Ranch, Texas

They call her Texas Lil and she calls her ranch the Diamond A. If you are a business group, family, or individual looking to savor some mighty friendly Texas hospitality, with a Western flair, for a day or an evening, better keep reading. Texas Lil is all Texan and has that marvelous "Ya'll come back now" personality that goes with being a good Texan. Originally, Lil got her start in the corporate catering business. Before too long she recognized that her clients wanted a relaxed ranch atmosphere to hold company and business gatherings. With no shortage of ideas and energy, it wasn't long before she found her Diamond A Ranch just outside Justin, a small town between Denton and Fort Worth. Today, her ranch offers a host of day and evening activities for groups and individuals alike. If you are in Texas or traveling that way and want to enjoy the West, Texas-style, give the ranch a call. If by chance you are held up by the Diamond A gang when you arrive, tell these "ole" boys they can holster their pistols. Texas Lil sent you!

Address: P.O. Box 656K, Justin, Texas 76247
Telephone: (800) LIL-VILL (545-8455), (817) 430-0192; Fax: (817) 430-0984
Location: 24 miles northwest of Dallas/Ft. Worth Airport, 30 miles north of Ft. Worth
Memberships: Dallas and Fort Worth Chambers of Commerce
Medical: Denton Medical Center, 12 miles
Conference: 1,000
Guest Capacity: 2,500
Accommodations: For small groups only, Lil offers two packages—camping out in sleeping bags under the stars or her 3-day, 2-night tepee experience.
Rates: • $. Rates vary greatly with individual and group packages. Call ranch for details.
Credit Cards: None. Cash, traveler's checks, or corporate checks for groups.
Season: Year-round
Activities: Individuals and families: most arrive before noon and will engage in a luncheon and afternoon activity program including hourly horseback riding, swimming (seasonal), fishing (Lil provides the water and the fish, you bring the rest), softball, and volleyball. A late afternoon hayride tops off the day. Group (tours, travel clubs, bus tours, and corporate groups): participation in a variety of activities depending on the group package chosen. Ask about the following packages: Texas Trail Ride and Campout, Texas Lil's Cookout, Day at a Dude Ranch, Texas Experience, and the Cowboy Breakfast.
Children's Programs: No specific program. Special activities can be arranged for children's groups. Old-fashioned playground with giant tree slide, trampolines, swings, horseshoe pitching, cable trolley, bucking barrel, tire swings.
Dining: Specialize in Texas-style barbecues and steaks. Everything is home-baked. A private club (The Longhorn Saloon) is open to guests and serves mixed beverages, beer, and wine.
Entertainment: Country music with guitar-picking, singing cowboys. Country swing dancing, shoot-outs, wild outlaws, arena games with competitions and prizes, rodeos, and wild west shows.
Summary: The Diamond A Ranch is a day ranch offering customized western packages/activities for groups and individuals. Plenty of Texas hospitality and exciting Western fun located in the Dallas-Ft. Worth Metroplex. Nearby Six Flags Over Texas, Southfork Ranch, historic West End District of Dallas, and the old stockyards of Ft. Worth.

Y.O. Ranch, Texas

Y.O. Ranch is in the heart of the Texas hill country near San Antonio. It is one of Texas' largest working ranches and the largest exotic wildlife ranch in North America. The Y.O. is famous for its herd of 1,500 Texas longhorns and over 10,000 animals, representing 55 species, that inhabit 40,000 acres of ranchland. Visitors come to see native white-tailed deer and turkeys, as well as giraffe, ostrich, wildebeest, scimitar-horned oryx, addax, European fallow deer, Japanese sika, axis, aoudad, Iranian red sheep and Indian black buck antelope, zebra, and African Watusi cattle. The Y.O. is very conservation-oriented and runs a wonderful educational program for children. At its 2,200-foot elevation, the Y.O. is dry and temperate most of the year. Evenings are usually cool.

Address: Drawer K, Mountain Home, Texas 78058
Telephone: (512) 640-3222; Fax: (512) 640-3227
Airport: San Antonio International and Kerrville; small 2,200-foot airstrip at the ranch
Location: 2 hours northwest of San Antonio off I-10, 45 minutes northwest of Kerrville
Memberships: International Wildlife Ranchers' Association, Texas Longhorn Breeders Association
Medical: Sid Peterson Memorial Hospital, Kerrville
Conference: Up to 1,500 for an afternoon or evening visit with meal. Ask about the ranch's sister property, the Y.O. Hilton, in Kerrville.
Guest Capacity: 35 overnight
Accommodations: Four renovated log cabins, each over a century old with names like Wells Fargo, Boone, Crockett, and Sam Houston. Each is individually decorated with Old West relics and furnishings and sports Texas Historical Markers. Each has a fireplace, gas and electric heat/air-conditioning, and a front sitting porch. There are also four rooms in the former Schreiner home. There are no telephones or televisions in any of the rooms.
Rates: • $-$$. American Plan. Children 6 to 12

half-price, children under 6 free. Wildlife tours, horseback riding, photo safaris, and hunting rates available.
Credit Cards: Visa, Mastercard, American Express
Season: Year-round. Closed Christmas Eve and Christmas Day.
Activities: Most come here to relax, enjoy the marvelous Texas hospitality, and to view all the animals. Limited horseback riding opportunities on a reservation basis only. You should book this before you arrive. Rides go out for a minimum of one hour. Most guests go on the daily guided wildlife tours or relax and swim in the beautiful Y.O. pool with adjoining hot tub. The ranch offers an excellent photographic safari. Excellent adventure nature trail. Texas longhorn cattle drive each spring. Limited year-round hunting is available.
Children's Programs: Ranch adventure camp June, July, and August. Ask ranch about environmental programs for children 9 to 14 during the school year.
Dining: Breakfast, lunch, and dinner served at the Chuckwagon Dining Room. Serve yourself buffet-style—all you can eat. Be sure to try their world famous Y.O. Ranch-style Beans. Liquor available or BYOB.
Entertainment: Game viewing from pool deck. Piano, pool table, and shuffleboard. Wait until you see the main lodge. Ask about the Y.O. Social Club and other special events.
Summary: Famous 100-year-old, 40,000-acre working cattle/wildlife ranch with 10,000 deer/antelope from around the world and large herd of Texas longhorns. The Y.O. is rich in history and serves up tremendous Texas hospitality. Photo safaris and cattle drive each spring. Summer camp for children. Limited big game hunting. Special note: The Y.O. has a family landowner program. Ask ranch for details. Nearby attractions include The Alamo, LBJ State Park, Cowboy Artists of America Museum. Video available.

See color photos, page 240

Hargrave Cattle and Guest Ranch, Montana

Hargrave Cattle and Guest Ranch, Montana

See page 120

Grapevine Canyon Ranch, Arizona

Grapevine Canyon Ranch, Arizona

See page 12

West Fork Meadows Ranch, Montana

West Fork Meadows Ranch, Montana

See page 140

Reid Ranch, Utah

Reid Ranch, Utah

See page 244

Teton Ridge Ranch, Idaho

Teton Ridge Ranch, Idaho

See page 98

Peaceful Valley Lodge and Ranch Resort, Colorado

Peaceful Valley Lodge and Ranch Resort, Colorado

See pages 66, 345

Peaceful Valley Lodge and Ranch Resort, Colorado

Peaceful Valley Lodge and Ranch Resort, Colorado

See pages 66, 345

Peaceful Valley Lodge and Ranch Resort, Colorado

See pages 66, 345

Rimrock Ranch, Wyoming

Rimrock Ranch, Wyoming

See page 283

Spanish Springs Ranch, California

Spanish Springs Ranch, California

See page 39

Lost Valley Ranch, Colorado

Lost Valley Ranch, Colorado

See page 64

Don K Ranch, Colorado

Don K Ranch, Colorado

See page 51

Fryingpan River Ranch, Colorado

Fryingpan River Ranch, Colorado

See pages 57, 320, 342

Tumbling River Ranch, Colorado

Tumbling River Ranch, Colorado

See page 81

Rafter Six Ranch Resort, Alberta, Canada

Rafter Six Ranch Resort, Alberta, Canada

See page 296

Flathead Lake Lodge, Montana

Flathead Lake Lodge, Montana

See page 118

C Lazy U Ranch, Colorado

C Lazy U Ranch, Colorado

See pages 46, 340

Bitterroot Ranch, Wyoming

Bitterroot Ranch, Wyoming

See page 254

Wit's End Guest and Resort Ranch, Colorado

Wit's End Guest and Resort Ranch, Colorado

See page 86

Wit's End Guest and Resort Ranch, Colorado

See page 86

Wit's End Guest and Resort Ranch, Colorado

Wit's End Guest and Resort Ranch, Colorado

See page 86

Wit's End Guest and Resort Ranch, Colorado

Wit's End Guest and Resort Ranch, Colorado

See page 86

Wit's End Guest and Resort Ranch, Colorado

Wit's End Guest and Resort Ranch, Colorado

See page 86

Hunewill Circle H Ranch, California

Hunewill Circle H Ranch, California

See page 35

Lone Mountain Ranch, Montana

Lone Mountain Ranch, Montana

See pages 129, 349

Red Rock Ranch, Wyoming

Red Rock Ranch, Wyoming

See page 282

Vermejo Park Ranch, New Mexico

Vermejo Park Ranch, New Mexico

See page 330

British Columbia Guest Ranch Association

Cataloochee Ranch, North Carolina

Cataloochee Ranch, North Carolina

See page 157

Diamond D Ranch, Idaho

Diamond D Ranch, Idaho

See page 92

Prude Ranch, Texas

Prude Ranch, Texas

See page 175

Rock Springs Guest Ranch, Oregon

Rock Springs Guest Ranch, Oregon

See page 166

Circle Z Ranch, Arizona

See page 8

North Fork Guest Ranch, Colorado

North Fork Guest Ranch, Colorado

See page 63

Baker's Bar M Ranch, Oregon

Baker's Bar M Ranch, Oregon

See page 163

Paradise Guest Ranch, Wyoming

Paradise Guest Ranch, Wyoming

See page 278

Paradise Guest Ranch, Wyoming

Paradise Guest Ranch, Wyoming

See page 278

Lost Creek Ranch, Wyoming

See page 274

Lost Creek Ranch, Wyoming

See page 274

Lost Creek Ranch, Wyoming

Lost Creek Ranch, Wyoming

See page 274

Elktrout Lodge, Colorado

Elktrout Lodge, Colorado

See page 319

Mountain Sky Guest Ranch, Montana

See page 130

Cherokee Park Ranch, Colorado

Cherokee Park Ranch, Colorado

See page 44

Wilderness Trails Ranch, Colorado

Wilderness Trails Ranch, Colorado

See page 85

Diamond J Ranch, Montana

Diamond J Ranch, Montana

See pages 114, 326

Western Hills Guest Ranch, Oklahoma

Western Hills Guest Ranch, Oklahoma

See page 162

Elk Mountain Ranch, Colorado

Elk Mountain Ranch, Colorado

See page 54

Skyline Guest Ranch, Colorado

Skyline Guest Ranch, Colorado

See pages 76, 346

Tanque Verde Ranch, Arizona

Tanque Verde Ranch, Arizona

See page 21

Flying U Ranch, British Columbia, Canada

Flying U Ranch, British Columbia, Canada

See page 302

Gros Ventre River Ranch, Wyoming

Gros Ventre River Ranch, Wyoming

See page 266

The Lodge at Chama, New Mexico

The Lodge at Chama, New Mexico

See pages 148, 329

The Lodge at Chama, New Mexico

The Lodge at Chama, New Mexico

See pages 148, 329

Pinegrove Resort Ranch, New York

Pinegrove Resort Ranch, New York

See page 151

Elk Canyon Ranch, Montana

Elk Canyon Ranch, Montana

See page 113

Busterback Ranch, Idaho

Busterback Ranch, Idaho

See pages 91, 348

The Hills Health and Guest Ranch, British Columbia, Canada

The Hills Health and Guest Ranch, British Columbia, Canada

See pages 301, 351

Crescent H Ranch, Wyoming

Crescent H Ranch, Wyoming

See page 332

Crescent H Ranch, Wyoming

Crescent H Ranch, Wyoming

See page 332

Alisal Guest Ranch, California

Alisal Guest Ranch, California

See page 26

The Spur Cross Ranch, Nevada

The Spur Cross Ranch, Nevada

See page 145

Y.O. Ranch, Texas

Y.O. Ranch, Texas

See page 178

Lazy K Bar Guest Ranch, Arizona

Lazy K Bar Guest Ranch, Arizona

See page 14

Trail Creek Ranch, Wyoming

See page 288

Pack Creek Ranch, Utah

Pack Creek Ranch is one of a growing number of country ranch inns. Fifteen miles southeast of Moab and within easy driving distance of Arches and Canyonlands national parks, this rustic hideaway is in the foothills of the 12,721-foot La Sal Mountains. Hosts Ken and Jane Sleight met some years ago on a white water raft trip. In 1987, they bought their 300-acre ranch to complement a lifetime devoted to river running and horse packing on the Colorado Plateau. The property offers a cool retreat from the desert sun and superb views of canyon country.

Address: Box 1270 K, Moab, Utah 84532
Telephone: (801) 259-5505
Airport: Grand Junction, Colorado, 100 miles; commercial flights to Moab Airport, 15 miles
Location: 15 miles southeast of Moab, 4 hours south of Salt Lake City
Memberships: Utah Guide and Outfitters Association, Western River Guide Association
Medical: Allen Memorial Hospital in Moab, 16 miles
Conference: 50
Guest Capacity: 50
Accommodations: Nine red-roofed cabins are of log or log-sided construction. Each has a living room, full kitchen, hide-a-bed, electric blankets or quilts, and carpeting; most have fireplaces. Cabins vary in size, sleeping from 2 to 12 people. There are also several private cabins available. Ask ranch for details. Laundry can be sent out.
Rates: • $-$$. Lunch and horseback riding not included.
Credit Cards: Visa, MasterCard, American Express, Discover
Season: January through October. Cabins available year-round. Restaurant open to public January through October.
Activities: Some arrive and do absolutely nothing but relax. Others hike or ride in the canyons or the La Sal Mountains or swim in the pool. Overnight pack trips to mountain hideaway ("South Mountain Cabin") and exciting river rafting trips. Ken is extremely knowledgeable about the natural history of the area and, as a first-rate white water guide, has exciting rafting adventures to share. You can also ask Ken or Jane about their backpacking and horse packing trips. Scenic flights, jeep trips, mountain bike (BYO) tours, and fishing are available. Cross-country skiing in the winter.
Children's Programs: Children welcome but no special program.
Dining: Continental breakfast. Lunch by request. Candlelight dinners include fresh seafood, homemade dill rolls, Swedish cream topped with raspberries. Crab, pasta, and fresh fruit salads, barbecued chicken, steaks, and vegetarian specialties. Wine available.
Entertainment: Few organized activities. You may hear classical guitar or a poetry reading at dinner. Lots of books.
Summary: Come to Pack Creek to relax. If you need to be entertained, read on. Jane and Ken offer a low-key environment away from all social pressures. Host Ken Sleight is very knowledgeable about Utah's backcountry. Ranch is open to the public for dining and horseback riding. Much like a country ranch inn. Attractions nearby include Canyonlands National Park, the wild Colorado River.

Reid Ranch, Utah

The Reid Ranch is at 7,800 feet, on the slopes of the Uinta Mountains, once home to the Uinta Ouray Indians. Since it was originally homesteaded in the late 1800s, the property has had four owners, all of whom savored the abundance of wildlife and nature's tranquillity. Today, this modern ranch is owned by Mervin and Ethna Reid, both Ph.D.'s, and managed by their son, Gardner. Only two hours east of Salt Lake City, the ranch owns 400 acres and is surrounded by state and federal forest land. The Reids, both from Utah, have a very successful Reading Center that attracts people nationwide. They bought the ranch to host visitors from around the world and to establish a learning environment where individuals, teachers, students, and professionals could have fun studying in nature's setting. It is ideal for business conventions, executive meetings, and relaxing vacations. The ranch offers lodge facilities for seminars and family and group retreats.

Address: 3310 South 2700 East K, Salt Lake City, Utah 84109
Telephone: (800) 468-3274, (801) 848-5776 (summer); (801) 486-5083 (winter); Fax: (801) 485-0561
Airport: Salt Lake City International
Location: 50 miles east of Heber City off I-40, 100 miles east of Salt Lake City
Memberships: International Reading Association
Awards: United States Department of Education, Nationally Validated Reading and Computer programs
Medical: Heber City Hospital, 50 miles
Conference: 115; two 2,000-square-foot meeting rooms/dining rooms
Guest Capacity: 115
Accommodations: Two modern lodges and two newly built homes. One lodge has two rooms that sleep 26 each in bunk beds and a 2,000-square-foot dining/meeting room. The main 3-story lodge has 7 large bedrooms that sleep up to 7 adults each. The 24-foot cathedral ceilings, spacious entry, library with adult and children's books, large dining area, and decks provide a wonderful atmosphere.

Rates: • $. American Plan. Children's rates available; children under 5 free. Family, corporate, and group rates available. No minimum stay.
Credit Cards: American Express
Season: Mid-June through October
Activities: Adults and children can participate in activities like horseback riding (half-hour and hour rides). Fishing, hiking, fossil hunting, swimming in kidney-shaped heated pool and whirlpool spa, one lighted sports court for tennis, volleyball, and basketball. Photography, astronomy, and archery. Four-wheel-drive and fall hunting.
Children's Programs: Reading classes for 5 weeks each summer with teachers and counselors. Baby-sitting available.
Dining: Buffet breakfast and lunch; dinner under chandeliers on formally set tables. Barbecues, special meals on request, weekly cookouts. BYOB.
Entertainment: Sing-alongs, tractor hayrides, occasional forest ranger talks.
Summary: Group/conference ranch facility, great for church, business groups, family reunions, and individual family vacations. Seminars for teachers in teaching methods and leadership workshops for administrators, reading/computer camp for students, English and reading classes taught as a second language for adults. Nearby largest piñon and juniper forest in the world. Only east-west mountain range in the United States, Dinosaur National Monument. Spanish spoken fluently.

See color photos, page 182

Rockin' R Ranch, Utah

Since the 1870s, the Black family has raised cattle in southern Utah. The Rockin' R nestles in a valley surrounded by mountains on the outskirts of the little village of Antimony. In the fall, one may spot up to 1,000 deer in neighboring meadows. Burns Black, in his mid-sixties, is the patriarch of the ranch and has been a cowboy most of his life. Early in his ranching career, Burns realized that the best way to stay afloat in the cattle business was to diversify. That meant taking on dudes. In 1970 the ranch opened its doors to the public. A 21,000-square-foot, 3-story, barnlike lodge was completed in 1985. The Rockin' R is run by Burns, his wife, Mona, and their three sons. The Blacks also run about 1,000 cattle on 1,000 privately owned acres and 50,000 acres of leased grazing land. The Rockin' R is ideal for youth or church groups, family reunions, or business conferences. Small groups and individual families are welcome any time. Burns and his staff go out of their way to ensure guests are well looked after.

Address: Box 12 K, Antimony, Utah 84712
Telephone: (801) 624-3250
Airport: Bryce Canyon, 35 miles
Location: 60 miles south of Richfield off Highway 89, 200 miles south of Salt Lake City, 225 miles northeast of Las Vegas
Medical: Panquitch Hospital, 60 miles
Conference: 300
Guest Capacity: 300
Accommodations: The lodge is surrounded by several acres of lawn and features a full 3-story fireplace with a huge, rock-floor fire pit. There are 22 bedrooms, all carpeted, plus 2 large dormitories that sleep 55 each, some with private baths. Most guests use the large tiled rest rooms with both private and group showers. For larger groups, the overflow guests from the lodge sleep in 8 former Bryce Canyon log cabins or in the old ranch house. Laundry facilities.
Rates: • $. American Plan. Children's rates, with children under 4 free. Cattle drive and conference rates available; overnight stays available.

Credit Cards: Visa, MasterCard, American Express
Season: April through November
Activities: In summer almost everything is organized with sign-up sheets. The ranch specializes in cattle work and lake activities. Guests may participate in roundups at the 10,000-foot cow camp or take half-day or all-day rides. Pack trips and riding instruction. Basketball, canal baseball, football, lawn hockey, and tennis. Two and a half miles from the main lodge is 6-mile-long Otter Lake, voted No. 1 in the state for lake fishing, also offering sailboarding, canoeing, sailing, tubing, and waterskiing. Four-wheel drive. Seasonal elk and deer hunting.
Children's Programs: Supervised children's/youths' programs, excellent facilities for youth groups. June, July, and August summer camp. Baby-sitting available.
Dining: Very good cafeteria-style food in the lodge dining room. Parents and adults can eat privately in the solarium. Dutch oven chicken, barbecued steak with mushrooms, Rockin' R pizza, fresh fruit and vegetables, breakfast and supper rides. Restaurant open to public one night each week. Liquor is not served.
Entertainment: Hayrides, juke box dancing, cowboy singing several nights a week.
Summary: Excellent for small and large groups—youth, church, business, conference. Ranch may be booked exclusively for different-size groups. Cattle experience for those who desire. Near Lake Powell; Dixie National Forest; Bryce Canyon, Zion, and Capitol Reef National Parks. Video available on request.

Tavaputs Plateau Ranch, Utah

Tavaputs ("Rising Sun" in Ute) Plateau Ranch takes in some 15,000 acres along the rim and plateaus bordering Desolation Canyon. At 9,100 feet, the main guest lodge is surrounded by rolling meadows, steep mountains, and red rock canyons. The view is endless—the Uinta Mountains to the north, Colorado and Arizona to the east and south. Four generations of the Wilcox family have owned and operated Tavaputs Ranch. Today, it is run by Jenette and Don. This part of the country is full of early American folklore. Butch Cassidy and his wild bunch rode the same trails you will ride. Don is an expert on local history. Nearby are the remains of the Fremont Indian culture. Relaxing is easy here. Soft country music after a hearty dinner, combined with brisk night air, makes sleep effortless. If you arrive by car, the ranch will meet you in East Carbon City as the gates to the ranch are kept locked.

Address: Box 139 K, Green River, Utah 84525
Telephone: (801) 454-8955 (summer radio telephone); (801) 564-3463 (winter)
Airport: Salt Lake City, Utah; Grand Junction, Colorado
Location: 200 miles southeast of Salt Lake City, 65 miles east of Price
Memberships: Utah Cattleman's Association
Medical: Castleview Hospital, 65 miles; Life Flight helicopter available
Conference: 15
Guest Capacity: 15
Accommodations: A variety of accommodations for singles, couples, and families in the main building, as well as in several cabins that sleep up to 6. Each has private bath, carpeting, homemade comforters. The ranch makes its own electricity, and the ranch generator runs continuously.
Rates: • $$$. American Plan.
Credit Cards: None
Season: June through September
Activities: If you enjoy walking, you can take strolls through fields and aspen woods as well as ambitious hikes along the rim country or in the canyons. Four-wheel-drive trips to breathtaking vistas and canyons. Plenty of horseback riding on saddle mules and quarter horses—slow, easy rides taking in the scenery. Outdoor whirlpool.
Children's Programs: None. Older children are welcome. Children under 5 do not ride.
Dining: Great ranch food. Meals are carefully planned and well balanced. Stone-ground whole wheat breads and rolls, fresh scones, apple strudel. Roast beef, steaks, fresh fruits and vegetables. Special diets catered to with advance notice.
Entertainment: Depends on group. Occasional guitar music and sing-alongs.
Summary: If you want to truly get away from it all and be literally on top of the world, give Jenette and Don a call. Tremendous hospitality and kindness abound. Very, very remote ranch. The drive to Tavaputs is magnificent, but very slow going, and will take approximately an hour and a half by four-wheel-drive vehicle from East Carbon City. Spectacular views, lots of wildlife, and brilliant sunrises and sunsets. Wildlife photographers' paradise. Nightly bear watch. Fremont Indian pictographs, Butch Cassidy country. Western river expeditions.

Firefly Ranch, Vermont

In 1980, Marie Louise Link (she likes to be called "Issy"), not knowing the first thing about horses but having lots of people experience at her restaurant in upstate New York, began the Firefly Ranch. A native of Germany, she came to the United States in 1962. After 13 years in a successful but pressured restaurant business, she sought a way of relaxing. And so, Firefly was born. Taking only 8 guests at a time, Firefly serves warm and friendly New England hospitality in the Green Mountains with their rolling farmlands, beaver ponds, and woodland glades. The atmosphere is casual. Said one guest, "We felt not like guests but like members of the family." A stay at Firefly is much like finding a friend in a beautiful part of the country.

Address: P.O. Box 152 K, Bristol, Vermont 05443
Telephone: (802) 453-2223
Airport: Burlington International, 26 miles
Location: 16 miles northeast of Middlebury
Medical: Porter Hospital in Middlebury, 20 minutes
Guest Capacity: 8
Accommodations: Inn-type lodging with views from each of the three rooms. The main house overlooks Mount Abraham, Vermont's second-highest mountain, and sleeps eight. Double and single beds, shared baths, homemade quilts, electric blankets. Spa room with hot tub that seats five.
Rates: $-$$. American Plan. Two-day minimum for riding. Bed and breakfast during the winter months.
Credit Cards: None. Personal checks accepted.
Season: May to October (summer); December through March (winter)
Activities: In summer, there is unlimited English and Western riding. You may ride 5-6 hours per day. For those who are out all day, Issy will prepare a lovely picnic including homemade soup. Rides cater to intermediate and experienced riders. All rides accompanied by experienced guides. Lots of hiking and fishing off the property, spring-fed pond for swimming, hot tub, tennis nearby. In winter, Firefly turns into an informal ski lodge, offering coziness, cross-country skiing, snowshoeing, and downhill skiing at Mad River Glen and Sugar Bush, 12 miles away.
Children's Programs: No children please. Teenagers must definitely be experienced riders.
Dining: Wonderful fresh German-American food, complimentary cocktails and wine served. Vegetarian and macrobiotic and modified kosher diets catered to.
Entertainment: Most guests are too tired after an all-day ride to do anything except relax, eat, and climb into bed for deep sleep.
Summary: Ranch country inn/B&B. Bring your own horse. English riding lessons. Massage available by appointment only. Local arts and crafts shops, the University of Vermont Morgan Horse Farm in Middlebury. Tremendous shopping in the marketplace of downtown Burlington. Dutch, French, and German spoken.

Circle H Holiday Ranch, Washington

In 1988, Betsy, Jim, and son Jamie Ogden moved themselves, their antiques, and their donkey Petunia from suburban New York City to Thorp, Washington. The home they found for themselves was a private ranch located at the foothills of the Cascades. The 58-acre Circle H Holiday Ranch sits atop a gentle slope, surrounded by softly draping fir trees and a well-groomed lawn. The swimming pond, cabins, and barn spread below. The view on one side is of the Kittitas Valley, while the jagged, snow-covered peaks of the Stuart Mountain Range command your attention on the other. Guest ranching is a family affair at the Circle H. Grandma and Grandpa, the kids, even the family dog, are all welcome. In a completely unstructured environment, there are usually enough activities to keep everyone pleasantly worn out. Going to the Circle H is like the visits you used to make to your aunt and uncle's farm on the outskirts of town: familiar, friendly, and fun! The Circle H is a dude ranch in the old-fashioned sense, a bed and breakfast in the newest sense, and just plain fun in every sense.

Address: Route 1, Box 175K, Thorp, Washington 98946
Telephone: (509) 964-2000
Airport: Sea-Tac Airport, Seattle
Location: 101 miles east of Seattle just off I-90, 9 miles west of Ellensburg
Memberships: Cascade Mountain Lodging Association
Medical: Kittitas Valley Community Hospital, 15 miles
Conference: 25
Guest Capacity: 25
Accommodations: Take your pick of the Lone Ranger Cabin, which is connected to the Tonto Cabin, the Gene Autry Cabin, or the Roy Rogers Cabin, which is connected to the Dale Evans Cabin. Each has a separate bedroom and bathroom. A day-bed with trundle underneath, a kitchenette, and a dining area are in the living room. Originally bunk houses, the cabins have been restored with bleached, rough-sawn knotty pine that make the rooms light and warm. Painted floors showcase unusual rugs, and bed headboards are made from local tree limbs. Colorful Indian blankets are everywhere.

Rates: • $. American Plan Memorial Day to Labor Day. Children's rates and off-season bed and breakfast rates available. Horseback riding extra.
Credit Cards: Visa and MasterCard
Season: Year-round. Guest ranch season is Memorial Day weekend through Labor Day weekend. Bed and breakfast the rest of the year.
Activities: The main activity is horseback riding, with average rides lasting 2 hours. But those so inclined may also fish on a blue ribbon catch and release stream and raft on the nearby Yakima River. Swim in the freshwater pond (best done in the summer), take hikes in the hundreds of acres of adjacent wildlife habitat area, or merely admire the scenery and pet the goat, Ethel.
Children's Programs: No organized children's activities but plenty to do. A super-gentle old mare, which the kids can ride at no charge, stands out in the pasture. An enclosed play area has lots to do, but it is the hammock strung between two willow trees or the hay stacks where the kids most often will be found. Babysitting can be arranged.
Dining: During the guest ranch season, everyone eats together family-style on the patio or in the family room up at the main house. Hearty ranch breakfasts, saddlebag lunches that are either taken out on the trail or picnicked at some shady spot on the grounds, and full western ranch dinners. Everything is homemade by the friendly cook who everybody gets to know.
Entertainment: Outdoor barn dances. Hayrides in the woods on the back of the ranch pickup truck. Impromptu camp fires with marshmallows.
Summary: Ideal for the whole family and for family reunions. Lots of individual attention.

Flying L Ranch, Washington

In the mid-1940s, Les Lloyd, a forestry engineer, and his wife, Ilse, bought the Flying L Ranch to be their family home. Les was a consultant and traveled the world, assisting other countries on forest management. The Flying L opened its doors in 1960 and in the mid-1980s began year-round operation. The Flying L, a 160-acre retreat and wilderness launching pad, is surrounded by ponderosa pine and meadowlands of Glenwood Valley, with 12,276-foot Mount Adams 15 miles northwest. The ranch has played host to many interesting guests over the years. Today, the Lloyds' son, Darvel, a former university teacher, environmental educator, and accomplished mountain climber, runs the ranch. Most guests come from the Pacific Northwest and stay just a couple of days. Many art and business groups and organizations, like Audubon, have found the Flying L ideal for workshops and retreats. Guests bring their own horses.

Address: 25 Flying L Lane, Dept. K, Glenwood, Washington 98619

Telephone: (509) 364-3488

Airport: Portland, Oregon, 90 miles

Location: 35 miles north of Hood River, Oregon; 100 miles northeast of Portland; 265 miles southeast of Seattle

Memberships: Professional Innkeepers Association

Medical: Mid-Columbia Medical Center, 32 miles

Conference: 28

Guest Capacity: 35

Accommodations: The main lodge sleeps 12 to 15 in 6 rooms; a 2-story guest house sleeps 12 in 5 rooms; and 2-room cabins sleep 6 to 8. Rooms are named after famous Western personalities like Will Rogers, Charlie Russell, and Yakima Canutt. Guests cook for themselves or choose from wonderful restaurants nearby. Cooking facilities are provided. Complete meals can be arranged for groups.

Rates: • $. European Plan. Children's and weekly rates available. Two-night minimum on certain weekends and holidays.

Credit Cards: Visa, MasterCard, Diners Club, American Express. Personal checks and cash accepted.

Season: Year-round

Activities: In summer, bring your own horse; otherwise riding can be arranged with a local outfitter. Steelhead trout fishing in the Klickitat River. Three miles of ranch hiking trails and loop trails on national wildlife refuge. There are also many beautiful trails on Mount Adams; float trips on the wild White Salmon River can be arranged. Berry picking; mountain bike riding (must bring your own). In winter, cross-country skiing on marked and groomed ranch and forest service trails, Snowcat and snowmobiling in the Mount Adams backcountry. Year-round hot tub with mountain view.

Children's Programs: No special programs. Children are welcome.

Dining: Cook for yourself in several shared kitchens. The ranch serves a hearty breakfast including Mount Adams Huckleberry Hot Cakes. Restaurants in nearby Glenwood and Trout Lake. Full meal service can be arranged for groups of 12 or more.

Entertainment: Guests regularly gather in the cozy living room to visit by the lava rock fireplace. The Lloyds have a great collection of books on travel, history, wildlife, and mountaineering.

Summary: Ranch bed and breakfast. Bring your own horse. Short stays OK; great place to host workshops and family reunions.

Hidden Valley Guest Ranch, Washington

Hidden Valley Guest Ranch in eastern Washington offers a year-round getaway in a relaxing ranch atmosphere. The facility is nestled in the Swauk Valley in the foothills of the Wenatchee Mountains at 2,500 feet. On 750 acres of canyon and rolling range, the ranch has been continuously operated as a guest ranch since 1947, when Hollywood cowboy and entertainer Tom Whited carved Hidden Valley from an old homestead dating to 1887. Many original buildings, including the homestead cabin, form the nucleus of the lodging facilities. Today Hidden Valley is owned and operated by the Coe family. There is a casual atmosphere at the ranch, one that brings back memories of yesteryear.

Address: HC 61, Box 2060K, Cle Elum, Washington 98922
Telephone: (509) 857-2344
Airport: Cle Elum Municipal Airport, 8 miles; commuter flights via Seattle to Yakima; DeVere Field (private), 6 miles
Location: 8 miles northeast of Cle Elum off Highway 970, 85 miles east of Seattle
Memberships: Cascade Mountain Lodging Association
Awards: Northwest Best Places Two Stars
Medical: Kittitas Valley Community Hospital, 20 miles
Conference: 35
Guest Capacity: 35
Accommodations: One- to two-bedroom cabins and one 4-plex cabin, each with its own personality and names like Cedar, Aspen, Apple Tree, Spruce, or Elk Horn. Two are housekeeping units with mini-kitchens. The Coes call these units the Bunkhouse and can tell you what you will need. All are fully furnished with private bath and entry, carpeting, gas heating, some fireplaces, and porches.
Rates: • $. American Plan. Horseback riding, hayrides, and bar tab extra.
Credit Cards: Visa, MasterCard
Season: Year-round
Activities: In summer the riding program is open to the public. Rides last about 1½ hours, but there are also half-day and all-day rides. Heated pool, 10-person hot tub, hiking, wagon rides, chuck wagon barbecues, and breakfast rides. Fishing in Swauk Creek and trout farm nearby. Wildflower/bird-watching in conjunction with the Northern Cascade Institute. Good mountain biking, but BYO. In winter, cross-country skiing, sleigh rides, sledding, and snowshoeing. Bring your own gear.
Children's Programs: Family participation in all activities is encouraged. No organized children's program. Baby-sitting available with advance notice. Children under 6 do not go on trail rides. Children are the responsibility of their parents.
Dining: Guests eat in the cook house. Family-style dining served from a single entrée buffet; all you can eat. Home-baked bread and pies, hearty Western cuisine. Ranch specialties include Hidden Valley pork chops and Bruce's Mexican dishes. Vegetarian fare provided cheerfully on request. Beer and wine served.
Entertainment: Recreation lounge resembles a hunting lodge with fireplace, pool table, table tennis, honky-tonk piano, and loads of atmosphere. Gymkhana, poker rides, play days, Western fantasy weekends, overnight wagon trips for groups of 15 or more with advance notice. Gold panning and special events.
Summary: When they say "hidden," they're not kiddin'. Good food, good horses, and the down-right friendly Coe hospitality. No telephone, television, or hassles. Bird-watching, wildflowers, and photography workshops available. You may bring your own horse. Rodeos in Ellensburg; historic mining towns of Liberty, Roslyn, and Cle Elum nearby.

Woodside Ranch, Wisconsin

The 1,000-acre Woodside Ranch is open year-round and offers plenty of country-style activities for families. This is one of the few ranches in the country with a small buffalo herd. Woodside sits in the upper Dells on a high wooded hillside with panoramic views of the Lemonweir Valley. Woodside is a family-run guest ranch. It was started in 1925 by William Feldmann as a family retreat. Soon the Feldmanns and their half dozen children had friends wanting to be part of their fun. Each year it grew, until there were 21 cabins with fireplaces and a lodge. In 1952 the ranch was incorporated. It is managed today by the Feldmanns' youngest daughter and two grandsons. Guests from around the world come to experience the Feldmanns' Wisconsin hospitality. You are part of the family at Woodside.

Address: Highway 82, Box K, Mauston, Wisconsin 53948
Telephone: (608) 847-4275
Airport: Madison; small private airport in Mauston-New Lisbon, 11 miles
Train: Wisconsin Dells, 20 miles
Bus: Greyhound to Mauston, 4 miles
Location: 20 miles northwest of Wisconsin Dells, 70 miles north of Madison, 220 miles north of Chicago, 200 miles south of Minneapolis on Interstate 90/94.
Memberships: Wisconsin Innkeepers Association
Medical: Hess Memorial Hospital, 6 miles
Conference: 60
Guest Capacity: 150
Accommodations: Woodside offers rustic, informal accommodations. There are 21 one-, two-, and three-bedroom cabins with fireplaces. The main house has rooms with private baths that accommodate up to 4 people. All rooms have thermostatically controlled heat and air-conditioning. You must bring your own towels.
Rates: $. American Plan. Three-day, six-day, and weekly rates available. Minimum 3-day, 2-night stay. Children's rates.

Credit Cards: Visa, MasterCard
Season: Year-round
Activities: Summer recreation director on staff. Eight one-hour rides go out daily for novice to experienced riders. Daily breakfast rides, covered wagon and hayrides. Three tennis courts, miniature golf, volleyball, large sauna. Fishing, horseshoes, new outdoor heated pool, and paddle boats. Canoeing nearby. In winter, beginner alpine skiing with rope tow, night skiing, extensive cross-country skiing with 12 miles of tracked and 5 miles of skating trails, horseback riding, sleigh rides, ice skating. Ski equipment rental.
Children's Programs: Pony rides in ring for children of all ages. Supervised play school during the day.
Dining: Barbecues, buffalo cookouts; family-style meals with everyone assigned to a table; chicken dinners and buffalo steaks; Trading Post Cocktail Bar.
Entertainment: Square dancing, polkas, 1950s music, sing-alongs, camp fires with marshmallow roasts.
Summary: Family owned and operated ranch for families, featuring fireplace log cabins, year-round horseback riding, horse drawn wagon rides, sleigh rides. Winter program. Small buffalo herd. Adults-only week in August.

Absaroka Ranch, Wyoming

Authentic Western Ranch, Member–Dude Ranchers' Association

Absaroka Ranch is at the base of the spectacular Absaroka Mountains, yet just 25 minutes from the town of Dubois. The dirt road to the ranch offers exhilarating mountain views. The ranch hosts only 16 guests at a time. Budd and Emi Betts specialize in the personal touch. At 8,000 feet, the ranch is big on outdoor space, with thousands of acres and miles of trails, mountain streams, and valleys. Wildlife abounds; it is not uncommon to see elk, moose, deer, eagles, beaver, and even an occasional bear. The valley is surrounded by the Shoshone National Forest and wilderness, offering all the elements conducive to total rest and relaxation. If this kind of catches your fancy, better get on the telephone quickly—Budd and Emi book up almost a year in advance.

Address: Star Route, Dept. K, Dubois, Wyoming 82513
Telephone: (307) 455-2275
Airport: Jackson or Riverton via Denver or Salt Lake City
Location: 75 miles east of Jackson Airport, 16 miles northwest of Dubois off U.S. 26/287
Memberships: Dude Ranchers' Association
Awards: *Hideaway Report*: 1990 Family Guest Ranch of the Year
Medical: Emergency Clinic in Dubois, 16 miles
Guest Capacity: 16
Accommodations: Four cabins (Delta Whiskey, Six Point, Five Mile, and Detimore), are snug, heated, with one or two bedrooms and adjoining baths, comforters, full carpeting. One cabin with fireplace. All cabins have covered porches with views of the Wind River Mountains and the manicured lawn in front.
Rates: • $$. American Plan. Group, family, and children's rates available. Special rates for return guests.
Credit Cards: None
Season: Mid-June to mid-September
Activities: In summer, trail rides to high meadows, through forests, and to Trail Lake. Breakfast and evening cookout rides. Fishing in nearby lakes.

The trout streams are particularly challenging and best suited for experienced anglers. Limited fishing gear available. The ranch chef will gladly cook your fish for you. Hikers enjoy picnic lunches. Float trips in Jackson Hole can be arranged. Ask about walking and horse pack trips (the ranch has a brochure on these). Photo enthusiasts should bring lots of film. Swimming in crystal clear but chilly streams and lakes. Warm up in the redwood dry heat sauna.
Children's Programs: The "Gold Pinch Palace" recreation room with pool table, juke box, arcade games, and a 25-cent Coke machine. Children's games, instructional horseback rides, and game rides. Baby-sitting can be arranged (extra).
Dining: Delicious meals served family-style. Beef tenderloin and lasagna are two ranch specialties. Complimentary wine with dinner. BYOB.
Entertainment: Gymkhanas, square dancing, card games, horseshoes, camp fires, slide shows, weekly rodeos in Jackson.
Summary: Rustic, secluded, very personal and family-oriented. Walking and horse pack trips (ask for brochure), float trips. Saturday night in the Western town of Dubois, Yellowstone National Park, Teton National Park.

Bill Cody's Ranch Resort, Wyoming

At Bill Cody's Ranch, your hosts are none other than Bill Cody—the grandson of Col. William F. "Buffalo Bill" Cody—and his wife, Barbara. What makes this small ranch unique are colorful Bill Cody, who is in his late seventies, and the riding program, a no-nonsense operation. Bill is very strict with his guests and wranglers. The ranch is in the Shoshone National Forest, and Bill goes out of his way to ensure that guests have diverse riding opportunities, even to the point of trailering horses to other parts of the valley. Be forewarned—due to the terrain and the ranch's safety standards, horses are not allowed to trot or canter. Bill is a great storyteller, an art he learned while he was at Harvard Law School years ago. He has had a most interesting life. If you catch him at the right time, he may sit down and tell you just how the West was really won.

Address: 2604 Yellowstone Highway, Dept. K, Cody, Wyoming 82414
Telephone: (307) 587-6271
Airport: Cody, Wyoming, or Billings, Montana
Location: 26 miles west of Cody just off U.S. Highway 14/16/20
Awards: AAA 3 Diamond
Medical: West Park Hospital in Cody, 26 miles
Conference: 30
Guest Capacity: 76
Accommodations: The lodge and guest facilities are nestled in a valley shaded by tall pines. Guest cottages are log-sided with motel-like Western interiors. All are spotless and very comfortable. All rooms have private baths and thermostatically controlled heat; no television or telephone.
Rates: • $-$$. American Plan. All-inclusive packages, family and off-season rates available.
Credit Cards: Visa, MasterCard, American Express, Discover
Season: Year-round, including Thanksgiving, Christmas, and Easter
Activities: Scheduled and unscheduled riding is the main activity at the ranch. Rides go out morning, noon, and evening. Riders and horses are trailered to points near Yellowstone National Park to provide a variety of riding terrain, but horses are allowed to walk only. There is a small hot tub in the front yard, volleyball, horseshoe pitching, hiking, and fishing off the property on the North Fork of the Shoshone River. Two-hour float trips can be arranged with local professional rafting company.
Children's Programs: Children age 5 and older ride their own horses; baby-sitting available for children under age 5 while parents ride. Children are the responsibility of their parents.
Dining: Happy hour each evening at ranch lounge bar. Full-service, varied menus with daily steaks and fresh trout. Cookouts occasionally by the ranch stream.
Entertainment: Evening rides, unscheduled musical entertainment, which could be a cowboy singer or a guest with a guitar.
Summary: A friendly ranch that attracts many families who travel with their AAA tour book close at hand. Riding is the main activity. Many come for three days, some stay for up to a week. Buffalo Bill Cody's grandson. Strict riding program. Bill says, "It's your vacation, you can do as you want." River rafting, Buffalo Bill Historical Center, Yellowstone and Teton national parks.

Bitterroot Ranch, Wyoming

Authentic Western Ranch, Member–Dude Ranchers' Association

Bitterroot Ranch is bordered by the Shoshone National Forest to the north and the Wind River Indian Reservation to the east. The ranch is owned and operated by Bayard and Mel Fox. Bayard is a Yale graduate who has lived for many years in Europe, Africa, the Middle East, and the South Pacific. Mel was brought up on a farm in Tanzania and spent many years working with wildlife. Bayard and Mel place a strong emphasis on their riding program and provide two horses per guest, splitting rides into small groups according to ability. They provide both English and Western tack, offer a jumping course for advanced riders, and give formal instruction twice per week. They raise and train their pure-bred Arabian horses exclusively for the use of their guests. The riding terrain is extremely varied. Sagebrush, plains, grassy meadows, and colorful rocky gorges give way to forested mountains and alpine clearings. With the Absaroka Range at the back door, riders are immediately immersed in wilderness settings. Because of their international backgrounds, Mel and Bayard get many European guests. The Foxes run rides in 28 countries as well as several week-long riding tours in the United States. Bitterroot is a tremendous international and equestrian experience.

Address: Route 66, Box 1042 K, Dubois, Wyoming 82513
Telephone: (800) 545-0019 (nationwide); (307) 455-2778; Fax: (307) 455-2354
Airport: Riverton or Jackson
Location: 26 miles northeast of Dubois, 80 miles west of Riverton, 100 miles east of Jackson off Routes 287 and 26
Memberships: Dude Ranchers' Association
Medical: Medic in Dubois; Riverton Hospital, 80 miles
Guest Capacity: 25
Accommodations: Accommodations are provided in 11 cabins, many of which are old-time log cabins. Most have wood-burning stoves; all have electric heat, full bathrooms, and views of the mountains and river. The main lodge offers a big stone fireplace, piano, library and card room, pool room, and small bar. Laundry facilities.
Rates: • $$-$$$. American Plan. Group and children's rates available.
Credit Cards: None. Personal checks and traveler's checks accepted.
Season: Last weekend in May through third week in September
Activities: Besides a full English and Western riding program, with half-day and all-day rides, pack trips (extra), and optional riding instruction, there are week-long cross-country horseback rides: the Pony Express, Outlaw Trail, and Mountain rides. Telephone the ranch for more information. Bayard is a keen fly-fisherman. There is good catch-and-release fly fishing on the ranch in the East Fork of the Wind River, which is full of cutthroat trout. They also have two stocked trout ponds. Nature walks and hiking.
Children's Programs: Kiddie wrangler; no special programs. Young children ride at discretion of ranch.
Dining: As many of the guests are European, the standards of the cuisine are high. Complimentary wine with dinner.
Entertainment: Weekly square dancing in Dubois. Piano in main lodge.
Summary: Excellent equestrian program with both English and Western tack. Expert instruction. Raise own Arabians. Its sister company, Equitour, organizes exciting riding holidays in 28 different countries for riders of almost all abilities. Lots of single people and families, many Europeans. Fluent German and French spoken.

See color photos, page 196

Castle Rock Lodges Guest Ranch, Wyoming

Authentic Western Ranch, Member–Dude Ranchers' Association

Castle Rock Lodges Guest Ranch offers a host of wilderness adventures and travel opportunities in the magnificent South Fork Valley of the Shoshone River. It is bordered by the Shoshone River; by Castle Rock, which keeps a watchful eye over the property, pinnacles, and rocks of the desert; and by evergreen forests and distant snow-capped peaks. Hosts Nelson and Velta Wieters, their daughter, Robin, and an energetic and knowledgeable crew of young people will broaden your horizons and let you experience the magnificent wilderness and a variety of outdoor and travel programs.

Address: 412 County Road 6NS, Dept. K, Cody, Wyoming 82414
Telephone: (307) 587-2076 or (800) 356-9965
Airport: Cody
Location: 17 miles southwest of Cody
Memberships: Dude Ranchers' Association, American Camping Association, Western Association of Independent Camps
Medical: West Park Hospital in Cody, 17 miles; EMT or RN on staff at ranch
Conference: 32
Guest Capacity: 32
Accommodations: Ten log cabins sleep up to 6, feature handmade furniture, bright Pendleton blankets, and modern private baths with showers, and are decorated with Native American objects, pioneer era artifacts, and original paintings. All are insulated and heated and most have either wood-burning stoves or fireplaces. The octagonal main lodge has a peaked roof and is decorated in a similar fashion. Floor-to-ceiling windows offer wonderful views of the mountains. Free laundry service.
Rates: • $-$$. American Plan, all-inclusive. Children's and group rates.
Credit Cards: None
Season: June through September. Open for special programs in winter.
Activities: In summer, there is an unusually wide range of activities supported by a large staff. Horsemanship instructions, including half-day and all-day rides, overnight pack trips. Outdoor experiences include llama treks, kayaking, technical climbing, mountain biking, backpacking, tubing, archery, rafting, Yellowstone guided trips, sailing, sailboarding, heated outdoor swimming pool, and sauna. In winter, cross-country skiing and snowmobiling in Yellowstone.
Children's Programs: Daily organized activities. Swimming, arts and crafts, nature hikes, horseback riding, games, and skits. Children's tepees, game room, fishing pond. Baby-sitting available.
Dining: Guests enjoy the Saddle Saloon in the main lodge before dinner. BYOB. Western gourmet meals for all diets, prime rib, and shrimp, romaine strawberry salads with poppy seed dressing. Delicious Castle Rock peppermint layered brownies. No smoking in dining room.
Entertainment: Square dancing, musicians, cowboy balladry, clogging (a type of folk dancing), game room in main lodge, rodeo nights in Cody, Buffalo Bill Historical Center.
Summary: Families, couples, and single people enjoy Castle Rock for many reasons, particularly because of the diversity of activities offered. Unique ranch with multiple outdoor adventure programs. Professional growth seminars, stress-management workshops for corporate groups. Snowmobiling and cross-country skiing in the winter. Shoshone Tipi Village. Travel camp program for teenagers. Yellowstone National Park. Video available on request.

CM Ranch, Wyoming

Life is simple on the CM Ranch, but then that's what makes ranch life so wonderful. The ranch's objective is to provide comfortable headquarters where guests can relax and enjoy informal, wholesome pleasures in the magnificent mountain country of the West. The ranch is one of the oldest dude ranches in the United States, with a fine reputation that attracts guests from around the world. Charlie Moore founded the ranch in 1927. Thirty years later, the ranch was passed on to the Shoemakers. Today Pete and Lisa Petersen own and operate this wonderful ranch with a terrific staff. An altitude of 7,000 feet provides the CM with a climate ideally suited to summer vacations. Sunshine usually predominates, daytime temperatures are comfortably warm, and nights are cool enough to make wool blankets and sweaters feel delightful. Rock hounds and geology buffs will be fascinated with the extraordinary red sandstone and geological displays.

Address: P.O. Box 217 K, Dubois, Wyoming 82513
Telephone: (307) 455-2331 or (307) 455-2266
Airport: Jackson or Riverton; private, surfaced airstrip 3 miles outside Dubois, 10 miles from ranch (large enough for small private jets)
Location: 6 miles southwest of Dubois
Medical: Clinic in Dubois; hospital in Riverton, 75 miles
Conference: 25, small business groups
Guest Capacity: 50
Accommodations: Well-kept lawns surround fourteen log cabins that are spaced along Jakey's Fork, a stream that passes through the ranch. The cabins have electricity, wood-burning stoves, and small, comfortable porches. There are also three beautifully decorated log houses with full amenities that sleep up to 6—East House, West House, and Hardie House. Teenagers who come without their parents live in dormitory cabins and use a central bathhouse. The CM employs a young woman to do guest laundry and care for young children.

Rates: • $$. American Plan. Children's (under 12) rates available.
Credit Cards: None. Personal checks or cash accepted.
Season: Mid-June to September
Activities: You can ride, fish, hike, swim in the outdoor heated pool, picnic, or relax just with a book. No need to know how to ride before you come. There is excellent instruction provided. Horses are matched to your ability. Usually 6 guests on each ride. Rides go out twice a day except Sundays. Weekly all-day picnic rides to Whiskey Mountain, which is, as Pete says, "home to the largest herd of bighorn sheep in North America." Excellent pack trips to the ranch's hand-hewn log cabins on Simpson Lake in the Fitzpatrick Wilderness. Five miles of stream run through the property, so anglers can fish privately for brook, rainbow, and brown trout. Fishing guides available. Torrey, Ring, and Trail lakes are a short drive by auto. Tennis and golf nearby. Float trips on Snake River can be arranged. Parents must supervise their children at the pool.
Children's Programs: Kiddie wrangler, babysitting available (extra). No set program.
Dining: Wonderful dining room and exciting Western meals that are carefully planned and well balanced. Fresh mountain trout added to the menu frequently. Lots of homemade goodies. BYOB.
Entertainment: The large recreation building has several rooms for reading and games, two pianos, Ping-Pong, geology room, and small library, weekly square dancing, volleyball and softball with guests and crew.
Summary: One of the most beautiful really old-time historic ranches in North America. Tremendous warmth and personality. Second, third, and fourth generations come to the CM each summer. Great for families and large family reunions.

CM Ranch, Wyoming

CM Ranch, Wyoming

Crossed Sabres Ranch, Wyoming

Authentic Western Ranch, Member–Dude Ranchers' Association

Crossed Sabres Ranch was established in 1898 by Tex Holm as a stagecoach stop. As one walks around this historic ranch, you can imagine the old stagecoach with a team of six stout horses chomping at the bit as they wait for passengers. Crossed Sabres exudes life and rugged character the minute you lay eyes on the place. Besides the "years gone by" ambience, the ranch has a special feature: it is built alongside a wonderful stream that serenades all the cabins as it makes its way down the mountain. Fred and Alvie Norris sold their ranch in Montana in the late 1970s and bought Crossed Sabres. Fred could well have been a Western movie star with his blue eyes and mustache. He and Alvie have seen a lot of guests over their 30 years in the guest ranch business. Today, as before, families come to be rejuvenated and share in each other's joy and excitement. Many love to sit in the rocking chairs on the porch of the main house, listening, watching, and remembering. Crossed Sabres has Old West charm and two of the nicest ranchers—Fred and Alvie Norris.

Address: P.O. Box K, Wapiti, Wyoming 82450
Telephone: (307) 587-3750
Airport: Cody, Wyoming, or Billings, Montana
Location: 43 miles west of Cody
Memberships: Dude Ranchers' Association, Wyoming Outfitters Association
Medical: Cody Hospital
Guest Capacity: 45 to 50
Accommodations: All seventeen cabins, half of which are along Libby Creek, have names like Red Cloud, Yellow Hand, Indian Echo, and Rides on Clouds. Each is rustic but comfortable and heated. One hand-hewn pine rocking chair sits on each porch.
Rates: • $-$$. American Plan. Children's rates and children under age 2 free. Everything included.
Credit Cards: None. Personal checks or traveler's checks accepted.
Season: Late May to October
Activities: Short and long rides, picnic rides, very popular overnight pack trips. Because the terrain is rough, all riding is done at a walk. Rides may go out in groups of 10 to 15. Fishing for mountain trout in streams and Shoshone River. Float trips included. Guided tours of Yellowstone National Park by Fred, whose great-uncle was second administrator of the park. Plenty of hiking.
Children's Programs: No special program. Everyone does everything together. Baby-sitting available.
Dining: Wholesome family meals in the beautiful authentic old Western main lodge built in 1906 with unique burl posts and beams.
Entertainment: Cody rodeo, square dancing, movies, sing-alongs with wrangler, game room.
Summary: Historic old ranch, wonderful hosts, Fred's marvelous tour of Yellowstone. Ranch general store, Buffalo Bill Historical Center, old Trail Town.

Darwin Ranch, Wyoming

Authentic Western Ranch, Member–Dude Ranchers' Association

In a valley of its own, Darwin Ranch is one of the highest and most remote guest ranches in the Wyoming Rockies. It is a year-round hideaway surrounded by the magnificent Gros Ventre Wilderness. The property was first homesteaded by Fred Darwin in 1904. As the story goes, his Rough Rider friend, Teddy Roosevelt, gave Fred these 160 acres by presidential decree. In 1964, the old, rundown homestead was purchased and renovated. Today Darwin Ranch, at an altitude of 8,200 feet, welcomes 20 guests at a time during the summer and private gatherings of up to 12 people in the winter. Because the ranch is so small, there is great flexibility for guests and their desired activities. Though the ranch is secluded, guests can count on plumbing, electricity by a silent water turbine that runs 24 hours a day, a library, a piano, and a fine kitchen. Darwin Ranch offers an escape from hectic city life. It is today as it always has been—remote, serene, and beautiful.

Address: P.O. Box 511 K, Jackson, Wyoming 83001
Telephone: (307) 733-5588
Airport: Jackson. Call ranch for charter flights to ranch airstrip or helicopter flights from Jackson Airport.
Location: 30 miles east of Jackson, 50 miles northwest of Pinedale
Memberships: Dude Ranchers' Association
Medical: St. John's Hospital in Jackson, Kjerstad Medical Evac Helicopter
Conference: 16
Guest Capacity: 20, summer; 12, winter
Accommodations: Four rustic, comfortable log cabins. One with four bedrooms and two baths can sleep eight. Each private cabin has its own bath (the old-fashioned kind), hot and cold running water, wood stoves, and sitting porches. No telephones. The main lodge with its vaulted ceilings has handmade furniture, large stone fireplace, sitting room, informal bar, dining room, and kitchen. From the lodge, there is a 360-degree view of wilderness.

Rates: $-$$. American Plan. Minimum stay policy during winter and high season in summer.
Credit Cards: None. Personal checks or cash accepted.
Season: Mid-June to early November; late December to early April
Activities: Individualized and nonstructured. In summer, enjoy this wilderness wonderland on foot or by horseback. Daily riding, fishing, pack trips. Experienced riders can ride without a guide once they have demonstrated competence. In winter, guided cross-country tours, snowshoeing. Dogsled excursions can be arranged with advance notice. Five-person rustic log sauna by the ice-cold Gros Ventre River.
Children's Programs: Children are welcome, but they are the sole responsibility of parents. Many guests bring their own nannies.
Dining: Continental cuisine. To discuss menus and food preferences before you arrive, call the ranch chef. Gourmet meals in the winter, even Chinese.
Entertainment: The main lodge has a piano, lots of books and games, and a stereo tape deck with a variety of classical tapes and records. Most guests entertain themselves.
Summary: Rustic and isolated wilderness ranch, very relaxing. Activities tailored to guests. Fluent French, Mandarin and Taiwanese, and some German spoken.

David Ranch, Wyoming

Authentic Western Ranch, Member–Dude Ranchers' Association

The David Ranch is a working cattle operation that was established in 1938 by Milton David. Located on an 8,000-foot mountain plain, the ranch is framed by three mountain ranges—the Wind River Mountains on the east, the Gros Ventre Range on the north, the Wyoming Range on the west—and Beaver Ridge to the south. It is open country with lots of room to breathe. Sublette County, where the ranch is located, is cattle country and is named after one of the early explorers and mountain men, Bill Sublette. Cattle ranches in this part of the country go way back and run thousands of head of cattle. The David Ranch leases its pasture land to some of these ranches and looks after about 750 head. Cattle work begins in late May and runs through September. Hosts Melvin and Toni David have been running the ranch since 1961. They have an excellent horse program and take great pride in teaching their guests about horsemanship. Adults and children are given tremendous appreciation for well-trained cow horses.

Address: Box 5, Dept. K, Daniel, Wyoming 83115
Telephone: (307) 859-8228
Airport: Jackson Hole, private planes to Pinedale
Location: 80 miles southeast of Jackson, 36 miles west of Pinedale off Highway 189
Memberships: Dude Ranchers' Association, Wyoming Outfitters Association
Medical: Pinedale Medical Clinic, 36 miles east
Guest Capacity: 10
Accommodations: The ranch has four log cabins. One large two-room cabin was built in 1982 of native logs and timbers. Trappers cabin is about 20 by 20 feet, with shower. The old School House cabin was rebuilt in 1986 and also has a full shower. The last cabin is the old ranch house with three bedrooms and two bathrooms. The main lodge houses the kitchen, dining room, and living room. Handmade quilts on each bed.
Rates: • $$. American Plan. Minimum one-week stay.

Credit Cards: American Express. Personal checks accepted.
Season: June to mid-September; mid-January to April
Activities: In the summer, there is cattle work and lots of horseback riding, including pack trips to the pristine Wyoming Range. Qualified guests may work with young horses being trained and may even get to do some cutting. If you are really good, Melvin may teach you how to rope. Two ranch ponds are full of rainbow trout and are great for fishing and canoeing. Hiking. In winter, weather permitting, cross-country skiing, snowshoeing, snowmobiling in a secluded winter wonderland. Ranch will only take one group at a time.
Children's Programs: No structured kids' program. Kids usually ride with parents. Children under age 8 not recommended.
Dining: Served in the ranch house, hearty, filling, ranch-style food, weekly cookouts. Everything is cooked from scratch. Ranch specialties include full turkey dinners, steak barbecues, homemade pies. BYOB.
Entertainment: You are on your own. Occasional old Western video movies and sing-alongs.
Summary: Working cattle ranch. Great for experienced riders and particularly for folks who want to learn and work with horses and cattle. Children under 8 not recommended. Both Melvin and Toni are extremely knowledgeable about local history. Superb horses. Jackson Hole for shopping and museums. Hunting in the fall.

Heart 6 Ranch, Wyoming

Authentic Western Ranch, Member–Dude Ranchers' Association

The cover of the Garnicks' Heart 6 Ranch brochure really says it all. "If you are lookin' for a life where the air is sweeter, the folks friendlier, and the gallopin' years slow to a trot, we're playing your tune." Heart 6 Ranch looks out over the Buffalo River Valley and on to the Teton Range. It is just five miles east of the gateway to Grand Teton and Yellowstone national parks. The Buffalo Valley is a lush, wide open valley and offers guests at Heart 6 a variety of ranch activities. The Garnicks are an easygoing Western family who serve down-right friendly hospitality. They love kids, families, and life. Billie and Bill, along with their son Cameron (who has six wonderful children), run the ranch. As Billie says, "We are mellow, easygoing folks who enjoy people who want to get away from it all." If you need a television or telephone in your cabin, this is not the ranch for you.

Address: P.O. Box 70 K, Moran, Wyoming 83013
Telephone: (307) 543-2477, (307) 739-9477, (800) 733-9407
Airport: Jackson
Location: 25 miles northeast of Jackson off Highway 26
Memberships: Dude Ranchers' Association
Medical: Hospital in Jackson
Conference: 50
Guest Capacity: 62
Accommodations: Fourteen comfortable log cabins decorated with western decor. One-, two-, and three-bedrooms sleep up to 12. Almost all have woodstoves or fireplaces. Each day your cabin basket is restocked with fruit, snacks, and juices. Cozy main lodge with large fireplace and picture windows. Laundry facilities.
Rates: • $-$$. American Plan. Family reunion and children's rates available. Snowmobile and hunting rates available on request.
Credit Cards: American Express, MasterCard, Visa, Discover, Diners Club
Season: June to mid-October, mid-December to mid-April. Open Easter.
Activities: In summer, riders sign up each eve-

ning for the ride they would like to take the next day. Morning, afternoon, and all-day rides everyday except Sunday. Ask the Garnicks about the Davis Mountain and Soda Fork rides. You may bring your own horse. Each summer the Garnicks have a forest service/naturalist on staff who teaches guests (kids, too) all about the flora and fauna. Hiking, swimming in heated pool or in the Buffalo River—ask about the "polar bear club." Lots of great fishing in the Buffalo and Snake rivers and in Jackson Lake. Fly-fishing guide and float trips available. Pack trips by prior arrangement. In winter, the Garnicks offer fabulous guided one- to five-day snowmobile trips into Yellowstone.
Children's Programs: Cameron Garnick has 6 children so your kids will always be in good company and well looked after—great for parents and single parents. Ask about their awards programs—wrangler, naturalist, and outdoorsman.
Dining: As Billie says, "It is not high gourmet because there are so many kids." Delicious, hearty ranch fare. Food served mainly banquet-style, some buffet. Prime rib, barbecued ribs, and trout almondine. Thursday night steak ride on Mt. Davis. Weekly breakfast ride and "polar bear swim." Happy hour each evening at 5:00 p.m. in the BYOB Beaver Slide Saloon.
Entertainment: Local guest speakers discuss area topics. Authentic Indian dancing, hayrides, talks by forest service personnel. Jackson Hole weekly rodeo and the best entertainment west of the Black Hills at the Garnicks' Jackson Hole Playhouse in Jackson.
Summary: Great family owned and operated ranch overlooking a lush river valley and to the distant Tetons. Terrific for families and single parents. The Garnicks' son has 6 children who will keep close tabs on your kids. Nothing fancy, just one heck of a guest ranch experience. Fly-fishing and photography workshops available. Pack trips and winter snowmobiling into Yellowstone. German and some French spoken.

Eaton Ranch, Wyoming

Authentic Western Ranch, Member–Dude Ranchers' Association

The Eaton Ranch is the granddaddy of dude ranches. Started in 1879 in North Dakota by three brothers, Howard, Willis, and Alden, the ranch relocated to its present site, 18 miles west of Sheridan, in 1904 to provide "more suitable and varied riding." More than once it has been said that dude ranching was born with the Eatons. Run now by the third and fourth generations of this old line Western family, this 7,000-acre ranch has 150 horses with daily rides for every type of rider. There is no end to the varied terrain. You can hike or ride through open rangeland and wildflower-studded trails that traverse the intricate Big Horn Mountains just west of the ranch. One guest said, "What makes the Eatons' ranch such a success is that it has just enough structure to draw a family together but enough beautiful wide open spaces to give us our reins."

Address: P.O. Box K, Wolf, Wyoming 82844
Telephone: (307) 655-9285 or (307) 655-9552
Airport: Sheridan
Location: 18 miles west of Sheridan
Memberships: Dude Ranchers' Association
Medical: Sheridan Memorial Hospital, 18 miles
Conference: 15 to 20 (June, late August, and September)
Guest Capacity: 125
Accommodations: Guests stay in one-, two-, and three-bedroom cabins suitable for large and small families, couples, and singles. Most have twin beds and all have private baths and gas heat. A few coal stoves. Several have living rooms with fireplaces and real old-fashioned outdoor iceboxes. Most of the original cabins were built by and named after many of the early guests. A post office is on the ranch. Laundry facilities available.
Rates: $$. American Plan. Children age 2 and under free, and other children's rates. Late June through early September, one-week minimum stay.
Credit Cards: Visa, MasterCard. Personal checks preferred.

Season: June to October
Activities: Tremendous riding program every day except Sunday afternoons. Once you know the countryside, you can ride on your own. Pack trips and riding instruction available. Fishing in Wolf Creek, which flows through the ranch, hiking through the beautiful countryside, bird-watching, and swimming in the heated outdoor pool. Golf nearby.
Children's Programs: No specific children's program. Children are the responsibility of their parents. Kids ride both ponies and horses.
Dining: Huge dining room. Hearty Western ranch cooking, barbecues, noon cookouts. BYOB.
Entertainment: Team roping, bingo, weekly country-western dancing at Howard Hall, the ranch's recreation building. Staff vs. guests softball games. Occasional rodeos in town. Books are available in the main ranch house.
Summary: First official dude ranch. The ranch exudes history and intrigue. Wonderful ranch store and post office. Ride on your own. Custer Battlefield, Fort Phil Kearney, polo tournaments in Big Horn, and the Bradford Brinton Museum in Big Horn, 20 miles away.

Eaton Ranch, Wyoming

Flying A Ranch, Wyoming

Authentic Western Ranch, Member–Dude Ranchers'
Association

In 1965, Lowell Hansen went to Wyoming on a hunting trip. He returned with the Flying A Ranch. Today, Lowell Hansen's Flying A offers the discerning adult a distinctive Western vacation. Located 50 miles southeast of Jackson Hole at 8,200 feet, the Flying A is near the base of the Gros Ventre Mountains in a wide open meadow. The drive into the ranch is slow and beautiful. You'll probably pass a hundred or more head of grazing cattle. Almost surrounded by the majestic Wind River Mountain Range, the ranch offers a casual Western atmosphere. You can ride through the quiet seclusion of groves of aspens and pines; fish in the abundant ponds and mountain streams; enjoy the wonder of moose, deer, and elk in their natural habitat; and finally, have your breath taken away by a spectacular sunset on the peaks. Built in 1929, the Flying A is a ranch that has undergone a complete renovation, allowing it to offer tastefully restored and exquisitely comfortable facilities. Under the guidance of Lowell's daughter, Debbie, the Flying A reopened for guests in 1989.

Address: Route 1, Box 7 K, Pinedale, Wyoming 82941
Telephone: (307) 367-2385 (summer); (800) 759-8687 (reservations only.) Don't be surprised if someone answers "Jack Rabbit Tours." Jack Rabbit Tours is owned by the Hansen family.
Airport: Jackson; airport for private planes in Pinedale; ranch has private 6,700-foot dirt airstrip. All pilots must telephone the ranch.
Location: 50 miles southeast of Jackson off Highway 191, 27 miles north of Pinedale
Memberships: Dude Ranchers' Association
Medical: St. John's Hospital in Jackson, medical center in Pinedale, helicopter service available
Guest Capacity: 12
Accommodations: Six completely renovated rustic cabins offer a unique Western experience. Each has a living room, modern bathroom (with a shower or tub/shower combination), full-size kitchen, bedroom, and a fireplace or wood-burn-

ing stove. All have electric heat. Amenities have been crafted with care—oak floors and native pine furniture, Ralph Lauren bedding with flannel sheets, and kitchens with everything from coffee makers to wine glasses. Each cabin has one or two private porches to relax on and enjoy the little stream that passes by, the view of the pond, the grassy meadows, and the Wind River Range.
Rates: • $$. American Plan. Special rates for multiple-week stays. Off-season rates.
Credit Cards: None
Season: Mid-June through September
Activities: Very unstructured. Trout fishing on the ranch property or mountain streams and lakes. Plenty of beautiful high country to be explored by hiking or riding. The riding program is tailored to the guests who are at the ranch. Because the ranch is surrounded by so much country, guests will experience exhilarating vistas and see all kinds of wildlife. Ask Debbie about her favorite rides to Jack Creek, Rock Creek, and Bartlett Canyon. Mountain bikes are also available.
Children's Programs: None. Adults only.
Dining: Three meals served with a casual, yet gourmet, flair. For that added touch, china is used for the daily settings. Weekly barbecues and fish fry. Each evening the ranch serves appetizers in their Gilded Moose Saloon, which overlooks the ranch pond and farther off, the Wind River and Gros Ventre mountain ranges.
Entertainment: Visiting with other guests, lots of R&R. Video library, horseshoes, volleyball, and croquet.
Summary: Small, adults-only guest ranch. Peaceful, remote setting. Do exactly as you like, no structured program. Warm and cozy accommodations with lovely interior decoration touches. An abundance of wildlife, trout fishing, and views of the Wind River Range. Tremendous wildflowers in July and part of August and the beautiful colors of changing aspen trees and abundance of wildlife in the fall. Close to Yellowstone and the Tetons.

Flying A Ranch, Wyoming

Flying A Ranch, Wyoming

Gros Ventre River Ranch, Wyoming

Authentic Western Ranch, Member–Dude Ranchers' Association

At 7,000 feet, Gros Ventre River Ranch is a great place to savor the mighty Tetons, take quiet walks, fish, ride, explore, or just relax and enjoy this year-round paradise. This old ranch has been in the guest ranching business since the early 1950s but was recently bought by Karl and Tina Weber. They have given the place a real face lift but without diminishing the Old West charm. In fact, the Webers and their fine staff have enhanced what was and created a world-class guest ranch. Guests will enjoy a new lodge with views that capture the splendor of the Tetons, magnificent wilderness scenery, and the rushing Gros Ventre River. While preserving the past, the Webers have made it possible for people from around the world to settle in and enjoy rustic elegance and nature at its best.

Address: P.O. Box 151 K, Moose, Wyoming 83012
Telephone: (307) 733-4138; Fax: (307) 733-4272
Airport: Jackson
Location: 18 miles northeast of Jackson
Memberships: Dude Ranchers' Association, Trout Unlimited, American Quarter Horse Association
Medical: St. John's Hospital in Jackson, 18 miles
Conference: 35; May to June, mid-September to October
Guest Capacity: 35
Accommodations: There are nine log cabins, five of them renovated, three new, all winterized, with electric mattress pads. The new cabins have 10-foot ceilings, fireplaces, sliding glass doors that open to decks with views of the Tetons, kitchenettes. Laundry facilities available. The magnificent lodge could well be on the cover of *Architectural Digest* and features two decks overlooking the Gros Ventre River with views to the distant Tetons, a lovely dining room, living room, and bar area. On the lower level is a rec room/conference room that opens out to a landscaped area overlooking the river.

Rates: $$-$$$$. American Plan. Children's and off-season rates.
Credit Cards: None. Cash, personal checks, and traveler's checks accepted.
Season: May through October; December through March, open at Christmas
Activities: In summer, horseback riding with slow, fast, half-day, all-day, and lunch rides. Pack trips into the backcountry. Fly-fishing in the legendary Snake River, Crystal Creek, or Gros Ventre River, which runs through the ranch (some fishing gear available). Ranch swimming hole, canoeing in Slide Lake, hiking, mountain biking at ranch. (Bikes available.) Golf and tennis 10 miles away. Winter activities include cross-country skiing (bring your own gear), snowmobiling, and downhill skiing in Jackson.
Children's Programs: No set programs. Kiddie wrangler. Children under 6 do not go on trail rides.
Dining: How about rack of lamb with mint sauce, salmon with avocado butter, perfectly grilled New York steaks? Breakfast includes steak, eggs, and hash browns. Complimentary wine with dinner. BYOB to guest happy hour.
Entertainment: Cards or quiet music. Weekly rodeos in Jackson, camp fires and marshmallow roasts, weekly cookouts with country-western singing by local entertainers.
Summary: World-class guest ranch. Excellent for small corporate groups. Magnificent view of the Tetons and Gros Ventre River. Grand Teton and Yellowstone National Parks, National Elk Refuge, the town of Jackson Hole, Gros Ventre Slide (largest landslide in United States history) with interesting geology and fossils.

See color photos, page 229

Gros Ventre River Ranch, Wyoming

Gros Ventre River Ranch, Wyoming

H F Bar Ranch, Wyoming

The H F Bar Ranch, one of the great old dude ranches in America, has preserved that old ranch feeling. Since the late 1920s, this 10,000-acre ranch has received distinguished guests from around the world. The ranch is owned and run today by Margi Bliss, along with her husband, Dave, and their daughter, Lily. The H F Bar's horse corrals, barns, and ranch headquarters haven't changed much over the years, nor have the surrounding pastures with native grasses rising to meet the timbered hills leading into the Big Horn Mountains. Margi has tried to keep things as they always have been—and guests keep returning year after year. Don't be surprised if you find out from Margi that they are booked months in advance.

Address: P.O. Box K, Saddlestring, Wyoming 82840
Telephone: (307) 684-2487
Airport: Sheridan
Location: 12 miles northwest of Buffalo, 35 southwest of Sheridan
Memberships: Ducks Unlimited, Rocky Mountain Elk Foundation
Medical: Family Medical Center, Buffalo
Conference: 95, audiovisual equipment available
Guest Capacity: 95
Accommodations: Guests stay in 26 older rustic cabins built from local timber. Each has its own charm, with names like Brookside, Meadowlark, and Round-Up. Each has a living room, fireplace, and one to five bedrooms. Ten are heated with propane or electricity. Most have that days-gone-by feeling. The ranch stream sings outside many of the cabins.
Rates: • $$. American Plan. Children's rates; children under age 3 half-price. The ranch encourages families to bring their own nannies and offers a 50 percent discount for them.
Credit Cards: None. Personal checks or traveler's checks accepted.
Season: Mid-June to mid-September
Activities: It's a relaxed atmosphere, and guests can do as they please. With 150 horses and 10,000 acres, there is plenty of riding for beginners as well as experienced horsemen, who can ride on their own unsupervised. Half-day and all-day rides, pack trips, and riding instruction available. Excellent fishing in the North and South forks of Rock Creek, which runs through the ranch. Swimming in heated pool, hiking, and "sporting clays" shooting (flush, driven pheasant, and double courses). Guns available.
Children's Programs: You can bring your own nanny. Hayrides, craft days, hamburger cookouts. Children's rides called the "Mosquito Fleet." Baby-sitters available with advance notice.
Dining: Each family is assigned its own table. Children may eat earlier and have their own menu. Sunday is lavish country fare, otherwise it's hearty, standard American cuisine with extraordinary desserts. Special diets catered to. BYOB.
Entertainment: Weekly country dancing to live music, roping, and occasional bronc riding at ranch, rodeos in town.
Summary: A great ranch for the entire family and children of all ages. Lots of high-quality family time here. "Sporting clay" shooting, fascinating geology with Indian sites on ranch, Big Horn Polo Club nearby.

High Island Guest Ranch, Wyoming

Authentic Western Ranch, Member–Dude Ranchers' Association

High Island Guest Ranch is the dream of a keen businessman from Massachusetts. Since the mid-1960s, George Nelson has operated a successful steel fabrication plant. When time permits, he goes West to hunt. Not long ago he bought 91,000-acre High Island and began running Hereford and Angus cattle. Soon his Eastern friends were asking if they could help with the cattle work. This is exactly how the guest ranching business was born almost a century ago. High Island has become known for its authentic cattle drives and May branding week. The ranch now takes summer guests and offers week-long stays at the upper ranch to individuals and families for daily riding and pack trips. You will experience a tremendous diversity of terrain, from 5,000-foot prairie to 11,000-foot mountains. This working cattle ranch is beautiful, remote, and rugged, in crisp mountain air, and surrounded by pungent sage. High Island is for those who want to experience the West the way it used to be but with a few modern conveniences.

Address: Box 71 K, Hamilton Dome, Wyoming 82427
Telephone: (307) 867-2374; Fax: (307) 867-2374
Airport: Cody
Location: 35 miles north of Thermopolis, 60 miles south of Cody
Memberships: Dude Ranchers' Association
Medical: Hot Springs Memorial Hospital, Thermopolis
Conference: 30
Guest Capacity: 30
Accommodations: The upper ranch is powered by propane. It has 4 to 5 rustic 4-wall canvas tents, one private cabin, and comfortable lodge rooms furnished with log beds, blanket rugs, and wood stoves. There are men's and women's outhouses and shower houses. Bring your own sleeping bag, towels, soap, and toiletries. The lodge, nestled in the timber, has a broad porch overlooking the camp fire and a trout stream called Rock Creek. The lodge features comfort-

able seating around the stone fireplace and a dining area accented by prints and numerous animal mounts. The lower ranch has a smaller lodge and bunk house, both with electricity.
Rates: • $$. American Plan. Children's rates available.
Credit Cards: MasterCard, American Express
Season: May to October; hunting season, October to November
Activities: Branding week; guests get to participate in all the cattle work including branding, castrating, dehorning, and doctoring calves. Spring and fall cattle drives. A 35-mile drive moving 220 head of cows, calves, and steers to new pastures. This is the real thing. For those who want to experience long days in the saddle, bedrolls, and hearty ranch food cooked over the camp fire on the trail, this will be an adventure you will never forget. Pack trips and unlimited riding packages are also available between the brandings and cattle drives. Fishing for cutthroat trout.
Children's Programs: Children 15 and older go on cattle drives. Children 12 and older are welcome on pack trips and horseback rides. This is not a ranch for children who need a tremendous amount of attention. No planned activities.
Dining: While on the trail, an old-fashioned chuck wagon pulled by two stout draft horses follows with plenty of fresh fruit, vegetables, cold drinks, cowboy coffee or tea. Almost everything is cooked on an open fire. Standard Western fare at the upper and lower lodges. No alcohol is served.
Entertainment: Listening to the call of the coyotes or cows calling for their young. Campfire sing-alongs. Occasional old-time cowboy singer or elk caller. Final barbecue and dance.
Summary: Old-fashioned cattle drives. Bring your own sleeping gear. If George is at the ranch, ask him to get out his banjo. Groups and corporations may rent ranch for entire weeks. (Author's note: If you go on the cattle drive, it is advisable to do a good bit of riding before you arrive.) Inexperienced riders not advised.

Hunter Peak Ranch, Wyoming

Authentic Western Ranch, Member – Dude Ranchers'
Association

Nestled in the pines at the base of Hunter Peak lies Hunter Peak Ranch at an elevation of 6,700 feet. Homesteaded in 1907, the ranch has evolved into a relaxing, family-oriented dude ranch. The hand-hewn lodge offers a warm and cozy atmosphere for guests, whether on vacation, as a family reunion, celebrating a wedding or anniversary, or attending business meetings. The lodge is appointed with Indian rugs, a beautiful cinnamon bear rug, head mounts of elk, deer, and antelope, tack, and antique tools. Hunter Peak is situated near the spectacular Sunlight Basin, Beartooth Plateau, and Yellowstone Park. The Clarksfork River divides the property with 20 acres on one side, home to the buildings and pastures, and 100 acres on the other side for pastures and irrigated hay meadows. A hand-powered trolley provides transportation across the river. The ranch is within the Shoshone National Forest and adjacent to the North Absaroka Wilderness Areas. Pack trips into these areas and Yellowstone Park are a highlight. Louis Cary is the third generation to be running the ranch, with his wife, Shelley, who is from Wisconsin. Guests appreciate Louis's life-long knowledge of the area—he knows a good deal about the local history and geography—and enjoy his tales and stories. One of the nice features of Hunter Peak is the flexible cooking and meal program. Because each cabin has its own kitchen, guests can eat in the ranch dining room or cook their own meals. Most choose to combine the cooking privileges.

Address: Box 1731 K, Painter Route, Cody, Wyoming 82414
Telephone: (307) 587-3711 (summer); (307) 754-5878 (winter)
Airport: Cody, Wyoming; Billings, Montana
Location: 65 miles north of Cody, 120 miles southwest of Billings
Memberships: Dude Ranchers' Association, Wyoming Outfitters Association
Medical: West Park County Hospital, 65 miles
Conference: 25

Guest Capacity: 35
Accommodations: The 30-year-old cabins, one log, the other framed and finished in wood paneling, are wood heated and close to the river. The log cabin sleeps two; the framed cabin sleeps six in two bedrooms. The main lodge was built in 1972 and has 6 rooms with carpeting and steam heat. No TV or telephone. Laundry facilities available.
Rates: $-$$. American and European plans.
Credit Cards: American Express. Traveler's checks, cash, and money orders accepted.
Season: June to mid-December
Activities: Activities are very flexible. Shelley and Louis try to cater to individual desires. Choose from hiking, scenic four-wheel-drive trips, hourly, half-, or all-day horseback rides, pack trips, and fishing for rainbow, cutthroat, brook, and golden trout. Big game hunting.
Children's Programs: No special program. Babysitting and child care available.
Dining: Enjoy home-cooked ranch food with Shelley and Louis, or cook for yourself in your own cabin. BYOB.
Entertainment: Small library in recreation room, also pool table and table tennis. Square dancing, outdoor volleyball, croquet, horseshoe pitching, baseball.
Summary: Small family ranch with flexible cooking and meal program. Sunlight Basin mountain highway called "Chief Joseph Highway," Beartooth Plateau, Daisy and Lulu mining area, Yellowstone National Park. In Cody, Buffalo Bill Historical Center and nightly rodeos.

Lozier's Box R Ranch, Wyoming

Authentic Western Ranch, Member–Dude Ranchers' Association

Since 1900, when the ranch was first homesteaded, the Lozier family has been operating this backcountry ranch, which maintains its pioneer atmosphere today. Modern log cabins are lighted by propane lamps and electric lights, and the delicious sparkling water comes by gravity from nearby springs. Irv and Robin take a maximum of 25 guests and interact with everyone as one large family. The ranch is nestled in a lush valley on the slopes of the Wind River Mountains. The ranch raises 300 head of cattle and 75 horses and mules, which are broken to ride on the ranch. As his father and grandfather did, Irv and his family offer fine guided pack and fall hunting trips. Nature lovers and hunters will be taken into some of the most spectacular, remote, mountainous areas, where big game animals live. The Loziers make no pretensions—they offer old-time Western living and hospitality. Ask about 2- to 10-day vacation packages and adults-only weeks.

Address: Box 100-K, Cora, Wyoming 82925
Telephone: (307) 367-2291 (inquiries); (800) 822-8466 (reservations); (307) For-Hunt (367-4868 for hunting); Fax: (307) 367-4757 (Be sure to put "Box R" on messages)
Airport: Jackson Hole
Location: 23 miles north of Pinedale off State Highway 352, 60 miles southeast of Jackson
Memberships: Dude Ranchers' Association; Wyoming Outfitters Association
Medical: Jackson Hospital, 60 miles
Guest Capacity: 25
Accommodations: Six log cabins and two large multiunit lodges. All have private baths, twin and queen-size beds. Rooms range from single cabins to family suites for up to six. Some lodge rooms have TV and share a recreation room and Jacuzzi. All arriving guests in the suites get a basket of fruit and a complimentary bottle of champagne.
Rates: • $-$$$. American Plan. Vacation packages available (call ranch for details). Three-day minimum stay.

Credit Cards: American Express, Discover
Season: June to September. Hunting August through October.
Activities: Seventy-five horses and mules are the ranch's pride and joy. Daily rides to month-long pack trips. Help with cattle and early morning wrangling of the ranch horse "cavy." Ride to alpine lakes (Rainbow, Lost Camp, Round, and Cliff lakes at 10,800 feet). Pack trips are the ranch's specialty. Trophy trout fishing for rainbows and German browns on the ranch's streams and 11 private ponds. Also, swimming and sunbathing at seven-mile-long Willow Lake with a wonderful sandy beach. Badminton, horseshoes.
Children's Programs: Children under 6 are not encouraged; children 6 and older may ride separately or with adults. Children's fishing pond and swing set.
Dining: Hors d'oeuvres and happy hour each evening. BYOB. Specialize in ranch beef, salads, and pastries. Lots of good food served on long, family-style tables.
Entertainment: Four horseshoe pits, rope "Oscar" the steer, spacious recreation room with table tennis, pool, darts, and indoor games. You are on your own after dinner.
Summary: True working ranch augmented with activities for the ranch guests. If you are coming here to be pampered, read on. Great for the active, outdoor recreationists and their families. Family pack trips and wagon treks to cow camps each Thursday through Saturday. Two-day to 10-day on-ranch and off-ranch vacation packages. Local rodeos and Pinedale Rendezvous. Ranch video available on request. Brochures in English, German, and French.

Lazy L & B Ranch, Wyoming

Authentic Western Ranch, Member–Dude Ranchers' Association

The Lazy L & B Ranch is named for its hosts, Leota and Bernard Didier. This family owned and operated ranch is tucked in a shaded cottonwood valley along the East Fork of the Wind River, adjoining the Wind River Indian Reservation. Colorful red rock hills embrace the cabins and corrals, many of which maintain the original mystique of this 1890 sheep and cattle spread. From its valley seclusion, the ranch stretches up and across five miles of cattle range and rolling hills to its mountain cow camp, where it is bordered by the Shoshone National Forest and Elk Refuge. Here, it has been said, people can ride all the way to Alaska without crossing private lands. If you like to ride and enjoy wonderful western hospitality, give the Didiers a call. As they say, "Where our ranch ends, the wilderness begins."

Address: Route 66 K, Dubois, Wyoming 82513
Telephone: (307) 455-2839
Airport: Jackson Hole or Riverton
Location: 50 miles east of Jackson Hole and Yellowstone entrance, 11 miles east of Dubois to East Fork Road
Memberships: Dude Ranchers' Association
Medical: Doctor in Dubois, hospital in Lander.
Guest Capacity: 30
Accommodations: The main lodge offers warm hospitality, reading, table games, or conversation by the fireplace. Twelve comfortable log cabins are arranged around the central yard or riverside. All have private baths or showers, electric heat and porches with views of the distant Absaroka and Wind River mountain ranges. Some have fireplaces or wood stoves. Knotty pine furnishings give the rooms a western flavor.
Rates: • $. American Plan. Children's, large family, and group rates available. No charge for nannies/baby-sitters.
Credit Cards: American Express. Personal checks accepted.
Season: June to September
Activities: Some guests relax and let the rest of the world go by. Most, though, come here to ride in small groups on 60 good horses. Riding is unlimited as to length and pace. It is dependent only on the rider's wishes and ability. Seasonal roundups, branding, and cattle drives with neighboring ranches. Anglers enjoy spinning or fly-fishing (weekly instruction) in the ranch's stocked ponds, in the East Fork, and in area lakes and streams. Swimming in the solar heated pool with deck. Ask about the scenic mountain overnight and three- to five-day pack trips. Well-equipped lapidary shop to shape antlers and gemstones gathered on the trail. Tennis in Dubois. Float trips in Jackson Hole can be arranged.

Children's Program: Children age 5 and over included in all ranch activities. Families with children under 5 may bring their own baby-sitter/nanny at no charge. Kids particularly enjoy the mountain overnight and the animals in the "petting farm." Young wranglers center with Ping-Pong, fooz-ball, and pocket pool.

Dining: Country cooking with some vegetables and salads fresh from the ranch garden. Children eat dinner with wranglers while parents enjoy a BYOB happy hour. Lunches may be served poolside, on the trail, or tailgate-style at the cow camp. Weekly mountain barbecue and poolside steak fry.

Entertainment: Sing-alongs, campfires, and cowboy poetry. Riflery, horseshoes, billiards, volleyball, hayrides, western movies, and dancing at the ranch or in the local and colorful cowboy bars.

Summary: Wonderful riding in varied and colorful terrain. Located in secluded valley. Cowboy poetry. Museum and art exhibit tours weekly. Nearby Grand Teton and Yellowstone parks. Video available.

Lazy L & B Ranch, Wyoming

Lost Creek Ranch, Wyoming

Lost Creek Ranch, a small, privately owned ranch, is a showplace of the Jackson Hole area. At 7,000 feet, it is surrounded by Grand Teton National Park and Bridger Teton National Forest. The spectacular lodge and cabins, with their expansive views, are furnished with the highest quality decor featuring custom-made furniture and original artwork. The cabin amenities and superb service make a stay at Lost Creek Ranch special for the entire family or for a corporate group. The lodge, with views from each window, entices you to gather with new and old friends in front of the massive stone fireplace, in the elegant yet comfortable and informal dining and living rooms, in the billiard and adult card room, or at the BYOB bar. Mealtime, whether a Dutch-oven cookout on Shadow Mountain, a picnic lunch on your fishing trip, or a gracious dinner in the dining room, is a culinary delight. The activities building offers a recreation room for young people, providing table tennis, bumper pool, and games. Amid the quality and comfort there is a genuine Western atmosphere where attire is casual. The decor, ideal setting, fresh mountain air, and attentive and caring staff create an ambience of luxury with old-fashioned personal service.

Address: P.O. Box 95 K, Moose, Wyoming 83012
Telephone: (307) 733-3435 (summer); (307) 856-6789 (winter); Fax: (307) 733-1954
Airport: Jackson via Denver or Salt Lake City
Location: 20 miles north of Jackson
Awards: Mobil 4 Star, America's Finest Restaurants, Grand Master Chefs of America
Medical: First aid office at ranch; St. John's Hospital in Jackson, 20 miles
Conference: 100. Five rooms: smallest accommodates 20; largest, 100.
Guest Capacity: 60
Accommodations: Guests stay in luxury 2-bedroom/2-bath (with tub and shower) cabins providing queen and single beds in all bedrooms. All cabins have refrigerators with ice makers, coffee and hot chocolate, and electric heat. The living room cabins have queen sleeper sofas, full kitchenettes, and fireplaces. Twice daily maid service. Beds are turned down each evening, and the "mint fairy" always leaves a surprise. Courtesy laundry service.
Rates: • $$$$. Full American Plan including service charge. Corporate group and off-season rates available.
Credit Cards: No
Season: June through September
Activities: Full riding program with personal instruction, heated swimming pool, tennis court, skeet range (bring your own gun), Snake River scenic float trips, cookouts, wagon rides, overnight campouts, guided hiking. Many guests enjoy the Yellowstone and Grand Teton National Park tours. Optional wilderness pack trips, fishing, and golf nearby.
Children's Programs: Under 6 do not ride. Game room, video programs, overnight campout, wagon rides. Baby-sitting available during dinner. Many families bring nannies.
Dining: Outstanding cuisine with two entrées served nightly. Wine list is available. Optional dinner hour for children. Special diets served by prior arrangement.
Entertainment: Weekly cookouts, camp fire sing-alongs, Indian dances, video programs, steer roping, Western swing dance, weekly gymkhana, weekly rodeo in Jackson.
Summary: World-class ranch resort with outstanding service and a panoramic view of the Tetons. Excellent for corporate/business retreats and seminars. Unique to Lost Creek is their AQHA regulation-size barrel racing and roping arena. Historic Western town of Jackson (art galleries, shopping, Western events such as shootouts and stagecoach rides), Yellowstone and Grand Teton national parks, National Elk Refuge. Language interpreters available.

See color photos, pages 216-218

Lost Creek Ranch, Wyoming

Lost Creek Ranch, Wyoming

Moose Head Ranch, Wyoming

Authentic Western Ranch, Member–Dude Ranchers' Association

The Mettlers' Moose Head Ranch is flanked by the spectacular and majestic Teton range. In Jackson Hole at an elevation of 6,870 feet, Moose Head is one of the few privately owned ranches left entirely within the boundaries of Grand Teton National Park. Commanding a sweeping vista of the 13,000-foot peaks of the Teton range, this ranch offers a wonderful Western vacation experience. Eleanor Mettler spends her winters in Florida, where she recharges her batteries before returning to the ranch to entertain guests from around the world all summer long. Moose Head was actually homesteaded back in 1923. As a boy, John Mettler fell in love with Jackson Hole and vowed someday to put down roots there. In 1967, he and his wife, Eleanor, bought Moose Head and have been running it ever since. "We were dudes ourselves so many years that we think we know what people want," says Eleanor. The ranch offers plenty of activities and takes no more than 40 guests at one time. Some guests enjoy it also because it serves as headquarters for things to see and do in the beautiful Jackson Hole area.

Address: P.O. Box 214 K, Moose, Wyoming 83012
Telephone: (307) 733-3141 (summer); (904) 877-1431 (winter)
Airport: Jackson
Location: 26 miles north of Jackson
Memberships: Dude Ranchers' Association
Medical: St. John's Hospital in Jackson
Guest Capacity: 40
Accommodations: Log cabins are scattered among the aspen, cottonwoods, spruce, and pines. Each of the 14 cabins offers privacy and comfort for singles and families (8 with adjoining living rooms). All have private baths with shower and tub, electric heating, and porches. Coffee and tea may be enjoyed in your cabin before breakfast.
Rates: $$$. American Plan.
Credit Cards: None
Season: Mid-June to late August

Activities: Supervised horseback rides go out twice daily with guests divided into small family groups. Families usually ride together on more than 10 different trails. Most are scenic rides. Occasionally, there is some cantering. Don't come here to do a lot of fast riding. There is trout fishing (catch and release) on the property in a series of several excellent stocked ponds with cutthroat trout up to 28 inches. Many fish off the property on the Snake River and other streams. Tennis and golf can be arranged at local clubs, as can scenic and white water float trips on the Snake River.
Children's Programs: Limited children's program. Baby-sitting available. No organized activities.
Dining: Breakfasts cooked to order. Buffet lunch. Dinner with one entrée unless special food is requested. Sunday cookout. BYOB.
Entertainment: As John Mettler used to say, "Do your own thing and relax."
Summary: Small family guest ranch, excellent for family reunions and corporate groups. Superb fly-fishing casting ponds, scenic and white water float trips. Hiking in the Tetons. Within Grand Teton National Park, and near Yellowstone National Park, Jackson, Teton Village, and Jackson rodeo.

The Ranch at Ucross, Wyoming

In a windswept valley in the foothills of northern Wyoming's Big Horn Mountains is The Ranch at Ucross. A road sign reads, "Ucross, Population 25, Elevation 4,085." Here, in the middle of nowhere, past and present meet. The Ranch at Ucross was founded by Apache Corporation and is operated by the Ucross Foundation. It caters to business/conference groups and has a wonderful artist-in-residence program. This attracts gifted artists from around the country who come to share their talents, relax in the peaceful solitude, and grow in their work, whether the visual, literary, or performing arts. This blend of country, business, and art provides an incredible environment for work, relaxation, and intellectual and artistic fulfillment. There is plenty of indoor and outdoor meeting space. A beautiful art gallery in the historic Red Barn, a couple miles down the road, rotates shows every six weeks. Traditional Western activities are offered, along with 5-station sporting clay shooting, big game hunting, and guided fly-fishing. Ucross has an upland game bird hunting preserve, which raises pheasants and Hungarian partridge for the fall/winter hunting season.

Address: 2673 U.S. Highway 14E, Dept. K, Clearmont, Wyoming 82835
Telephone: (800) 447-0194, (307) 737-2281; Fax: (307) 737-2211
Airport: Sheridan, commercial service available
Location: 27 miles southeast of Sheridan off Highway 14
Memberships: Meeting Planners International, International Association of Conference Centers
Medical: Johnson County Memorial Hospital, 17 miles
Conference: 50. Ask for conference brochure packet; large barn loft seats 100 for day meetings or banquets, and the board room seats 8. Private dining room seats 8.
Guest Capacity: 50
Accommodations: A total of 27 rooms. The two-story lodge has been authentically restored and is listed on the National Register of Historic Places. It has retained the warmth and charm of another era with modern conveniences and state-of-the-art amenities. The lawns and grounds are beautifully kept. Cottonwood and Piney Creek lodges next to the pool offer luxurious queen-size bedrooms, some with outside decks, all with amenities packets. Rooms also available in the Homestead house and the new six-bedroom hunting lodge with a beautiful gathering room with fireplace.
Rates: • $$-$$$. American Plan. Children's, corporate, group, and weekly rates available. Inclusive hunting and fishing packages.
Credit Cards: Visa, MasterCard, American Express. Master billings preferred for groups.
Season: Year-round
Activities: In summer, activities are tailored to each group. Let the reservations staff know what your group would like and they will arrange it. Horseback riding, fly-fishing with professional guides, or overnight pack trips. A seasonally heated swimming pool and two tennis courts, tennis racquets available. Three 18-hole golf courses in nearby Buffalo and Sheridan. Fall and winter hunting is particularly popular among corporate groups. Extensive hunting packages from September through February with hunting dogs and guides. Guns and ammunition available (extra charge).
Children's Programs: Ranch does not encourage children.
Dining: Continental and ranch breakfasts. Poolside summer buffets. Full menu. Specialties include steak, seafood, and pheasant. Fresh breads and pastries. Homemade vanilla and hazelnut ice cream. Extensive wine list. Wine and liquor served. Restaurant open to public.
Entertainment: No special evening programs.
Summary: Full-service resort ranch and conference center. No planned activities—best for 3- to 5-day stays. Upland game bird hunting with dogs. Artist-in-residence program.

Paradise Guest Ranch, Wyoming

Authentic Western Ranch, Member–Dude Ranchers' Association

Paradise Guest Ranch offers the traditional dude ranch activities with lots of riding and fishing. Along with this as Jim says, "We keep an ear to the ground as to what modern day guests need and expect." In the 1980s the ranch underwent extensive renovation. It lives up to its name "Paradise" for good reason, as it offers the rustic flavor of the Old West along with many modern conveniences. Dude ranches reflect the personality of the owners and hosts. Jim and Leah Anderson love what they do, and it shows. Once the prized hunting ground for the Sioux, Crow, and Cheyenne Indians, the ranch rests in a mountain valley next to the French and Three Rivers creeks, surrounded by tall forests of evergreens. The peace and tranquillity are only occasionally interrupted by the calls of wildlife or the exuberant sounds of families having fun. It is little wonder that the ranch brand is "FUN."

Address: P.O. Box 790 K, Buffalo, Wyoming 82834
Telephone: (307) 684-7876
Airport: Sheridan, Casper
Location: 46 miles south of Sheridan off Hunter Creek Road, 110 miles north of Casper, 176 miles south of Billings
Memberships: Dude Ranchers' Association, AAA, Mobil
Medical: Johnson County Memorial Hospital in Buffalo, 16 miles
Conference: 50; 2,400-square-foot meeting space off-season only
Guest Capacity: 65
Accommodations: Eighteen luxury one-, two-, and three-bedroom log homes, each with living room, kitchenette, fireplace, central heat, and deck overlooking pine-covered mountains, Fan Rock, and French Creek. All are recently renovated or new. Each day your hot chocolate, tea, and coffee basket will be filled. Nightly turn-down service. Laundry facilities.
Rates: • $$. American Plan. Children's rates and rates for pack trips.
Credit Cards: None. Personal checks accepted.

Season: Late May to October
Activities: Riding is the main activity. Half-day and all-day rides, pack trips. Rides tailored to individual guests; nine rides may go out each day. No more than 7 go out per ride. Walking, trotting, or loping rides. Rides with and without children. Instruction available on one of the 110 horses. Serious fishermen should bring their own equipment. Heated outdoor swimming pool and indoor whirlpool spa.
Children's Programs: Kiddie wrangler/activities counselor for kids 12 and under. Weekly overnight campout. Kids' rodeo in arena—gymkhana events. Children under 6 will be completely looked after if parents desire. These children can be led around the ranch on ponies by parents.
Dining: All you can eat, three meals a day, family-style. Real mule-drawn chuck wagon dinner and cookouts, home-baked breads. Wine available.
Entertainment: Square dancing, talent night, historical talks, sing-alongs, and recreation center. Thursday is parents' night off as kids are camping out; resident artist/musician entertains parents. French Creek Saloon with liquor license.
Summary: Jim and Leah's Paradise Ranch is one of the very top guest ranches in the business. Traditional dude ranch values with modern day convenience. Excellent for small corporate/business groups off-season. Trips to "Hole in the Wall" country, home of some of the West's early outlaws. Mares and mule colts bred and trained. Guided historical trips, general store. Video available.

See color photos, pages 214-215

Paradise Guest Ranch, Wyoming

Rafter Y Ranch, Wyoming

Not far from the Montana border, in north central Wyoming, is the Goodwins' Rafter Y Ranch. Surrounded by pioneer history, this 1,000-acre family-run dude/cattle ranch is nestled in the rolling foothills of the Bighorn Mountains. The Rafter Y leans more toward families and one big family atmosphere. The young college and high school staff exude friendliness and quickly make everyone feel like part of the Goodwin family. When there is cattle and ranch work (stacking hay bales, irrigating, fixing fences) to be done, guests may participate if they choose. Early risers may help wrangle the horses in the morning. You will also see lots of wild game and game birds on the ranch property. The Goodwins have a strict no hunting policy. As Ralph says, "The wildlife we have here are almost part of our family." Nothing fancy about the Rafter Y. Good food, a lovely setting, perhaps most of all a great ranch for families to gather and have fun together. Because of its size, the Goodwins can be very flexible with their program and accommodate the families and couples that are with them.

Address: 323 Wagon Box Road, Drawer K, Banner, Wyoming 82832
Telephone: (307) 683-2221 (summer); (904) 437-6934 (December-March)
Location: 23 miles south of Sheridan, 17 miles north of Buffalo, close to Interstate 90.
Medical: Sheridan Memorial Hospital, 23 miles
Memberships: Nature Conservancy
Guest Capacity: 17
Accommodations: Three old-fashioned green-roofed log cabins sleep a total of seventeen (2 two-bedroom and 1 three-bedroom). The cabins are backdropped by huge cottonwood/willow trees and Little Piney Creek. Each with full baths, living rooms, fireplaces, screened sleeping porches. Housekeeping each morning, nightly turn-down service with a surprise treat. Ice is delivered to cabins each afternoon. For the adventuresome there is also a sheepherder's wagon; kids and teenagers love this.

Rates: • $. American Plan, minimum of four days. Seven-day group, family reunion, and polo rates available. Nanny rates, too.
Credit Cards: None. Cash, personal checks, or traveler's checks accepted.
Season: Early July through August
Activities: Riding is the main activity every day except Sunday. Most guests ride each morning with a wrangler. Afternoons are usually filled with other nonriding activities: napping, reading, or visiting local historical sites are favorites. Good selection of ranch horses. As the Goodwins say, "Our horses are all speeds." Guests may help with ranch chores, play tennis, swim in stream-fed swimming hole, fish, or play golf nearby.
Children's Programs: No separate activities program. Families usually interact together. Children are the responsibility of their parents. Bring a nanny if you wish.
Dining: The Goodwins are very proud of their food. Buffet-style, one sitting; second helpings always available. Hilary's famous Rafter Y Sunday brunch. Occasional evening hors d'oeuvres and barbecues at Lake De Smet. Special diets arranged. BYOB.
Entertainment: Informal. Spontaneous softball, volleyball, soccer, and horseshoe games. Occasional sing-alongs. Local rodeos.
Summary: Wonderful small family owned and operated dude/cattle ranch offering a flexible schedule and individual attention. Very high percentage of return guests. Great for families and couples. Some ranch and cattle work. Sunday afternoon Big Horn Polo matches (this is attracting international players). Nearby equestrian center.

Rafter Y Ranch, Wyoming

Rafter Y Ranch, Wyoming

Red Rock Ranch, Wyoming

Authentic Western Ranch, Member–Dude Ranchers' Association

Nestled in a secluded valley high on the eastern slope of Jackson Hole's spectacular mountain country is Red Rock Ranch. This operating old-time cattle ranch is in the heart of the Gros Ventre Mountains and offers some of the best guest ranching in the business. With a first-rate string of horses, wranglers will take you through spectacular country where you are likely to see antelope, coyotes, moose, elk, deer, bald eagles, hawks, and mountain sheep. Nature lovers and photography buffs will have a field day. Of note are the October cattle roundup and weekly cattle work. Fly-fishermen will enjoy the stocked ranch pond and Crystal Creek, a fly-fishing, catch-and-release stream. Ask about the Crystal Creek Red Rock Ranch hand-tied flies.

Address: P.O. Box 9 K, Kelly, Wyoming 83011
Telephone: (307) 733-6288 (summer)
Airport: Jackson
Location: 30 miles northeast of Jackson
Memberships: Dude Ranchers' Association
Medical: St. John's Hospital, Jackson
Conference: 30, early June and September
Guest Capacity: 30
Accommodations: There are nine log cabins with electric heat and wood stoves, named after famous Indian tribes. The cabins were built in the 1950s, and each has a living room and twin and queen-size beds. Carpeting throughout with some Indian rugs. Small refrigerator in each unit and porches.
Rates: • $$. American Plan, includes all activities except pack trips and river trips. Group and off-season rates.
Credit Cards: None. Personal checks or cash accepted.
Season: June through mid-October
Activities: Some of the most unspoiled riding in the country. Morning, afternoon, and all-day rides. Monday morning orientation rides in arena. Slow, medium, and fast (if you past the test) rides. Ask Ken about the White Canyon ride. Four- to five-day pack trips into the Gros Ventre Wilderness. Swimming in heated pool, 8-person hot tub, hiking, and plenty of relaxing. River trips can be arranged. Fly-fishing in mountain streams and lakes for cutthroat trout, which the ranch will cook for you.
Children's Programs: Wranglers take kids on day rides looking for fossils, wading in creeks, or searching for cattle. Every Tuesday they take an overnight pack trip. Baby-sitters are not available. Age limit for riding is 6 years and older.
Dining: Home-raised beef, fresh baked bread. Some of the chefs have come from culinary institutes. Children eat before adults (optional). BYOB.
Entertainment: Hors d'oeuvres and drinks (BYOB) before dinner. Sing-alongs, weekly rodeo in Jackson, pickle ball (mini-tennis) court.
Summary: Fun, family-oriented guest ranch with lots of camaraderie. Unspoiled wilderness, plenty of horseback riding. Return guests rarely leave the ranch once they arrive. Laid-back, relaxing atmosphere. Working cattle ranch, 4- to 5-day pack trips, cattle roundup in spring and fall, horse-drawn surrey rides. Small ranch store with excellent cowboy hats. Grand Teton National Park, Yellowstone National Park, Snake River, Elk Refuge.

See color photos, page 204

Rimrock Ranch, Wyoming

Authentic Western Ranch, Member–Dude Ranchers' Association

The Rimrock Ranch is named after the magnificent rock formations surrounding the property. It is just 26 miles from Yellowstone National Park's east entrance and at the edge of the Shoshone National Forest. Your hosts, Glenn and Alice Fales, are natives of Wyoming and have been receiving guests since the late 1950s. Alice grew up on a ranch, and Glenn has spent most of his life as a cowboy. He is a superb guide, dude rancher, outfitter, and most of all, a tremendous human being. The ranch is one mile from the North Fork of the Shoshone River and near Buffalo Bill Lake—both of which offer superb fishing. The ranch kitchen will prepare the 2- to 3-pound trout that guests catch. Rimrock has a fine string of about 100 horses. Glenn's 5- to 10-day pack trips are famous, and guests come from all over the world. The log ranch house is a gathering spot at the end of the day and exudes rustic warmth and hospitality. Many like to just stretch out here and enjoy its history while reading a favorite book. Glenn and Alice are modest people and won't tell you they have hosted some of the world's VIPs. They run one of the best outfits in the business.

Address: 2728 North Fork Road, Dept. K, Cody, Wyoming 82414
Telephone: (307) 587-3970
Airport: Cody, Wyoming, or Billings, Montana
Location: 26 miles west of Cody
Memberships: Dude Ranchers' Association, Wyoming Outfitters Association
Medical: Cody Hospital, 26 miles
Guest Capacity: 32
Accommodations: Each of the nine log cabins (two of which can accommodate up to 8 people) is furnished with Western decor. Some have stone fireplaces. All have private baths with hot and cold running water. Each has a porch; all but one have carpeting. Heated with gas. Laundry facilities.
Rates: $-$$. American Plan. Pack trip rates available.
Credit Cards: None. Personal checks accepted.

Season: Last week in May through August. Always Sunday-Sunday.
Activities: All-day and half-day trail rides. Glenn says, "Guests should learn how to ride at three gaits—walk, trot, and canter." Plenty of loping for those riders who can handle it. Separate from ranch activities are horse pack trips into Yellowstone Park and Teton and Shoshone national forests. Fishing, swimming, and weekly river rafting in the North Fork of the Shoshone River.
Children's Programs: No special programs. Children's fishing pond. Children's rides. Babysitting available.
Dining: On or off the trail, healthy and hearty ranch cooking. Prime rib is a specialty. Special diets can be arranged.
Entertainment: Cookouts, sing-alongs, and singing cowboys several times a week. Shuffleboard, table tennis, cards, and billiards in the recreation room with lots of hanging memorabilia. Cody nightly rodeo and square dancing.
Summary: Glenn and Alice and their Rimrock Ranch are tops! They exemplify what the true meaning and spirit of dude ranching is all about. Excellent wilderness pack trips. Nearby attractions include Buffalo Bill Historical Center, July Fourth Buffalo Bill Stampede. Because Yellowstone National Park is so close, Glenn and Alice take guests on a tour through the park.

See color photos, page 187

R Lazy S Ranch, Wyoming

Authentic Western Ranch, Member–Dude Ranchers' Association

Beautiful scenery, a friendly staff, excellent food, and Western hospitality make the R Lazy S one of the great guest ranches in America today. Since 1947, the McConaughy family has operated this wonderful ranch, almost at the foot of the majestic Tetons, bordering Grand Teton National Park. In 1975, Howard and Cara Stirn purchased the McConaughys' interest. Since then, both the Stirns and the McConaughys have been hosts to families from all over. While it is close to Jackson and the world-class ski resort at Teton Village, the ranch still maintains its privacy and solitude. Being so close and yet so far gives guests many options for activities and excursions. If you plan to try to do everything, better stay three to four weeks. By the end of one week, you will have only begun. Regardless of how long you stay, you will enjoy the friendly spirit and the magnificent mountain scenery.

Address: Box 308 K, Teton Village, Wyoming 83025
Telephone: (307) 733-2655
Airport: Jackson
Location: 13 miles northwest of the town of Jackson, one mile north of Teton Village
Memberships: Dude Ranchers' Association
Medical: St. John's Hospital, 13 miles
Guest Capacity: 45
Accommodations: There are 12 beautifully modernized one-, two-, and three-bedroom log cabins, all with electric blankets and fabulous views, scattered beautifully around the ranch property among the aspen trees. All have one or two bathrooms, depending on size, some have living rooms; all have electric heaters or wood-burning stoves and lovely hanging baskets with colorful flowers. There are two teen dorms (boys and girls) that sleep 4 in bunk beds; each has a bathroom. The main lodge, with its cathedral ceilings, is a favorite gathering place at day's end. Laundry facilities available.
Rates: $$. American Plan. Minimum one-week stay.

Credit Cards: None. Personal checks accepted.
Season: Mid-June through September, adults-only after Labor Day
Activities: The nearby Snake River (mile from ranch buildings) and neighboring Teton Mountain trails offer many activities. The ranch offers a full riding program. Half-day and all-day rides with picnic lunches. No riding on Sundays. Pack trips and riding instruction available. An extensive fly-fishing program is available. Claire and Bob's daughter and son-in-law are partners in Westbank Anglers, a first-rate guide and fly-fishing shop 3 miles from the ranch. Fishing on the Snake, South Fork, Green, and North Fork rivers and streams, lakes, and stocked ranch pond. Hiking, swimming in ranch swimming hole, or tubing. River rafting, tennis, and golf can be arranged nearby. Waterskiing or scenic boat rides once a week on Jackson Lake.
Children's Programs: The ranch is unable to accommodate children under 6 years of age. Kiddie wranglers with programs for kids and teenagers. Children eat together in own dining room. Gymkhanas.
Dining: The lovely dining room looks out to meadows and the Tetons beyond. Family-and buffet-style food. Ranch hosts Sunday welcome happy hour. Weekly cookouts. BYOB.
Entertainment: Kids' marshmallow roasts, hayrides to cookouts and around the ranch. Jackson Rodeo, volleyball, softball, and horseshoes. Nature walk and fishing clinic.
Summary: Wonderful family ranch. Spectacular setting looking to the Tetons. Adults only after Labor Day for peak fly-fishing season. R Lazy S is great for single parents and their children. Ask the ranch about their R Lazy S cookbook. Shopping, rodeo, and melodrama in town of Jackson. Teton Village with its mountain tram, Yellowstone National Park.

Savery Creek Thoroughbred Ranch, Wyoming

Savery Creek Thoroughbred Ranch is the home of Joyce Saer and caters to no more than two families at a time. Joyce is a soft-spoken woman who has four grown children—a physician, a veterinarian, a navy flyer, and a daughter in real estate. She has spent much of her life in Europe, particularly in Spain, is an outstanding horse-woman and trainer of winning thoroughbreds—and she has the trophies to prove it. Guests stay with Joyce in her house. The ranch is in one of the last unspoiled, untouristy areas in Wyoming, where cattle and sheep still graze, streams have not been dammed, air is not polluted, wildlife has not been eliminated, and industry and man have not taken over. The name "Wyoming," an Indian word meaning "mountains and valleys alternating," could have originated in the Savery Valley. Savery Creek Thoroughbred Ranch is for experienced English and Western riders wishing to savor the Old West in total privacy, low-key, unregimented, Western comfort, with lots of warmth and hospitality.

Address: Box 24 K, Savery, Wyoming 82332
Telephone: (307) 383-7840
Airport: Steamboat Springs, Colorado. Ranch has private, dirt airstrip (call for information). Paved landing field at Dixon 11 miles.
Location: 70 miles south of Rawlins, 60 miles north of Craig, 280 miles from Denver
Medical: Craig Hospital, 60 miles; clinic at Baggs, 20 miles.
Guest Capacity: 6+
Accommodations: The house is beside Savery Creek in cottonwood trees facing the beautiful Savery Valley. There are three guest bedrooms upstairs, attractively furnished with antiques. One is spacious, overlooking the creek, with fireplace, king-size four-poster bed, sitting area, and private bath and entry. The other two bedrooms have queen-size beds and share a bathroom. For the adventurous, there are two covered wagons.
Rates: • $$. American Plan. Rates on request. Special rates for children.

Credit Cards: American Express. Personal checks and traveler's checks accepted.
Season: May to October; winter months by special arrangement
Activities: This is a riding ranch with 1 to 3 horses per guest. The horses are exceptional. It is possible to ride in three directions without seeing another person. Savery Creek is best-suited for intermediate and advanced riders and caters to expert riders especially. If there is a beginner rider in the family, be sure to talk with Joyce about her program. Western and English saddles, jumping, and jumping lessons available. Opportunity to compete in Area IX combined training events and school your own horse and/or yourself for cross-country and through water. Fly-fishing on Savery Creek, the Little Snake, or on Hog Park Reservoir. Tennis, swimming in Savery Creek, hiking, badminton, and seasonal hunting.
Children's Programs: Very small children allowed by special arrangement only. The ranch is best-suited for children who can ride. There are no facilities for babies and toddlers.
Dining: Superb meals, specializing in leg of lamb, sherry chicken, green salads, fresh fruit, home-grown vegetables, cookouts. Fine chardonnays and cabernets served.
Entertainment: Cowboys practice once a week at Dixon Arena; evening conversation and bridge; large selection of books, classical music, newspapers and magazines including *The New Yorker* and *Wall Street Journal*.
Summary: Large ranch with small intimate accommodations offering unlimited riding opportunities catering to experienced riders (both English and Western) and a very limited number of guests. Experts in their fields (both professional and creative) find Savery Creek particularly enjoyable. Superb cuisine, Red Desert riding trip, individualized service. Nearby Savery Museum, Encampment Museum, old mining towns, Steamboat Springs, Overland Trail, wildflowers, fossils and wildlife, Medicine Bow National Forest. Spanish and some French spoken.

Seven D Ranch, Wyoming

Authentic Western Ranch, Member–Dude Ranchers' Association

The Seven D Ranch is a cozy haven in the midst of a magnificent wilderness. It was bought in the late 1950s by Dewey and Lee Dominick, a surgeon and his wife. Today, the family tradition continues under their son and daughter-in-law, Marshall and Jane. Mrs. Dominick still plays an active role, welcoming new and old friends to her family ranch. The ranch is in the remote and beautiful Sunlight Basin deep within Shoshone National Forest. It is surrounded by the Absaroka Mountains and has vast pastures where the horses are turned out each night to play and graze. The Seven D appeals to all ages. For those who wish to relax, the ranch offers the peace of a mountain hideaway. Those with more energy may want to take a leisurely morning or afternoon ride, cast for trout, or hike into the Absaroka Wilderness. And those with more get-up-and-go, may enjoy a full day of riding, fishing, or a wilderness pack trip into Yellowstone Park. Most of all there is a wonderful atmosphere of camaraderie, laughter, and energetic participation. If you have ever wondered where Marlboro Country is, many of the photographs were taken at the Seven D.

Address: P.O. Box 100 K, Cody, Wyoming 82414
Telephone : (307) 587-3997 (summer); (307) 587-9885 (winter)
Airport: Cody
Location: 50 miles northwest of Cody via Chief Joseph Scenic Highway (Hwy. 296), and Sunlight Basin Road, a beautiful 1 hour drive.
Memberships: Dude Ranchers' Association
Medical: Cody Hospital
Conference: 35
Guest Capacity: 35
Accommodations: Twelve rustically comfortable cabins are spaced apart in a beautiful aspen grove and have names like Trapper, Aspen, Buffalo, Waldorf, and the Fireplace cabin. Cabins vary from one to four bedrooms each, with private baths and wood stoves. Fire starter and wood provided. Guests enjoy these stoves during delightfully cool summer evenings. Laundry facilities available.

Rates: • $$. American Plan. Children's and off-season rates available. Pack trip and hunting rates available.
Credit Cards: None. Personal checks or cash accepted.
Season: Early June through September; fall hunting
Activities: Eighty excellent riding horses. Rides every day except Sunday. Your choice of long, short, half-day, or all-day rides. Riders are accompanied by experienced wranglers on beautiful and varied trails. Instruction available. Two- to ten-day horse pack trips by advance arrangement into the North Absaroka Wilderness and Yellowstone Park for groups of 6 or fewer. This has been a trip of a lifetime for many. Fishing on and off the property, four-wheel-drive trips, trap shooting (guns provided), hiking, and fall hunting trips may be arranged. Volleyball, soccer, and baseball. Float trips available in Cody.
Children's Programs: Day care for infants; counselors for children age 5 to age 12. Pony rides for children under age 5.
Dining: Excellent ranch food, topped only by the beautiful old ranch dining room. Marshall's famous Chilean-style lamb roast, ranch-raised beef. Special diets catered to with advance notice. BYOB.
Entertainment: Books at the main lodge. Recreation room with piano, table tennis, billiards, square dancing with live caller. Gymkhanas, horseshoes. Some occasionally go to the rodeos in Cody.
Summary: The Seven D is one of the great old guest ranches. The Dominick family exudes warmth and plenty of Western hospitality. Excellent wilderness pack trips. September is adults-only month. Health, birding, and photography workshops.

Spear-O-Wigwam Ranch, Wyoming

Authentic Western Ranch, Member–Dude Ranchers' Association

Arrival at Spear-O-Wigwam by auto is picture perfect! As you peer through the log-framed entrance supporting the oversized cast iron ranch brand, it may seem that you are on a dirt runway and about to take off into the wild blue yonder. Fear not. It is only the dirt road leading straight to the ranch. As your car rumbles over the cattle guard, be prepared. You are about to take off on a tremendous ranch vacation. Spear-O-Wigwam was established in the early 1920s by the Willis Spear family, who entertained many Eastern friends. An early guest was Ernest Hemingway who, in 1928, completed *A Farewell to Arms* at the ranch. Hemingway was overheard saying one day, "There are two places I love, Africa and Wyoming." The ranch is southwest of Sheridan, in the Big Horn National Forest near the Cloud Peak Primitive Area. At 8,300 feet, the air is clear, mountain water pure, summer days cool, and the scenery spectacular. Write or call for the brochure.

Address: Box 1081 K, Sheridan, Wyoming 82801
Telephone: (307) 674-4496 (summer); (307) 672-0002 (winter). No telephone at the ranch, only two-way radio.
Airport: Sheridan via Denver
Location: 30 miles southwest of Sheridan
Medical: Sheridan Memorial Hospital, 30 miles
Memberships: Dude Ranchers' Association
Conference: 32
Guest Capacity: 32
Accommodations: Guests stay in seven old-fashioned (generate own electricity), beautiful log cabins with hardwood floors, one to four bedrooms each, all with private baths, heat, and Western decor. Cabins are known by such names as Hemingway, Porcupine, Chipmunk, and Bears Den, to name a few. The main lodge has a huge fireplace, library, bar, and dining room. Laundry facilities available.
Rates: $-$$. American Plan. Children's, group, and off-season rates available.
Credit Cards: None

Season: Mid-June to mid-September. Winter by reservation only and accessible only by snowmobile or snowcat.
Activities: Informal program. Riding every day—your choice of half-day or all-day rides. Families with the ability may ride on their own. Pack trips to remote Beaver Lake, with its own permanent tent camp. Trout fishing in streams or lakes (flies and licenses available), kiddie pond, excellent hiking and nature photography, weekly picnic rides, breakfast cookouts, and evening barbecues. Swimming and boating on nearby Park reservoir.
Children's Programs: No separate program. Families are encouraged to participate as families. Baby-sitters can be arranged for small children. Some families bring their own baby-sitters. Cribs available.
Dining: Lovely, old-fashioned dining. Meals served family-style at one long table seating 32. Excellent Western cuisine featuring spaghetti, prime rib, shrimp, fried chicken, home-baked breads, and desserts. BYOB.
Entertainment: Rodeos in Sheridan and Buffalo, weekly polo in Big Horn, 20 miles away. Happy hour, spectacular sunsets, recreation room with pool table, table tennis, and cards; occasional songfest. No television. Jim may yodel or sing a few songs.
Summary: The ranch has a magnificent setting. Abundant wildlife and wildflowers of the Big Horn Mountains. Pets are allowed, but arrangements must be made in advance. Several nearby battlefields and historic sites in the Sheridan and Buffalo areas.

Trail Creek Ranch, Wyoming

Authentic Western Ranch, Member–Dude Ranchers' Association

Trail Creek Ranch is very special to me. It is the ranch where my parents took my sister and me as young children. It is here that a seed was planted which blossomed into my love for this incredible way of life. I am proud to say that Trail Creek Ranch is responsible for this guidebook. Back in the 1940s, a young Olympic skier named Betty Woolsey bought a rundown ranch at the foot of Teton Pass, 8 miles from Jackson. With her tenacity and tremendous spirit, Betty transformed the ranch into a gold mine of charm. It is one of the prettiest family-oriented ranches in the country and offers sincere Western hospitality. To the east, the property consists of a lush green hay meadow; the rest is towering timber with many bridle trails and crystal clear streams, bordered by national forest. Trail Creek is a working ranch, raising hay that supports a fine string of horses and pack mules. Daily riding and overnight pack trips are the main activities. Betty has touched many lives over the years. Together with her exceptional staff, she continues to greet guests, make new friends, and offer the very best in the West.

Address: P.O. Box 10 K, Wilson, Wyoming 83014
Telephone: (307) 733-2610
Airport: Jackson via Salt Lake City or Denver
Location: 2 miles west of Wilson, 8 miles west of Jackson
Memberships: Dude Ranchers' Association
Medical: St. John's Hospital, Jackson
Guest Capacity: 25 (summer); 10-12 (winter)
Accommodations: The main lodge and cabins overlook the meadow and beyond to Sleeping Indian, a beautiful mountain in the Gros Ventre Range. The cabins, with names like The Ritz (a large family cabin with a loft), Willi's, The Suite, and The Compound, are interspersed among aspens and pines. All have full baths. There are several rooms in the main house/lodge and separate boys' and girls' bunk houses for teenagers.
Rates: • $-$$. American Plan. Everything included except pack trips.
Credit Cards: None. Personal checks accepted.

Season: Mid-June to mid-September (summer); February and March (winter)
Activities: One of the best riding programs in the country. In summer, riding is the only scheduled activity. All rides, fast, medium, and slow, go out in groups of 4 to 5 twice a day. There are also all-day luncheon rides to Ski Lake and Grand Teton Park. Pack trips are special at Trail Creek, with families or groups going out for one- to ten-day trips into the high country (arranged in advance.) Fishing in the Snake River, nearby lakes, and ranch pond. Canoeing, hiking, swimming in heated pool. River rafting with local outfitter. In winter, Betty takes no more than 10 to 12 guests, who enjoy cross-country and nearby downhill skiing.
Children's Programs: No formal program, but kids have the times of their lives. Kids may ride together if they wish. Parents with young children are encouraged to bring their own babysitter or nanny. The ranch has no baby-sitting program.
Dining: A ranch garden supplies lettuce, asparagus, and herbs for family meals of roast beef, pork chops, baked ham, roast chicken, fish, soups, and salads. BYOB.
Entertainment: Guests are pretty much on their own. Many go to the Stagecoach Bar in Wilson for country-western dancing or into Jackson. Jackson rodeo three times a week.
Summary: One of the all-time great family-oriented guest ranches, second to none. Lovely setting and great people. The Tetons, Yellowstone National Park, Jackson, National Elk Refuge. Be sure to buy a copy of Betty's *Off the Beaten Path*. French and German spoken.

See color photo, page 242

Trail Creek Ranch, Wyoming

Triangle X Ranch, Wyoming

Authentic Western Ranch, Member–Dude Ranchers' Association

Four generations of Turners have run this spectacular high country guest ranch. Known for its beauty, hospitality, and caring spirit, Triangle X has just about everything one could ask for, including a million-dollar view. Just outside Moose, Triangle X is situated on the eastern slope of Jackson Hole and has panoramic views of the awesome Teton Range and Snake River Valley. The ranch was established in 1926 by Mr. Turner, Sr., as a cattle and hunting ranch. Today, the Turner family runs a first-rate operation. Their repeat business (one guest has been coming for over 40 years) proves it. One must book almost a year in advance. Some of the ranch's unique features are the river rafting program and its well-supervised Little Wrangler program for kids 5 to 12 and under. This program makes the Triangle X a perfect family stay.

Address: Star Route Box 120K, Moose, Wyoming 83012
Telephone: (307) 733-2183
Airport: Jackson
Location: 25 miles north of Jackson
Memberships: Dude Ranchers' Association, Wyoming Outfitters Association
Medical: St. John's Hospital in Jackson
Conference: 50, off-season only
Guest Capacity: 75
Accommodations: Guests stay in one-, two-, or three-bedroom log cabins with private baths, warm wool blankets, and porches. Cabins are very clean (with polished wood floors), comfortable, and ranch cozy. Laundry facilities available. Small ranch gift shop with hats, Indian jewelry, and river rafting desk.
Rates: • $-$$. American Plan, one-week minimum stay
Credit Cards: None. Personal checks or traveler's checks accepted.
Season: May to November; January to April
Activities: In summer, riders enjoy tremendous vistas and a variety of trails to the tops of timbered mountains, through wildflower meadows, over sagebrush, and along the Snake River. Breakfast rides and weekly Dutch oven suppers. Scenic, medium, and faster rides. Hiking, tremendous Snake River rafting program, trout fishing, excellent hunting during the fall for elk, moose, and deer. Wilderness pack trips into the high country. In winter, cross-country skiing across the vast parklands, some groomed trails. Snowmobiling on adjacent national forest.
Children's Programs: Kiddie wrangler with riding lessons, arts, crafts, and swimming trips to the lakes. Children under 5 do not ride.
Dining: Meals are hearty and delicious, served family-style in a wonderful dining room with commanding views overlooking the Tetons. Children dine separately.
Entertainment: Camp fires with old-fashioned sing-alongs, Western guitar music, square dancing, rodeos in Jackson, weekly slide shows of local history.
Summary: Magnificent views of the Grand Tetons, wonderful family-oriented ranch. Great Snake River raft trips. Snowmobiling and sleigh rides in winter. Teton National Park, Chapel of Transfiguration, Yellowstone National Park, National Elk Refuge, Jackson Hole, and Jackson Lake.

TX Ranch, Wyoming

The TX Ranch on the Wyoming-Montana border is a real cattle ranch that takes dudes. It is for those who wish to really experience the Old West and know what being saddle sore means. After a week with the Tillett family (Lloyd, Abbie, and their children) at one of their four cow camps, you will be able to say to anyone that you did it—the real way with the right stuff. You were a cowboy! If you have always wanted to sleep under the stars and shower with water that was heated on the camp fire, poured into a bag that leaks down on you while you soap up, then get on the phone and reserve a spot. Better hurry, though. Abbie gets calls from all over. If you really get into the action, better help yourself to a container of Copenhagen tobacco. It goes in your shirt pocket. Two things to remember: just a pinch between cheek and gum, and should you swallow the juice, as one cowboy told me, "Don't worry, you'll never have any worms." As they say at the TX, "You will not just visit the West—you'll live it!"

Address: P.O. Box 453 K, Lovell, Wyoming 82431
Telephone: (406) 484-2583
Airport: Billings
Location: 60 miles south of Billings, 2 hours by car. Call ranch for details—you will not find the ranch on your own.
Medical: Deaconess Hospital in Billings; emergency helicopter service available
Guest Capacity: 20
Accommodations: On arrival, you will be taken to one of the four cow camps. For the length of your stay, you will live in a tent. You will experience one of the greatest feelings of your life—falling asleep soon after you've eaten, listening to the coyotes' lullaby. The ranch provides everything but sleeping bag and personal gear. Ranch will send you a full packing check list. It would be a good idea if you brought a pair of spurs.
Rates: • $. American Plan. Children's rates available.
Credit Cards: American Express
Season: April through August

Activities: Remember the song from the television series *Rawhide*? "Keep them rollin', rollin'. . ." Activities revolve totally around cattle work. Depending on the time of the year, guests get involved in herding, branding, dehorning, castrating, doctoring, gathering strays, and trailing cattle to new pastures.
Children's Programs: Children are welcome. Children under age 6 not advised. Several of the Tilletts' grandchildren are always around, so children always feel at home. Parents should keep in mind the TX is not for all children.
Dining: Food has never tasted so good! After a long day in the saddle, you will savor all the hearty food cooked over the camp fire. Big cowboy breakfasts; lunch varies (may be a sandwich or big meal). Roast turkey, steak, ham, and mashed potatoes, cakes, apple or banana cream pies, and, yes, to top it all off, cowboy coffee at the nightly bonfire. BYOB.
Entertainment: Most guests are so wonderfully worn out that they drop off to sleep long before finishing all their cowboy coffee.
Summary: This is an authentic working ranch. This is a working vacation experience. Plenty of cattle work, lots of riding, and great hosts. (Author's note: You should be in good physical condition and should have put some riding time in before you arrive.)

Black Cat Guest Ranch, Alberta, Canada

The Black Cat Guest Ranch is hidden in the forest on the eastern slopes of the Canadian Rocky Mountains and Jasper National Park. Jerry and Mary Bond and their daughter and son-in-law, Amber and Perry Hayward, have been hosting guests since 1970. People come from around the world to stay in the beautifully rustic, 2-story, 16-room, cedar-sided lodge; each room looks out to the spectacular Rockies. The lodge is the center of attraction, next to the surrounding wilderness area, and features many comforts. Among them are a large living room with picture windows, fireplace, piano, comfortable chairs, and well-stocked library, all in a warm, home-like atmosphere. Outside lies a breathtaking wilderness in which an abundance of wildlife can be seen. The Black Cat Ranch is the perfect place for adults and older children to relax and escape from the hectic pace of everyday life to the seclusion of a mountain wilderness ranch.

Address: Box 6267 K, Hinton, Alberta, Canada T7V 1X6
Telephone: (403) 865-3084
Airport: Edmonton International, 3 hours; Hinton-Jasper air strip for private airplanes
Location: 350 miles west of Edmonton, 5 hours northwest of Calgary, 15 miles northwest of Hinton off Highway 40 North.
Medical: Hinton Hospital, 20 minutes
Memberships: Alberta Guest Ranch Association
Conference: 30, September through May only
Guest Capacity: 40
Accommodations: The lodge is modern but rustic looking. Each guest room is carpeted and has a fully equipped bath. All the rooms open to a balcony overlooking the front range of the Rockies. Motel-like with a Western twist.
Rates: $. American Plan. Children's, senior citizens', and special rates available.
Credit Cards: Visa, MasterCard. Personal checks accepted.
Season: Year-round. Open Thanksgiving, New Year's, and Easter.

Activities: In summer, guided trail rides, superb marked hiking trails, swimming, canoeing and fishing on Jarvis Lake (15 miles) or down the Athabasca River (5 miles), cookouts. In winter, hiking and riding trails become terrific cross-country ski trails, which are machine-groomed single track. Night skiing and excellent double track trails at Athabasca Nordic Center nearby. Guests find Christmas and New Year's a memorable experience. Both winter and summer, enjoy the outdoor hot tub.
Children's Programs: The ranch is oriented to adults and older children. No baby-sitting or children's program.
Dining: Home-cooked, family-style meals with fresh bread and desserts daily. Vegetarian and special diets on request. BYOB.
Entertainment: Lounge with dart board and other games. In the fall the ranch features "murder mystery weekends."
Summary: Complete home-style family comfort in the wilderness. The only sounds you may hear are the horse bells. Spring and fall art workshops—watercolor, photography, creative writing. Elderhostel programs for seniors. Spectacular drive to Columbia Ice Field and Jasper National Park.

Brewster's Kananaskis Guest Ranch, Alberta, Canada

The Kananaskis Guest Ranch is the Brewster family's original homestead. Established in 1923 by Missy Brewster, it is owned and operated by fifth-generation Brewsters. The ranch is an hour west of Calgary in spectacular Kananaskis country right on the edge of the Bow River and at the end of Banff's mountain corridor. This area has been known to produce gusts of wind that bring cool summer breezes and drifts of winter snow. *River of No Return* and *Little Big Man* were both filmed here. The modern lodge and several of the cabins overlook the Bow River. If, for some reason the Brewsters are not around when you arrive, keep an eye out for "JD." He will make you feel right at home.

Address: General Delivery, Dept. K, Seebe, Alberta, Canada T0L 1X0
Telephone: (403) 673-3737 (summer); Fax: (403) 762-3953
Airport: Calgary International, 60 miles
Location: 28 miles east of Banff, 45 minutes west of Calgary off the Trans-Canada Highway
Memberships: Alberta Guest Ranch Association
Medical: Canmore Hospital, 15 minutes
Conference: 60; Lyster seminar building; Brewster Donut Tent especially for barbecues up to 1,000
Guest Capacity: 66
Accommodations: Twenty-nine cabins and chalet accommodations. One- or two-bedroom units feature cedar interiors with antique dressers and nightstands, wall-to-wall carpeting, double and single beds, full shower and bath. Some cabins are original Brewster family dwellings. The main lodge houses the X Bar X cocktail lounge and a fully licensed dining room.
Rates: • $. American Plan. Includes 2 hours of horseback riding a day; bed and breakfast and children's rates available. Barbecue rates and seminar packages available.
Credit Cards: Visa, MasterCard. Traveler's checks accepted.
Season: May through mid-October
Activities: Hourly, half-day, and all-day rides.

A favorite is riding to the ridge on Yamnuska Mountain. Overnight pack trips to the historic Brewster Company ranch in the Devil's Head Mountain area. Riding is also available at the family's Lake Louise Stables (in Banff National Park) where you can ride to the spectacular Lake Agnes or Plain of Six Glacier. Four golf courses within 30 minutes of the ranch; guests must make their own golf arrangements. Ranch will advise guests on local courses. Indoor heated whirlpool. Heli-hiking and touring and white water rafting trips down the Bow River. For groups of 100 or more the ranch will organize on-site rodeos with many local cowboys.
Children's Programs: No children's programs. Parents must supervise children.
Dining: Conference and group menus include British Columbia salmon steak fries, barbecued baron of beef, and lobster, in the scenic dining room overlooking the Bow River. Enjoy prime rib, steaks, and European specialties. Wine and liquor are served.
Entertainment: The lounge just off the dining room features a pool table, country music, piano, and television. Hardwood floors, small bar, and stone fireplace make for a cozy atmosphere.
Summary: Brewster's Kananaskis Guest Ranch is a division of Brewster's Rocky Mountain Adventures based in Banff. This family-run company offers a host of activities and tours in the Kananaskis, Banff, and Lake Louise areas. If you are planning a trip from the ranch to Banff and Jasper, these are the people to talk to. Groups and corporations should ask the Brewsters about their famous donut tent for barbecues. Also ask about their daughter Lori's country-western single.

Homeplace Guest Ranch, Alberta, Canada

The Homeplace Ranch is a year-round, low-key guest ranch in the Canadian Rocky Mountain foothills, 30 miles southwest of Calgary. The ranch is bordered by several beautiful ranches and the Kananaskis Forest Reserve. Mac Makenny offers guests a way of life for which southern Alberta is known. Every week a small number of people share the traditions, heritage, recreation, and natural beauty that constitute this unique life-style. There is abundant wildlife (deer, elk, moose, beaver, and grouse and other wild birds) and native flowers and trees. Camera buffs and artists ought to bring their gear. At Homeplace, the staff-guest ratio is high. Mac welcomes you to his home and makes every effort to see that you are well looked after. If you are from another country, he may raise your flag to welcome you.

Address: Site 2, Box 6, RR1, Dept. K, Priddis, Alberta, Canada T0L 1W0
Telephone: (403) 931-3245; Fax: (403) 931-3245
Airport: Calgary
Location: 30 miles west of Calgary, 50 miles east of Banff
Memberships: Alberta Guest Ranch Association, Alberta Outfitters Association
Medical: Foothills Hospital in Calgary, 30 miles
Conference: 12, winter only; Alberta barbecue for 150
Guest Capacity: 12
Accommodations: Guests are comfortable staying in the lodge in 8 small private rooms. All rooms are finished in cedar. Guest bedrooms are on both levels of the two-story lodge. All have private baths; some with twin futon beds, others with four-poster beds. Some of the rooms step out to balconies or decks. There is a hot tub outside on the back lower deck of the lodge.
Rates: • $-$$. Full American Plan. Rates vary depending on the season.
Credit Cards: None
Season: Year-round
Activities: In summer, full riding program. Excellent horses from gentle to spirited polo ponies.

Wonderful all-day and half-day rides through neighboring ranches and along ridgetops with wonderful vistas. Pack trips, riding instruction available, (many come from Calgary for daily instruction), fishing, and hiking. Eighteen- and 9-hole golf and tennis nearby. In winter, cross-country skiing, sleigh rides, downhill skiing at Banff, 45 minutes away.
Children's Programs: No planned program. Children under 7 do not ride.
Dining: Food is a key ingredient to a successful ranch. There is lots of homemade everything here, from applesauce muffins to fresh blackberry pie and big beef barbecues. Special food prepared on request.
Entertainment: Hay wagon rides, square dancing, dances, and exhibition polo in Calgary.
Summary: Very small guest ranch run by the Makenny family. Warm hospitality. Close and yet so far from Calgary. Branding weekends end of May and first of June, Calgary Stampede early July. Nature from the saddle workshops.

TL Bar Ranch, Alberta, Canada

The TL Bar Ranch is located in the province of Alberta along the Red Deer River in the beautiful Valley of the Dinosaurs. This working cattle and quarter horse ranch is owned and operated by Tom and Willie Lynch. Horseback riding is the main activity, with miles of scenic trails to explore. Fishermen will enjoy fishing the Red Deer River at the back door of the ranch. For rock and archaeology lovers, the Tyrrell Museum of Palaeontology is just 45 miles away. Guests live and, if they wish, work right along with the Lynches and experience firsthand what a working cattle and horse ranch is all about. Guests become one of the family here, and all ages are welcome to share and enjoy this way of life. One couple from Germany wrote, "The last seven days at the TL Bar Ranch were the highlight of our impressive trip across British Columbia and Alberta. We find it hard now to leave this treasure of peace and hospitality."

Address: Box 217 K, Trochu, Alberta, Canada T0M 2C0
Telephone: (403) 442-2207
Airport: Calgary International
Location: 100 miles northeast of Calgary, 10 miles east of Trochu on Highway 585
Medical: Trochu Hospital, 10 miles
Memberships: Alberta Country Vacations Association
Guest Capacity: 10
Accommodations: Guests stay with the Lynch family in their log ranch home, which accommodates 4 with shared bath. There is a large living room with a stone fireplace. For those who wish, there is satellite television. A cottage nearby sleeps 4 to 6 with private bath. No daily maid service. If you stay longer than a week, Willie will do your laundry.
Rates: $. American Plan. Off-season weekend rates available.
Credit Cards: None. Cash and traveler's checks accepted.
Season: May through October, including Canadian Thanksgiving

Activities: Riding must be kept to a slower pace because of the rough terrain. Riding arena on ranch for those who wish to try their hand at gymkhana events. Hiking, swimming, canoeing on Red Deer River—very quiet and relaxing with lots of deer, beaver, geese, ducks; picnic lunch provided; 9-hole golf nearby. Fishing for gold eye, perch, and pickerel.
Children's Programs: No special programs, but kids are welcome. Willie will watch your kids.
Dining: Nothing fancy, just good, old-fashioned ranch cooking.
Entertainment: Do your own thing. Television, pool table, cookouts, rodeos in surrounding towns.
Summary: Very low-key, small family ranch with wonderful Canadian hosts. Mostly just riding, relaxing, and visiting with friendly people. Rustic campground for tents, trailers, and motor homes. Tyrrell Museum of Palaeontology.

Rafter Six Ranch Resort, Alberta, Canada

At the threshold to the Rockies lies the Rafter Six Ranch Resort. Whether you stay for a day or a week, the ranch offers boundless activities and down-home Western hospitality. Because of its natural beauty and western atmosphere, Rafter Six has become a major location for movies and commercials. You never know who may be on the trail ride with you. Step back in time. Here the hustle and bustle are behind you, and fresh mountain air, pine-scented forests, and sparkling river waters are abundant. In 1976, a real estate agent and an interior decorator-designer, both from Calgary, discovered the old Rafter Six. Gloria and Stan traded high heels and oxfords for tennis shoes and cowboy boots. With a lot of hard work, they rebuilt this old ranch and turned it into one of Alberta's finest. Today you will savor delicious food and magnificent scenery, make friends, and experience for yourself pure country living. The Stoney Indian Reservation is to the east and Bow Valley Park to the west. On this historical site, over 100 years ago, the Rafter Six horse brand was used by Colonel Walker of the Northwest Mounted Police. Some of the log buildings are modern but maintain the rustic charm of days gone by. Everyone becomes a part of the living history at the Rafter Six Ranch.

Address: P.O. Box K, Seebe, Alberta, Canada T0L 1X0
Telephone: (403) 673-3622; Fax: (403) 673-3961
Airport: Calgary
Location: 45 miles west of Calgary off Trans-Canada Highway
Memberships: Alberta Guest Ranch Association
Awards: AAA 2 Diamond, Gold Award Alberta Hotel Association
Medical: Hospital in Canmore
Conference: 40
Guest Capacity: 60
Accommodations: Five historic cabins, each with shower units, double and twin beds, and carpeting. One of these is a honeymoon cabin with a bed of native logs. The 3-story log lodge has guest rooms, some with balconies, on the second and third floors. Each room has a hand-painted mural, as do many of the doors, each created by Stan, his father, and brother.
Rates: • $-$$. American Plan. Ranch packages and children's rates available. Open to public, hourly rides available.
Credit Cards: Visa, MasterCard, American Express, Enroute
Season: May through October, including Canadian Thanksgiving
Activities: One-, two-, and four-hour trail rides, all-day rides, hay and carriage rides, breakfast and supper rides and overnight pack trips, heated outdoor pool, indoor whirlpool, and hiking. Eighteen-hole golf, fishing, and river rafting nearby. Heli-hiking and touring.
Children's Programs: Play area. Baby-sitting available. Petting zoo with cow, goat, sheep, ducks, geese, chickens.
Dining: Award-winning dining room with much of Stan's artwork. Rafter Six specializes in steaks, ribs, and buffalo. Guests can select from a varied menu. Mad Trappers Dining Room and Bearspaw Lounge, Saturday night hoedowns.
Entertainment: Western entertainment (shoot-outs, Indian dancing, ranch display rodeos, "mini-Calgary stampede," guest fun time rodeo), Calgary Stampede in July, powwows at Indian reservation.
Summary: Some of the best scenery in the world is in Kananaskis country. Very Western with all log construction. Appeals to a wide variety of people—families, couples, and singles. Many movies have been shot at the ranch and in the surrounding areas. Outdoor chapel overlooking Kananaskis River. Cowley's Passing of the Legends (an Indian Legends Museum). Stan and Gloria have extensive knowledge of and background in Indian history and culture, plus a great museum. Book shop on the ranch. French and German spoken.

See color photos, page 193

Rafter Six Ranch Resort, Alberta, Canada

Big Bar Guest Ranch, British Columbia, Canada

In a gentle valley between the Marble Mountains and Big Bar Mountain, just six hours by car from Vancouver, is Brian and Kathleen Gunn's Big Bar Guest Ranch. Brian, an international engineering consultant, and Kathleen, bought Big Bar in 1988 after returning from several years overseas. They were interested in combining their love of the outdoors with Western hospitality. After a good deal of searching, they found their ranch overlooking Big Bar Creek, the neighboring OK Cattle Ranch, and the crown land that surrounds them. Here the pace is slow and the riding wonderful. Explore, relax, and recharge. Most of all, enjoy the peaceful solitude and the Gunn's warm and friendly hospitality.

Address: Box 27K Jesmond, Clinton, B.C., Canada V0K 1K0
Telephone: (604) 459-2333; Radiophone: (604) 395-7101; Fax: (604) 459-2333 (call before sending Fax)
Airport: Kamloops, 115 miles. Several small air strips nearby.
Location: 1 hour by car northwest of Clinton, 270 miles northeast of Vancouver
Memberships: British Columbia Guest Ranch Association
Medical: 100 Mile House Clinic, 60 miles, Ashcroft Hospital
Conference: 32
Guest Capacity: 44
Accommodations: Twelve guest rooms in the new two-story main lodge. All with private baths. Six rooms have bunk lofts for children. Two rustic log cottages with kitchens, full baths, woodburning stoves, and covered porches overlooking the creek. The original homestead lodge has a cozy fireside lounge and billiard room. Just outside is the hot tub overlooking Mount Bowman and the distant Marble Mountains.
Rates: • $-$$. American Plan
Credit Cards: Visa, MasterCard
Season: Year-round
Activities: May through November: one to two-hour or all-day horseback rides on cattle range land or through the forest, canoeing and trout fishing on Big Bar Creek, mountain biking (rentals available), hiking, sightseeing trips to Fraser River for game viewing or gold panning. December through February: Cross-country skiing on groomed trails, ice fishing, ice skating, sleigh rides.
Children's Programs: No special program. Children ride at the discretion of the wrangler. Children under 8 ride in corral only.
Dining: Hearty ranch food in fully licensed family-style dining room.
Entertainment: Read your favorite book, impromptu music. Fireside chats.
Summary: Small family-operated guest ranch overlooking Big Bar Creek. Views overlooking the rolling cattle range land, Mount Bowman and the Marble Mountains.

Cariboo Rose Guest Ranch, British Columbia, Canada

Cariboo Rose is a small adult-oriented ranch where you will enjoy the life-style of a bygone era—unspoiled wilderness, scenic lakes, hearty home-cooked meals, and of course, old-fashioned Western hospitality. The ranch is surrounded by the wilderness of the Marble Mountains and the gentle lake and meadow country for which the Southern Cariboo is famous. Following a day in the saddle, take in the breathtaking mountain view over a cool drink on the porch or a leisurely soak in the hot tub. The day's events and cool mountain air serve to guarantee an evening of restful sleep and pleasant dreams. Host Karl J. Krammer was born in Austria, the son of a blacksmith and farrier, and studied mechanical engineering before moving to British Columbia. After a long search he found this ranch and bought it in 1987. Karl and Teresa have kept the ranch small, taking only 10 guests at a time. At the Cariboo Rose you can enjoy peace and tranquillity. Listen to hoofbeats on a mountain path, saddle leather creaking, or the sound of horse bells. Most of all, leave civilization behind and pause for a week or more to recharge.

Address: P.O. Box 160 K, Clinton, B.C., Canada V0K 1K0

Telephone: (604) 828-6959 (ranch); (604) 459-2255 (office)

Airport: Vancouver. Charter and helicopter flights available.

Train: B.C. Rail from North Vancouver to Clinton

Location: 4 hours northwest of Vancouver by car, 1 hour by air; 15 miles northwest of Clinton

Memberships: British Columbia Guest Ranchers Association, Cariboo Tourist Association

Medical: Ashcroft Hospital, 40 miles

Guest Capacity: 10

Accommodations: Guests stay in the privacy of their own small cabins, fully equipped with bathroom and showers, queen or twin-size beds and cozy comforters. A few steps away, the ranch house provides the opportunity to social- ize in the loft-style game room or relax in front of a cozy fire.

Rates: • $$. American Plan.

Credit Cards: Visa, American Express

Season: April through October, including Canadian Thanksgiving and Easter

Activities: The ranch caters to those with a serious interest in riding and horsemanship. Half-day and all-day rides with lunch camps on the trail. Rides are tailored to be as easy or as challenging as required. Catch and release trout fishing in nearby pond, or catch and keep on Big Bar Lake. Hiking, canoeing, sauna and whirlpool hot tub. Five-day Western riding clinics are offered in April, May, and October. The indoor, covered riding arena is available for informal riding instruction throughout the season.

Children's Programs: This is an adult-oriented ranch.

Dining: Hearty, family-style meals including roast beef with Yorkshire pudding, baked chicken and Fettucine Alfredo, lasagna, homemade desserts, and cowboy coffee, all served in the dining room with a beautiful mountain view.

Entertainment: Loft-style game room with pool table, board games, and dart board.

Summary: Very private and personal with a warm "at home" feeling. Quality horseback riding in small groups. Rides go into the unspoiled wilderness of the Marble Mountains. Well-trained horses, western riding clinics geared for the beginner, local rodeos in May and August. Fluent German spoken.

Elkin Creek Guest Ranch, British Columbia, Canada

Located in British Columbia's Chilcotin country is Elkin Creek Guest Ranch. The Nemaiah Valley is a corridor of natural beauty with the coast range mountains and distant Mt. Tatlow rising over 10,000 feet. Unique to Elkin Creek is its proximity to Vedan Lake, almost a stone's throw from the main lodge. Right in front of the ranch itself are hay fields with generously wooded sloping terrain behind. In operation since 1987, this 640-acre ranch offers a host of riding and lake activities for families, couples, and single people. Elkin Creek is, without question, one of British Columbia's finest new ranches combining western hospitality with incredible natural beauty. Unlike many, the ranch brochure will give you a wonderful eye-opening feel for this scenic part of British Columbia and the ranch setting.

Address: 221 Rondoval Crescent, Dept. K, North Vancouver, B.C., Canada V7N 2W6 (Office); General Delivery, Drawer K, Nemaiah Valley, B.C., Canada V0L 1X0 (Ranch)

Telephone: (604) 984-4666; Fax: (604) 984-4686 (Office). (604) H497533 (ranch radio telephone. Ask operator for Alexis Creek Channel).

Airport: Williams Lake and 4,300-foot-long dirt airstrip at ranch (call for details)

Location: 48 miles south of Alexis Creek, 120 miles southwest of Williams Lake, B.C.

Memberships: British Columbia Guest Ranch Association, Cariboo Tourist Association

Medical: Medical clinic at Alexis Creek, 48 miles; Cariboo Memorial Hospital at Williams Lake, 120 miles

Conference: 40

Guest Capacity: 35

Accommodations: Seven traditionally built log cabins, each consisting of two double bedrooms, two separate bathrooms, a comfortably appointed living room, and separate storage rooms. Individually controlled electric heat in all cabins. The main lodge houses the dining room, lounge, and Western-style bar.

Rates: • $$-$$$. American Plan. Gold-panning and overnight pack trips extra. Children's rates available.

Credit Cards: Visa, MasterCard, American Express. No personal checks.

Season: May to mid-November

Activities: Unlimited horseback riding with picnic lunches on the trail. Beginner, intermediate and advanced trails with hourly, half-day and all-day rides. Pack trips, wagon rides. Lake activities include fishing, motorboating, sailing, windsurfing, canoeing, and swimming. Hiking, indoor game room, sauna, and seasonal ranch activities.

Children's Programs: None. Children are the responsibility of parents. Small children not recommended.

Dining: Good, hearty ranch meals served family-style. Special diets upon request. Barbecues and cookouts. Full bar.

Entertainment: Games room with regulation size pool table, Ping Pong table, shuffleboard, fooseball table, darts, and assorted board games.

Summary: Wide variety of riding opportunities and lake activities. Guest participation encouraged with cattle work. April branding, fall cattle round-up, range riding. Photo-safaris and wildlife observation of mountain goats, cougar, black bear, deer, moose, and beaver.

The Hills Health and Guest Ranch, British Columbia, Canada

Pat and Juanita Corbett, realizing the desire of people to combine fitness with pleasure, in 1984 created the Hills Health and Guest Ranch on the historic Cariboo Trail. The Hills offers a combination of comfort, independence, and a range of horseback activities. A 2-story lodge houses exercise-fitness facilities, beauty and body treatments, dining room, indoor pool, meeting room, and gift shop. Summer and winter guests may choose to take part in aerobics, stretch and flex classes, aqua fit, and no-bounce aerobics. The ranch also offers full personal care from facial treatments to massage, herbal wraps, waxing, clay packs, manicures, and pedicures. If that's not enough, you can go for a hayride pulled by two huge draft horses and then dine on gourmet cuisine prepared by a Swiss chef.

Address: C-26, 108 Ranch 100 Mile House, Dept. K, B.C., Canada V0K 2E0
Telephone: (604) 791-5225; Fax: (604) 791-6384
Airport: Williams Lake via Vancouver International
Location: 8 miles north of 100 Mile House off Highway 97, 295 miles north of Vancouver
Memberships: British Columbia Guest Ranchers Association, Cross-Country Division of the Canadian West Ski Areas Association
Medical: 100 Mile House, 8 miles
Conference: 200; 4,300-square-foot meeting space
Guest Capacity: 114
Accommodations: The Hills is perched on one of the Cariboo hilltops. As you drive up the hill, you first encounter the 2-story logsided main lodge. Around the bend on either side of the ridge are 20 A-frame, 2-level modern cabins, with kitchens and two decks. These comfortable chalets are on either side of a road, with the "sunrise" cabins on the left and the "sunset" cabins on the right. Each cabin looks out over virgin Cariboo country. You may rent a chalet and cook your own meals or take part in the full American plan. Laundry service.
Rates: • $-$$. American Plan. Many vacation packages available, including spa package. Children's and group rates.
Credit Cards: Visa, MasterCard
Season: Year-round
Activities: In summer half-day horseback riding with cowboy breakfast served at Willy's Wigwam. One- to 2-hour and all-day "mountain top" rides with lunch. Indoor 20 by 40-foot heated pool, 2 Jacuzzis, and 2 saunas open to public members as well as guests. Fitness programs include aerobics studio, weight room, hydrogym, weights, tanning salon, massage and beauty salon, and exercise rooms. Superb Swiss fitness, nutritional and kinesiology counselors. Fishing at nearby lakes for rainbow, eastern brook, and lake trout. Hiking. PGA par 72 golf course and 5 tennis courts nearby. Winter: Cross-country ski trails, sleigh rides, snowshoeing. See cross-country section.
Children's Programs: Supervised program. Kiddie wrangler. Children under 6 ride with parents. In winter, kids' ski school. Baby-sitting available. (Summer and winter.)
Dining: The Hills' fine restaurant, Trail's End, is open to the public and is overseen by a superb Swiss chef. He offers a range of dishes from delicate culinary delights to low-calorie spa cuisine and ranch-style meals, depending upon the package. Fully licensed bar. Mostly European wines served.
Entertainment: Fitness workshops, horse-drawn hayrides, television in each chalet, sing-alongs in "Willy's Wigwam" (a tepee in the woods), some of Canada's best live country music in dining room 3 nights with wonderful local singer Bob Dalrymple.
Summary: An affordable family guest ranch as well as a health and fitness ranch spa in western Canada. Wonderful musical entertainment. Numerous lakes, historic gold mining, Cariboo Trail, 108 Lake Historic Ranch. Williams Lake Stampede July 4th. Anaheim Lake Stampede in early July (in the Old West country of British Columbia). French, German and Italian spoken.

See color photos, page 235

Flying U Ranch, British Columbia, Canada

The Flying U Ranch, oldest guest ranch in Canada, is on the north shore of beautiful 15-mile Greenlake. The ranch was established by rodeo personality Jack Boyd. As early as 1924, two Western movies were made here, directed by A. D. "Cowboy" Kean. Guests have come from 28 countries and most states and provinces of the United States and Canada. Those who come all the way from Europe usually stay 3 to 6 weeks. The ranch is owned and operated by the Fremlin Seniors, four sons and their wives, who moved to British Columbia from California and Nevada in 1980. This talented family includes a university professor, artist, lawyer, house builder, and musician. The ranch has a history of the early Indians and fur trappers who traded and trapped in these parts. Just ask the Fremlins; they'll be glad to tell you about it. On 40,000+ acres, the Flying U has been preserved and the spirit of the early West lives on.

Address: Box 69 K, N. Greenlake, 70 Mile House, B.C., Canada V0K 2K0
Telephone: (604) 456-7717
Airport: Vancouver International; 3,000-foot grass airstrip on ranch. Land and sea charter flights available to ranch.
Train: B.C. rail from North Vancouver to Flying U Station, 5 miles away. This is very popular.
Location: 20 miles south of 100 Mile House, 5 hours northeast of Vancouver by car
Memberships: Texas Longhorn Association, Wilderness Tourism Counsel, B.C. Cattleman's Association
Awards: Listed in *Best Places*
Medical: 100 Mile House Hospital, 20 miles
Conference: 65
Guest Capacity: 65
Accommodations: Guests stay in 23 "chinker" log cabins (sleeping 2-8), arranged in a "U" shape around the main lodge. All these rustic cabins are heated with wood stoves and feature hand-hewn log furniture and sitting porches. Separate men's and women's shower house with shower and bathroom amenities and 15-person sauna. Covered porches with rocking chairs.
Rates: • $. American Plan. Children's, weekday, weekend, and group rates. Two-day minimum.
Credit Cards: Visa, American Express
Season: April to November
Activities: Upon arrival, each guest is assigned a horse according to his or her ability. Guests are given a trail map and are free to ride alone or with other guests. The Flying U has 120 horses and thousands of acres. Riders may saddle up from 9:00 a.m. to 4:00 p.m. each day, including Sunday. Fishing, swimming, and canoeing on Greenlake. Hiking.
Children's Programs: Children participate with parents. Baby-sitting available.
Dining: The Flying U has an authentic Western saloon separate from the main lodge. Cocktails are served to the sounds of the circa 1880 nickelodeon. Mealtime at the lodge is announced with the clanging of the old rail. Family and friends eat together ranch-style. Weekly outdoor lunch and dinner barbecues. Beer and a selection of wine available with meals.
Entertainment: Movies, horse-drawn hayrides, barbecues, and bonfires are topped off with an old Western whoop-de-doo Wednesday and Saturday nights, when Pete tunes up the 8-piece Flying U Band.
Summary: Canada's oldest guest ranch, on beautiful Greenlake, terrific hosts, and their Flying U Band. Guests may horseback ride without supervision. One hundred Texas longhorns on ranch, small Flying U Western Historical Museum, general store. Authentic Western saloon. A little Japanese, German, French, and Spanish spoken.

See color photos, page 228

Flying U Ranch, British Columbia, Canada

Flying U Ranch, British Columbia, Canada

Mount Robson Guest Ranch, British Columbia, Canada

Mount Robson Guest Ranch is a small historic ranch that has been run by the same family since 1922. It is one of the few places left where you can actually live in buildings of pioneer construction. While the ranch has added electricity, a nostalgic oil lamp remains in each of the cottages. Breathtaking Mount Robson's snow-capped peak towers over the ranch—anywhere you look the views are spectacular. Mount Robson is the highest peak in the Canadian Rockies rising 12,972 feet and offers tremendous hiking, riding, and nature watching opportunities. You will see numerous hummingbirds. You might even see moose, black bear, and deer as well as salmon spawning at Rearguard Falls.

Address: Box 301, Hargreaves Road, Dept. K, Valemount, B.C., Canada V0E 2Z0
Telephone: (604) 566-4370
Airport: Kamloops or Prince George
Location: 200 miles north of Kamloops, 180 miles southeast of Prince George, 1 hour drive west of Jasper on Highway 16
Memberships: High Country Tourist Association, Valemount Historic Society
Medical: Valemount Medical Center, 25 miles
Guest Capacity: 30
Accommodations: Six authentic original cabins sleep 4 to 6 people, each with bedroom, bath, and fully equipped kitchen. Complimentary coffee and tea provided. Camping facilities available with picnic tables and small metal grills. RVs are welcome, up to 10.
Rates: $. Weekly, seniors' and group rates available. Meals not included.
Credit Cards: Visa
Season: June through mid-September
Activities: No planned activities. Horseback riding. Hourly and day rides, white water and family float rafting on the Fraser River. In August you can float through the salmon spawning riverbeds. Wilderness pack trips, helicopter rides, and canoeing will be organized happily by the ranch. Hiking, bird-watching, salmon spawning grounds. Fishing nearby.
Children's Programs: None; children are the responsibility of their parents.
Dining: Home-cooked meals served family-style in the main ranch house. Fresh vegetables. Steak, roasts, poultry and ham. Fresh ranch raspberries and delicious desserts.
Entertainment: Do your own thing; most guests are in awe of the view.
Summary: A wonderful ranch for those who love to hike and take in breathtaking beauty of Mount Robson on their own. Pioneer buildings on ranch, RV sites, Mount Robson Provincial Park. George Hicks Park at Valemount, salmon spawning and information center at Mount Robson. August blueberries and raspberries for picking.

Springhouse Trails Ranch, British Columbia, Canada

Springhouse Trails Ranch is the home of Werner and Suzi Moessner, two very kind and friendly people who moved to British Columbia from Stuttgart in 1978. Werner grew up on a farm. As a young man, he started a construction firm, which is still run by his son and daughter. In the late 1970s, the Moessners flew to British Columbia, rented an RV, and began looking at ranches. They found Springhouse Trails, and Werner spent two years rebuilding the ranch. In 1980 they took their first guests. At 3,000 feet, the property overlooks a small lake, grass-covered rolling hills, and open meadows. They grow many of their own vegetables and serve fresh eggs from their twenty chickens. Werner and Suzi pretty much let you do as you please. Many of the guests are Europeans who enjoy the fact that the Moessners are bilingual. In fact, they like it so much, they stay for 3 to 6 weeks at a time. In traditional German fashion, the property and accommodations are immaculate, the food hearty, and yes, there is beer available.

Address: Box 2 K, Springhouse Trails R.R. 1, Williams Lake, B.C., Canada V2G 2P1
Telephone: (604) 392-4780; Fax: (604) 392-4780
Airport: Williams Lake Airport via Vancouver International; private planes to Springhouse airport
Location: 11 miles southwest of Williams Lake on Dog Creek Road, 6 hours northeast of Vancouver by car
Memberships: British Columbia Guest Ranchers Association
Medical: Williams Lake Hospital
Conference: No
Guest Capacity: 30
Accommodations: Guests stay in 4 log cabins with full kitchens and two large, 1-story, new complexes. One is a dorm building that has a common hallway with 10 rooms and 2 end units with full kitchen facilities for those making extended visits. The second building has individual units with separate entrances. Also available are 12 RV hookups, with shower and laundry facility.
Rates: • $. American Plan. European Plan, RV, tenting, and children's rates available.
Credit Cards: Visa, MasterCard, American Express
Season: May to September
Activities: Informal program. Ride, hike, walk, canoe, or just relax as you wish. Most guests ride with other guests or alone. Guided riding is available. Werner assigns horses according to a rider's ability, with hour rides and all-day picnic rides available.
Children's Programs: No children's programs, but kids are welcome. If a 2-year-old can ride, Werner will put him on a horse.
Dining: The ranch has a large, separate fully licensed restaurant with views and a fireplace in the center. Hearty ranch food, including favorites such as German schnitzel and barbecues twice a week. Wine (mostly Canadian) and liquor are served. Special coffees (Spanish, Swiss, Irish, Monte Cristo, and Rudesheimer iced coffee).
Entertainment: Nothing formal. Guests usually make their own.
Summary: Bilingual German hosts with many European guests. Many guests stay up to 3 weeks and longer. RV hookups. Ride on your own, Indian arts and crafts, Indian rodeos, Williams Lake Stampede Rodeo.

Sundance Guest Ranch, British Columbia, Canada

In British Columbia's high semiarid desert country with sun-drenched sagebrush, the Sundance Ranch looks out to Cornwall and the Glossy Mountains high above the Thompson River. The ranch ran cattle in the late 1800s and began taking dudes in the 1940s. In 1978, Stan Rowe, one of Canada's leading business equipment salesmen, bought Sundance and fulfilled a boyhood dream. Stan and his family had been guests at the ranch since the early 1960s. When it was offered for sale, the Rowes didn't take much time to decide they wanted it. Stan and his wife and their grown children have made their operation one of Canada's most successful. Sundance runs 100 horses over 20,000 acres. Most guests come to ride. Stan and his crew run a first-rate riding program. No one gets on a horse without cowboy boots (which can be rented at the ranch office). When you have proven that you can really ride, ask about the Sioux Lookout ride. Stan cares about his horses and will not put overweight riders on them; when you telephone they will ask your height and weight. Sundance is for those who like to ride and enjoy the high desert country—summers are hot.

Address: Box 489 K, Ashcroft, B.C., Canada V0K 1A0
Telephone: (604) 453-2422/2554
Airport: Kamloops (1-hour drive)
Location: 200 miles or 4-hour drive north of Vancouver, 55 miles west of Kamloops along the Trans-Canada Highway
Medical: Ashcroft Hospital, 6 miles
Memberships: British Columbia Guest Ranchers Association
Awards: 1987 British Columbia Resort Operator of the Year
Conference: 60
Guest Capacity: 70
Accommodations: Twenty-eight simply decorated rooms connected by the sprawling L-shaped extension of the ranch house with covered walkways. Some rooms open to the parking area and riding arena, others to pastures over-looking a small herd of buffalo and the arid hills. All rooms are carpeted, have private bath/shower, air-conditioning; one deluxe suite with king-size bed and wood stove. Lawns are trimmed, and flowers abound in the summer. For more rustic, secluded accommodations, ask about Chi Springs.

Rates: • $-$$. Full American Plan. Children's rates available.
Credit Cards: Visa, MasterCard
Season: March through October. New Year's Eve program, open Thanksgiving and Easter.
Activities: Summer riding season March through October. Gentle trail horses to frisky mounts; two rides per day, 2 to 3 hours each. Sioux Lookout ride. Ask the ranch about "Topping Off" in March, lots of riding excitement. Hiking, tennis, swimming in 45-foot outdoor heated pool, volleyball, horseshoe pitching, float trips available nearby.
Children's Programs: Children eat lunch and dinner together before adults. Children under 8 do not go on trail rides but may be led around in arena by parents or guardian. Children's lounge and game room. Wide-screen video movies. Baby-sitting available.
Dining: Weekly candlelight dinners. Varied menus. Will cater to special requests. Barbecues, cookouts, and buffalo hip roasts on patio. The five-sided dining room has a lovely view and is licensed for beer and wine service. BYOB bar lounge for adults.
Entertainment: Game room for adults with pool tables, card tables, and darts. Gymkhanas with ribbons for 1st, 2nd, and 3rd places, nearby rodeos. Country-rock dance Saturday nights.
Summary: Family owned and operated. Especially popular with families. Many young couples and singles visit Sundance as well. Riding is the main activity. April branding at nearby Chataway Ranch, "Topping Off" in March, cowboy boot rentals available, small herd of buffalo, town of Ashcroft, Ashcroft Museum. Some French and German spoken.

Teepee Heart Ranch, British Columbia, Canada

Teepee Heart Ranch is in the shadows of British Columbia's Coast Range Mountains and in the heart of Chilcotin cattle country. This outback (the closest town is 85 miles), primitive ranch is famous for its one- and two-week pack trips and weekly fly-fishing trips to the Sherwood Lake fishing camp 30 miles away. This outfitting ranch was started in the 1940s by pioneers Frank and Duane Witte. The name "Teepee Heart" comes from the registered ranch brand, which is literally a tepee and a heart. Naturally, the ranch is noted for its tepees at some of the base camps. Hans Burch bought the Teepee Heart Ranch in 1983. Today he runs an excellent string of Tennessee walkers for most of his trips. If you have never ridden one of them, it is like being in a rocking chair.

Address: Box 6 K, Big Creek, B.C., Canada V0L 1K0
Telephone: (604) 392-5015
Airport: Williams Lake, 85 miles; Big Creek airport for private planes, 10 miles
Location: 85 miles west of Williams Lake. Call ranch for directions.
Memberships: British Columbia Guest Ranchers Association, Caribou Tourist Association
Medical: Williams Lake Hospital, 85 miles. Emergency helicopter service available.
Conference: No
Guest Capacity: 12
Accommodations: Guests sleep in 4 rustic log cabins that sleep from 4 to 6. Each is equipped with wood heaters, propane stoves, and dishes but no running water. A diesel generator provides electricity. Bathroom facilities consist of outhouses; guests are welcome to use the shower in the main ranch house.
Rates: • $$. American Plan. Housekeeping rates available.
Credit Cards: None
Season: June through September
Activities: In summer, camping in alpine meadows, lots of riding on fine trailwise Tennessee walkers. Seven- to 16-day wilderness pack trips. Fly-fishing trips on horseback. Privately owned fishing camp where you will sleep in two lakeside cabins.
Children's Programs: None. Young children not recommended on weekly pack trips.
Dining: Hearty Canadian country meals. Pack trip meals cooked on an open fire—steak, chicken, trout. BYOB.
Entertainment: Depends on staff and guests.
Summary: Remote rustic ranch specializing in wilderness pack trips. Best suited for horsemen and horsewomen looking for a wilderness experience. You should be in good physical shape and enjoy backcountry riding. You may sleep in Indian tepees while you are on the trail. Local Indian lore, fossil hunting, clean air, wildlife photography, Taylor Windfall gold mine. German spoken.

Top of the World Guest Ranch, British Columbia, Canada

Top of the World is just that—on top of the world. It sits in a valley; the farther up you go, the more rugged it gets. Most guests cannot believe the splendor, the wide open country, and the beauty of this 45,000-acre cattle/guest ranch. Lloyd and Rowena Jones, whose family has been in ranching for four generations, have a wealth of knowledge about horses, cattle, and the area history. Trail rides follow the old stagecoach route from Fort Steele to Golden, past the remnants of corrals that once trapped wild horses, to falls that cascade from peaks and through meadows. You may help with branding, fencing, salting, and moving cattle to summer pastures. At the end of the day, you can sit on your cabin porch with a cool drink watching the sun set behind the Purcell Mountains. The last rays remind you that you are, indeed, on Top of the World.

Address: Box 29 K, Fort Steele, B.C., Canada V0B 1N0
Telephone: (604) 426-6306
Airport: Cranbrook, via Calgary or Vancouver
Location: 16 miles north of Cranbrook, 135 miles south of Banff, 200 miles southeast of Calgary, 180 miles north of Spokane
Memberships: British Columbia Guest Ranchers Association
Medical: Cranbrook Hospital, 16 miles
Conference: 45, October through March
Guest Capacity: 35
Accommodations: Six log cabins are in a semicircle around the 2-story log lodge. Each summer the Joneses plant lots of flowers and mow an acre of grass—plenty of room for children to play. Each cabin has carpeting, twin and queen beds, woodstove and electric heat, private baths with tubs and showers, and covered porches. Four rooms on the second floor of the lodge have private baths, and spectacular views. All accommodations furnished with antiques and homestead furnishings. Main lodge has a large deck where guests relax and watch myriad hummingbirds.

Rates: • $. Full American Plan. Winter, children's, large family, and group rates.
Credit Cards: Visa
Season: April through September; open most holidays
Activities: Summer riding program for all levels. Better riders may help with cattle. Morning, afternoon, and some moonlight rides. Weekly breakfast rides. Yearly cattle drives. Three lakes on property; Loon Lake is the favorite for rowboats or canoes. Lots of hiking, volleyball, and horseshoes. Swim in Lake Wasa, 5 miles away. Have an ice cream cone on the way home. Tired riders enjoy the Jacuzzi hot tub under the stars. Eighteen-hole golf at area courses. In winter, cross-country skiing and downhill skiing nearby.
Children's Programs: Children are the responsibility of parents. Baby-sitting available with advance notice. Children under 6 ride in arena only.
Dining: "We are not gourmet, we are ranch," says Rowena. Top of the World grows its own vegetables and serves ranch beef. Fresh eggs, fruit, well-balanced meals. Buffet lunches. Dinners are more formal, topped off with fresh berry pies. Weekly cookouts. BYOB.
Entertainment: Pony chuck wagon races in nearby towns, occasional rodeos, piano in lodge, occasional sing-alongs. Recreation room with pool table, Ping-Pong, and darts.
Summary: Great Western hospitality, superb food, and excellent horses. Working cattle ranch, yearly cattle drives, golf nearby. Ranch abounds in wildlife. This is the wintering ground for elk and sheep. Also, thousands of nesting birds find their way to Top of the World. Historic Fort Steele, Bavarian town of Kimberley with Caminco Gardens. Ski tram and fish hatchery.

Tyax Mountain Lake Resort, British Columbia, Canada

Tyax Mountain Lake Resort, a magnificent luxury hideaway, is tucked in the breathtaking wilderness of the Chilcotin Mountains. This rustically handsome lodge, one of the largest log structures in North America, is made from hand-hewn spruce logs, with ceilings soaring to 30 feet. Summers here are hot and sunny, and winters afford some of the best downhill helicopter skiing and cross-country skiing in the world. Owner/operator Gus Abel runs a first-class operation. (Gus has a Master Ocean-going Degree—he used to pilot supertankers.) He has brought many European amenities to Tyax. You can hot tub under the stars, sleep under eider down, and wake to views of the lake and mountains with the smell of fresh-baked bread from Dutch ovens. Tyax offers a vacation of a lifetime.

Address: Tyaughton Lake Road, Dept. K, Gold Bridge, B.C., Canada V0K 1P0
Telephone: (604) 238-2221; Fax: (604) 238-2528
Airport: Vancouver International; charter float plane service to Tyax Lake
Location: Five hours by car north of Vancouver
Memberships: British Columbia Guest Ranchers Association, Federation of B.C. Wilderness
Medical: Lillooet Hospital, 60 miles
Conference: 80; 2 conference rooms, 1,120 square feet and 651 square feet; spring, fall, and winter
Guest Capacity: 100
Accommodations: Twenty-eight comfortable suites feature balconies with views of the lake and pine-studded mountains. Four modern log chalets with fireplace, kitchen, and 3- and 4-bedrooms. All rooms are furnished in pine. The lodge has a large sun deck, lounge and Western bar, conference room, and lower level fitness center. Laundry service available.
Rates: • $$-$$$$. Seasonal rates available, group discounts. Meals and activities extra. Almost everything is à la carte.
Credit Cards: Visa, MasterCard, American Express

Season: Year-round, including Thanksgiving, Christmas, and Easter
Activities: Summer activities include horseback riding, with hourly, daily, and overnight pack trips. Lake and stream fishing for Dolly Varden, kokanee, Eastern brook, cutthroat, and rainbow trout. Fly-fishing in remote lakes. Helicopter hiking. Fly out with a float plane for fishing. Gold panning and mountain biking. Tennis court, sailing, sailboarding, canoeing, lake swimming, whirlpool, and sauna. Winter: cross-country skiing on well-groomed trails, helicopter skiing, snowmobiling, ice skating, ice fishing, sleigh rides. Rent skis, skates, snowshoes, snowmobiles at Tyax.
Children's Programs: Disney movies, ponies, paddleboats, and kids bikes. Baby-sitting on request.
Dining: Restaurant with wonderful homecooked meals overlooking Lake Tyaughton. Full menu. Tyax specialties: leg of lamb, T-bone steaks, barbecued chicken. Children's menu. Extensive wine list and full liquor license.
Entertainment: Billiard and table tennis room, dance area with live music, camp fires, cookouts.
Summary: Mountain lake retreat. The Tyax helicopter or float plane will take you to wilderness areas for summer and winter sports. Eight RV sites available. Brolone ghost town, pioneer mines. French, German, and Japanese (summer only) spoken.

Fly-Fishing
Ranches

Introduction

This fly-fishing section was designed for the novice as well as the expert angler. If you have never had a fly-rod in your hands, do not worry about it. Fifty percent of the people who visit these lodges are people just like you. For one reason or another, they have dreamed about fly-fishing but have never taken the time to try it. The other 50 percent may be intermediate to expert anglers. Regardless of your level of skill or aptitude, you will have a fun and exciting time. Those of you who are experts will be challenged. Those of you who don't know the difference between one fly and another will have the time of your life. Remember this, the ranches listed here are doing what they do for two reasons—they love people and they love to fish. They are running their operations for you and will do everything possible (within reason, of course) to ensure that your time with them is both pleasurable and exhilarating.

Fly-fishing is booming. If you doubt my words, look at some of the major outdoor wear/sporting goods companies and mail order catalogs. You will see complete sections, and sometimes entire catalogs, devoted to water and fish and all the exciting equipment that goes with them.

Fly-fishing, like golf, is a very exacting sport, and to become an expert takes a tremendous amount of skill, patience, and dedication. Those unfamiliar with the sport might wonder why anyone would put on a pair of waders that come up to your Adam's apple and stand in the middle of a cold, whirling stream, casting a long, colored line back and forth. But millions of people around the world have found that once they try it, they are likely to get hooked. Besides the marvelous array of equipment and the thrill of hooking and landing a trophy-size fish or even a small one, fly-fishing offers men, women, and children a chance to get out into nature and away from the pressures of daily living.

Realizing the demand for quality fly-fishing retreats where people can receive guidance and instruction, not to mention camaraderie, I have included some of the top fly-fishing lodges in the United States. While many of the ranches in this guide offer fly-fishing and are located on or near superb trout waters, this section is devoted to those that offer top instruction and guide service.

In selecting a facility, you must first decide where in North America you would like to go. Read the descriptions and write or call for a brochure. Some of the brochures are very modest, so do not judge the facility solely on this basis. As with all ranches in this guide, remember that each is unique and represents the personality of the host. Ask for references and find out if the level of instruction is sufficient to help you achieve your expectations. Every property in this section will show you a wonderful fishing experience.

Even though it is an exacting sport, the basics of fly-fishing are not difficult to master. A tremendous amount of information is available in books and videos. I highly recommend that you contact a fly-fishing school before embarking on a fly-fishing vacation. Most of the leading instructors of this sport would agree that if you can master, or at least become familiar with, the techniques of fly casting before you leave, your overall experience will be much more enjoyable and fulfilling. The easiest way to find out about these schools is to contact your local fly-fishing store/outfitter.

Before buying any equipment, check with the lodge to see what you will need to bring. Many have their own shops and can take care of most of your needs. Don't be afraid to ask questions. The more you learn about this sport, the more fun you will have.

Now go out and tie one on.

Author's Note: You will notice that some of the ranches and lodges have under their name "Orvis-Endorsed Lodge." Each of these properties has been endorsed by the world-renowned Orvis Company. This retail/mail order company is dedicated to enriching lives and providing not only top merchandise but also first-rate service. Toward this end, Orvis has developed this Orvis-Endorsed Lodge program as a special service to its customers. These fly-fishing lodges and ranches are monitored by Orvis personnel and must maintain high standards. Thus, Orvis can recommend each and every one with confidence. We are delighted to include this Orvis endorsement and feel that it complements and enriches our goal of providing you with the very best fly-fishing opportunities.

Crystal Creek Lodge, Alaska

Orvis-Endorsed Lodge

You have probably dreamed about Alaska—and with good reason. It is big, fresh, wild, free, and filled with adventure. This is a land of mountains, tundra, glaciers, and lakes, where the scenery is overwhelming and the wildlife untamed. Located amid all of this is Crystal Creek Lodge. Terry Eberle created this premiere Alaskan fishing retreat to complement a life of adventure. He offers men and women alike an Alaskan adventure/fishing experience second to none. At Crystal Creek, you will be treated like a king and get to see and fish as much of Alaska as you could possibly want in a week. If you are one of those who likes to really rough it or doesn't like to fly, this probably is not the place for you. The lodge offers all upscale amenities, and fly-out service each day with your guide is a major part of this exhilarating Alaskan experience.

Address: P.O. Box 3049 K, Dillingham, Alaska 99576 (summer); 3819 E, Drawer K, LaSalle, Phoenix, Arizona 88504 (information and reservations)
Telephone: (800) 525-3153, (602) 437-8780
Location: Bristol Bay area, Southwest Alaska; 320 miles southwest of Anchorage, 15 miles northwest of Dillingham
Memberships: Federation of Fly-Fishermen
Awards: Orvis-Endorsed Lodge
Medical: Kannaknek Hospital in Dillingham, 20-minute helicopter flight
Conference: 20
Guest Capacity: 20
Accommodations: The 9,800-square-foot main lodge is the center of operation. There are thirteen double occupancy rooms on two levels (1-7 lower, 8-13 upper); room 3 is the most spacious. Each is modern with full amenities including queen-size beds, full bathrooms (tub and shower combination) with plenty of hot water, even though the lodge is powered by its own generator, and individual temperature controls. Because during the summer months it is light almost 20 hours a day, there are "blackout" shades in each room. Daily maid and laundry service is provided. The lodge also has changing and boot-drying rooms.
Rates: • $$$$. Full American Plan. Saturday to Saturday with six days fishing and seven nights lodging. Includes everything except round-trip airfare to Dillingham, fishing licenses, flies/lures, and liquor (drinks during happy hour and wine with dinner included).
Credit Cards: Visa, MasterCard
Season: Mid-June to mid-September
Activities: The lodge is located right on Lake Nunavaugaluk, which is in the center of southwest Alaska's Bristol Bay area, known for its large salmon runs and trophy class fishing. There are five planes and two helicopters to take you and your guide to remote fishing areas. Here you will fish for king, chum, sockeye, pink, and silver salmon, rainbow and lake trout, arctic char, arctic grayling, Dolly Varden, and northern pike. Fully equipped tackle shop in lodge. Call for more details.
Children's Programs: Children are welcome. Not recommended for children under 10.
Dining: Breakfast is cooked to order. After breakfast the chef will ask you for dinner preference from three different entrées that change daily. Streamside sack lunches (you give your lunch order the night before), and occasionally your guide will prepare fresh-caught salmon. Happy hour at 5:00 p.m. (complimentary open bar) with hors d'oeuvres. Wine served with dinner.
Entertainment: After a full day of fishing and flying, most guests are delightfully worn out.
Summary: Crystal Creek Lodge offers excellent personal service, comfort, and superb daily fly-in/fly-out fishing in seven aircraft. You will see an abundance of wildlife. Ask about the bear sanctuary and the scenic helicopter flights to Wood-Tikchik State Park. If you desire, your legal limit of freshly caught salmon will be cleaned, vacuum-packed, and frozen for your trip home. (Author's Note: You should definitely like to fly and enjoy fishing. Avid photographers should bring plenty of film.)

PJ's Lodge, Arkansas

It may look like a country club setting, but this red cedar lodge on the banks of the White River, overlooking the Ozark National Forest, is fast becoming one of the most popular fly-fishing retreats in the country. PJ's (named after Paul and Joyce Campbell, your hosts and the owners) octagonal, 11-room lodge with 18-foot ceilings was completed in 1986. Campbell, an artist whose works used to line the wharf on Cannery Row in Monterey, California, and his wife, Joyce, moved from California and built the lodge. "It's new but old," says Joyce. "We've tried to combine modern conveniences with 30ish period furnishings." The lodge was built purposely at the center of 100 miles of productive Arkansas trout water. PJ's is the only lodge in the area that offers complete services for the fly-fisherman with fly-fishing schools year-round.

Address: P.O. Box 61 K, Norfork, Arkansas 72658
Telephone: (501) 499-7500
Airport: Little Rock; Baxter County Municipal Airport for private planes, and commuter service via St. Louis
Location: 145 miles north of Little Rock, 20 miles southeast of Mountain Home
Medical: Calico Rock Hospital, 15 miles
Conference: 20; 700-square-foot facility
Guest Capacity: 22
Accommodations: The lodge is a cross between a mountain retreat and a mountain country club situated at the edge of a pasture. Dwarfed by towering elm, oak, and ash trees, the lodge overlooks the river and Ozark National Forest. There is a centrally located lounge and 11 guest rooms with double and twin beds, all with hardwood floors and rough-hewn cedar siding looking out to the neighboring pasture and hills. The sliding glass doors in each room look out to a cedar walkway lined by marigolds, pansies, petunias, and snapdragons, which Joyce plants each spring. Laundry facilities available.
Rates: $$-$$$$. American Plan. Does not include fishing guides, license, or tackle.
Credit Cards: None. Checks or cash accepted.

Season: Year-round, including Thanksgiving and Easter. Closed Christmas and from late January to mid-February.
Activities: This is a fly-fishing lodge offering some of the finest trout fishing in the country. You can also fly-fish for striped bass. Paul offers one- to three-day fishing clinics and schools with nationally known instructors. Guides and float and canoe trips can be arranged. Nonanglers enjoy hiking, canoeing, and antique hunting. Expect temperatures in July and August to be in the mid-90s. November through mid-January offers exceptional trophy fishing for trout and landlocked stripers.
Children's Programs: None. Recommended for children over 12 who like to fish.
Dining: The restaurant, open to the public on weekends, is more gourmet than country. Among the specialties are trout with peppers and onions, Cajun or curry trout, and Cornish game hen. Local vegetables are served freshly steamed. Joyce grew up in the bakery business and has some fabulous gourmet desserts. BYOB.
Entertainment: Evening story swapping, like the 38 lb. 9 oz. German brown that was caught recently on the North Fork River, 8 miles away—that's for real. Paul or one of his guides usually ties flies in the evening.
Summary: Year-round fly-fishing lodge with schools and clinics taught by national and internationally known instructors. Ozark Folk Center, Blanchard Springs and Caverns, treasure hunting in local antique shops, and the lovely local mountain scenery.

Arcularius Ranch, California

Arcularius Ranch is one of the premier catch and release, wet and dry fly-fishing ranches in California. Since 1919, the Arcularius family has run this 1,000-acre cattle ranch and has been concerned stewards of their property. In the main lodge, numerous photo albums pay tribute to guests who have come to enjoy this fishing haven, including such notables as the late Herbert Hoover. The ranch is near Mammoth Mountain and fifty-three miles northeast of Bishop (famous for its annual Mule Days). It maintains almost five miles of private stream on the Owens River, one of the richest fly-fishing streams in the country, where record 5-pound to 7-pound rainbow and German brown trout have been landed. Astounding as it may sound, some 50,000 fish inhabit this five-mile stretch of water, all of them wild trout, not hatchery transplants. John Arcularius limits the number of fishermen as well as the number of fish you can pull out of the river. One guest commented, "It's a great place and the fishing is the icing on the cake."

Address: Route 1, Box 230 K, Mammoth Lakes, California 93546
Telephone: (619) 648-7807 (summer); (805) 238-3830 (winter)
Airport: June Mammoth Airport; Reno International, 150 miles
Location: 14 miles due northeast of Mammoth Lakes off Highway 395, 53 miles northeast of Bishop, 150 miles south of Reno
Medical: Mammoth Lakes Hospital, 14 miles
Guest Capacity: 50
Accommodations: Fifteen one- to six-bedroom housekeeping cabins, with knotty pine interiors and very clean kitchens, equipped with everything you need. All cabins (except the Bob Steel Cabin) have bathrooms with showers, heaters, and electricity; some have porches. No daily maid service, but sheets will be changed on request. In the main lodge there is a tackle shop, small country grocery store, common living room for all guests, a pool table, and selection of fly-fishing videos.

Rates: $. Check with ranch for rates.
Credit Cards: None. Personal checks accepted.
Season: Late April to November
Activities: Catch and release fly-fishing only on Hot Creek. Fishing also on Crowley Lake and lakes of the eastern Sierras. Most of the guests fish morning, noon, and into the twilight hours. Guides are available if arranged in advance. Bring your own equipment. Recommended flies—Adams Fly, Elk Hair Cadis, Gold Ribs, Hairs Ear, Pheasant Tail Nymph, Maribu Streamer. If you don't fish, you can relax or hike into the nearby Sierras.
Children's Programs: None
Dining: You are on your own in the cooking department. Cabins have cooking facilities, and groceries should be purchased before you arrive. Many nice restaurants are just fourteen miles away.
Entertainment: Tell your big fish stories in the main lodge. Fishing videos.
Summary: Very peaceful ranch next to the pines with high desert scenery. John reports 85 percent repeat customers each summer. One guest has returned every year since 1923. High-quality adventures in fly-fishing. Recommended for experienced anglers. Catch and release only; John is very strict and conservation minded. Nearby Bodie ghost town, Devil's Post Pile, Mammoth Resort (14 miles), and Mono Lake (10 miles).

Elk Creek Lodge, Colorado

Orvis-Endorsed Lodge

In describing their vacation at Elk Creek Lodge, one couple wrote, "It was a fishing vacation dreams are made of." And so it is. Since 1930 the Wheeler family has owned over 20,000 acres in northwestern Colorado. In previous years, the family ran an extensive cattle operation. In 1989, Bill Wheeler, with the support of his Kansas-based family began work on a long-time family dream. Elk Creek Lodge opened its doors to the world in early 1990. What makes the Wheelers' fishing operation so unique is the fact that guests have access to so much private land and fishing water. Elk Creek runs right past the lodge with over 100 log-dammed pools. Guests also fish on six private miles of the White River, on Trapper Lake (the second largest natural lake in Colorado), as well as on a variety of streams, rivers, and high mountain lakes. For those with real adventure in their blood, Elk Creek offers fly-out fishing (1½ hours to first cast) to Utah's Green River, known for its great dry fly-fishing and 10,000 trout per mile. Together with manager Steve Herter and a great staff, Bill and his wife, Melise, will give you the fishing vacation of a lifetime.

Address: P.O. Box 130K, Meeker, Colorado 81641
Telephone: (303) 878-4565
Airport: Steamboat Springs, Aspen, and Grand Junction
Location: 2 hours north of Aspen, 180 miles west of Denver, 250 miles east of Salt Lake City
Memberships: Trout Unlimited, Rocky Mountain Elk Foundation, Nature Conservancy, Ducks Unlimited
Awards: Orvis-Endorsed Lodge
Medical: Meeker Hospital, 20 miles
Conference: 25. Excellent for corporate retreat. Sleeping accommodations in various ranch quarters.
Guest Capacity: 15
Accommodations: Guest quarters vary depending on the size of the group. Most stay in one of four suites, three with lofts. All have vaulted ceilings, electric blankets, flannel sheets, private baths, and common porches. Families with children may stay in the two-bedroom with kitchen Cowboy House. Spill-over from larger corporate groups stay at the lower K/K Ranch.
Rates: • $$$-$$$$. Full inclusive package rates. Preferred package is 5 days, 6 nights with two days of fly-out fishing. Nonfishing spouse, group (over 6), and corporate rates.
Credit Cards: Visa, MasterCard
Season: July through September; hunting September to mid-November
Activities: All anglers, expert and beginner, will have a unique fishing experience. However, if you are an expert who likes to make sure everyone knows you are tops to the detriment of beginners, this is not the place for you. Wide variety of fishing. Professional and friendly guides. Fully stocked tackle shop. Horseback riding from Trappers Lake (ask about the ride and mountain lake fishing). Hiking, mountain biking, nature photography, and trap shooting. Elk hunters, ask Bill about his fall hunting program.
Children's Activities: Children under 12 are not recommended. Best for children who really wish to learn or are already enthusiastic about fly-fishing.
Dining: Elk Creek takes great pride in its cuisine. Guests eat together at one large table. All meals served individually. Hosted dinners, California wines served. Variety of shore/fishing lunches. Weekly guides, hosted barbecue night along Elk Creek.
Entertainment: Fishing movies, casting demonstrations, fly-casting "golf" course, horseshoes.
Summary: Exciting new fly-fishing lodge with a tremendous variety of fly-fishing on private waters. Fly-out fishing to Utah's Green River. Excellent for both beginners and experts.

Elktrout Lodge, Colorado

Orvis-Endorsed Lodge

Elktrout Lodge is one of America's premier fly-fishing retreats. At 7,375 feet, this fly-fisherman's haven was founded by a group of businessmen who were also anglers dedicated to providing unsurpassed quality trout fishing in a totally private environment. The property includes five miles of private Gold Medal water on the Colorado River. These waters are full of large brown and rainbow trout. In addition, surrounding streams and lakes hold tremendous numbers of brook and rainbow trout. One can also float on high mountain lakes for an angling thrill beyond compare — 18- to 24-inch rainbows, browns, and brooks that weigh up to 10 pounds. Guests who hook these become members of the highly coveted Elktrout "21" Club. Beginners are welcome; Elktrout offers an extensive instructional program. Professional guides are selected for their friendliness, teaching ability, and fly-fishing know-how. Besides the superb fly-fishing, Elktrout provides handsome accommodations and meals. Ask about the excellent private fall hunting program.

Address: P.O. Box 614 K, Kremmling, Colorado 80459
Telephone: (303) 724-3343
Airport: Denver; private planes and small jets at Kremmling Municipal Airport, 5,500-foot paved runway
Location: 110 miles northwest of Denver, 50 miles south of Steamboat Springs, 70 miles east of Vail
Memberships: Trout Unlimited
Awards: Orvis-Endorsed Lodge, *Hideaway Report*
Medical: Kremmling Hospital, 2 miles
Conference: 20
Guest Capacity: 20
Accommodations: Eight-bedroom, hand-hewn log lodge. All rooms have private baths. Lodge overlooks the Colorado River Valley and hay meadows. The owners' "Executive Cabin," a beautiful two-bedroom log home, is available when the owners are not in residence. All beds have electric blankets. In the two-story living room of the main lodge are a tremendous fireplace and a wet bar, where guests relax and share fishing stories. Tasteful antique Western furnishings.
Rates: • $$$$. American Plan (guides included). Special rates for nonfishing spouses. Off-season rates available.
Credit Cards: None. Personal checks accepted.
Season: Late May to mid-November
Activities: Fly-fishing is the main activity. Elktrout has some of the finest private trout fishing in the western United States. All fishing is on private water exclusive to the lodge's guests: five miles of Colorado River, three miles of Blue River, a Gold Medal stream, lakes, and small streams. All fishing must be done with provided fishing guides. Tackle shop on premises. Equipment rental available. For nonfishing spouses/guests, the management will make arrangements for horseback riding, hiking, tennis, golf, shopping, or sight-seeing, but guests must provide their own transportation.
Children's Programs: None. Recommended for children who enjoy or want to learn how to fly-fish.
Dining: Bountiful meals. Huge breakfasts. Lunch is usually eaten on the river. Elegant evening dining with crystal and china, illuminated with antique oil lamps and candles. Four-course dinners, with complimentary California cabernet and chardonnay. Once a week, there is a marvelous authentic chuck wagon dinner on the Blue River with entertainment. Fruit, cookies, and beverages always available.
Entertainment: Fly-tying and fishing videos. Most guests prefer to fish, and fish, and fish. Rodeo in September.
Summary: World-class fly-fishing with expert guides. Great for families, couples, and singles who enjoy lots of fly-fishing. Excellent for groups and corporate retreats. Rocky Mountain National Park nearby.

See color photos, page 219

Fryingpan River Ranch, Colorado

Authentic Western Ranch, Member–Dude Ranchers'
Association • Orvis-Endorsed Lodge

The Fryingpan River Ranch is a small, family ranch located on the upper waters of the renowned Fryingpan River looking out over pretty Nast Lake. The ranch offers guided and unguided fishing on the Fryingpan and Roaring Fork rivers, as well as many of the high lakes surrounding the ranch. After fishing the gold medal catch and release waters of the Fryingpan below Ruedi Dam or floating the Roaring Fork, many guests find the wild trout and challenging waters of the upper Fryingpan a welcome diversion. Nast Lake, less than one hundred yards from the lodge, is full of brook and rainbows eager to add to the confidence of beginners and experts alike. A Fryingpan River Ranch vacation is perfect for those families where some members are avid fishermen and others prefer guest ranch activities.

Address: 32042 Fryingpan Road, Drawer K, Meredith, Colorado 81642
Telephone: (303) 927-3570; Fax: (303) 927-3570 (call first)
Airport: Aspen or Denver
Location: 31 miles up the Fryingpan River from Basalt, Colorado; 1¼ hours from Aspen
Memberships: Colorado Dude and Guest Ranch Association, Dude Ranchers' Association
Awards: Orvis-Endorsed Lodge
Medical: Aspen or Glenwood Springs, 50 miles
Conference: 36
Guest Capacity: 36
Accommodations: Guests stay in six cabins and two lodge suites. Each cabin has its own special charm. Some offer views of Nast Lake, while others overlook the Fryingpan River. Two are secluded in the pines away from the main activity of the lodge and conference center. Most rooms and cabins were redecorated in 1987-88. Pine and antique furnishings reflect the heritage of the ranch, accented with art collected by Jim and Paula. Each cabin or suite has its own private bath and excellent beds. The hot tub overlooking Nast Lake is available year-round. No smoking in any of the buildings.

Rates: $$-$$$$. American Plan. Rates available with and without guide service. Rates vary depending on the season.
Credit Cards: Visa, MasterCard. Personal checks and traveler's checks accepted.
Season: Year-round
Activities: Fishing guests who select a vacation with guides will fish a variety of waters—the gold medal catch-and-release fishing below Ruedi Dam, floats or walk-wade fishing on the Roaring Fork, and a variety of private water on both of these rivers. Above the ranch are eight miles of pristine, seldom-fished, never-stocked water where wild fish and wild country combine for an unforgettable experience. Nast Lake sits less than a hundred yards from the lodge and is full of brook and rainbow trout. Fishing is also available in the high lakes and streams that surround the ranch. For the not-so-serious angler, the ranch offers a full horse program including instruction, half- and full-day rides, and a breakfast ride once a week. Overnight pack trips are available. Guided hiking, as well as mountain bikes, trap and rifle shooting, along with archery, river rafting, and four-wheel-drive trips are available. Some swim in Nast Lake. The hot tub at the end of the day soothes casting arms as well as tired riders.
Children's Programs: No children's programs.
Dining: Hearty and healthy varied ranch menus include beef, lamb, pork, chicken, and trout. Wild game is occasionally served. Early fishing breakfasts. Special diets catered to with advance notice. BYOB.
Entertainment: Well-stocked library, VCR with a selection of fishing videos, and a cozy log lodge.
Summary: A great fly-fishing vacation for the whole family! Excellent for those who love to fish morning, noon, and night, and for those members of the family who would rather ride, hike, paint the wildflowers, or just relax. Great hosts—Paula is a fabulous wildlife artist. Nearby attractions include the town of Aspen, 75 minutes away.

See color photos, page 191

Fryingpan River Ranch, Colorado

Fryingpan River Ranch, Colorado

Three Rivers Ranch, Idaho

Orvis-Endorsed Lodge

Three Rivers Ranch is one of the top catch-and-release fishing lodges in North America. You can expect a first-class fishing program. Hosts and owners Don and Lonnie Allen combine Idaho hospitality and mountain know-how (Lonnie has the pizzaz; Don has the mountain and fishing savvy). The ranch is licensed to guide on some of the most famous fishing rivers in North America, including the Madison, Henry's Fork, and the South Fork of the Snake River. Three Rivers is about an hour's drive northeast of Idaho Falls. You'll see the Idaho side of the sawtoothed Grand Tetons towering in the distance as you drive to the ranch from Jackson.

Address: P.O. Box 856 K, Warm River, Ashton, Idaho 83420
Telephone : (208) 652-3750; (208) 652-7819
Airport: Idaho Falls
Location: 52 miles northeast of Idaho Falls, 9 miles from Ashton off Highway 47
Memberships: Outfitters and Guides of Idaho, Nature Conservancy, Trout Unlimited, Ducks Unlimited, Elk Foundation
Awards: Orvis-Endorsed Lodge
Medical: Ashton Hospital, 9 miles
Conference: 24
Guest Capacity: 24
Accommodations: Guests stay in five rustic cabins (two have recently been rebuilt), under tall shade trees along Robinson Creek, and in six rooms at Three Rivers Ranch House overlooking Warm River, a separate facility accommodating up to twelve, which is excellent for corporate, business, or family groups. All cabins have porches, Western antiques, carpets, and electric heat. All cabins and rooms have private baths and showers.
Rates: • $$$$. American Plan. Day trips and weekly packages available.
Credit Cards: American Express
Season: Late May to mid-October
Activities: Fishing days can be arranged to satisfy the desire of each angler. Most guests split their time wading and floating. Fishing options are limitless. Programs are designed for beginners, intermediates, and advanced fishermen. All flies are hand-tied by guides at the ranch. Individual instruction is given as needed. All Three Rivers guides are pros, and there are never more than two guests to each guide. Nonfishing spouses enjoy guided tours of the area, shopping (Jackson and West Yellowstone), or just plain old relaxing. Hiking, trail rides, pack trips, and overnight fishing float trips on the South Fork of the Snake River are available but extra.
Children's Programs: Children over age 14 only
Dining: Except for most lunches, which are eaten riverside with fishing guides, meals are served either in the handsome lodge filled with antiques and memorabilia or at the ranch house. The evening meal is a special part of the day. Each evening Don and Lonnie host a happy hour. Prime rib with Idaho potatoes and Cornish game hen are just two of the wonderful dishes. Rum cakes and, apple pie. All guests enjoy the weekly old-time steak barbecue—a time to tell your fishing tale of the week on a wonderful deck overlooking Robinson Creek.
Entertainment: Guests either visit after dinner, sipping on a little brandy while swapping fish stories, or retire after a long day.
Summary: Superb fly-fishing and excellent guides. Tackle shop on property. Area attractions include Yellowstone Park, Mesa Falls, tours in the Targhee National Forest, the town of Jackson, Railroad Ranch, and Harriman State Park.

Falcon, Inc., Maine

Orvis-Endorsed Lodge

Spencer Lake Lodge, Hardscrabble Lodge, and Drop Camps are all part of Falcon, Inc.—a new wilderness lodging company based in Bangor and specializing in remote wilderness retreat fishing and hunting. Set in Maine's western mountains and North Country, the Falcon properties are surrounded by thousands of acres of privately managed woodlands with majestic views and quiet natural isolation. The Falcon program can be experienced three ways, ranging from total rugged luxury to roughing it at Drop Camps. Whichever you choose, you will be enveloped in spectacular Maine backcountry in the heart of excellent fishing and hunting. Falcon's premier property is Spencer Lake Lodge, an expansive six-bedroom log lodge with cathedral ceilings, a granite fireplace, and a host of VIP activities all included in the fare. The second property is Hardscrabble, a smaller, more intimate lodge offering excellent fishing and hunting without a lot of extras. This is a happy medium for sportsmen who want quality guided fishing and hunting in beautiful surroundings. For those who like to commune with nature and don't need luxuries, at least for a few days, Falcon's Drop Camps take advantage of the full wilderness experience.

Address: P.O. Box 1899 K, Bangor, Maine 04402-1899
Telephone: (207) 990-4534; (800) 825-8234
Airport: Bangor International, 120 miles
Location: Spencer Lake, 120 miles west of Bangor; Hardscrabble Lodge, 130 miles northwest of Bangor
Memberships: Maine Professional Guide Association, Main Sporting Camp Association
Awards: Orvis-Endorsed Lodge
Medical: Jackman, 14 air miles
Conference: 12 (Spencer Lake Lodge)
Guest Capacity: 26 (both lodges)
Accommodations: Luxurious Spencer Lake Lodge offers six private, soundproof rooms with baths, 122 feet of deck overlooking Spencer Lake, private patio doors opening onto a deck, and a fully stocked fly-tying bench. Hardscrab-

ble Lodge, on a point that affords a beautiful panoramic view of upper Spencer Lake, is a rustic lodge that can accommodate 14 guests in its 5 comfortable private cabins. At the Drop Camps, which are selected for the quality of fishing and hunting, you must bring your own food, clothing, sleeping gear, fishing, and hunting equipment. Falcon supplies the rest, including canoes and boats.
Rates: • $-$$$$. Call ranch for packages. Corporate/group and children's rates available. Minimum stay policy. Licenses extra.
Credit Cards: Visa, MasterCard, American Express
Season: Year-round
Activities: General fishing begins early April and runs through September. True Maine wilderness fishing for brook trout, lake trout, and landlocked salmon, much of it on cold water lakes and ponds, accessible by four-wheel drive or float plane. Hunting season normally begins early September. Superb trophy white-tailed deer hunting in both locations. All Falcon locations are in prime bear country. Maine is one of the premier bear hunting states in the country. Winter activities are cross-country skiing, snowshoeing, ice fishing. Snowmobile weekend packages available.
Children's Programs: None. Children should be about 12 and are usually old enough to fish.
Dining: Ranges from gourmet to cook-your-own trout, depending on which property you choose. Fine wines and preferred beverages provided.
Entertainment: Most just relax and enjoy each other's company.
Summary: Executive retreat, luxury lodge, Drop Camp tents. Superb fishing and hunting. Prior to arrival, each lodge guest is contacted about preferences concerning culinary, fine wine, beverage, and other needs. Maine is alive with bear and moose. Video available on request.

Big Hole River Outfitters, Montana

Craig Fellin owns and operates a small fly-fishing operation. Craig offers a superb fly-fishing experience in the ranch country of southwestern Montana. This small lodge borders Beaverhead National Forest. The scenery is magnificent, and it is not uncommon to see moose, elk, deer, and mountain goats. The beautiful Wise River flows through the ranch, so you can cast to rising trout almost from your doorstep. Within minutes your guide can float you down the Big Hole, one of the most scenic rivers in the West, famous for its large, wild trout. The Beaverhead River nearby boasts some of the largest trout in Montana. Horseback trips to numerous high mountain lakes can be arranged for cutthroat and grayling. Craig's philosophy is simple: take only 12 guests and give them the best fishing trip of their lives. To do this, Craig prefers guests who can stay with him for 6 nights and 5 days.

Address: P.O. Box 156 K, Wise River, Montana 59762
Telephone: (406) 832-3252
Airport: Butte via Salt Lake City
Location: 45 miles southwest of Butte
Memberships: Montana Trout Foundation, Trout Unlimited, Fishing Floating Outfitters Association of Montana
Medical: St. James Hospital, Butte
Guest Capacity: 12
Accommodations: Guests stay in either the new log lodge with two bedrooms, a duplex cabin, or a two-bedroom log cabin along the Wise River. All have electric heat, twin and queen beds, some with electric blankets. The two smaller cabins have screened porches. The newest log cabin has a full kitchen, wood-burning stove, living room, dining room, and open front porch.
Rates: • $$$-$$$$. American Plan. Six-night and five-day packages only.
Credit Cards: None
Season: May to mid-October
Activities: The fly-fishing program is tailored to guests' level of experience. Beginners and advanced fishermen are welcome. Personal and patient instruction for beginners is one of Craig's specialties. Each group will be challenged. One guide to a maximum of two guests. Guided float or wading trips on the Big Hole, Beaverhead, and Wise rivers. Excellent fly-fishermen should ask Craig about Poindexter Slough, a classic spring creek. Horseback trips to a mountain lake can be arranged by a local outfitter. No rental equipment available; however, Craig has a very well stocked fly shop with Winston rods. On those days you care not to fish, your fishing guide will take you on a wonderful sightseeing trip.
Children's Programs: Young children not advised. Craig encourages teens who want to learn about fly-fishing. Ask Craig about his special father/son and father/daughter weeks.
Dining: Country family-style meals. Lunches are served streamside with cloth napkins and tablecloths. Happy hour before dinner. Fine dining by candlelight with soft music in the new lodge. Wines served.
Entertainment: After a relaxing dinner, most people are so pleasantly tired that they are ready to drift off to sleep. Some, though, enjoy fishing in the evening within steps from the main lodge.
Summary: Top fly-fishing with personalized, caring service. Craig has been featured on the Today Show, ESPN's "Fishing the World," and in *Condé Nast Traveler.* Nearby attractions include Dillon Rodeo, hot springs, Big Hole Monument Battlefield, historic wilderness mining mill.

Eagle Nest Lodge, Montana

Orvis-Endorsed Lodge

In 1981, Alan Kelly opened a new chapter in his life. With his family's support, he began Eagle Nest Lodge, with excellent trout fishing during the summer months and game-bird hunting in the fall. Alan was a U.S. Fish and Wildlife Service biologist who was responsible for the fishery supplying one of the nation's richest trout streams, the Big Horn River. With his thorough knowledge of fish, the Big Horn River, and his love for this part of the country, Alan and his wife, Wanda, are able to provide Eagle Nest Lodge guests with superb service, lots of personal attention, and world-class fishing. Alan and Wanda take only 10 guests at a time. The Big Horn River is clear and cold year-round, yet never freezes. Fly hatches are almost continuous and at times unbelievably abundant. Alan also offers terrific fall hunting for upland birds, including pheasant, partridge, and sharptail grouse. Montana's grandeur, vastness, and diversity provide a backdrop for unforgettable experiences. Eagle Nest Lodge is for magnificent fly-fishing and upland bird hunting. Alan and Wanda love what they do, and it has earned them a great reputation and many loyal guests. Their southern warmth and hospitality show in everything they do. Smokers, be forewarned. There is a strictly enforced no smoking policy in the main lodge.

Address: P.O. Box 470 K, Hardin, Montana 59034
Telephone: (406) 665-3799; Fax: (406) 665-3762
Airport: Logan International Airport, Billings, 50 miles
Location: 3 miles south of Hardin, 50 miles east of Billings off Interstate 90
Memberships: Trout Unlimited, American Museum of Fly-Fishermen
Awards: *Hideaway Report*, Orvis-Endorsed Lodge
Medical: Hardin Hospital, 3 miles
Conference: 10
Guest Capacity: 10
Accommodations: The two-story, log Eagle Nest Lodge was built in 1985. It is set back from the river and features large bedrooms with two single beds and a bath in each. There is a great trophy-studded dining room with an outside screened porch and old-fashioned swing. Rocking chairs are provided.
Rates: • $$$$. American Plan. Weekly all-inclusive packages only. No day trips.
Credit Cards: None. Personal checks accepted.
Season: Mid-April to mid-November
Activities: Most fishing takes place on the Big Horn River. All fishing guests are guided in drift boats with stream wading. There is fishing year-round here, but the best months are May through October. Alan will tell you exactly what you need to bring and what he can supply. At Eagle Nest, there is an Orvis fly shop. Alan makes it clear there are only five things to do: fish in the summer, hunt in the fall, eat like a king, sleep like a baby, and enjoy the peace of Mother Nature.
Children's Programs: Children 13 and older are welcome, but make sure they really like fly-fishing.
Dining: Excellent gourmet, 4-course meals featuring garden vegetables, fresh baked bread, and scrumptious desserts.
Entertainment: Fly-fishing and shooting instruction.
Summary: Alan suggests that guests learn how to fly cast and/or shoot before arrival so that they will enjoy optimum fishing and/or hunting. Excellent fly-fishing and fall bird hunting. No smoking in main lodge. Custer Battlefield is nearby. French spoken.

Diamond J Ranch, Montana

Authentic Western Ranch, Member–Dude Ranchers' Association • Orvis-Endorsed Lodge

If you are looking for a fly-fishing experience that combines excellent fishing with a wonderful guest ranch program, the Diamond J may just be the answer. So many times, anglers will have a member of the family who does not fish. Many families have forgone summer vacations together just for this reason. More often than not, husbands have gone off fishing, leaving their families behind. The Diamond J Ranch is the perfect solution. If you are a die-hard angler, the ranch is situated in the center of some of the best Blue Ribbon streams in Montana. If other members of your family wish to horseback ride, play tennis, hike, or just relax, they can do it. Everyone can be happy at the Diamond J. This marvelous ranch is run by the terrific Combs family. Peter and Jinny, along with their grown children, Tim and Ginger, offer something for the entire family—anglers and nonanglers alike.

Address: P.O. Box 577 K, Ennis, Montana 59729
Telephone: (406) 682-4867; Fax: (406) 682-4106
Airport: Bozeman
Location: 14 miles east of Ennis off Highway 287, 60 miles south of Bozeman
Memberships: Dude Ranchers' Association
Awards: Orvis-Endorsed Lodge
Medical: Ennis Hospital, 14 miles
Conference: 36 (June and September)
Guest Capacity: 36
Accommodations: There are 10 cozy log cabins, each with hardwood floors, a rock fireplace, matching furniture, and beds. Each has a full bath with separate shower stalls and a cast iron tub. Cabins have their own writing desks and porches.
Rates: • $$-$$$. American Plan. Call ranch for specifics.
Credit Cards: MasterCard
Season: June through September
Activities: The ranch is in the Madison River Valley and very close to its crown jewel, the Madison River. Many take side trips to fish the Beaverhead, Big Hole, Missouri, Jefferson, Gallatin, and Yellowstone Park waters (Firehole and Gibbon).

The ranch has its own little stream they call Jack Creek and a two-acre lake. Most fishing takes place from June through September with wet flies and salmon fly hatches in June. Dry fly-fishing July and August and streamer fishing for spawning browns in September. Available trips include wading, floating, belly tubes on mountain lakes, rivers, and springs. Full guide service available. Usually one guide per two guests. Full tackle shop in Ennis. All trips are tailored individually to each guest. Nonfishing members of the family will enjoy full horseback riding, tennis, and hiking. Do as much or as little as you wish.

Children's Programs: No set program. Kiddie wrangler with instruction. Kids usually ride together. Baby-sitting available.

Dining: Sack and barbecue lunches on shore for all those who fish. Anglers on overnight float trips get to experience the tent "chalet." Back at the ranch, family-style hearty dining in three (they prefer no smoking) dining rooms. BYOB happy hour.

Entertainment: Campfires, sing-alongs, and a great library. The Combses subscribe to the best-sellers list.

Summary: An excellent fly-fishing ranch for the entire family. Those who love to fish are in excellent hands. And for those who do not stay awake at night dreaming about fly-fishing, the ranch has a host of nonfishing activities.

See color photos, page 223

Diamond J Ranch, Montana

Diamond J Ranch, Montana

Parade Rest Ranch, Montana

Parade Rest Ranch is in the heart of some of North America's best fly-fishing. With Grayling Creek literally at the back door and blue ribbon trout streams surrounding it, Parade Rest is a parade of outdoor activities, natural beauty, and, for those more inclined, lots of rest. Here there is no timetable or regimented activity list. Your time is your own, and you may do as much or as little as you wish. Walt and Shirley Butcher have been in the guest ranching business since the late 1970s. They are in their late sixties and extend true Western hospitality in all respects. Life at "PR" is informal. The dress code is whatever is comfortable, and, for the most part, that means an old pair of jeans. Mornings and evenings are cool, with midday temperatures in the mid- to high 80s. Parade Rest is a small dude/fly-fishing ranch run the old-fashioned way.

Address: 7979 Grayling Creek Road, Drawer K, West Yellowstone, Montana 59758; Winter: Sunrise RV Resort, 1403 West Broadway, Space 17K, Apache Junction, Arizona 85220
Telephone: (406) 646-7217 (summer); (602) 983-2653 (winter)
Airport: West Yellowstone, or Gallatin Field at Bozeman; also, commuter flights from Salt Lake City to West Yellowstone
Location: 8 miles northwest of Yellowstone, 90 miles south of Bozeman off Highway 191
Medical: West Yellowstone
Conference: 60
Guest Capacity: 60
Accommodations: Fifteen turn-of-the-century log cabins with one to four bedrooms each. They radiate Western warmth and are cheerfully furnished. All are named after the famous fishing rivers nearby. Ask Shirley about the Homestead cabin and her favorite Grayling single. All have porches, wood-burning stoves, full baths, and comfortable beds; the newest, three-story cabin is Aspen North. Several are along Grayling Creek. Nightly turn-down service. The Gallatin Lodge is a happy gathering spot for reading,

visiting, playing games, and listening to music.
Rates: • $-$$$. Full American Plan. Children's, corporate, off-season, and fly-fishing guide rates available.
Credit Cards: Visa, MasterCard, American Express
Season: Mid-May through September
Activities: Very few areas in the country offer such a diversity of fine fishing. Through the ranch flows one and a half miles of Grayling Creek, an excellent fly-fishing stream. Within minutes are the Madison, Gallatin, Firehole, and Gibbon. Full guide service is available. Just let Shirley know what you would like to do and she will arrange it for you. Also, ask her about the 3-day fly-fishing schools. Parade Rest is well known by all the local guides. Horseback riding is geared to your desires. Rides are accompanied by a wrangler and vary from an hour to all day. White water and scenic raft trips. Ask Shirley about the wilderness float trip. Ten-person hot tub outside Gallatin Lodge overlooking Grayling Creek.
Children's Programs: No special programs. Children are welcome. Kids will not have enough time in the day to do everything they would like. Children are the responsibility of parents.
Dining: Even if you are late from your fishing excursion, dinner will be waiting for you and your guide. The warm and friendly atmosphere is matched by great, hearty ranch cooking. Packed lunches are available to those wishing to ride, fish, raft, or explore all day. All meals are served all-you-can-eat, buffet-style in a central dining room. BYOB.
Entertainment: Nothing special. Many of the die-hard fishermen eat dinner, then go back out for more fishing. Cookouts on Monday and Friday nights. Western entertainment. Volleyball, basketball, and horseshoes.
Summary: Great fishing, hearty food, a relaxed atmosphere. Sincere Western ranch hospitality.

The Lodge at Chama, New Mexico

The unspoiled, picturesque San Juan Mountains of northern New Mexico are home to the 32,000-acre Lodge at Chama ranch. The ranch has been in one family since 1950, and today it maintains the highest standards of excellence in fishing, special hunting, and lodging amenities. Both lake and stream fly-fishing are the highlights of guest activities from June to October. Rainbow, brown, brook, and cutthroat trout thrive in this pristine environment of isolated, high-country lakes and miles of crystal-clear streams. Heavy-bodied fish from 16 inches to 25 inches will test your fishing skills. Your fishing guide will put you where the fish are, share some of his Chama fishing secrets, and help to give you the fishing experience of a lifetime. Hunters, be sure to talk with General Manager Frank Simms about the world-class fall and winter hunting/lodging program.

Address: Box 127K, Chama, New Mexico 87520
Telephone: (505) 756-2133; Fax: (505) 756-2519
Airport: Albuquerque International, private jets to Pagosa Springs. Call regarding ranch airstrip.
Location: 100 miles north of Santa Fe, 90 miles west of Taos
Awards: *Hideaway Report*: 1986 Fishing/Hunting Lodge of the Year; *Hideaway Report*: 1990 Best Sporting Retreat
Medical: Hospital in Espanola, emergency helicopter service available
Conference: 24 in board meeting room
Guest Capacity: 24
Accommodations: The handsome, 13,500-square-foot lodge offers panoramic views of the beautiful Chama Valley and snow-capped Colorado peaks from its twelve rooms. The huge living room is dominated by a 20-foot-wide rock fireplace, original Western art and sculpture, and fish and wildlife mounts. There are ten luxurious rooms with private baths, sitting/desk areas, lofty ceilings, large closets, and up-scale amenities. Two spacious junior suites, named Roadrunner and Bear, have fireplaces, vanity baths, televisions, and lounging areas.

Rates: $$$$. Full American Plan. Special fly-fishing and hunting packages available on request.
Credit Cards: None
Season: May to October for fishing. Mid-September to January for hunting. Conferences and viewing of wildlife (elk, mule deer, bear) year-round.
Activities: Private lake and stream fishing. Some waters reserved for catch and release only. Fishing equipment available; however, most people bring their own gear. Self-guided nature trail from lodge. Hiking, picnics, wildlife tours, photography trips. Guided ranch trail rides. Non-fishing spouses enjoy off-ranch activities including narrow gauge train rides, shopping tours to Taos or Santa Fe, and white-water rafting. After a full day of outdoor activities, you may relax in a ten-person, indoor, hydrotherapy whirlpool or enjoy a sauna. Superb fall elk and mule deer hunting on limited basis.
Children's Programs: None, unless the entire facility has been reserved for private use. Thus, you are assured of an adult atmosphere when you visit The Lodge at Chama.
Dining: Trail lunches and fishermen's special shore lunches. Excellent varied cuisine for all three daily meals. Ranch specialties include steaks, chops, trout, and fowl as well as New Mexican specialties made with wonderful chilies grown in New Mexico. Home-baked bread, rolls, desserts, and pastries.
Entertainment: Wide-screen television offers network programs, VCR movies, and fishing and wildlife videos.
Summary: Tremendous personal service. Excellent fishing and corporate retreat. You will come as guests and leave as friends. Elk and deer are frequent sundown visitors to the Lodge grounds. Spectacular sunsets.

See color photos, pages 230-231

Vermejo Park Ranch, New Mexico

In northeastern New Mexico is a 600,000-acre paradise called Vermejo Park Ranch. Since the turn of the century, this privately owned retreat has played host to professional, corporate, and creative individuals who have sought refuge from the stresses and strains of city life. Vermejo Park is, without question, one of the world's most unique wilderness sanctuaries offering those who come abundant wildlife and beauty as far as the eye can see. Because of its size, Vermejo offers anglers tremendous lake fishing in addition to 25 miles of mountain streams. Experts, intermediates, and beginners will enjoy the diversity and many fishing challenges. German brown, brook, rainbow, and the rare Rio Grande cutthroat are all here. Each summer the ranch hosts a fly-fishing clinic with internationally known instructors. Those who come, anglers, naturalists, hikers, photographers, hunters, historians, families, and corporate groups, will experience the best of the best. Vermejo Park Ranch—a tradition of excellence.

Address: P.O. Drawer E, Dept. K, Raton, New Mexico 87740
Telephone: (505) 445-3097, 445-5028; Fax: (505) 445-3474
Airport: Private aircraft and small jets to Crews Field, Raton, New Mexico; commercial flights to Albuquerque, New Mexico, or Denver (call for details)
Location: 45 miles west of Raton on Highway 555, 225 miles northeast of Albuquerque, 240 miles south of Denver
Memberships: Rocky Mountain Elk Foundation, Safari Club International
Medical: Miner's Colfax Medical Center, 40 miles
Conference: 60
Guest Capacity: 75
Accommodations: Seven newly remodeled turn-of-the-century guest homes with 3 to 12 bedrooms, some with fireplaces. All are carpeted, with twin beds, amenity basket, and oversized cotton towels. A newly constructed main log-style lodge houses a complete tackle shop, great

room, dining room, and lounge. The self-sufficient, full-service, 6-room Costilla Lodge at 10,000 feet is 28 miles away and is available for groups of 12 people. At either location, you will enjoy magnificent sunsets.
Rates: $$$$. Full American Plan. Fishing guides and vehicles extra. All-inclusive hunting packages and group rates available. Children age 12 and under, 50% off.
Credit Cards: None. Personal checks accepted.
Season: Summer: June to early September; October to December (elk and deer hunting); mid-April to mid-May (turkey hunting)
Activities: At check-in, the front desk will brief you on all the activities available. Full range of fly- and spinning-reel fishing. Lakes are stocked continually throughout the year. You can expect to catch 1-lb. to 5-lb. fish. All but a few lakes are accessible by car. The high lakes at 12,000 feet can only be reached by four-wheel drive, on horseback, or on foot. Trolling boats on many of the lakes. The tackle shop has over 200 flies. Limited fly- and spinning rods. Favorite flies: Royal Wulff, Damsel Nymph, Woolly Bugger, and the ranch's own Wonder Fly. Horseback riding and skeet shooting (guns and ammunition provided) are also available.
Children's Programs: No formal children's programs. Children are the responsibility of their parents. Ask about the NRA program at Whittington Center for children ages 13-17.
Dining: You will dine in a spacious area complete with fireplace, elk antler chandeliers, and Southwest-style furnishings. Dinner menu changes daily from western to southwestern favorites to gourmet meals. Picnic lunches available.
Summary: Executive world-class fishing and hunting retreat. Excellent for those who love fishing or just want to get away from it all, enjoying the serenity of 600,000 acres of private land with 21 lakes and 25 miles of fishing streams with an abundant amount of wildlife: elk and deer and over 140 varieties of birds (seasonal). Historical sites around the ranch. Call for details on fall and spring hunting packages.

See color photos, page 205

Morrison's Rogue River Lodge, Oregon

Morrison's Lodge was built in the mid-1940s on the banks of the Rogue River, now a federally designated wild and scenic river. The lodge is sixteen miles downriver from Grants Pass, amid groves of evergreen and oak. Morrison's is owned and operated by the Hanten family (B.A., Elaine, and daughter Michelle), and is well known for its blend of country style and gourmet cuisine with traditional family-style service. The big fishing season on this stretch of the Rogue is in the fall, with the best steelhead fishing September through November and salmon fishing in September. The lodge has maintained a fine reputation for fishing and retains some of the best licensed guides in the area. Morrison's uses traditional dory fishing boats for guided fishing, all equipment provided. For the bank or wading fisherman, the Rogue has easy access for fly-fishing (nonguided). Bank and wade fishermen must provide their own equipment. During the fishing season the lodge will make jet boat runs to spot fly-fishermen in prime fly casting waters each morning and evening. Though Morrison's traditionally has been an anglers' lodge, today it is equally popular with families, outdoorsmen, and romantics, especially in the summer. A major attraction is white water rafting, with one- to four-day trips available.

Address: 8500 Galice Road, Dept. K, Merlin, Oregon 97532
Telephone: (503) 476-3825; (800) 826-1963
Airport: Medford Commercial Airport, 1 hour; private planes, Josephine County Airport, 8 miles
Location: 46 miles northwest of Medford, 16 miles northwest of Grants Pass off I-5
Memberships: Oregon Guides and Packers
Awards: Orvis-Endorsed Lodge
Medical: Two hospitals in Grants Pass, 16 miles
Conference: 32
Guest Capacity: 32
Accommodations: Nine red-trimmed cottages and four rooms inside the lodge. All cottages, with comfortable furnishings, are on the second story with carports underneath. All feature a deck looking over a well-kept lawn, pines, and the Rogue River. All have private bath, wall-to-wall carpeting, air-conditioning, fireplaces, and television; four are equipped with full kitchenettes for summer housekeeping. The newly remodeled rooms in the lodge feature country decor and private baths. All accommodations receive daily maid service.
Rates: • $-$$$. Modified American Plan or Housekeeping Plan in summer. American Plan in fall. Rates vary depending on the season. Special fishing packages available.
Credit Cards: Visa, MasterCard, American Express
Season: May to November
Activities: Fall steelhead and salmon fishing. Summer white water rafting trips. One-day scenic float trips; 2- to 4-day trips through the wild and scenic section of the Rogue; 2- and 3-day white water trips to rustic lodges; and 4-day camping trips available. Heated swimming pool, hot tub, two tennis courts, putting green, and walking trails. Nearby jet boating and golf.
Children's Programs: No special programs. Children are the responsibility of their parents.
Dining: Four-course menu nightly, family style in the dining room or on the spacious redwood deck viewing the river, weather permitting. Entrées may include grilled leg of lamb, roast duck with plum sauce, or salmon with a green chile butter sauce. Beer, wine, and liquor served.
Entertainment: In-circuit movie is shown nightly.
Summary: Family owned and operated. Very homey atmosphere. Lots of return guests. Wide range of clientele—the young and the young-at-heart. Women particularly enjoy fishing here. Excellent fall steelhead fishing from dory boats. Summer white water rafting. As for the cuisine, Michelle says, "Don't come here to lose weight." Shakespeare Festival in Ashland, Crater Lake National Park. Video available of white water rafting trips.

Crescent H Ranch, Wyoming

Orvis-Endorsed Lodge

Crescent H Ranch was built in the late 1920s. Today, this 1,700-acre property is a world-class fly-fishing guest ranch, surrounded by the breathtaking magnificence of the Jackson Hole Valley. In 1963, Don Albrecht bought the old ranch as a summer retreat. In 1973, the Crescent H resumed receiving guests. With the guiddance of Vern Bressler, an experienced fish biologist and fly-fisherman, the ranch developed its international reputation. The Crescent H is run by Albrecht's son, Scott. "We specialize in personal service coupled with traditional Western hospitality," says Scott. "People who stay in elegant, metropolitan hotels will be comfortable here, but we offer a swing on the porch instead of a television in the room." Don't expect marble floors and taxis waiting for your summons, though. Do expect to experience magnificent rustic elegance, mouth-watering cuisine, and an excellent fly-fishing program.

Address: Box 347 K, Wilson, Wyoming 83014
Telephone: (307) 733-3674; Fax: (307) 733-3674
Airport: Jackson Hole
Location: 5 miles west of Jackson on Fall Creek Road
Memberships: Trout Unlimited, Jackson Chamber of Commerce
Awards: Original Orvis-Endorsed Lodge in North America
Medical: St. John's Hospital, Jackson Hole
Conference: 40
Guest Capacity: 30
Accommodations: There are about thirty log buildings on the ranch, all in harmony with the surroundings. There are ten darkly stained, charming log cabins in a large semicircle above the main lodge, each set on a gentle slope with views. Cabins have one, two, or three bedrooms, all decorated in a hunter green motif. Each has a shower, marble-topped bedside tables, carpeting, brass beds, and baskets of fresh fruit for new arrivals. The handsome log main lodge reflects the elegant rustic spirit here, with 30-foot ceilings, two stone fireplaces, wagon wheel lamps,

and bronze sculptures.
Rates: • $$$-$$$$. American Plan. Children's, group, corporate, and fly-fishing packages and schools available.
Credit Cards: None. Personal checks accepted.
Season: Late May through September
Activities: The fly-fishing program is under the direction of Ed Ingold. Experienced guides will show you the tremendous variety of fishing opportunities in the Jackson Hole area. The ranch owns more than seven miles of private spring creeks, with native cutthroat up to 22 inches. These challenge even the experienced fisherman. Float the Snake River through Grand Teton National Park or fish for large browns and rainbows in the Green River. Ranch guests also fish the nearby South Fork (in Idaho) and the Firehole and Yellowstone rivers in Yellowstone National Park. Horseback riding; half-day and all-day rides with riding instruction if desired. Rides go out seven days a week with no more than 8 riders per guide. Children under age 5 are led around the ranch. Weekly breakfast cookout rides. Two professional tennis courts, swimming in free-form, oval, heated pool, hiking, guided nature walks, float trips, and 18-hole golf nearby.
Children's Programs: Summer: Teenage boys' fly-fishing and backpacking program. Babysitting available. Daily children's program.
Dining: Elegant cuisine. Specialty game, fresh fish, two nightly entrées, and mouth-watering desserts. Fine wine and liquor served. A weekly Grand Barbecue overlooking the Snake River with cowboy music.
Entertainment: Nature and fly-fishing videos. Jackson weekly rodeo.
Summary: Premier fly-fishing and guest ranch with private fishing guides, Liar's Den fly shop, superb cuisine, rustic elegance. Be sure to ask Scott about his sister ranch called Firehole Ranch and the fishing opportunities there. Town of Jackson, Teton village, Yellowstone, and Grand Teton National Parks. Orvis fly-fishing schools and equipment.

See color photos, pages 236-237

Crescent H Ranch, Wyoming

Cross-Country Skiing Ranches

Introduction

Unlike northern Europeans, who grew up with the sport, North Americans have discovered cross-country skiing only in the past few years. Many people used to think of Nordic skiing, as it is sometimes called, not as a sport but as an occupational necessity. It was one of those things done by mountain climbers and National Geographic crews working on stories in the Antarctic.

Now cross-country skiing is taking the winter by storm. It is one of the fastest-growing winter activities, offering an alternative to downhill skiing for the entire family and the most wonderful combination of natural beauty, winter grace, and camaraderie. Health experts have given it their stamp of approval, recognizing cross-country skiing as the number one sport for low-impact cardiovascular exercise. It is more beneficial than jogging, high-impact aerobics, and marathon running. With Americans' renewed desire for fitness and spending time with family, cross-country skiing offers fun and good exercise in nature's winter beauty.

Skinny skiing, as some call it, is a friendly sport and not difficult to learn. It just takes practice. The better your skills, the more you will enjoy it. In the past few years, the choices in equipment have exploded. There are skis for tracking, skating, telemarking, and touring, not to mention the variety of boots, bindings, and clothing.

Cross-country skiing is suitable for the whole family. In this guide, I have included only those facilities that offer excellent, full-service programs, with instruction and guides available. All have created wonderful winter programs filled with many activities and unique skiing experiences. And each facility has its own individual charm and personality.

When making inquiries with your prospective host, you should ask the following: How much instruction is offered, and is the cost included in the package? Does the program include instruction for beginners as well as advanced skiers? If you are taking children, ask about activities for children. You might also wish to inquire about groomed trails, particularly machine-set tracks, as these are becoming a more fundamental part of the ski vacation. Cross-country skiing expert Jon Weisel of Nordic Group International explains grooming like this: "Grooming transforms walking on skis into gliding over snow. It involves reworking snow with special grooming machines to provide consistent skiing conditions. On groomed trails, beginners learn more quickly and have a greater sense of accomplishment rather than breaking trail on their own. Groomed trails allow skiers to travel farther and enjoy the thrill of speed with the option of control. Most of all, groomed trails give those who are a bit more timid and perhaps less athletic, the opportunity to venture out on their own before tackling deep untracked powder."

Make sure the facility sends you a clothing and equipment list well in advance. Ask if the facility provides any equipment. If you have more questions about equipment, talk with qualified cross-country ski outfitters in your area.

Finally, regardless of whether you are a single person, a couple, or a family, and you go to one of these ranches to cross-country ski or not (many have been known to stay for a week and do nothing but relax, rest, read, sunbathe, take a sleigh ride, snowshoe, or sit in the Jacuzzi or in front of a warm and cozy fire enjoying fondue and a glass of wine), you will have one of the most wholesome winter vacations of your life. Great food, great people, great fun. And on a clear day, you might be able to see forever!

The Aspen Lodge Ranch Resort, Colorado

High in the beautiful Rocky Mountains just outside Estes Park is a resort ranch that offers seclusion, outstanding scenery, and wonderful skiing. The Aspen Lodge provides a unique environment for the winter enthusiast. Away from the hustle and bustle of the big ski resorts, this small, uncrowded resort is a masterpiece of amenities. The newly constructed lodge, over 30,000 square feet, is one of the largest log structures in Colorado. It features 36 guest rooms, massive moss rock fireplaces, exquisite meeting rooms, and a lobby that will take your breath away. There are also beautifully appointed cabins that are cozy, warm, and spaciously designed, making them perfect for couples and families. Featuring 15 kilometers of cross-country trails, with many acres of untracked trails in Rocky Mountain National Park, the Aspen Lodge is suited for both beginner and expert. Their complete rental center and available instruction can help the beginner quickly advance to high comfort levels in days.

Address: 6120 Highway 7-K, Estes Park, Colorado 80517
Telephone: (303) 586-8133; (800) 332-MTNS (6867); Fax: (303) 586-8133, ext. 403
Airport: Denver
Location: 65 miles northwest of Denver off Highway 25, 7 miles south of Estes Park
Memberships: Colorado Dude and Guest Ranch Association, Cross-Country Ski Area Association
Awards: Mobil 3 Star, AAA 3 Diamond
Medical: Full hospital, 7 miles
Conference: 150, with excellent conference facilities; seven meeting rooms, some with fireplaces, all with windows and porches.
Guest Capacity: 150
Accommodations: The lodge features several hospitality suites and can accommodate up to 150 guests. Choose from thirty-six beautiful lodge rooms or twenty-one multiroom cabins with porches. The Executive Haus features wet bar, living room/library meeting area with fireplace, and 2 bedrooms. Each is designed with comfort in mind. No matter which accommo-

dations you choose, their rustic yet elegant motif ensures a pleasurable stay.
Rates: • $-$$. American Plan based on double occupancy. Rentals extra; special Christmas package available.
Credit Cards: Visa, MasterCard, American Express, Diners Club, Discover
Season: December through March
Activities: Excellent cross-country skiing with rentals and instruction available. The ranch caters primarily to backcountry skiing. If you are looking for tracked trails, this is not the ranch for you. Intermediate and expert skiers will enjoy guided tours to Wild Basin of Rocky Mountain National Park. There are no set tracks or skating trails. Romantic sleigh rides both day and evening, snowmobile tours, ice skating, tobogganing, racquetball, sauna, hot tub, weight and exercise room in sports club that is also open to the public.
Children's Programs: On request. Baby-sitting available.
Dining: The dining room, Ptarmigan's, looks out to Long's Peak. It features fine American/Western cuisine, with seafood buffet and wild game. Children's menu available. Breakfast buffets ensure that everyone has plenty to eat before hitting the trails.
Entertainment: No regularly scheduled entertainment. Special Christmas program. Children enjoy sleigh rides with Santa.
Summary: Ranch resort ideal for conference, group, and family retreats. Some wheelchair access. Video available on request.

C Lazy U Ranch, Colorado

On 2,000 acres in the heart of the Colorado high country, the C Lazy U Ranch offers an outstanding winter vacation program. Fully supervised children's program all season long. Knicker Knickerland, a unique winter playground for children (adults may enter if accompanied by a child), provides for hours of outdoor fun. Cross-country skiing at the ranch is a never-to-be-forgotten experience. Of note, too, is the wonderful Christmas and New Year's celebration each year. If you can make a reservation, you and your family will have the old-fashioned Christmas you have always dreamed about. The holiday spirit comes alive when Santa arrives in his red horse-drawn sleigh. Then everyone enjoys a magnificent turkey dinner. No matter when you go, you will find a warm and caring staff and miles of skiing trails. Ski touring is the specialty and can be enjoyed by all members of the family. All tours are gauged to the level of the individual. Both beginner and advanced skiers will find challenging terrain. For the adventurous, there are usually miles of untracked powder in the backcountry areas. Full instruction and guide service are included. Over 25 kilometers of machine-groomed trails meander throughout the property.

Address: P.O. Box 379 K, Granby, Colorado 80446
Telephone: (303) 887-3344; Fax: (303) 887-3917
Airport: Denver
Train: Granby
Location: 6½ miles northwest of Granby, 90 miles west of Denver
Memberships: Cross-Country Ski Association
Awards: Mobil 5 Star, AAA 5 Diamond
Medical: Granby Medical Clinic
Conference: 35
Guest Capacity: 40-90
Accommodations: Eighteen fully insulated, comfortable units. Suites vary from one- to three-room family units with baths and carpeting. Some have fireplaces and jacuzzi bathtubs.

Daily fresh fruit; fireplace restocked every day.
Rates: • $-$$. American Plan. Everything but the bar tab is included.
Credit Cards: None. Personal checks accepted.
Season: Mid-December through March
Winter Activities: Fifteen kilometers of groomed trails for ski skating; 25 kilometers of groomed trails for ski tracking. Ice skating, sledding, inner tubing, horse-drawn sleigh rides. Full indoor luxurious health spa with whirlpool and sauna. New championship racquetball court. Downhill skiing nearby at Silver Creek and Winter Park, transportation provided. All ski equipment, skates, and racquetball provided.
Children's Programs: Full children's program all winter.
Dining: Excellent cuisine, including homemade corn chowder or beef barley soup, rack of lamb, chicken Jerusalem, orange roughy, ice cream pie. Full service bar.
Entertainment: Christmas and New Year's programs. Game room. Country-Western singing, ice skating party with bonfire and schnapps.
Summary: Excellent Christmas program. Full winter activities. Spanish, French, and German spoken.

See color photos, page 195

The Home Ranch, Colorado

Authentic Western Ranch, Member–Dude Ranchers' Association

The Home Ranch is one of the premier cross-country skiing havens in North America. Host-owner Ken Jones, along with a very competent and friendly staff, combines the best of two worlds—rustic elegance and winter adventure. Here, guests from around the world gather to enjoy what the Home Ranch has to offer. In the beautiful Elk River Valley in the small town of Clark, not far from Steamboat Springs, this ranch provides a gracious combination of Western warmth and lively outdoor activity. The ski trails that radiate from the property give skiers varied terrain, rolling valleys, and glistening forests. If that is not enough, a short drive to Steamboat will put you on downhill slopes that will challenge even the most advanced skier.

Address: P.O. Box 822 K, Clark, Colorado 80428
Telephone: (303) 879-1780; Fax: (303) 879-1795
Airport: Steamboat Springs and Hayden
Location: 18 miles north of Steamboat Springs
Memberships: Colorado Cross-Country Ski Association, Relais and Chateaux, Colorado Dude and Guest Ranch Association, Dude Ranchers' Association
Awards: Mobil 4 Star Award, AAA 4 Diamond Award, Relais and Chateaux
Medical: Routt Memorial Hospital
Conference: 25
Guest Capacity: 40
Accommodations: Guests stay in seven secluded cabins and six beautiful lodge rooms furnished with antiques, Indian rugs, original artwork, down comforters, and robes. Each cabin has its own wood stove and a private enclosed outdoor whirlpool.
Rates: • $$$-$$$$. American Plan.
Credit Cards: Visa, MasterCard, American Express
Season: Late December to early April, open Christmas
Activities: This ranch offers more than 50 kilometers of tracked trails throughout the valley, 20 kilometers of which are groomed for telemark practice. The instructor-guides are qualified to teach all levels of cross-country skiing. One of the more popular excursions is lunch at the llamasary. Guests ski or take the sleigh about 1 mile up to the mountain cabin, have a lunch of gourmet Western fare, and return to the main house. Heated outdoor swimming, snowshoeing, and sauna. Equipment is available for both adults and children. Downhill skiing and hot air balloon rides at Steamboat.
Children's Programs: Arts and crafts. Except at Christmas, there usually are not many children here.
Dining: Excellent meals with many Home Ranch specialties, such as breast of duck, fresh fish, filet mignon, European dishes, praline cheesecake. BYO wine and liquor (ranch will pick up with advance notice).
Entertainment: Well-stocked library, grand piano, recreation hall, Home Ranch Band "The Mustangs."
Summary: One of the prettiest ranches in North America. Famous ski town of Steamboat Springs nearby. French spoken.

Fryingpan River Ranch, Colorado

Authentic Western Ranch, Member–Dude Ranchers' Association • Orvis-Endorsed Lodge

Looking for a winter getaway in the Colorado Rockies with thousands of acres of untracked snow, beautiful white-studded pine trees, and old-fashion mountain hospitality? Welcome to the Fryingpan River Ranch. Located about 25 miles from the small town of Basalt, the ranch is a haven for singles, couples, and families who wish to experience peace and solitude, coupled with all the trappings that go with romantic winter splendor. What makes this ranch unique is that it is on the 10th Mountain Hut and Trail System, a 300-mile backcountry network of trails linking the wilderness surrounding Aspen, Vail, and Leadville. This trail system was fashioned after the European Haute Route system and is maintained by volunteers of the 10 Mountain Trail Association. They call this hut-to-hut skiing, and for many, the ranch is a one- or two-night stop-over. Others prefer to make the Fryingpan River Ranch their home base and venture out each day exploring remote valleys and tree-lined mountains. Skiers and nonskiers alike will enjoy the warmth and kind hospitality that Jim and Paula share with those who visit them.

Address: 32042 Fryingpan Road, Drawer K, Meredith Colorado 81642
Telephone: (303) 927-3570; Fax: (303) 927-3570 (call first)
Airport: Aspen or Denver
Location: 31 miles up the Fryingpan River from Basalt, Colorado, 1¼ hours from Aspen
Memberships: Colorado Dude and Guest Ranch Association, Dude Ranchers' Association, Colorado Cross-Country Ski Association
Awards: Orvis-Endorsed Lodge
Medical: Aspen or Glenwood Springs, 50 miles
Conference: 25
Guest Capacity: 25
Accommodations: Four cabins and two lodge rooms, each with private baths and decorated in a cozy country motif. The spirit of winter and Christmas comes alive in the main lodge. A fire is always burning.
Rates: • $-$$. American Plan.

Credit Cards: Visa, MasterCard. Personal checks and traveler's checks accepted.
Season: Year-round
Activities: There are a variety of winter activities. Expert cross-country skiers will find unlimited skiing opportunities. The ranch will arrange for guides. Instruction is available for both beginner and intermediate skiers. Many like snowshoeing on the historic Colorado Midland Railroad grade. Ice skating and snowmobiling. Equipment and snowmobiles can be arranged with advance notice. For those die-hard anglers, be sure to talk with Jim about his winter fly-fishing program.
Children's Programs: Children are welcome, but there are no organized children's programs. Paula has two great kids, so your children will feel at home.
Dining: The ranch is getting quite a reputation for its scrumptious cuisine. All meals have a Western flair and are prepared in a healthful way. Lunch is served in the lodge or on the trail. Ask about lunch al fresco at Sellers Meadow. Dinner may start with an appetizer of smoked pheasant followed by trout, wild turkey, beef, or lamb, accompanied by wild or domestic rice, and homemade bread. BYOB.
Entertainment: Most of the guests are pretty well worn out at the end of a full day of skiing and a wonderful dinner. Some, though, will read by the fire (there is a good selection of books), watch a movie from the video library, or gaze at the heavens from the outdoor hot tub.
Summary: Historic family owned and operated guest ranch located on the 10th Mountain Hut and Trail System. Great for those who enjoy backcountry skiing and for those who simply want to get away from it all in the middle of winter. Ask about the Christmas week and Jim's winter fly-fishing program. German spoken. (Author's note: While exhilarating and beautiful, backcountry skiing is not for everyone. You should be in reasonably good physical shape and enjoy the challenges of knee-deep untracked powder.)

See color photos, page 191

Fryingpan River Ranch, Colorado

Latigo Ranch, Colorado

Cross-country skiers who keep returning to Latigo Ranch are drawn by the relaxed atmosphere, spectacular scenery, superb cuisine, and warm hospitality of the owners. Latigo is off the beaten track, tucked on the side of Kasdorf Mountain in a corner of Arapaho and Routt national forests. With a 100-mile panorama of the Continental Divide and a quarter million acres of national forest bordering it, Latigo Ranch offers the recreational skier a variety of scenery and skiing. Latigo machine grooms and packs 35 kilometers of single track through meadows and pine and aspen forests. The trails are ideal for the beginner as well as advanced skier. There is also unlimited backcountry and telemark skiing for the more adventurous. Since the ranch lies at 9,000 feet on top of Colorado's Gore Range, snow conditions are ideal. Most of the winter, several feet of dry powder make it just perfect for telemarking. Hosts Kathie Yost and Lisa George have both been schoolteachers (music and English). Randy George has a degree in chemical engineering as well as an M.B.A. Jim Yost has a Ph.D. in anthropology and has taught anthropology and linguistics at the University of Colorado. Thus, a stay at Latigo is not only a recreational heaven but also a stimulating intellectual experience. Above all, Latigo offers a low-key and relaxing ambience. People leave here feeling like they have been with family at their private winter retreat.

Address: Box 237 K, Kremmling, Colorado 80459
Telephone: (800) 227-9655 (toll-free outside Colorado); (303) 724-9008; Fax: (303) 724-3449
Airport: Steamboat Springs in Hayden, Stapleton International in Denver
Train: Granby
Location: 16 miles west of Kremmling, 55 miles southeast of Steamboat Springs, 130 miles west of Denver
Memberships: Colorado Cross-Country Ski Association

Medical: Kremmling Memorial Hospital, 16 miles
Conference: 35 if staying overnight
Guest Capacity: 35
Accommodations: Three carpeted, contemporary, log duplex cabins, three bedrooms on each side with sitting room, electric heat, and wood-burning stove.
Rates: • $-$$. American Plan. Group rates available.
Credit Cards: Visa, MasterCard, American Express
Season: Mid-December to early April, open Christmas
Activities: Tubing, sledding, cross-country skiing. Snowmobiling can be arranged but is extra. Bring your own ski gear, or rentals are available in Kremmling.
Children's Programs: No special program. Children's lessons available. Baby-sitting by prior arrangement.
Dining: Breakfast grill service, hot lunch (sack lunch by arrangement), family-style dinner. Can cater to special diets. BYOB.
Entertainment: VHS player available, pool, and Ping-Pong.
Summary: After an invigorating day of exercise, skiers can soothe tired muscles in the whirlpool, unwind with a game of pool, or relax with a book in front of a fireplace. Be sure to ask about and see Jim's movie on Ecuador, *Nomads of the Rain Forest*, that was shown on Nova. Spanish spoken.

Peaceful Valley Lodge and Ranch Resort, Colorado

The Boehm family arrived in the valley in 1953 and began building toward their dream of a ski lodge for winter recreation and a ranch for promoting the beauty of the Rockies in the summer. While the ranch hosts many families during the winter months, many conference groups come here as well. Guests can choose from a variety of winter activities, including snow coach tours, cross-country skiing, horse-drawn sleigh rides, a trip to nearby Rocky Mountain National Park or nearby downhill skiing, or just relaxing in front of the fire or enjoying the indoor sauna and whirlpool. Advanced cross-country skiers may be shuttled into the depths of the Roosevelt National Forest, where unbroken powder skiing is at its best. Winter in the Rockies is not complete without experiencing a traditional horse-drawn sleigh ride. The Boehms' single horse-drawn sleigh rides are wonderful. For the family or a larger group, there is a sleigh drawn by a team of Percherons. The combined Western hospitality and European charm of the Boehm family and the commitment of both owners and staff to personal attention assure guests of a most memorable winter vacation.

Address: Star Route, Box 2811 K, Lyons, Colorado 80540
Telephone: (303) 747-2881, (800) 95-LODGE (955-6343 for reservations only); Fax: (303) 747-2167
Airport: Denver Stapleton International Airport.
Train: Denver, shuttle service available
Location: 60 miles northwest of Denver on Highway 72
Memberships: Cross-Country Ski Areas Association, Colorado Cross-Country Ski Association, Colorado Dude and Guest Ranch Association
Awards: AAA 3 Diamond, Mobil 3 Star
Medical: Longmont Community Hospital
Conference: 80; full conference facilities. Extensive conference brochure available on request.
Guest Capacity: Winter, 80
Accommodations: Accommodations at the lodge include cozy lodge rooms, modern cha-let rooms, and comfortable cabins with fireplaces, some with hot tubs. Deluxe rooms with Jacuzzi tubs. Coin-operated laundry machines.
Rates: • $$-$$$. Includes lodging and three meals. Children's, conference, ski package, and bed and breakfast rates available.
Credit Cards: Visa, MasterCard, American Express, Diners Club
Season: Early December through April. Lodge open year-round. Open all holidays.
Activities: There are no groomed trails; however, there are miles of cross-country wilderness skiing opportunities. Beginners and intermediate skiers will find the trails from Peaceful Valley to the national forest excellent for cross-country skiing. Downhill skiing and cross-country lessons at nearby Eldora, 24 miles away with groomed cross-country ski trails. Full indoor pool and spa facilities.
Children's Programs: Children are welcome, but there is no children's program available in winter.
Dining: Large, home-cooked, family-style meals are served in the dining rooms with a great view of the mountains.
Entertainment: Game room with pool, table tennis, video games, and ski movies. Christmas is especially festive at Peaceful Valley.
Summary: Excellent backcountry cross-country skiing. The Boehms combine their Austrian and Kentuckian heritages, blending Western culture, European charm, and Southern hospitality. Excellent winter conference center. Winter video available. German spoken.

See color photos, pages 184-186

Skyline Guest Ranch, Colorado

Authentic Western Ranch, Member–Dude Ranchers' Association

Do you yearn for a classic ski lodge, where you can sit around the potbelly stove, sip hot cider, and eat freshly made cookies after a fabulous day of skiing? You will find that experience at Skyline Guest Ranch. The beauty of the mountains and the warmth of the Farny family will set you aglow. Skyline Guest Ranch is just 3 miles from the Telluride Ski Resort, where you will find incredible terrain for alpine and Nordic skiing. The resort has 10 lifts, one of which is used for Nordic access to the mountaintop, where they have groomed and set 30 kilometers of trails. If one wishes to ski at the ranch, there are 3 kilometers of set track and marked trails for the backcountry skier. A guide may be hired for skiing back to the ranch on fresh, untracked powder from the ski area. Skyline is noted for its spectacular setting: you can see three 14,000-foot peaks from the front porch. Skyline feels secluded enough, yet it is only eight miles from the wonderful historic mining ski town of Telluride.

Address: Box 67 K, Telluride, Colorado 81435
Telephone: (303) 728-3757
Airport: Telluride
Location: 8 miles from Telluride
Memberships: Dude Ranchers' Association, Colorado Dude and Guest Ranch Association
Medical: Telluride Medical Center, 8 miles
Conference: 35
Guest Capacity: 35
Accommodations: Each of the ten lodge rooms has its own comfortable bed with down comforter and sheepskin bed pad, its own thermostat control, and a private bath. Attached to the lodge is a new log addition with two apartments equipped with kitchenettes. There are four housekeeping cabins, each with a kitchen for those who wish to have their home away from home. They can accommodate from two to six skiers. Suntan lotion and lip gloss provided. No smoking in any buildings.
Rates: • $-$$. European Plan. Breakfast included.

Credit Cards: Visa, MasterCard, Discover, American Express
Season: Early December to early April, open Christmas
Activities: Alpine and Nordic skiing, machine-groomed single-track trails (6 km). Cross-country equipment available, and instruction is available with advance notice. Snowmobiling up to old mining ghost town can be arranged (extra). Snowshoeing (BYO). Small retail store. Wonderful hot tub and sauna.
Children's Programs: None, but children are welcome.
Dining: The kitchen cooks a hearty skier's breakfast with a special each morning. You are on your own for lunch; however, there are wonderful apres-ski delicacies and hot cider. Dinners are prepared by the Farnys' daughter, Cindy, a French-trained chef. Some claim the food is the best in Telluride, so reservations should be made in advance.
Entertainment: Cozy evening fires at the ranch and local entertainment in Telluride. Be sure to see Mountain Splendor, a multi-image slide show.
Summary: Small and friendly classic ski lodge/ranch with excellent food close to the famous ski town of Telluride. The wonderful Farny family, incredible setting surrounded by 14,000-foot mountain peaks. Great for both cross-country and downhill skiing. German and French spoken.

See color photos, page 226

Vista Verde Guest and Ski Touring Ranch, Colorado

Authentic Western Ranch, Member–Dude Ranchers' Association

You may hear sleighbells ringing, hear children laughing, and watch them kicking up their heels in the snow while their parents relax in a hot whirlpool, soaking tired muscles. Welcome to Winton and Frank Brophy's Vista Verde Guest and Ski Touring Ranch. Just down the road from the world-renowned ski town of Steamboat Springs, Vista Verde offers a network of neatly groomed and marked trails. A 20-kilometer trail system on the ranch's 600 acres winds through forests and meadows, offering challenges to expert and beginner skiers. This is double tracked with some skating lanes. There is an additional 40-kilometer marked trail network on the adjoining 1.3 million acres of the Routt National Forest. The forest also has unlimited opportunities for telemark and backcountry powder skiing. Certified instructors and superbly kept trails make Vista Verde a cross-country skiers' haven. For those who like ranch work, the Brophys welcome help with feeding sixty head of horses and gathering morning eggs. Holidays at the ranch are special for the entire family.

Address: Box 465 K, Steamboat Springs, Colorado 80477
Telephone: (800) 526-7433 or (303) 879-3858
Airport: Yampa Valley Regional Airport, 40 miles, serviced directly by American, America West, Northwest Airlines, and Continental. Steamboat Springs, 20 miles away, served by Continental Express.
Train: Amtrak to Glenwood Springs
Location: 25 miles north of Steamboat Springs
Memberships: Cross-Country Ski Area Association, Colorado Cross-Country Ski Association, Dude Ranchers' Association
Awards: Mobil 3 Star
Medical: Steamboat Springs Hospital, 25 miles
Conference: 25
Guest Capacity: 25
Accommodations: Six cozy and fully insulated, two- to three-bedroom log cabins with central heat and fireplaces, full baths, and kitchens. The cabins are tastefully furnished with antiques, calico curtains, and carpeting.
Rates: • $-$$. American and European plans. Group rates available. Some activities are à la carte.
Credit Cards: None
Season: Mid-December to mid-March
Activities: Cross-country skiing, sleigh rides, snowshoeing, dog sledding, ice fishing, ice climbing. Sports and spa building with 12-person whirlpool, sauna, exercise bicycle, and cold pool. Cross-country equipment rentals available. The Brophys have a nice low-key Christmas program.
Children's Programs: No special program, but kids are welcome.
Dining: Home cooking is the fare, whether gourmet or hearty Western dishes, fondue, famous Vista Verde winter stew, or sauerbraten. Trailside chili lunch at remote cabin. The pastures provide beef, and the ranch chicken house provides eggs for the breakfast table. Homemade breads, pies, and pastries enhance every meal. Some guests prefer to cook in their cabins.
Entertainment: Piano, sing-alongs weekly, puzzles, cards, daily sleigh rides.
Summary: Terrific backcountry touring. Excellent food, lodging, and personalized service. Ask the Brophys about their adventure week package, which includes dog sledding, ice climbing, and backcountry side tours. French, Chinese, and German spoken.

Busterback Ranch, Idaho

Authentic Western Ranch, Member–Dude Ranchers' Association

Busterback Ranch is a world-class cross-country ski ranch in the winter and a beautiful small guest ranch in the summer. In the magnificent Sawtooth Valley, not far from Sun Valley, this little gem is a hideaway for those who savor privacy and appreciate nature's magic. The ranch got its name in the early 1920s. The story goes that the wife of the original owner used to say, "We came to the mountains for fun. Now we just bust our backs working." Not so today. The only work you will do here is savor the magnificence of your surroundings and the comfort of your cozy beds. While the ranch specializes in its superb winter program, it features fine summer activities as well. It is a working ranch with eleven hundred head of cattle. The ranch is unique and committed to providing the highest quality recreational experience for a limited number of guests. Kevin and Roberta, along with their fine staff, serve up great hospitality in the splendor of Idaho's magnificent Sawtooth Mountains. After skiing, soak in the hot tub or bake in the Finnish sauna. Massages are also available.

Address: Star Route, Dept. K, Ketchum, Idaho 83340
Telephone: (208) 774-2271
Airport: Boise, Twin Falls, Hailey Airport near Ketchum
Location: 40 miles north of Ketchum/Sun Valley
Memberships: Dude Ranchers' Association, Cross-Country Ski Association
Medical: Moritz Community Medical Center, 40 miles; Salmon River Emergency Clinic, 20 miles
Conference: Up to 20
Guest Capacity: 20
Accommodations: Choose from five newly designed rooms in the main lodge, three of which share two bathrooms, or the three comfortable log cabins with wood stoves, electric baseboard heaters, and reading lights. Each room has big rough-hewn queen-size pine beds with woods-

man plaid throws. Each room enjoys a beautiful vista. Complimentary shampoo and conditioner.
Rates: • $$$. American Plan. Rates for children vary; age 4 and under, free.
Credit Cards: Visa, MasterCard. Personal checks accepted.
Season: Late November to early May, including Christmas, Thanksgiving, and Easter
Activities: Master the graceful telemark turn on fresh Idaho powder, or develop your technique along 58 kilometers of skating and double set tracks, which are professionally designed and maintained by sophisticated grooming equipment. Tours and instruction are available with PSIA instructors. Daily lessons include skating, track, or telemark. Guided tours are available to Alturus or Petit Lake. Telemark skiing on 9,000-foot Galena Summit for accomplished skiers. Lessons for children and adults are fun and relaxed. A learner's loop is just outside the living room. Full rental equipment is available.
Children's Programs: Baby-sitting available. Children welcome, but there are no specific programs.
Dining: Hearty breakfasts with fresh fruit, yogurt, cereal, and juices. Lunches are homemade soups, breads, cookies, fresh fruit, vegetables, cheeses, and locally smoked fish and meats. Dinner is served in the White Cloud Lounge in front of the big fireplace and features roast rack of Idaho lamb, pork tenderloin in jalapeño pepper glaze, California seafood stew, chicken breasts with tequila and lime. Everyone's favorite desserts include Roaring Meg's Chocolate Cake, poached pears, and cheesecakes with fresh fruit.
Entertainment: Wine tastings and guest lectures. Idaho swing dancing in Stanley.
Summary: Super cross-country skiing, combined with tremendous hospitality. World-famous Sun Valley for alpine skiing and shopping. The atmosphere at Busterback is extremely friendly and very informal.

See color photos, page 234

Lone Mountain Ranch, Montana

Authentic Western Ranch, Member–Dude Ranchers' Association

The Schaaps' and Ankenys' Lone Mountain Ranch is a wonderful destination for vacationing Nordic skiers. Early each week, the Schaaps host a wine and cheese party to welcome guests. Lone Mountain Ranch offers a variety of skiing opportunities right from each cabin's doorstep. The double-wide, machine-tilled, and tracked trail system winds 75 kilometers through meadows, across ridges, and up deep Rocky Mountain valleys. In addition, miles of ungroomed trails lead guests to spots where they can ski and carve telemark turns in untracked powder. Every effort has been made to design a trail system to please every level of skier. Many of the guests participate in optional all-day guided ski trips into the backcountry of Yellowstone or the Spanish Peaks surrounding the ranch. All trips are led by guides who are knowledgeable about skiing, the winter environment, and the area's natural history. One of the more popular trips leads skiers to the interior of Yellowstone by snow coach. Guests then disembark for backcountry skiing through the geyser basins, perhaps catching a glimpse of wintering elk and grazing buffalo. The ranch recommends that all beginners take lessons to help develop the skills needed to enjoy this lifetime winter sport.

Address: P.O. Box 69 K, Big Sky, Montana 59716
Telephone: (406) 995-4644; Fax: (406) 995-4670
Airport: Bozeman
Location: 40 miles south of Bozeman
Memberships: Cross-Country Ski Area Association, Dude Ranchers' Association, Montana Outfitters Association
Awards: Orvis-Endorsed Lodge, *Family Circle* magazine's choice as 1990 Top Ranch Family Vacation Destination
Medical: Bozeman Deaconess Hospital
Conference: 50
Guest Capacity: 60
Accommodations: Twenty-three fully insulated 1- and 2-bedroom cabins with comfortable beds, electric heat, modern bathrooms with tub/shower, and rock fireplace or Franklin stove.

Rates: • $$-$$$. American Plan. Children under age 2, free.
Credit Cards: Visa, MasterCard
Season: Early December to early April
Activities: Seventy-five kilometers of tilled and tracked cross-country trails through meadows, across ridges, and up valleys. Miles of ungroomed trails. Retail and rental cross-country shop. Lessons, naturalist guide, and trips to Yellowstone backcountry. Outdoor whirlpool. Nightly sleigh rides open to the public.
Children's Programs: None in the winter. Full children's program in summer.
Dining: Tremendous new log dining room open to the public. The food has received rave reviews. Guests enjoy an old-fashioned sleigh ride to dinner and the famous on-the-snow trail buffet lunch as part of their meal package. Everyone's favorite is the North Fork cabin dinner. A twenty-minute sleigh ride up to this beautiful cabin is just the beginning. The cabin is lit by kerosene lanterns, and food is cooked on a magnificent 100-year-old wood cookstove. Guests enjoy a prime rib dinner and musical entertainment before their ride back to the ranch. The weekly trail buffet lunch is presented on a huge snow bar, with fare ranging from salmon pâté and other appetizers to roast beef or turkey, boiled shrimp, cheese, fresh fruits and vegetables, homemade breads, and a huge variety of desserts, hot beverages, and beer and wine. Guests ski to a scenic spot on the trail system to enjoy this feast.
Entertainment: Throughout the winter, there are many evening programs, including naturalist presentations on grizzly bears, the fires of Yellowstone, and the greater Yellowstone ecosystem. Once a week there is a classical and folk music program by a couple who play guitar, flute, and Celtic harp.
Summary: World-class cross-country skiing. Sleigh rides and dining room open to the public. Winter guided fly-fishing trips. Big Sky Ski Resort for downhill skiing. Winter video available.

See color photos, page 203

Woodside Ranch, Wisconsin

Woodside Ranch is a year-round operation. The winter season runs from December to mid-March. During this time, Woodside takes only weekend guests, except during the Christmas and Easter holidays, when the ranch is open full-time. Woodside is run by Lucille Nichols and her nephews, Ray and Rick Feldmann. Unlike most guest ranches in southern Wisconsin, guests here can ski from their cabins. A cross-over loop runs behind the twenty cabins. There are five main loop trails and several advanced trails with names like Half Way Hut and Prairie View Run. Beginners will enjoy loops one and two and Coyote Run. There are two warming huts on the trail system, both with fireplaces, great for having a picnic lunch. For backcountry skiing, there are more than seven hundred acres of mixed hardwood and pine forests. Prairie View Run, for advanced skiers, is about 80 percent open country and resembles the alpine parks of the Rocky Mountains.

Address: Highway 82, Box K, Mauston, Wisconsin 53948
Telephone: (608) 847-4275
Airport: Madison, Wisconsin; small private airport in Mauston-New Lisbon, 11 miles
Train: Wisconsin Dells, 20 miles away; Greyhound bus to Mauston, 4 miles
Location: 5 miles east of Mauston, 20 miles northwest of Wisconsin Dells, 220 miles north of Chicago, 200 miles south of Minneapolis on Interstate 90/94
Memberships: Wisconsin Innkeepers Association
Medical: Hess Memorial Hospital, 6 miles
Conference: 60
Guest Capacity: 125
Accommodations: Twenty one-, two-, and three-bedroom log cabins and white-sided cottages behind the main lodge, with names like Abe Lincoln, Fireside, Last Frontier, and Old 99. All have fireplaces and thermostatically controlled heat, double beds, and bunk beds. The main lodge has 14 rooms that sleep two to four people, with private baths.
Rates: $. American Plan. Rates vary depending on the plan you choose. Children's rates available.
Credit Cards: Visa, MasterCard
Season: December to March for skiing
Activities: There are more than 12 miles of marked ski trails, all machine groomed for single set track. There are also 5 miles of skating trails. A 1,000-foot downhill slope with a rope tow is available for beginner skiers and telemarkers. Night skiing is offered. Free downhill and cross-country ski instruction. Experts and beginners will find the cross-country terrain challenging. All skiing facilities are open to the public. Downhill and cross-country equipment can be rented at Woodside. Horse-drawn sleigh rides, horseback riding, ice skating, and tubing. Large steam sauna.
Children's Programs: Pony rides in ring for children of all ages. Supervised kinder school. Christmas week games for kids.
Dining: Meals are served family style at long tables. Filling ranch breakfasts, homemade soups and chili, ski lunch buffet, roast beef and roast chicken; occasionally buffalo is served.
Entertainment: Trading Post lounge with hot buttered rum, hot cider, and hot chocolate. The Round Up Room, which is part of the ranch Trading Post, has arcade games, table tennis, ski movies, and Saturday night barn dance with social and square dancing.
Summary: Family owned and operated ranch for families featuring log cabins with fireplaces. Weekend and holiday cross-country skiing, beginner downhill skiing, ski-in/ski-out access to cabins, night skiing. Horseback riding, sleigh rides, the Trading Post souvenir shop. Antiques and shopping in small towns of New Lisbon, Adams Friendship, Mauston.

The Hills Health and Guest Ranch, British Columbia, Canada

Pat and Juanita Corbett had a vision of creating one of the most extensive cross-country ski complexes in North America. Today, their facility, perched on a hill, is nearly in the center of a maze of trails that wind in all directions. The Hills is part of a community-wide 200-kilometer trail system. The complex has hosted such major Canadian events as the Cariboo Marathon (Western Canada's largest with more than 1,000 skiers), the Canadian Junior Championship B.C. Cup Race, the Kahlua Treasure Hunt on skis, the Timex, and the Skiathlon. At the Hills, you can ski hut to hut and among other lodge facilities. Pat and Juanita have opened membership at the Hills to the community. With a membership, families can use the indoor pool, two whirlpools, dressing rooms, and saunas. They keep busy at the Hills; they like what they do and it shows. Their staff is extremely friendly and helpful. Juanita's Kentucky warmth and charm are contagious.

Address: C-26, Dept. K, 100-Mile House, B.C., Canada V0K 2E0
Telephone: (604) 791-5225; Fax: (604) 791-6384
Airport: Williams Lake, British Columbia
Train: 100 Mile House
Location: 8 miles north of 100 Mile House off Highway 97, 50 miles south of Williams Lake, 290 miles north of Vancouver
Memberships: Canada West Ski Areas Association, British Columbia Guest Ranch Association
Medical: 100 Mile House Hospital, 8 miles
Conference: 200; 4,300-square foot meeting space
Guest Capacity: 114
Accommodations: Twenty chalets (sunrise or sunset views) line the ridge, with a road up the middle. Each has a full kitchen, small living/dining area, color television, upstairs and downstairs bedrooms, porch, and daily maid service.
Rates: • $-$$. European/American packages available. Children's and group rates available.
Credit Cards: Visa, MasterCard

Season: December through March (open Christmas)
Activities: Full cross-country ski program, 200 kilometers of machine-groomed and double-tracked trails, 20 kilometers of skating trails, ski shop with rentals/sales and ski school, sleigh rides, full spa facilities. Winter spa facilities include exercise room, aerobics, power walking, weights, massage, facials, pedicures, and nutritionist.
Children's Programs: Swimming classes (all ages), baby-sitting available.
Dining: Fully licensed dining room. Superb Swiss chef prepares wonderful meals in the Trails End Dining Room. Weight Watchers spa meals available.
Entertainment: The weekend dinner music is one of the most delightful features of the Corbetts' operation. Several very talented professional musicians are part of the musical family. European wine served.
Summary: Full cross-country ski program with double-tracked trails with full ski shop and instruction. Professional musical entertainment, spa facilities. German, French, and Italian spoken.

See color photos, page 235

Tyax Mountain Lake Resort, British Columbia, Canada

At Tyax Resort, winter is a time of reflection and contemplation. The forest, lake, and mountains are covered with snow, often up to four feet deep. On clear nights, you can hear the lonely cry of a timber wolf as you sit in the outside Jacuzzi. During the day you can get away from it all, snowshoe in knee-deep powder, and enjoy crystal clear skies and a virgin timbered winter wonderland. At day's end, return to the luxurious log lodge and warm your feet by the open fireplace. The rooms are warm and spacious, and most overlook Lake Tyaughton. Around the resort, you will find twenty miles of set track and groomed cross-country ski trails. If you want to go farther, there are unlimited miles of trails, some of which will take you above the tree line to virgin alpine meadows. Tyax has guides for mountain touring, as well as for heli-skiing. Cross-country and telemark skis are available for rental at the lodge. Because of its remoteness, there are no lifts. A helicopter will bring you to 8,000 feet. You can rent ice skates, snowshoes, toboggans, and snowmobiles. At Tyax you can join a sleigh ride or just relax.

Address: Tyaughton Lake Road, Dept. K, Gold Bridge, B.C., Canada V0K 1P0
Telephone: (604) 238-2221; Fax: (604) 238-2528
Airport: Vancouver; direct charter ski plane flights available
Train: British Columbia Rail from Vancouver to Lillooet
Location: About 5 hours north of Vancouver
Memberships: British Columbia Guest Ranch Association
Medical: Lillooet Hospital, 60 miles
Conference: 80
Guest Capacity: 100
Accommodations: Tyax is one of the largest log lodges in western North America and overlooks beautiful Tyaughton Lake. There are twenty-eight rooms on three floors. Each has pine furnishings, twin or queen-size beds, down comforters, and balconies. The lodge also features a winter bar and giant native rock fireplace with built-in Dutch ovens. Outside, a spacious sun deck with whirlpool overlooks the lake. There are also four luxurious lakefront log chalets with full kitchens and fireplaces.
Rates: • $$-$$$$. American Plan. Modified American and European plans available. Special chalet rates. Almost everything here is à la carte.
Credit Cards: Visa, MasterCard, American Express
Season: January through late April; also Thanksgiving, Christmas, and Easter
Activities: Cross-country ski trails are groomed with single track set. Full instruction available. Guests enjoy lake ice skating and often play hockey and broomball. Two big thrills are heli-skiing and mountain snowmobiling. Bring your own downhill equipment. There are also ice fishing, tobogganing, snowshoeing, snowmobiling, and horse-drawn sleigh rides. Fitness center with massage and aerobics. Cross-country and ice skating equipment can be rented at store on property.
Children's Programs: No special program. Baby-sitters available.
Dining: The restaurant seats 100 guests, has a 30-foot-high ceiling, and a stone fireplace. Looking out the large windows, you see the lake, forest, and mountains. Specialties include rack of lamb, T-bone steak, barbecued salmon, and cheesecake. Extensive wine list, specializing in Australian wines.
Entertainment: Special hot rum drinks in Western bar, dance floor with live music, campfires and cookouts, billiard and table tennis room.
Summary: Spectacular "à la carte" world-class wilderness resort, helicopter skiing, snowmobiling, sleigh rides, massage. Convenience store with souvenirs, clothes, and snacks. French and German spoken. Video available on request.

Ranches, Listed Alphabetically

Special Ranch Features

Accessible Only by Boat, Horseback, Helicopter, Plane, or Train
Kachemak Bay Wilderness Lodge, Alaska
Phantom Ranch, Arizona
Muir Trail Ranch, California
Tall Timber, Colorado
Allison Ranch, Idaho
Mackay Bar Ranch, Idaho
Shepp Ranch, Idaho
Stonebraker Ranch, Idaho
Klicks' K Bar L Ranch, Montana
The Horse Ranch, Oregon

Adults-Oriented Ranch (some are adults-only, some have adults-only weeks/months)
Grapevine Canyon Ranch, Arizona
Scott Valley Ranch, Arkansas
Howard Creek Ranch, California
C Lazy U Ranch, Colorado
Colorado Trails Ranch, Colorado
Lake Mancos Ranch, Colorado
Wilderness Trails Ranch, Colorado
Double JJ Ranch, Michigan
Triple Creek Ranch, Montana
The Lodge at Chama, New Mexico
Pinegrove Resort Ranch, New York
Firefly Ranch, Vermont
Woodside Ranch, Wisconsin
Flying A Ranch, Wyoming
Lozier's Box R Ranch, Wyoming
The Ranch at Ucross, Wyoming
R Lazy S, Wyoming
Savery Creek Thoroughbred Ranch, Wyoming
Seven D Ranch, Wyoming
Black Cat Guest Ranch, Alberta, Canada
Cariboo Rose Guest Ranch, British Columbia, Canada
Sundance Guest Ranch, British Columbia, Canada

Airstrip (on or near ranch)
Grand Canyon Bar Ten Ranch, Arizona
Kay El Bar Ranch, Arizona
Rancho de los Caballeros, Arizona
Wickenburg Inn, Tennis and Guest Ranch, Arizona

Coffee Creek Ranch, California
Drakesbad Guest Ranch, California
Flying AA Ranch, California
Hunewill Circle H Ranch, California
Spanish Springs Ranch, California
Trinity Mountain Meadow Resort, California
Wonder Valley Ranch Resort, California
Elktrout Lodge, Colorado
Everett Ranch, Colorado
4UR Ranch, Colorado
Outdoor Resorts River Ranch, Florida
Allison Ranch, Idaho
Mackay Bar Ranch, Idaho
Shepp Ranch, Idaho
Double JJ Ranch, Michigan
Diamond J Ranch, Montana
Hargrave Guest Ranch, Montana
Lazy K Bar Ranch, Montana
Nez Perce Ranch, Montana
Nine Quarter Circle Ranch, Montana
Cottonwood Ranch, Nevada
Western Hills Guest Ranch, Oklahoma
Flying M Ranch, Oregon
The Horse Ranch, Oregon
Morrison's Rogue River Lodge, Oregon
Western Dakota Ranch Vacations, South Dakota
Dixie Dude Ranch, Texas
Flying L Ranch, Texas
Y.O. Ranch, Texas
Hidden Valley Guest Ranch, Washington
Woodside Ranch, Wisconsin
CM Ranch, Wyoming
Darwin Ranch, Wyoming
Flying A Ranch, Wyoming
Savery Creek Thoroughbred Ranch, Wyoming
Cariboo Rose Guest Ranch, British Columbia, Canada
Flying U Ranch, British Columbia, Canada
Springhouse Trails Ranch, British Columbia, Canada
Teepee Heart Ranch, British Columbia, Canada
Tyax Mountain Lake Resort, British Columbia, Canada

Bring Your Own Horse
Price Canyon Ranch, Arizona
White Stallion Ranch, Arizona
Spanish Springs Ranch, California
Trinity Mountain Meadow Resort, California
Aspen Canyon Ranch, Colorado
Rawah Ranch, Colorado
Idaho Rocky Mountain Ranch, Idaho
Bear Mountain Guest Ranch, New Mexico
Ridin-Hy Ranch, New York
Roundup Ranch Resort, New York
The Horse Ranch, Oregon
Flying W Ranch, Pennsylvania
Firefly Ranch, Vermont
Flying L Ranch, Washington
Hidden Valley Guest Ranch, Washington
Heart Six Ranch, Wyoming

Cattle Roundups, Cattle Drives
Grapevine Canyon Ranch, Arizona
Hunewill Circle H Ranch, California
Spanish Springs Ranch, California
Elk Mountain Ranch, Colorado
Everett Ranch, Colorado
Lost Valley Ranch, Colorado
Wilderness Trails Ranch, Colorado
Circle Bar Guest Ranch, Montana
Hargrave Guest Ranch, Montana
Schively Ranch, Montana
Sweetgrass Ranch, Montana
Western Dakota Ranch Vacations, South Dakota
Y.O. Ranch, Texas
Rockin' R Ranch, Utah
David Ranch, Wyoming
High Island Guest Ranch, Wyoming
Lozier's Box R Ranch, Wyoming
Red Rock Ranch, Wyoming
TX Ranch, Wyoming
Homeplace Guest Ranch, Alberta, Canada
Top of the World Guest Ranch, British
  Columbia, Canada

Cross-Country
The Aspen Lodge Ranch Resort, Colorado
C Lazy U Ranch, Colorado
Fryingpan River Ranch, Colorado
The Home Ranch, Colorado
Latigo Ranch, Colorado
Peaceful Valley Lodge and Guest Ranch,
  Colorado
Skyline Guest Ranch, Colorado
Vista Verde Guest and Ski Touring Ranch,
  Colorado

Busterback Ranch, Idaho
Lone Mountain Ranch, Montana
Woodside Ranch, Wisconsin
The Hills Health and Guest Ranch, British
  Columbia, Canada
Tyax Mountain Lake Resort, British Columbia,
  Canada

English Riding
Price Canyon Ranch, Arizona
Spanish Springs Ranch, California
C Lazy U Ranch, Colorado
Colorado Trails Ranch, Colorado
Pinegrove Resort Ranch, New York
Timberlock, New York
Firefly Ranch, Vermont
Bitterroot Ranch, Wyoming
Savery Creek Thoroughbred Ranch, Wyoming

Executive Conference
Grapevine Canyon Ranch, Arizona
Rancho de la Osa, Arizona
Rancho de los Caballeros, Arizona
Tanque Verde Ranch, Arizona
White Stallion Ranch, Arizona
Wickenburg Inn Tennis and Guest Ranch,
  Arizona
Alisal Guest Ranch, California
Spanish Springs Ranch, California
Aspen Canyon Ranch, Colorado
The Aspen Lodge Ranch Resort, Colorado
C Lazy U Ranch, Colorado
Colorado Trails Ranch, Colorado
Coulter Lake Guest Ranch, Colorado
Don K Ranch, Colorado
Elk Trout Ranch, Colorado
4UR Ranch, Colorado
Fryingpan River Ranch, Colorado
The Home Ranch, Colorado
Longs Peak Inn and Guest Ranch, Colorado
Lost Valley Ranch, Colorado
Peaceful Valley Lodge and Guest Ranch,
  Colorado
Rawah Ranch, Colorado
Sylvan Dale Ranch, Colorado
Tall Timber, Colorado
Vista Verde Guest and Ski Touring Ranch,
  Colorado
Wind River Ranch, Colorado
Wit's End Guest Ranch and Resort, Colorado
Outdoor River Resort, Florida
Busterback Ranch, Idaho
Double JJ Ranch, Michigan

Diamond J Ranch, Montana
Flathead Lake Lodge, Montana
Lone Mountain Ranch, Montana
Mountain Sky Guest Ranch, Montana
Nine Quarter Circle Ranch, Montana
Pine Butte Guest Ranch, Montana
Triple Creek Ranch, Montana
West Fork Meadows Ranch, Montana
The Bishop's Lodge, New Mexico
The Lodge at Chama, New Mexico
Hidden Valley Mountainside Resort, New York
Pinegrove Resort Ranch, New York
Roaring Brook Ranch and Tennis Resort, New York
Rocking Horse Ranch, New York
Roundup Ranch, New York
Catalouchee Ranch, North Carolina
Western Hills Guest Ranch, Oklahoma
Flying M Ranch, Oregon
Rock Springs Guest Ranch, Oregon
Dixie Dude Ranch, Texas
Flying L Ranch, Texas
Garrett Creek Ranch, Texas
Lazy Hills Guest Ranch, Texas
Mayan Dude Ranch, Texas
Prude Ranch, Texas
Y.O. Ranch, Texas
Reid Ranch, Utah
Bill Cody's Ranch Resort, Wyoming
Crescent H Ranch, Wyoming
H F Bar Ranch, Wyoming
Lost Creek Ranch, Wyoming
Paradise Ranch, Wyoming
The Ranch at Ucross, Wyoming
Black Cat Guest Ranch, Alberta, Canada
Rafter Six Ranch, Alberta, Canada
The Hills Health and Guest Ranch, British Columbia, Canada
Sundance Guest Ranch, British Columbia, Canada
Tyax Mountain Lake Resort, British Columbia, Canada

Fly-Fishing

Crystal Creek Lodge, Alaska
PJ's Lodge, Arkansas
Arcularius Ranch, California
Elk Creek Lodge, Colorado
Elktrout Lodge, Colorado
Fryingpan River Ranch, Colorado
Three Rivers Ranch, Idaho
Falcon, Inc., Maine
Big Hole River Outfitters, Montana

Diamond J Ranch, Montana
Eagle Nest Lodge, Montana
Lone Mountain Ranch, Montana
Parade Rest Ranch, Montana
The Lodge at Chama, New Mexico
Vermejo Park Ranch, New Mexico
Morrison's Rogue River Lodge, Oregon
Crescent H Ranch, Wyoming

Foreign Language

Northland Ranch Resort, Alaska-Spanish
Circle Z Ranch, Arizona-Spanish
Rancho de la Osa, Arizona-Spanish
Tanque Verde Ranch, Arizona-Spanish, French, Japanese
Alisal Guest Ranch, California-Spanish, French, German, Italian
Circle Bar B Ranch, California-Spanish
Coffee Creek Ranch, California-Spanish, Dutch, German
Highland Ranch, California-French, Italian
Howard Creek Ranch, California-Italian, Dutch, German
Quarter Circle U Rankin Ranch, California-Spanish
Spanish Springs Ranch, California-Spanish
Cherokee Park Ranch, Colorado-Russian, German
C Lazy U Ranch, Colorado-Spanish, French, German
Fryingpan River Ranch, Colorado-German
The Home Ranch, Colorado-French
Peaceful Valley Lodge and Guest Ranch, Colorado-German
Rawah Ranch, Colorado-Norwegian
Skyline Guest Ranch, Colorado-French, German
Sylvan Dale Ranch, Colorado-Spanish
Idaho Rocky Mountain Ranch, Idaho-Spanish
Turkey Creek Ranch, Missouri-French
Circle Bar Guest Ranch, Montana-French
Diamond J Ranch, Montana-Spanish
Eagle Nest Lodge, Montana-French
Flathead Lake Lodge, Montana-Interpreters available
Hargrave Guest Ranch, Montana-German
Lazy K Bar Ranch, Montana-French, Spanish
Pine Butte Guest Ranch, Montana-German
West Fork Meadows Ranch, Montana-German
The Bishop's Lodge, New Mexico-Spanish, French, German
Pinegrove Resort Ranch, New York-Spanish

Rocking Horse Ranch, New York-
  Spanish, German
Baker's Bar M Ranch, Oregon-Spanish
Dixie Dude Ranch, Texas-Spanish
Lazy Hills Guest Ranch, Texas-Spanish
Mayan Dude Ranch, Texas-Spanish
Prude Ranch, Texas-Spanish
Reid Ranch, Utah-Spanish
Firefly Ranch, Vermont-German
Bitterroot Ranch, Wyoming-French
Darwin Ranch, Wyoming-German, Mandarin,
  Taiwanese, French
Heart Six Ranch, Wyoming-German
Lost Creek Ranch, Wyoming-French, German,
  Spanish
Red Rock Ranch, Wyoming-German
Savery Creek Thoroughbred Ranch, Wyoming-
  Spanish, French
Seven D Ranch, Wyoming-Spanish
Trail Creek Ranch, Wyoming-French, German
Rafter Six Ranch, Alberta, Canada-French,
  German, Japanese
Cariboo Rose Guest Ranch, British Columbia,
  Canada-German
Flying U Ranch, British Columbia, Canada-
  German, French, Spanish
The Hills Health and Guest Ranch, British
  Columbia, Canada-German, French, Dutch,
  Italian
Springhouse Trails Ranch, British Columbia,
  Canada-German
Sundance Guest Ranch, British Columbia,
  Canada-German, French
Teepee Heart Ranch, British Columbia,
  Canada-German
Tyax Mountain Lake Resort, British Columbia,
  Canada-French, German, Japanese

Handicapped/Wheelchair Accessible
Blue Spruce Lodge and Guest Ranch, Montana

Horse Drives
Spanish Springs Ranch, California
Diamond J Ranch, Montana

Hot Springs
Drakesbad Guest Ranch, California
Muir Trail Ranch, California
Deer Valley Ranch, Colorado
4UR Ranch, Colorado
Waunita Hot Springs Ranch, Colorado
Idaho Rocky Mountain Ranch, Idaho
Klicks' K Bar L Ranch, Montana
Baker's Bar M Ranch, Oregon

Large Outdoor Business/Group Barbecues
Rancho de los Caballeros, Arizona
Sylvan Dale Ranch, Colorado
Double JJ Ranch, Michigan
Ponderosa Ranch, Nevada
Rocking Horse Ranch, New York
Allen Ranch, Oklahoma
Flying M Ranch, Oregon
Garrett Creek Ranch, Texas
Prude Ranch, Texas
Texas Lil's Diamond A Ranch, Texas

Large Tours
Tanque Verde Ranch, Arizona
Outdoor Resort River Ranch, Florida
Double JJ Ranch, Michigan
Ponderosa Ranch, Nevada
Pinegrove Resort Ranch, New York
Allen Ranch, Oklahoma
Western Hills Guest Ranch, Oklahoma
Prude Ranch, Texas
Texas Lil's Diamond A Ranch, Texas
Rockin' R Ranch, Utah

Pets Allowed
Price Canyon Ranch, Arizona
Coffee Creek Ranch, California
Spanish Springs Ranch, California
Lane Guest Ranch, Colorado
Indian Creek Ranch, Idaho
Flying M Ranch, Oregon
Hunter Peak Ranch, Wyoming
Spear-O-Wigwam Ranch, Wyoming
Flying U Ranch, British Columbia, Canada

Ranch Inn Bed and Breakfasts
Howard Creek Ranch, California
Sylvan Dale Ranch, Colorado
Idaho Rocky Mountain Ranch, Idaho
Bear Mountain Guest Ranch, New Mexico
Western Dakota Ranch Vacations, South Dakota
Lazy Hills Guest Ranch, Texas
Pack Creek Ranch, Utah
Firefly Ranch, Vermont
Flying L Ranch, Washington
Savery Creek Thoroughbred Ranch, Wyoming

Ranch Resort
Rancho de los Caballeros, Arizona
Tanque Verde Ranch, Arizona
Wickenburg Inn Tennis and Guest Ranch,
  Arizona
Alisal Guest Ranch, California
The Aspen Lodge Ranch Resort, Colorado

C Lazy U Ranch, Colorado
Colorado Trails Ranch, Colorado
Lane Guest Ranch, Colorado
Longs Peak Inn and Guest Ranch, Colorado
Lost Valley Ranch, Colorado
Peaceful Valley Lodge and Guest Ranch, Colorado
Tall Timber, Colorado
Wit's End Guest Ranch and Resort, Colorado
Outdoor Resorts River Ranch, Florida
Double JJ Ranch, Michigan
El Rancho Stevens, Michigan
Turkey Creek Ranch, Missouri
Flathead Lake Lodge, Montana
Mountain Sky Guest Ranch, Montana
The Bishop's Lodge, New Mexico
Hidden Valley Resort, New York
Pinegrove Resort Ranch, New York
Ridin-Hy Ranch Resort, New York
Roaring Brook Ranch and Tennis Resort, New York
Rocking Horse Ranch, New York
Roundup Ranch Resort, New York
Western Hills Guest Ranch, Oklahoma
Rock Springs Guest Ranch, Oregon
Flying L Ranch, Texas
Lost Creek Ranch, Wyoming
The Ranch at Ucross, Wyoming
Tyax Mountain Lake Resort, British Columbia, Canada

Ride on Your Own without Wrangler (generally for experienced riders only, at ranch's discretion)

T-Lazy-7 Ranch, Colorado
Bakers Bar M Ranch, Oregon
Western Dakota Ranch Vacations, South Dakota
Hidden Valley Guest Ranch, Washington
Darwin Ranch, Wyoming
Eaton Ranch, Wyoming
HF Bar Ranch, Wyoming
Rafter Y Ranch, Wyoming
Spear-O-Wigwam Ranch, Wyoming
Flying U Ranch, British Columbia, Canada
The Hills Health and Guest Ranch, British Columbia, Canada
Springhouse Trails Ranch, British Columbia, Canada

RVs

Price Canyon Ranch, Arizona
Everett Ranch, Colorado
Outdoor Resorts River Ranch, Florida

Bear Mountain Guest Ranch, New Mexico
Pisgah View, North Carolina
Allen Ranch, Oklahoma
Western Hills Guest Ranch, Oklahoma
Flying M Ranch, Oregon
Flying W Ranch, Pennsylvania
Western Dakota Ranch Vacations, South Dakota
Prude Ranch, Texas
TL Bar Ranch, Alberta, Canada
The Hills Health and Guest Ranch, British Columbia, Canada
Mount Robson Guest Ranch, British Columbia, Canada
Springhouse Trails Ranch, British Columbia, Canada
Tyax Mountain Lake Resort, British Columbia, Canada

Travel Industry Awards

Kachemak Bay Wilderness Lodge, Alaska
Lazy K Bar Guest Ranch, Arizona
Rancho de los Caballeros, Arizona
Tanque Verde Ranch, Arizona
White Stallion Ranch, Arizona
Wickenburg Inn Tennis and Guest Ranch, Arizona
Alisal Guest Ranch, California
Howard Creek Ranch, California
The Aspen Lodge Ranch Resort, Colorado
C Lazy U Ranch, Colorado
Colorado Trails Ranch, Colorado
Deer Valley Ranch, Colorado
Elk Mountain Ranch, Colorado
Elktrout Lodge, Colorado
The Home Ranch, Colorado
Latigo Ranch, Colorado
Longs Peak Inn and Guest Ranch, Colorado
Lost Valley Ranch, Colorado
Peaceful Valley Lodge and Guest Ranch, Colorado
Tall Timber, Colorado
Vista Verde Guest and Ski Touring Ranch, Colorado
Waunita Hot Springs Ranch, Colorado
Wilderness Trails Ranch, Colorado
Wind River Ranch, Colorado
Turkey Creek Ranch, Missouri
Eagle Nest Lodge and Outfitters, Montana
Flathead Lake Lodge, Montana
Mountain Sky Guest Ranch, Montana
Triple Creek Ranch, Montana
The Bishop's Lodge, New Mexico

Roaring Brook Ranch and Tennis Resort,
New York
Rocking Horse Ranch, New York
Roundup Ranch Resort, New York
Cataloochee Ranch, North Carolina
Snowbird Mountain Lodge, North Carolina
Western Hills Guest Ranch, Oklahoma
Lazy Hills Guest Ranch, Texas
Mayan Dude Ranch, Texas
Hidden Valley Guest Ranch, Washington
Absaroka Ranch, Wyoming
Bill Cody's Ranch Resort, Wyoming
Lost Creek Ranch, Wyoming
Rafter Six Ranch Resort, Alberta, Canada
Flying U Ranch, British Columbia, Canada
Sundance Guest Ranch, British Columbia,
Canada

Working Cattle

Northland Ranch Resort, Alaska
Grand Canyon Bar Ten Ranch, Arizona
Grapevine Canyon Ranch, Arizona
Price Canyon Ranch, Arizona
Rancho de los Caballeros, Arizona
Sprucedale Ranch, Arizona
Flying AA Ranch, California
Hunewill Circle H Ranch, California
Quarter Circle U Rankin Ranch, California
Spanish Springs Ranch, California
Aspen Canyon Ranch, Colorado
Everett Ranch, Colorado
Lost Valley Ranch, Colorado
Sylvan Dale Ranch, Colorado
Vista Verde Guest and Ski Touring Ranch,
Colorado
Wilderness Trails Ranch, Colorado
Busterback Ranch, Idaho
C-B Ranch, Montana
Circle Bar Guest Ranch, Montana
G Bar M Ranch, Montana
Hargrave Guest Ranch, Montana
Lazy K Bar Ranch, Montana
Schively Ranch, Montana
63 Ranch, Montana
Sweet Grass Ranch, Montana
Cottonwood Ranch, Nevada
Logging Camp Ranch, North Dakota
Western Dakota Ranch Vacations, South Dakota
Prude Ranch, Texas
Y.O. Ranch, Texas
Rockin' R Ranch, Utah
David Ranch, Wyoming
High Island Guest Ranch, Wyoming
Lozier's Box R Ranch, Wyoming

Rafter Y Ranch, Wyoming
Red Rock Ranch, Wyoming
TX Ranch, Wyoming
TL Bar Ranch, Alberta, Canada
Flying U Ranch, British Columbia, Canada
Top of the World, British Columbia, Canada

Workshops

Kachemak Bay Wilderness Lodge, Alaska-
Photography
Tanque Verde Ranch, Arizona-Naturalist
White Stallion Ranch, Arizona-Elderhostel
PJ's Lodge, Arkansas-Fishing
Circle Bar B Guest Ranch, California-Dinner
Theater
Hunewill Circle H Ranch, California-
Watercolor
Trinity Mountain Meadow Resort, California-
Photography
Bar Lazy J, Colorado-Fishing
Elktrout Lodge, Colorado-Fishing
4UR Ranch, Colorado-Fishing
The Home Ranch, Colorado-Photography
Latigo Ranch, Colorado-Photography
Peaceful Valley Lodge and Guest Ranch,
Colorado-Naturalists, Crafts
San Juan Guest Ranch, Colorado-Photography
7W Guest Ranch, Colorado-Horsemanship
Skyline Guest Ranch, Colorado-Photography
Wind River Ranch, Colorado-Naturalist
Double JJ Ranch, Michigan-Corporate
Management
Boulder River Ranch, Montana-Fishing, Art
Circle Bar Guest Ranch, Montana-Art
Flathead Lake Lodge, Montana-Photography, Art
Hargrave Guest Ranch, Montana-Women and
Art, Photography
Lakeview Guest Ranch, Montana-Outfitting/
Horsemanship
Pine Butte Guest Ranch, Montana-Nature
Photography, Bears, Birds, Mammal Tracking,
Writing
63 Ranch, Montana-Photography
Cottonwood Ranch, Nevada-Photography
Bear Mountain Guest Ranch, New Mexico-
Birding, Pottery, Archaeology
Roundup Ranch Resort, New York-Riding,
Nature, Wildlife Seminars
Western Hills Guest Ranch, Oklahoma-Horse
Care/Riding
Reid Ranch, Utah-Reading, Computers
Hidden Valley Guest Ranch, Washington-Bird-
watching, Wildflowers, Photography

Castle Rock Lodges Guest Ranch, Wyoming-
  Multiworkshops
Crescent H Ranch, Wyoming-Fly-fishing
  School June and September
Heart Six Ranch, Wyoming-Fly-fishing,
  Photography
High Island Guest Ranch, Wyoming-Basket
  Weaving
Lozier's Box R Ranch, Wyoming-
  Horsemanship
Seven D Ranch, Wyoming-Health,
  Birding, Photography
Black Cat Guest Ranch, Alberta, Canada-Art,
  Photography, Writing
Cariboo Rose Guest Ranch, British Columbia,
  Canada-Photography Safari
Mount Robson Guest Ranch, British Columbia,
  Canada-Elderhostel

Appendix

Associations

Colorado Dude and Guest Ranch Association
P.O. Box 300K
Tabernash, CO 80478
(303) 887-3128
1 (800) 441-6060 (outside Colorado)

The Dude Ranchers' Association
P.O. Box 471K
LaPorte, CO 80535
(303) 493-7623

Alberta Guest Ranch Association
Box 6267 K
Hinton, Alberta Canada T7V 1X6

British Columbia Guest Ranch Association
P.O. Box 4501 K
Williams Lake, British Columbia, Canada V2G 2V8
1 (800) 663-6000 (Tourism British Columbia)

Bureaus of Tourism

Alabama
(800) ALABAMA (252-2262)
(Nationwide, AK and HI)

Alaska
(907) 465-2010
(907) 586-8399 FAX

Arizona
(602) 542-8687

Arkansas
(501) 682-7777
(800) 643-8383

California
(916) 322-1397
(800) 862-2543 (ext. A1003)

Colorado
(303) 592-5510
(800) 433-2656

Connecticut
(203) 566-3948
(800) 282-6863

Delaware
(302) 736-4271
(800) 441-8846

District of Columbia
(202) 789-7000

Florida
(904) 487-1462

Georgia
(404) 656-3590

Hawaii
(808) 923-1811

Idaho
(208) 334-2470
(800) 635-7820

Illinois
(312) 917-4732
(800) 223-0121 (nationwide)
(312) 280-5740 (Chicago only)

Indiana
(317) 232-8860
(800) 2-WANDER

Iowa
(515) 281-3100
(800) 345-IOWA

Kansas
(913) 296-2009
(800) 252-6727

Kentucky
(800) 225-TRIP (225-8747)
(800) 255-PARK

Louisiana
(504) 342-8100 (in state)
(800) 334-8626 (out of state)
(504) 342-3207 FAX

Maine
(207) 289-2423
(800) 533-9595 (out of state)

Maryland
(301) 333-6611
(800) 543-1036 (all U.S.)
(800) 282-6632 (Baltimore City)

Massachusetts
(617) 727-3201

Michigan
(517) 373-0670
(800) 5432-YES

Minnesota
(612) 296-5029 (Twin Cities)
(800) 652-9747 (in state)
(800) 328-1461 (out of state)

Mississippi
(601) 359-3297
(800) 647-2290

Missouri
(314) 751-4133
(800) 877-1234

Montana
(406) 444-2654
(406) 444-2808 FAX
(800) 541-1447

Nebraska
(402) 471-3796
(800) 228-4307 (out of state)
(800) 742-7595 (in state)

Nevada
(702) 885-4322
(800) 237-0774

New Hampshire
(603) 271-2666 or
(603) 271-2665

New Jersey
(609) 292-2470
(800) JERSEY-7

New Mexico
(505) 827-0291
(800) 545-2040 (out of state)

New York
(518) 474-4116 (in state)
(800) 225-5697 (continental U.S.)

North Carolina
(919) 733-4171
(800) VISIT-NC

North Dakota
(701) 224-2525 (local Bismark)
(800) 437-2077 (out of state)
(701) 472-2100 (in state)

Ohio
(614) 466-8844
(800) BUCKEYE
(800) 848-1300 (out of state)
(800) 282-1085 (in state)

Oklahoma
(405) 521-2409 (in state)
(800) 652-6552 (out of state)

Oregon
(503) 373-1270
(800) 547-7842 (out of state)
(800) 543-8838 (in state)

Pennsylvania
(717) 787-5453
(800) VISIT-PA (847-4872)

Rhode Island
(401) 277-2601
(800) 556-2484 (Maine, Virginia, North Ohio)

South Carolina
(803) 734-0122

South Dakota
(605) 773-3301
(800) 843-1930 (out of state)
(800) 952-2217 (in state)

Tennessee
(615) 741-2158

Texas
(512) 462-9191
(800) 8888-TEX (all U.S.)
(800) MEET-TEX (Canada)

Utah
(801) 538-1030

Vermont
(802) 828-3236

Virginia
(804) 786-4484 (questions)
(800) VISITVA (answering service and general information)

Washington
(206) 586-2088/2102 (travel counseling)
(800) 544-1800 (all U.S. and Canada)

West Virginia
(304) 348-2286
(800) 624-9110

Wisconsin
(608) 266-2161
(800) ESCAPES (WI, IL, MI, IA, MN)
(800) 432-TRIP (out of state)

Wyoming
(307) 777-7777
(800) 225-5996

Alberta, Canada
(800) 661-8888 (outside Alberta)
(403) 427-4321 (local)
(800) 222-6501 (Alberta)

British Columbia, Canada
(604) 387-1642/660-2861
(800) 663-6000

Western Museums

Gene Autry Western Heritage Museum
4700 Zoo Drive, Los Angeles, CA 90027
(213) 667-2000

Buffalo Bill Historical Center
P.O. Box 1000, Cody, WY 82414
(307) 587-4771

Buffalo Bill Museum
P.O. Box 1000, Cody, WY 82414
(307) 587-4771

Amon Carter Museum
P.O. Box 2365
Fort Worth, TX 76113
(817) 738-1933

Cowboy Artists of America Museum Foundation
1550 Bandera Highway
Box 1716
Kerrville, TX 78028
(512) 896-2553

Cowboy Hall of Fame and Western Heritage Center
Campus of N.M. Junior College
5317 Lovington Highway
Hobbs, NM 88240
(505) 392-4510, Ext. 371

Eiteljorg Museum
500 West Washington St.
Indianapolis, IN 46204
(317) 636-WEST (9378)

Gilcrease Museum
1400 Gilcrease Museum Road
Tulsa, OK 74127
(918) 582-3122

Joslyn Art Museum
2200 Dodge Street
Omaha, NE 68102
(402) 342-3300

Montana Historical Society
225 N. Roberts
Helena, MT 59620
(406) 444-2694

Museum of Fine Arts
107 W. Palace
Santa Fe, NM 87503
(505) 827-4455

Museum of Indian Arts and Culture
710 Camino Lejo
Santa Fe, NM 87503
(505) 827-8941

Museum of International Folk Art
706 Camino Lejo
Santa Fe, NM 87503
(505) 827-8350

Museum of Western Art
1727 Tremont Place
Denver, CO 80202
(303) 296-1880

National Cowboy Hall of Fame
1700 N.E. 63rd Street
Oklahoma City, OK 73111
(405) 478-2250

The R. W. Norton Art Gallery
4747 Creswell Avenue
Shreveport, LA 71106
(318) 865-4201

Palace of the Governors
On the Plaza, W. Palace
Santa Fe, NM 87504
(505) 827-6483

Phoenix Art Museum
1625 N. Central Avenue
Phoenix, AZ 85004
(602) 257-1222

Plains Indian Museum
P.O. Box 1000
Cody, WY 82414
(307) 587-4771

Pro Rodeo Hall of Fame and Museum of the American Cowboy
101 Pro Rodeo Drive
Colorado Springs, CO 80919
(719) 593-8847 / 593-8840

Frederic Remington Art Museum
303 Washington St.
Ogdensburg, NY 13669
(315) 393-2425

Sid Richardson Collection of Western Art
309 Main Street
Fort Worth, TX 76102
(817) 332-6554

The Rockwell Museum
111 Cedar St.
Corning, NY 14830
(607) 937-5386

C.M. Russell Museum
400 13th Street North
Great Falls, MT 59401
(406) 727-8787

Stark Museum
P.O. Box 1897
Orange, TX 77630
(409) 883-6661

Whitney Gallery of Western Art
P.O. Box 1000
Cody, WY 82414
(307) 587-4771

Wildlife of American Western Art
110 N. Center Street
P.O. Box 2984
Jackson, WY 83001
(307) 733-5771

Cody Firearms Museum
P.O. Box 1000
Cody, WY 82414
(307) 587-4771

Woolaroc Museum
Route 3
Bartlesville, OK 74003
(918) 336-0307

Wagon Trains

In addition to a ranch vacation, you may want to consider a wagon train adventure. The wagon train operators listed below offer wonderful trips that take you back to the time when pioneers crossed the plains. In most instances, you will travel by covered wagon, experiencing the bumps and splendor of days gone by. You will dine on delicious fresh chuck-wagon food and enjoy some modern conveniences including showers and rest rooms. (This varies considerably so check with the outfitter.) Sleep under the stars, listen to the distant howls of coyotes, smell pungent sage, and, most of all, relive history. Each of these outfitters will happily send you information and references.

National Trail Ride and Wagon Train Association
Art Howell
P.O. Box 8625 K
Gadsden, AL 35902
(800) 633-2270 (for general information only)

Bar T Five Outfitters
Bill and Joyce Thomas
P.O. Box 3415 K
Jackson, WY 83001 (307) 733-5386

Flint Hills Overland Wagon Train Trips
Ervin E. Grant
Box 1076 K
El Dorado, KS 67042
(316) 321-6300

Fort Seward Wagon Trains, Inc.
Phylis Klein Knecht
Box 244 K
Jamestown, ND 58402
(701) 252-6844

Honeymoon Trail Co.
Mel Heaton
Honeymoon Trail Co., Dept. K
Moccasin, AZ 86022
(602) 643-7292

Overland Wagon Train
Charlie Messenger
5915 U.S. 30 K
Cheyenne, WY 82001
(307) 638-6888

Oregon Trail Wagon Train
Gordon and Patty Howard
Route 2, Box 502 K
Bayard, NE 69334
(308) 586-1850

Peterson's Wagons West
Everett and Pat Peterson
Box 1156 K
Afton, WY 83110
(800) 447-4711

Wagons Ho, Inc.
Ruth and Frank Hefner
P.O. Box 60098 K
Phoenix, AZ 85082
(602) 230-1801; (602) 977-7724

Western Dakota Ranch Vacations
HCR1, Dept. K
Wall, SD 57709
(605) 279-2198
(10-person minimum)

Western Stores

The American cowboy's worldwide appeal stretches beyond the rodeo arenas and the guest/cattle ranches that open their doors so that others may enjoy great Western hospitality. Today, many folks are interested in collecting one-of-a-kind cowboy and Indian memorabilia—woolly chaps, ten-gallon hats, Indian crafts, saddles, spurs, bits, bridles, even Western furniture and home accessories. In our travels, we have come across several cowboy boutiques that specialize in old "cowboy gear" and relics from days gone by. If you are passing through one of these towns, you may just want to stop by. Whether you purchase anything is up to you. My guess is that you will probably not leave empty-handed. Happy trails and happy shopping.

Edison's American West Gallery
Alan Edison
620 Sun Valley Rd.
P.O. Box 3130
Ketchum, ID 83340
(208) 726-1333

Cry Baby Ranch
Judy Trattner/Roxanne Thurman
1428 Larimer Square
Denver, CO 80202
(303) 623-3979

Old West Antiques
Brian and Diane Lebel
1212 Sheridan Avenue
Cody, WY 82414
(307) 587-9014

Old Taos
Steve Eich
108 Teresina Lane
Taos, NM 87571
(505) 758-7353

Arrow Smith Relics of the Old West
Mark Arrow Smith
402 Old Santa Fe Trail
Santa Fe, NM 87501
(505) 989-7663

Billy Martin's
812 Madison Avenue
New York, NY 10021
(212) 861-3100

Ranch Camps

One of the most exciting experiences for any young person is to spend the summer, or at least part of the summer, at a Ranch Camp. Since the first edition of *Ranch Vacations* was published, I have been asked repeatedly about ranch camps. Many parents are looking for summer camps for their children. Today, ranch camps provide a healthy, happy, summer environment that will, without a doubt, broaden each child's experiences. These camps provide opportunities for youngsters to be in the outdoors and exposed to refreshing challenges, both educationally and developmentally. It would be impossible to list all the ranch camps throughout North America. Remembering the old adage "less is more," I have chosen to list below just a few camps. Each has a fine reputation and has been in the ranch camp industry for many years. As with all the other ranch properties in this guide, I recommend that you contact the camp and talk with them directly. Ask for references. Each of the camps listed below would be delighted to provide you with all the information that you will need to help you select the best ranch camp for your child.

Brush Ranch Camp
P.O. Box 5759K
Santa Fe, NM 87502
(505) 757-8821

Cheley Colorado Camps
P.O. Box 6525K
Denver, CO 80206
(303) 377-3616

Jameson Ranch Camp
Box K
Glenville, CA 93226
(805) 536-8888

Teton Valley Ranch Camp
Jackson Hole
Box 8K
Kelly, WY 83011
(307) 733-2958

Top 20 PRCA Rodeos
Professional Rodeo Cowboys Association
101 Pro Rodeo Drive
Colorado Springs, Colorado

PRCA Media Dept.
(719) 593-8840

Date	City	Event
Mid-January	Denver, CO	National Western Stock Show and Rodeo
Late January	Fort Worth, TX	Southwestern Exposition and Stock Show Rodeo
Early February	El Paso, TX	Southwestern International Rodeo
Early February	San Antonio, TX	San Antonio Livestock Exposition Rodeo
Mid-February	Houston, TX	Houston Livestock Show and Rodeo
Late February	Tucson, AZ	La Fiesta de los Vaqueros
Mid-March	Pocatello, ID	Dodge National Circuit Finals Rodeo
Mid-May	Cloverdale,B.C.,Canada	Cloverdale Rodeo
Mid-June	Reno, NV	Reno Rodeo
Early July	Pecos, TX	West of the Pecos Rodeo
Early July	Calgary, Alberta, Canada	Calgary Stampede
Early July	Greeley, CO	Greeley Independence Stampede
Late July	Cheyenne, WY	Cheyenne Frontier Days
Mid-July	Salinas, CA	California Rodeo
Early August	Dodge City, KS	Dodge City Days Rodeo
Mid-August	Colorado Springs, CO	Pikes Peak or Bust Rodeo
Early September	Albuquerque, NM	New Mexico State Fair Rodeo
Mid-September	Pendleton, OR	Pendleton Round-up Rodeo
Late September	San Francisco, CA	Grand National (Cow Palace) Rodeo
Early December	Las Vegas, NV	National Finals Rodeo

Annual Western Events in the
United States and Alberta and British Columbia, Canada

The following is a selection of annual Western events. These events and dates are subject to change. Telephone the appropriate office of tourism listed to verify dates.

Date	City	Event
ALABAMA		
Late January	Town Creek	National Field Trials
Late February	Birmingham	Harper and Morgan Rodeo
Early March	Gadsden	Alabama Wagon Train
	Opp	Opp Jaycee Rattlesnake Rodeo
Late March	Montgomery	Southeastern Livestock Exposition Rodeo and Livestock Week
Mid- to Late April	Bridgeport	Indian Day
	Clayton	Little Britches Rodeo
	Decatur	Annual Racking Horse Spring Celebration
Late June	Clayton	Stetson Hoedown Rodeo
Late July	Selma	Selma Jaycee's Annual Southeast Championship Rodeo
Early August	Gadsden	Boys Club Annual Rodeo
Mid- to Late August	Gadsden	Cherokees of Northeast Alabama Indian Powwow Festival
Mid-September	Huntsville	Ole Time Fiddling and Bluegrass Convention
Late September	Winfield	Mule Days
	Decatur	Racking Horse World Celebration
Late September– Early October	Mobile	Greater Gulf State Fair and PRCA Rodeo
Early October	Montgomery	South Alabama State Fair
	Birmingham	Alabama State Fair
	Athens	Annual Tennessee Valley Old Time Fiddlers Convention
Early November	Montgomery	Southern Championship Charity Horse Show
Late November	Atmore	Annual Porch Band and Creek Indians' Thanksgiving Day Powwow
ALASKA		
February	Anchorage	Anchorage Fur Rendezvous
Early April	Juneau	Annual Alaska Folk Festival
Late May	Delta Junction	Buffalo Wallow Statewide Square Dance Festival
Mid-August	Palmer	Alaska State Fair Rodeo and Parade
	Kodiak	Alaska State Fair and Rodeo
	Fairbanks	Tanana Valley State Fair
	Haines	Southeast Alaska State Fair
Early July	Delta Junction	Buffalo Barbecue

Early July	Skagway	Soapy Smith's Wake
Mid-July	Fairbanks	Golden Days
	Whitehorse	Horse Show
Mid-November	Fairbanks	Annual Athabascan Fiddling Festival

ARIZONA

January	Phoenix	Arizona National Livestock Show and Old Timers Rodeo
Mid-January	Tucson	Turquoise Pro Rodeo Circuit Finals
Late January to Early February	Scottsdale	Parada del Sol Parade and Rodeo
February	Phoenix	A-Z National Horse Show
	Tucson	Tucson Winter Classic Horse Show and Grand Prix World Cup
	Tucson	Jumping Horse Fiesta Horse Show
	Goodyear	Estrella Rodeo
Mid-February	Yuma	Yuma Jaycees Silver Spur Rodeo
	Scottsdale	All Arabian Horse Show and Sale
	Wickenburg	Gold Rush Days and Rodeo
Late February	Tucson	La Fiesta de los Vaqueros Rodeo
Early March	Phoenix	World Championship Jaycees' Rodeo of Rodeos
Mid-April	Globe/Miami	Copper Dust Stampede Rodeo
May	Payson	Old Time Rodeo Cowboys Reunion
Late May	Tombstone	Wyatt Earp Days
June	Payson	Annual Junior Rodeo
	Alpine	Annual Rodeo, Parade, and Barbecue
June-August	Flagstaff	Hopi and Navajo Craftsman Exhibitions
Early June	Sonora	Quarter Horse Show
Mid-June to Early July	Flagstaff	Festival of Native American Arts
Early July	Springerville	Round Valley Rodeo and Parade
	Prescott	Frontier Days and World's Oldest Rodeo
	Window Rock	Fourth of July celebration PRCA Rodeo & Pow Wow
Late July	Snowflake	Pioneer Days Celebration
August	Williams	Cowpunchers' Reunion Rodeo
Late August	Payson	World's Oldest Continuous PRCA Rodeo and Parade
September	Tucson	Old Pueblo Horse Show
	Window Rock	Navajo Nation Fair
	Payson	State Championship Old Time Fiddlers Contest
Early September	Tombstone	Wild West Days
	Taylor	Sweet Corn Festival
	Window Rock	Annual Navajo Nation Fair and Rodeo
Late September	Sonora	PRCA Rodeo, Santa Cruz County
	Willcox	Rex Allen Days
Early October	Scottsdale	Wrangler Jeans Rodeo and Showdown

Mid-October	Tombstone	Helldorado Days
Early November	Sells	Sells All-Indian Rodeo
Late October– Early November	Phoenix	Cowboy Artists of America Exhibition
November	Phoenix	Native American Arts Show
Early December	Mesa	Fiesta del Sol Rodeo

ARKANSAS

Mid-April	Cabot	Old West Daze
Early May	Booneville	Booneville Riding Club Spring Rodeo
Late May–	Fort Smith	Annual Old Fort Days Rodeo
Early June	Shirley	Annual Homecoming and Rodeo
Early June	Calico Rock	IRA Championship Rodeo
	Huntsville	Hawgfest pig race, rodeo, music
	Newport	Riverboat Days and State Catfish Cooking Contest (Rodeo)
Mid-June	Mountain View	Western Music Weekend
	Booneville	Riding Club Rodeo
	Calico Rock	Annual IRA Championship Rodeo
	Dardanelle	Annual PRCA Rodeo
	Siloam Springs	Annual Rodeo and Parade
Early July	Springdale	Annual Rodeo of the Ozarks
	Caraway	Annual Community Picnic and Rodeo
Early August	Mena	Polk County Rodeo
	Crossett	Annual Rodeo Roundup Day
	Crossett	Annual PRCA Rodeo
	Crossett	Annual Miss Rodeo Arkansas Pageant
Late August	Foreman	Little River County Fair and Rodeo
Late August– Early September	Clinton	Arkansas Championship Chuck Wagon Races
	Malvern	Hot Spring County Fair and Rodeo
Mid-September	Fort Smith	Arkansas/Oklahoma State Fair
	Harrison	Northwest Arkansas District Fair and PRCA Rodeo
	Mountain View	Arkansas Old Time Fiddlers Association State Championship Competition
	DeQueen	Annual Sevier County Fair and Rodeo
	Jonesboro	Annual Northeast Arkansas District Fair Rodeo
	Marshall	Annual Searcy County Fair and Rodeo
Late September	Pine Bluff	Annual Southeast Arkansas Livestock Show and Rodeo
Late September– Early October	Texarkana	Annual Four States Fair and Rodeo
Early October	Little Rock	Arkansas State Fair and Livestock Show
	Marshall	Falling Water Trail Ride
	Pea Ridge	International Mule Jump

CALIFORNIA

Late January	Red Bluff	Red Bluff Bull Sale
Mid-February	Kernville	Whiskey Flat Days
Late February	Palm Springs	Mounted Police Rodeo and Parade
Mid-April	Bakersfield	Kern County Horse Show Classic on the Green
Late April	Red Bluff	Roundup Rodeo and Parade
	Auburn	Wild West Stampede (PRCA)
	Clovis	Clovis Rodeo
May	Marysville	Marysville Stampede
Mid-May	Redding	Redding Rodeo Week (PRCA)
	King City	Salinas Valley Fair
	Cottonwood	Cottonwood Rodeo
	Angels Camp	Calaveras County Fair, Frog Jumping Jubilee and Rodeo
Late May	Bishop	Mule Days Celebration
	Yucca	Valley Grubstake Days and PRCA Rodeo
Late May to Early June	Santa Maria	Annual Elks Rodeo and Parade
June	Anderson	Shasta District Fair/Rodeo
	Quincy	California State High School Rodeo Championships
Early June	Livermore	World's Fastest Rodeo
	McKinleyville	Pony Express Days
Mid-June	Middletown	Middletown Days
Late June	Diamond Springs	Hangtown Annual Pioneer Days Celebration
July	Santa Barbara	Horse and Flower Show (PRCA)
	Fortuna	Fortuna Rodeo, "Oldest, Longest, Most Westerly"
	Orick	Orick Rodeo
Early July	Folsom	Folsom Championship PRCA Rodeo
	Lakeport	Lake County Rodeo
Mid-July	Merced	Merced County Fair
Late July	Susanville	Doyle Days Rodeo
	Ruth	Ruth Rodeo
Late July to Early August	Paso Robles	California Mid-State Fair
Early August	Santa Barbara	Old Spanish Days
	Grass Valley	Nevada County Fair
	Quincy	Plumas County Fair
Mid-August	Susanville	Lassen County Fair
Mid-August to Early September	Sacramento	Cal State Fair
Late August	Lancaster	Antelope Valley Fair, Alfalfa Festival and Rodeo
September	Coulterville	Annual Gunfighters Rendezvous
Early September	Barstow	Calico Days Stampede Rodeo

Late September	Ridgecrest	Western Heritage Mining Days
Mid-October	Paso Robles	Pioneer Days
Early October	Calico	Calico Days
Mid-October	Kernville	Kernville Stampede
	City of Industry	Industry Hills Annual Charity Pro Rodeo
	Palms	Pioneer Days Celebration and PRCA Rodeo
Late October	San Francisco	Grand National Rodeo and Horseshow and Livestock Exposition
November	Brawley	Cattle Call and Rodeo
Early November	Death Valley	Annual Death Valley Encampment
Mid-December	Clovis	Lex Connelly Memorial Rodeo
Late December	Red Bluff	New Year's Eve Pro Rodeo and Celebration

COLORADO

Early January	Denver	National Western Stock Show and Rodeo
Mid-January	Steamboat Springs	Cowboy Downhill
May to September	Durango	Durango Pro Rodeo
Mid-June	Grand Junction	Colorado Stampede Rodeo
	Colorado Springs	Little Britches Rodeo
	Ute	Mountain Rodeo
Late June	Grand Junction	Colorado Stampede
	Glenwood Springs	Roaring Fork Rodeo
	Greeley	Independence Stampede Greeley Rodeo
Late June to Late August	Snowmass	Snowmass Stables Rodeo
July	Canon City	Royal Gorge Rodeo
	Loveland	Jaycees' Rodeo
	Estes Park	Arabian Horse Show
Early July	Greeley	Biggest Fourth of July Rodeo
	Steamboat Springs	Cowboys' Roundup Rodeo
Mid-July	Estes Park	Rooftop Rodeo
Late July	Boulder	Powwow Rodeo and Horse Show
	Monte Vista	Ski-Hi Stampede, Ski-Hi Park
	Fairplay	Burro Days
	Gunnison	Cattlemen's Days, Rodeo and Celebration
Early August	Colorado Springs	Pikes Peak or Bust Rodeo
	Evergreen	Mountain Rendezvous
	Leadville	International Pack Burro Race Championships
	Aspen	Aspen Rodeo
	Evergreen	Rodeo weekend
Mid-August	Loveland	Larimer County Fair and Rodeo
Late August	Pueblo	Colorado State Fair, Livestock Show and Rodeo
	Glenwood Springs	Garfield County Fair and Rodeo

DISTRICT OF COLUMBIA

October	Largo, MD (D.C.)	Washington International Horse Show

FLORIDA

Mid-January	Davies	5-Star Pro Rodeo Davies Series Rodeo (PRCA)
Early February	Homestead	Homestead Championship Rodeo
	Fort Pierce	Cattleman's Day Parade and Shrine
Early February	West Palm Beach	Winter Equestrian Festival
Early March to	Tampa	Florida State Fair PRCA Rodeo
Mid-February	Kissimmee	Annual Edition Silver Spurs Rodeo
	Hollywood	Seminole Tribal Fair and Rodeo
Late February	Homestead	Frontier Days Rodeo
Mid-March	Tampa	Winter Equestrian Festival
Early April	Tampa	Volvo Federation Equestrian International World Cup Finals
Late June	Kissimmee	82nd Edition Silver Spurs Rodeo
Late September	Tallahassee	Native American Heritage Festival
	Titusville	North Brevard Area Rodeo
Early October	Pensacola	St. Anne's Autumn Round-Up
Mid-October	Orlando	Pioneer Days
Late November	Ocula	Thanksgiving Arabian Show
	Davies	Sunshine State Pro Rodeo Championship

IDAHO

Mid-January	Boise	National Snaffle Bit Futurity
Late January	Sun Valley	Sun Valley Winter Carnival
Mid-March	Pocatello	Dodge National Circuit Finals Rodeo
Late April	Lewiston	Lewiston Rodeo: Dogwood Festival
Mid-June	Weiser	National Old Time Fiddlers' Contest
Early July	Salmon	Salmon River Days Rodeo
Mid-July	Nampa	Snake River Stampede
	Driggs	Fourth Annual High Country Cowboy Festival
August	Caldwell	Caldwell Night Rodeo
	Fort Hall/Blackfoot	Shoshone-Bannock Indian Festival Rodeo
Late August	Blackfoot	Eastern Idaho Fair
	Ketchum	Ketchum Wagon Days Celebration
Early September	Lewiston	Lewiston Roundup

ILLINOIS

Mid-January	Peona	"World's Largest Rodeo"

INDIANA

October	Lafayette	Feast of the Hunter's Moon

IOWA

Late May	Fort Madison	Trading Post Days and Buckskinners Rendezvous
Late May–Early June	Cherokee	Cherokee Rodeo
Early June	Fort Dodge	Frontier Days

Mid-June	Albia	Iowa High School Rodeo Finals
Late June	Edgewood	Edgewood Rodeo Days
Early July	Bloomfield	Fort Bloomfield IRCA Rodeo
	Lake City	Top Rail Saddle Club Rodeo and Western Days
Mid-July	Woodbine	Rodeo Days
Late July	Lenox	Lenox Rodeo
Early August	Carson	Carson Rodeo
	Sidney	Iowa Championship Rodeo
	Toledo	Double "D" Rodeo
Early September	Fort Madison	Tri-State Rodeo Festival

KANSAS

Early May	Hays	Annual Spring Rodeo, FHSU
Early June	Fort Scott	Good Ol' Days Celebration
	Dodge City	Longhorn Steer Drive
	Garden City	Beef Empire Days
Late July	Wichita	Mid-America Intertribal Indian Powwow
Early August	Dodge City	Dodge City Days (PRCA Rodeo)
Mid-August	Abilene	Central Kansas Free Fair and Wild Bill Hickok Rodeo
Early September	Topeka	Railroad Days
	Medicine Lodge	Indian Summer Days
Early October	Medicine Lodge	Indian Peace Treaty Pageant (Every 3 years starting 1991)

KENTUCKY

Early and Mid-February	Bowling Green	Kyana Quarter Horse Show
Mid-February	Bowling Green	Championship Rodeo
Early March	Bowling Green	Kyana Quarter Horse Show
	Bowling Green	Spring Festival Horse Show
Late March	Florence	Turfway Festival & Jim Beam Stakes
	Benton	Tater Day Rodeo and National Championship Horse and Mule Pulls
	Winchester	Point-to-Point Races
Early April	Lexington	Ha'Penny Horse Trials
Mid-April	Lexington	Spring Horse Affair
	Henderson	Tri-Fest Firemen's Rodeo
Late April	Lexington	Rolex Kentucky International 3-Day Event
	Lexington	High-hope Steeplechase
Early May	Louisville	The Kentucky Derby
	Louisville	The Kentucky Oaks
	Lexington	Kentucky Spring Premier Saddlebred Show
Mid-May	Lexington	Kentucky Spring Hunter/Jumper Show
	Florence	Mason-Dixon Steeplechase
Late May	Lexington	Kentucky Dressage Association
	Carter County	Grayson Memory Days Jaycees Horse Show

	Prospect	Hard Scuffle Steeplechase
	Bowling Green	Bluegrass Paint Horse Show
	Georgetown	Rotary Horse Show
Early June	Lexington	The Egyptian Event
	Bowling Green	Appaloosa Horse Show
	Hartford	AQHA Horse Show
Mid-June	Bowling Green	Saddlebred Horse Show
	Olive Hill	Carter County Horse Show
Early July	Lexington	Lexington Junior League Horse Show
Mid-July	Lexington	Paint Horse National Show
	Grayson County	Official Kentucky State Championship Old Time Fiddlers Contest
	Hartford	World Championship Rodeo
Early August	Lexington	Greater Eastern Appaloosa Regional Show
	Lexington	Wild Horse & Burro Adoption & Exposition
Mid-August	Lexington	Bluegrass Festival Hunter/Jumper Show
	Louisville	Kentucky State Fair, Horse Show and Rodeo
	Harrodsburg	Pioneer Days Festival & Old Time Fiddler's Contest
Late August	Lexington	Kentucky Hunter/Jumper Association Horse Show
	Lexington	Lexington Grand Prix
Late August–Early September	Lexington	Yamaha All-Arabian Combined Classic

LOUISIANA

Mid-January	Lake Charles	Calcasieu Parish Livestock Show
Late January	Lake Charles	Southwest District Livestock Show and Rodeo
Late February	Covington	Dixie Trail Riders
Late March	Lake Charles	Silver Spur Riders Club
Late April	Lake Charles	Silver Spur Riders Club
Late May	Lake Charles	Silver Spur Riders Club
Late July	Lake Charles	Silver Spur Riders Club
Late August	Lake Charles	Silver Spur Riders Club
Late August–Early September	Lake Charles	McNeese Classic Livestock Show and Louisiana Classic Agricultural Expo
Mid-September	Lake Charles	Tennessee Walking and Racking Horse Show
Late September	Lake Charles	Silver Spur Riders Club
October	Angola	Angola Prison Rodeo
Mid-October	Raceland	LaFourche Parish Agriculture Fair and Livestock Show
	Loranger	Old Farmer's Day
Late October	Lake Charles	Silver Spur Riders Club
Late November	Lake Charles	Silver Spur Riders Club

MAINE
January	Kingfield	White White World

MARYLAND
Early June	Pinefield	Piscataway Indian Festival and Powwow
Early July	McHenry	Annual American Indian Intertribal Cultural Organization Powwow
Early August	Cordova	Old St. Joseph Jousting Tournament and Horse Show
Late September	Timonium	Eastern National Livestock Show

MICHIGAN
Mid-February	Traverse City	VASA Cross-Country Ski Race
Late May	Shakopee	Eagle Creek Rendezvous

MINNESOTA
Late February	Kenyon	Horse and Cutter Day
Early March	New Ulm	Horse and Mule Parade
Late April	St. Paul	Minnesota Horse Exposition
Early May	Crookston	Great Northern Horse Extravaganza
Mid-June	Lake Benton	Saddle Horse Days
Mid-May	Bagley	Minnesota High School Rodeo
Late May	New London	Little Britches Rodeo
Early June	Worthington	High School Rodeo
Mid-June	Granite Falls	Western Fest Rodeo
	Buffalo	Buffalo Rodeo
Early July	Park Rapids	Mississippi Headwaters Rodeo
	Hamel	Hamel Rodeo
Mid-July	Isanti	Rodeo Jubilee Days
	Hawley	Hawley Rodeo
Mid-August	Hutchinson	McLeod County Rodeo
Mid-October	Crookston	Midwest International Horse Show

MISSISSIPPI
Early February	Jackson	Jackson Dixie National Livestock Show and Rodeo and Western Festival
Mid-July	Natchez	Choctaw Rodeo
Late July- Early August	Phil	Neshoba County Fair

MISSOURI
Late June	Kansas City	Kansas City Rodeo
Early September	Independence	Santa-Cali Gun Days
Mid-September	Sikeston	PRCA Rodeo
Early November	Kansas City	American Royal Livestock, Horse Show and Rodeo

MONTANA
Early February	Billings	Northern Rodeo Association Finals

	Seeley Lake	OSCR 50K Nordic Ski Race
	Helena	Race to the Sky Sled Dog Race
Mid-February	Anaconda/Butte	Big Sky Winternational Sports Festival
Mid-March	Great Falls	C. M. Russell Auction of Original Western Art
	Missoula	Montana State Expo
Early April	Whitefish	Whitefish North American Cross-Country Ski Championships
Early May	Missoula	Western Heritage Days
Mid-May	Conrad	Whoop-up Trail Days
	St. Ignatius	Buffalo Feast and Pow Wow
	Miles City	Miles City Bucking Horse Sale
Late May	Virginia City	Spring Horseback Poker Run
June	Hardin	Custer's Last Stand Re-enactment
Early June	Forsyth	Forsyth Horse Show and Rodeo
Mid-June	Bozeman	College National Finals Rodeo
	Lewistown	Snowy Mountain Regional Fiddlers Contest
Late June	Virginia City	Buffalo Runners Shootin' Matches
	Stevensville	Western Days
	Hamilton	Hamilton Old Timers Rodeo
Early July	Red Lodge	Home of Champions Rodeo
	Butte	Butte Vigilante Rodeo
	Roundup	Musselshell Valley July 4th Celebration and Rodeo
	Butte	Vigilante Rodeo
Mid-July	Browning	North American Indian Days
	Wolf Point	Wolf Point Wild Horse Stampede
Late July	Lewistown	Central Montana Horse Show Fair and Rodeo
	Helena	Last Chance Stampede and Fair
	Libby	Libby Logger Days
	Deer Lodge	Grant-Kohrs Ranch Annual Celebration
	Red Lodge	Red Lodge Mountain Man Rendezvous
Early August	Missoula	United Peoples Pow Wow and Encampment
	Glendive	Dawson County Fair and Rodeo
Mid-August	Big Timber	Montana Cowboy Poetry Gathering
	Crow	Agency Crow Fair
	Billings	Montana Fair
	Plentywood	Sheridan County Fair and Rodeo
	Kalispell	Northwest Montana Fair and PRCA Rodeo
	Deer Lodge	Tri-County Fair
Late August	Roundup	Roundup Cattle Drive
	Plains	Sanders County Fair and Rodeo
	White Sulpher Springs	Labor Day Rodeo and Parade
Early September	Reedpoint	Running of the Sheep-Sheep Drive
Mid-September	Great Falls	Annual Old Timers Rodeo
Late September	Libby	Nordicfest

October	Billings	Northern International Livestock Exposition and Rodeo
Early October	Moise	Bison Roundup (National Bison Range)
November	West Yellowstone	Cross-Country Fall Camp

NEBRASKA

Mid-June	Hastings	Cottonwood Prairie Festival
	North Platte	Celebration and Buffalo Bill Rodeo
July	Burwell	Nebraska's Big Rodeo
Early July	Crawford	Crawford Rodeo
	Chadron	Fur Trade Days and Buckskin Rendezvous
Late July	Winnebago	Indian Pow Wow
Mid-August	Ogallala	Ogallala Roundup Rodeo
Late August	Sidney	Cheyenne County Fair
	Gordon	Sheridan County Fair and Rodeo
September	Bayard	Chimney Rock Pioneer Days
Mid-September	Ogallala	Indian Summer Rendezvous
Late September	Omaha River	City Roundup and World Championship Rodeo

NEVADA

Every other weekend except during August	Mesquite	Peppermill Year-Round Roping Competition
Early January	Elko	Cowboy Poetry Gathering
	Reno	Biggest Little Cutting in the World Horse Competition
Mid-January	Reno	Miller Team Roping Horse Competition
Early March	Ely	Bristlecone Chariot Races
Mid-March	Reno	National Reined Cowhorse Association Hackamore Futurity
	Reno	Romagnola Cattle Show/Sale
	Reno	Beefmasters Cattle Show/Sale
Late April	Reno	Miller Team Roping Horse Competition
	Reno	Angus Cattle Show/Sale
Early May	Reno	Angus Cattle Show/Sale
Mid-May	Reno	Nevada Junior Livestock State Show
	Reno	Comstock Arabian Horse Show
Late May	Reno	Silver State Morgan Horse Show
May to June	Las Vegas	Helldorado Rodeo
June	Wells	Wells Bustin' and Dustin' PRCA Rodeo
Early June	Reno	Pacific Coast Cutting Horse Association Competition
	Carson City	Annual Kit Carson Rendezvous and Wagon Train Days
	Ely	White Pine Rodeo
Mid-June	Reno	Reno Rodeo Carson City Historic Pony Express Ride

Late June	Reno	Reno Grand Prix Jumping Classic Horse Competition
July	Fallon	All Indian Stampede and Pioneer Days
Early July	Fallon	Nevada International Invitational Rodeo
Mid-July	Reno	Comstock Arabian Horse Show
Early August	Reno	Peruvian Paso Horse Show
Late August	Reno	Paint-O-Rama Western States Horse Show
	Reno	Pacific Coast Quarter Horse Spectacular Horse Show
	Ely	White Pine Country Days Fair and Pony Express Horse Races
September	Virginia	City Virginia City Camel Races and 1880 Grand Ball
	Winnemucca	Nevada Oldest Rodeo & Western Art Round-Up Show and Sale
	Winnemucca	Winnemucca Parade and Rodeo
	Sparks	Western States Indian Rodeo Regional Finals
Mid-September	Reno	National Reined Cowhorse Association Snaffle Bit Futurity Horse Competition
	Ely	White Pine Silver Stampede
	Carson City	Open Horse Show
Late September	Reno	National Team Penning Finals Horse Competition
	Ely	Whitepine High School Rodeo
Early October	Reno	Western Open Cutting Horse Competition
Late October	Carson City	Nevada Day Celebration
Early November	Reno	North American Indian Championship Rodeo
Mid-November	Reno	National Old Timers Finals Rodeo
December	Las Vegas	National PRCA Finals Rodeo
Early December	Las Vegas	NFR Bucking Horse and Bull Sale

NEW JERSEY

Late May through Late September (Every Saturday)	Woodstown	Woodstown Weekly Rodeo (PRCA)
Late May through Late September	Netcong	Wild West City—Replica of Dodge City

NEW MEXICO

Early January	Red River	Red River Winterfest
Late February	Chama	High Country Winter Carnival
Late February	Angel Fire	Angel Fire Winter Carnival Festival Weekend
Late March	El Paso/Shakespeare	New Mexico Renegade Ride
Mid-April	Truth or Consequences	Ralph Edwards Fiesta and Rodeo
Mid-May	Deming	Fiddlers' Contest

Late May	Silver City	Endurance Horse Ride
	Cloudcroft	Mayfair Hayrides and Rodeo
Early June	Clovis	Pioneer Days Celebration and PRCA Rodeo
	Fort Sumner	Old Fort Days
	Mescalero	Apache Indian Maidens' Puberty Rites and Rodeo
	Las Vegas	Rails and Trails Days
	Farmington	Sheriff Posse Rodeo
Mid-June	Cloudcroft	Western Roundup
	Dulce	All-Indian Rodeo
	Taos	San Antonio Corn Dance
	Gallup	Lions Club Western Jubilee Week and Rodeo
Late June	Taos	Rodeo de Taos
	Tucumcari	Pinata Festival and Lions Club Rodeo
Late June–Early July	Clayton	Rabbit Ear Roundup Rodeo
Early July	Cimarron	Cimarron Rodeo
	Eunice	Eunice Fourth of July Celebration and Junior Rodeo
	Santa Fe	Rodeo de Santa Fe
	Taos	Taos Pueblo Powwow
Mid-July	Carlsbad	Western Days and AJRA Rodeo
	Dulce	Little Beaver Roundup Rodeo
	Galisteo	Galisteo Rodeo
Late July	Taos	Fiesta de Santiago y Santa Ana
August	Lovington	Lea County Fair and PRCA Rodeo
	Gallup	Inter-Tribal Indian Ceremonial and Rodeo
Early August	Los Alamos	Los Alamos County Fair and Rodeo
Mid-August	Capitan	Lincoln County Fair
	Santa Fe	Indian Market
	Albuquerque	Bernalillo County 4-H Fair and Rodeo
September	Albuquerque	New Mexico State Fair and Rodeo
	Santa Fe	Fiesta de Santa Fe
Early September	Socorro	Socorro County Fair and Rodeo
	Ruidoso	Downs All-American Futurity
	Clayton	Hayden Rodeo
Late September	Lovington	Days of Old West Ranch Rodeo
	Las Cruces	Southern New Mexico State Fair and Rodeo
	Roswell	Eastern New Mexico State Fair and Rodeo
	Deming	South-Western New Mexico State Fair
	Taos	The Old Taos Trade Fair
	Taos	San Geronimo Day Trade Fair
Mid-October	Carlsbad	Alfalfa Fest (mule races, largest parade, and hayride)
Late October	Truth or Consequences	Old-Time Fiddlers Contest

Mid-November	Hobbs	Llano Estacado Party and Cowboy Hall of Fame and Western Heritage Center Introduction Banquet
Late November	Albuquerque	Indian National Finals Rodeo
Late December	Taos	The Matachines Dances at Taos Pueblo

NEW YORK

July through September	Lake Luzerne	Adirondack Championship Rodeo
Early August	Attica	Attica Rodeo
Mid-September	Lake Ontario	Trout and Salmon Derby, Niagara River

For Dates Contact:
American Horse Show Association
598 Madison Avenue
New York, NY 10022 (212) 736-6314

	New York City	New York State National Horse Show at Madison Square Gardens
	Syracuse	New York State Fair International Horse Show
	Lake Placid	I Love New York Horse Show

NORTH CAROLINA

Mid-January	Raleigh	Midwinter Quarter Horse Show
Early February	Raleigh	Southern National Draft Horse Pull
Late March	Raleigh	North Carolina Quarter Horse Association Spring Show Championship Rodeo
	Pinehurst	Kiwanis Charity Horse Show
	Raleigh	Great Smokies Pro Rodeo
	Oak Ridge	Oak Ridge Easter Horse Show & Fiddlers Convention
	Fayetteville	Annual Shrine Club Rodeo
Early April	Blowing Rock	Annual Opening Day Trout Fishing Derby
	Southern Pines	Moore County Annual Pleasure Horse Drive Show
	Pembroke Spring	Racking Horse Show
	Pinehurst	Harness Horse Racing Matinee
	Raleigh	Appaloosa Horse Show
Mid-April	Raleigh	Easter Bunny Quarter Horse Circuit
	Tryon	Tryon Thermal Belt Chamber of Commerce Annual Horse Show
Late April	Asheville	Carolina Mountains Arabian Show
Early May	Statesville	Tarheel Classic Horse Show
	Asheville	Southern Horse Fair
Mid-May	Burnsville	Annual Jaycees Championship Rodeo
	Monroe	Mid-Atlantic Championship rodeo
	Raleigh	NC All Arabian Horse Show
	Southern Pines	Sandhills Combined Driving Event
Late May	Union Grove	Old Time Fiddlers' and Bluegrass Festival
	Raleigh	Southern States Morgan Horse Show

	Tryon	Tryon Horse Show
Early June	Raleigh	Capitol Dressage Classic
	Wilmington	Sudan Horse Patrol Coastal Plains Horse Show
Mid-June	Love Valley	Junior Showdown
	Raleigh	Appaloosa Horse Show
Late June	Love Valley	Frontier Week Rodeo
	Andrews	Annual Wagon Train
	Raleigh	NC Hunter Jumper Association Show
	Pembroke	Racking Horse Show
Early July	Hayesville	Clay County Rodeo
	Sparta	Annual Lions Club Horse Show
Mid-July	Love Valley	Junior Showdown
	Raleigh	NC State 4-H Horse Show
	Waynesville	Waynesville Lions Club Horse Show
Late July	Waynesville	Trail Riders Horse Show
	Raleigh	NC All Amateur Arabian Horse Show
	Raleigh	Raleigh Summer Hunter Jumper Show
	Asheville	Carolina Mountains Summer All Arabian Horse Show
	Blowing Rock	Blowing Rock Charity Horse Show
	Tryon	Tryon Thermal Belt Chamber of Commerce Annual Horse Show
Early August	Robbins	Annual Farmer's Day & Wagon Train
	Waynesville	Fraternal Order of Police Horse Show
Early September	Mocksville	Lake Myers Rodeo
Mid-September	Monroe	Mid-Atlantic Championship rodeo
	Raleigh	NC State Championship Charity Horse Show
Late September	Asheville	Carolina Mountains Fall All Arabian Horse Show
Early November	Pinehurst	Fall Horse Carriage Drive
Late November	Raleigh	Eastern Quarter Horse of NC-Show & Futurity

NORTH DAKOTA

Early March	Valley City	North Dakota Winter Show and Rodeo
Mid-April	Grand Forks	Native American Days
Late May	Medora	Dakota Cowboy Poetry Gathering
Early June	Bottineau	Old Time Fiddlers Contest
	Trugby	North Dakota State Championship Horse Show
Mid-June	Williston	Fort Union Trading Post Rendezvous
Late June	Jamestown	Fort Seward Wagon Train
	Mandan	Frontier Army Days
Early July	Dickinson	Rough Rider Days
Early August	Sentinel Butte	Champions Ride Rodeo, Home on the Range for Boys

Mid-August	West Fargo	Pioneer Days
September	Bismarck	United Tribes International Pow-Wow

OHIO

Mid-January	Dayton	World's Toughest Rodeo
October	Columbus	All-American Quarter Horse Congress

OKLAHOMA

Mid-January	Oklahoma City	International Finals Rodeo
Late January	Tulsa	Longhorn World Championship Rodeo
February-May	Oklahoma City	Parimutuel Thoroughbred Horse Racing
February-December	Sallisaw	Parimutuel Mixed Breed Horse Racing
Early February	Guthrie	Bullmania
Late February	Guthrie	Timed Event Championship of the World
Mid-March	Oklahoma City	4-H and FFA Junior Livestock Ranch Rodeo
Late March	Tulsa	Oklahoma Quarter Horse Spring Show
Early April	Guthrie	Lazy E Reining Classic
	Fairview	Farm and Ranch Day
Mid-April	Guthrie	Lazy E Spring Barrel Racing Futurity, 89er Day Celebration and Rodeo
	Oklahoma City	Centennial Horse Show
Late April	Waurika	Rattlesnake Hunt
	Mangum	Rattlesnake Hunt
May-July	Oklahoma City	Parimutuel Quarter Horse Racing
Early May	Guthrie	Ben Johnson Pro Celebrity Rodeo
	Guymon	Pioneer Day Celebration and Rodeo
Late May	Guthrie	Oklahoma Cattlemen's Range Roundup
	Boise City	Santa Fe Trail Daze
June-September	Bixby	Moonlight Horseback Rides
Early June	Claremore	Will Rogers Stampede Rodeo
Mid-June	Pawhuska	Ben Johnson Memorial Steer Roping Contest
Early July	Oklahoma City	Hunter-Jumper Horse Show
Mid-July	Pawhuska	International Roundup Club Cavalcade
	Tulsa	Palomino World Show, National Pinto Horse Show
Late July	Shawnee	National High School Finals Rodeo
Early August	Tulsa	American Junior Quarter Horse World Finals
Mid-August	Vinita	Will Rogers Rodeo
Late August	Oklahoma City	National American Miniature Horse Show
	McAlester	Oklahoma State Prison Rodeo
September-December	Oklahoma City	Parimutuel Thoroughbred Horse Racing
Early September	Guthrie	Women's National Finals Rodeo

Mid-September	Oklahoma City	Rodeo and Horse Show of the State Fair of Oklahoma
Late September	Tulsa	Rodeo and Horse Show of the Tulsa State Fair
	Chelsea	Bushyhead's World's Richest Calf Roping
Early October	Oklahoma City	Grand National and World Championship Morgan Horse Show
Mid-October	Guthrie	National Finals Ranch Rodeo
	Oklahoma City	Festival of the Horse
Late October	Guthrie	PRCA Prairie Circuit Finals Rodeo
Early November	Claremore	Will Rogers Days
	Oklahoma City	World Championship Quarter Horse Show
	Guthrie	U.S. Team Roping Championship
Late November	Guthrie	National Finals Steer Roping
December	Bixby	Holiday Rides
Early December	Oklahoma City	World Championship Barrel Racing Futurity
Mid-December	Oklahoma City	Sunbelt Cutting Futurity Horse Show
Late December	Tulsa	Holiday Circuit Quarter Horse Show

OREGON

Mid-January	Portland	"World's Toughest Rodeo"
	Salem	Oregon Stallion Showcase
Late January	Portland	AG Show
Mid-May	Tygh Valley	Tygh Valley Rodeo
	Rogue Valley	Rogue Valley Roundup
Early July	St. Paul	St. Paul Rodeo
	Molalla	Molalla Buckeroo
Mid-July	Prineville	Crooked River Roundup
	Philomath	Frolic and Rodeo Festival
Late July	Joseph	Chief Joseph Days Rodeo
Early August	Madras	Jefferson County Fair and Rodeo
Late August	Grant County	Grant County Fair and Rodeo
	Salem	Oregon State Fair and Rodeo
Mid-September	Pendleton	Pendleton Roundup
Mid-October	Klamath Falls	Klamath Basin Horse Show
Late October	Madras	Cutting Horse Show
Early November	Hillsboro	Pacific International Livestock Show

PENNSYLVANIA

Late May	Devon	Devon Horse Show and County Fair
Early June	New Castle	Pennsylvania Appaloosa Association Horse Show
Mid-June	Meridian	Butler Rodeo
	New Castle	Arabian Horse Show
	New Castle	Tri-State Reining Association Horse Show
Late June	Shartlesville	Professional Rodeo

	Kellettville	Trail Ride
	Ridgeway	Independence Day Festival
Mid-July	Benton	Frontier Days and Rodeo
Late July	Mercer	Jefferson Township Fair
	Driftwood	Tom Mix Roundup
	Kellettville	Allegheny Mountain Championship Rodeo
	New Castle	Quarter Horse Association Horse Show
	New Castle	Lawrence County Charity Horse Show
Mid-August	No. Washington	North Washington Rodeo
	New Castle	Quarter Horse Association Horse Show
Late August	Shartlesville	Professional Rodeo
Early September	Coatesville	Buffalo Bill Days & Western Horse Show
Mid-October	Harrisburg	Pennsylvania National Horse Show
Late October	Harrisburg	Pennsylvania 4-H Horse Show
	Uniontown	Old-Time Fiddlers State Championship

SOUTH CAROLINA

Late March	Aiken	Steeplechase and Hunt Meet
	Santee	Elloree Trials
Early May	Inman	IPRA World Championship Rodeo
Early August	Blacksburg	Ed Brown Rodeo
Late September	Inman	IPRA World Championship Rodeo
Early October	Olanta	Fall Festival and Rodeo
Early November	Camden	Colonial Cup International Steeplechase Racing

SOUTH DAKOTA

Late January	Rapid City	Black Hills Stock Show and Rodeo
Early June	Lake City	Fort Sisseton Historical Festival
Early July	Belle Fourche	Black Hills Roundup
Late July	Mitchell	Corn Palace Stampede Rodeo
Early August	Deadwood	"Days of '76"
Early October	Custer State Park	Buffalo Roundup Days

TENNESSEE

Late April	Paris	World's Biggest Fish Fry Rodeo
Mid-May	Nashville	Iroquois Steeplechase
Early June	Wartrace	Strolling Jim Memorial Horse Show Heyday
Late June	Smithville	Old Time Fiddlers' Jamboree and Crafts Festival
Late July	Clarksville	Walking Horse Show
Early August	Murfreesboro	International Grand Championship Walking Horse Show
Late August	Gray	Appalachian Fair Shelbyville Tennessee Walking Horse National Celebration
Late September	Memphis	Midsouth Fair and Exposition, Rodeo

TEXAS

Mid-January to Early February	Bandera Fort Worth	Bandera County Junior Livestock Show Southwestern Exposition Stock Show and Rodeo
Early February	El Paso San Antonio	Southwestern Livestock Show and Rodeo Annual Livestock Show and Rodeo
Mid-February to Early March	Houston	Houston International Livestock Show and Rodeo
Late February to Early March	Brownsville	Charro Days
Spring Weekends	Kerrville	Longhorn Trail Drive
March	Lubbock	ABC Rodeo
Mid-March	San Angelo Shamrock	Stock Show and Rodeo St. Patrick's Day Celebration
Late March	Palestine	Dogwood Trials Festival and Rodeo
April-September	Mesquite	Mesquite Rodeo (Every Friday and Saturday)
Early April	Woodville	Dogwood Festival: Western Weekend Rodeo
Mid-April	San Antonio	Fiesta San Antonio
Mid-May to Mid-September	Amarillo	Cowboy Morning
May	Dallas	Western Days PRCA Pro Rodeo
Early May	Del Rio	PRCA Rodeo and Bull Riding
Mid-May	Laredo	Frontier Days
Late May	Bandera	Funtier Days and Parade
Early June	Fort Worth	Chisholm Trail Roundup
Late June	Stamford Pecos	Texas Cowboy Reunion West of Pecos Rodeo (PRCA Approved)
Mid-July	Pampa	Top O' Texas Rodeo Denison Western Days
Early August	Dalhart	XIT Rodeo and Reunion
Mid-September	Fort Worth	Pioneer Days Celebration
Late September	Dallas	State Fair Texas Rodeo and Livestock Show
Early October	Gonzalez	Come and Take it Celebration
Early October	Waco	Heart O' Texas Fair and Rodeo
Early December	Forth Worth	World Championship National Cutting Horse Futurity
Late December	Fort Worth Odessa	Texas Pro Rodeo Circuit Finals Rodeo Sand Hills Hereford and Quarter Horse Show and Rodeo

UTAH

Mid-January	Snow Basin Ogden	Utah Winter Games Winter-Hof Festival
January	Moab	Annual Winter Festival
Early June	Roosevelt	Rough Rider Days
June	Ogden	National Old Time Fiddle Contest

Mid-June	Helper	Butch Cassidy Days
	Coalville	Annual Coalville Fishing Derby and Balloon Rally
Mid-June	Moab	Canyonlands PRCA Rodeo/Butch Cassidy Days
Late June	Vernal	Amateur Rodeo
	Ft. Duchesne	Celebration "Ute Indian Powwow"
	Price	Black Diamond Stampede PRCA Rodeo
Early July	Oakley	Oakley Rodeo
Mid-July	Salt Lake City	"Days of '47" Celebration and Rodeo
	Vernal	Dinosaur Roundup Rodeo
	Nephi	Annual Ute Stampede
Late July	Ogden	Pioneer Days Rodeo and Celebration
	Logan	Festival of the American West
	Wellington	Wellington Rodeo
Early August	Morgon	Morgon County Rodeo and Fair
	Kaysville	Davis County Fair and Livestock Show
	Trichfield	Sevier County Fair Garden City Annual Bear Lake Raspberry Days
	Castle Dale	Emery County Fair Logan Cache County Fair and Rodeo
	Price	Carbon County Fair and International Day
	Spanish Fork	Utah County Fair Heber City Wasatch County Fair and Rodeo
Mid-August	Minersville	Beaver County Fair
	Tooele	Tooele County Fair
	Monticello	San Juan County Fair and Junior Livestock Show
	Hurricane	Washington County Fair
	Duchesne	Duchesne County Fair and Rodeo
	Park City	Park City Ride 'n' Tie
	Park City	North American Supreme Championship Sheep Dog Trials
	Orderville	Kane County Fair
	Coalville	Summit County Fair
	Ogden	Weber County Fair
	Junction	Piute County Fair
	Loa	Wayne County Fair
	Randolph	Rich County Roundup Days
Late August	Tremonton	Box Elder County Fair and Rodeo
	Manti	Sanpete County Fair
Early September	Cedar City	Iron County Fair
	Moab	Annual La Sal Mountain Horse and Rider Endurance Race
	Parowan	Iron County Fair Park City Lewis Field Rodeo Challenge
	Hooper	Tomato Days and Rodeo
	Cedar City	Southwest Livestock Show
	Salt Lake City	Utah State Fair
	Brigham	Peach Days

Mid-September	St. George	Dixie Roundup
Early November	St. George	Southern Utah Endurance Ride
Mid-November	Moab	Western Poetry Writers Party and Reading Celebration
	Ogden	PRCA Rodeo Late November
	Moab	Mountainman Rendezvous
	Santa Clara	Thanksgiving Day Rodeo
Mid-December	Salt Lake City	Crossroads of the West Gun Show

VERMONT

Late May	Manchester	Annual Bennington County Horse Show
Early to Mid-July	Killington	Killington Mountain Horse Show
Mid-July	Killington	Vermont Summer Classic-Equestrian Summer Showcase
Late July	Waitsfield	Valley Class-Equestrian Summer Showcase
Late July to Early August	Waitsfield	Sugarbush Horse Show
Early August	Waitsfield	Mad River Festival-Equestrian Summer Showcase
	Bellows Falls	Annual Vermont State Championship Old Time Fiddlers' Contest
Mid-August	Stowe	Midsummer Festival-Green Mountain Equestrian Finale
Late August	Stowe	Midsummer Festival-Green Mountain Equestrian Finale
Late September	Bridport	Krawczyk Horse Farm Open Barn and Sale

WASHINGTON

Early June	Roy	Roy Pioneer Rodeo
	Bickleton	Alder Creek Picnic and Rodeo
Mid-June	Bremerton	Little Britches Rodeo
	Colville	Fort Colville Days and Rodeo (PRCA)
Late June	Sedro Woolley	Logger Rodeo
	Darrington	Darrington Timber Bowl Rodeo
Early July	Oakville	Oakville Rodeo
Mid-July	Cheney	Cheney Rodeo (PRCA)
Late July	Deer Park	Deer Park WRA Rodeo
Mid-August	Omak	Stampede and Suicide Race (PRCA)
Late August	Bremerton	Kitsap County Fair
Late August-Early September	Walla Walla	Southeastern Washington Fair & Frontier Days
	Ellensburg	Ellensburg Big 4 PRCA Rodeo
Early September	Puyallup	Western Washington Fair and Rodeo
Mid-September	Othello	Othello PRCA Rodeo
Late September	Ridgefield	Northwest Cutting Horse Association Annual Futurity Festival

WISCONSIN

Early January	Milwaukee	"World's Toughest Rodeo"
Late February	Cable	American Birkebeiner (cross-country ski event)
May to September	Black River Falls	Indian Powwows
Early May	Statewide	Fishing Season Opener
June	Fond du Lac	Walleye Weekend Festival on Lake Winnebago
	Milwaukee	Wonago World Championship Rodeo
July	Manawa	PCRA Rodeo Madison All-American Rodeo of Rodeos (PRCA)
	Spooner	Heart of the North Rodeo (PRCA)
	Lake Michigan	Fishing Contest and Festivals Shore
	Eagle	Summer of the Farm
Early September	Sauk City-Prairie du Sac	State Cow Chip Throwing Contest
	Praire du Chien	Villa Louis Carriage Classic

WYOMING

Early January	Ft. Washakie	Eastern Shoshone PowWow
	Lander	Wyoming State Winter Fair
Mid-January	Torrington	Shriners' Invitational Cutter Races
February	Riverton	Wild West Winter Carnival
Early February	Gillette	Coors PRCA Rodeo
Mid-February	Casper	WRA Rodeo
Early March	Casper	WRA Rodeo
Late March	Cheyenne	LCCC Golden Eagle Rodeo
Early May	Rock Springs	All Girl Rodeo
Mid-May	Rock Springs	Flaming Gorge Fishing Derby
	Rock Springs	Sweetwater Frontier Days
Late May	Shoshoni	Old Timer's Fiddlers' Contest
	Jackson	Old West Days
	Jackson	Jackson Hole Shoot Out
	Dubois	Annual Pack Horse Race
	Douglas	All Girl Roping
	Riverton	Wyoming Indian High School PowWow
	Ethete	Yellowcalf memorial PowWow
	Ft. Washakie	Shoshone Relay Association Horse Races
All Summer	Cody	Cody Nite Rodeo
June	Saratoga	Saratoga Cutting Horse Contest
Early June	Hulett	Hulett Rodeo
	Casper	Pack Horse Races
	Casper	Cowboy State Games
	Greybull	Days of '49
	Gillette	Cowboy State Games
	E. Wilkins St. Park	Pack Horse Races
	Douglas	All Girl Roping

	Gillette	Old Timer's Rodeo
	Gillette	WCHA Cutting Horse Show
	Greybull	Days of '49
	Evanston	Bear River Spring Classic Horse Show
	Douglas	Wyoming Paint Horse Show
	Sheridan	Big Horn Mountain Horse Show
Mid-June	Cody	Frontier Festival BBHC
	Encampment	Woodchoppers' Jamboree
	Gillette	High Energy Quarter Horse Show
	Grand Targhee	Annual High Country Cowboy Festival
	Ten Sleep	Wyoming Junior Rodeo
Late June	Cody	Plains Indian Powwow
	Lander	Wind River Indian Reservation Summer Rodeo and Pow-wow Days, Fort Washakie
	Lovell	Mustang Days Celebration
	Douglas	Jackalope Days and High School Rodeo Finals
	Cody	Powwow at Buffalo Bill Historical Center
	Pinedale	Western Heritage Festival
	Ft. Washakie	Eastern Shoshone PowWow and Rodeo
	Cody	Annual Plains Indian PowWow
	Pinedale	Roundup Rodeo
Early July	Afton	Parade and Night Rodeo
	Green River	Flaming Gorge Days
	Cody	Cody Stampede Days
	Ten Sleep	Ten Sleep Rodeo
	Laramie	Laramie Jubilee Days
	Lander	Pioneer Days and July Fourth Parade
	Guernsey	Old Timer's Rodeo
	Jackson	Fourth of July Celebration
	Big Piney	Chuck Wagon Days
	Pinedale	Chuck Wagon Days
	Buffalo	Wild West Show
	Medicine Bow	Medicine Bow Days
	Jackson	Mountain Man Rendezvous
Mid-July	Jackson	Cowboy Poetry Gathering
	Sheridan	Sheridan WYO Rodeo Sundance Memorial Youth Rodeo
	Wright	Wright Roundup and Rodeo
	Lusk	Legend of Rawhide / Vigilante Day
	Pinedale	Green River Rendezvous
Late July	Riverton	Riverton Rendezvous
	Jackson	Teton County Fiddle Contest
	Jackson	Teton County Fair
	Cheyenne	Cheyenne Frontier Days
	Gillette	Old Timer's Rodeo
	Rock Springs	Red Desert Rodeo
August	Wheatland	Platte County Fair and Rodeo
Early August	Casper	Central Wyoming Fair
	Lusk	Niobrara County Fair, Rodeo and Dance
Mid-August	Riverton	Fremont Fair and Rodeo

	Buffalo/Sheridan	Bozeman Trail Days
	Sheridan	Eric Mygard Memorial Woodchopper's Rodeo
	Dubois	Wind River Rendezvous
	Douglas	National Old Timer's Rodeo
Late August	Douglas	Wyoming State Fair/Mixed Team Roping
	Jackson	Old Timer's Rodeo
	Jackson	Trout Unlimited National Convention
	Buffalo	Johnson County Fair and Rodeo and Klondike Rush
Early September	Evanston	Little Britches Rodeo
	Evanston	Cowboy Days Rodeo
	Cheyenne	Cowboy All Weather 1000
	Meeteetse	Labor Day Rodeo
Late October	Casper	PRCA Pro Rodeo
	Gillette	Snaffle Bit Futurity
Late November	Gillette	NRCA Rodeo
Late December	Ft. Washakie	Eastern Shoshone PowWow
	Casper	Cowboy Shootout

ALBERTA

Late March	Edmonton	Northlands Super Rodeo (PRCA)
Mid-April	Lethbridge	Whoop-Up Quarter Horse Circuit
	Trochu	FCA Indoor Rodeo
Late April	Red Deer	Silver Buckle Rodeo
	Grande Prairie	Whispering Pines Rodeo
Late May	Red Deer	Westerner Spring Quarter Horse Show
Early June	Calgary	The National Horse Show, Spruce Meadows
Late June	Ponoka	Ponoka Annual Stampede
Early July	Calgary	The Invitational Horse Show, Spruce Meadows
	Calgary	Calgary Exhibition and Stampede
Mid-July	Red Deer	Westerner Days
	Edmonton	Edmonton's Klondike Days
Late July	Medicine Hat	Exhibition and Stampede
	Lethbridge	Whoop-Up Days
Early September	Calgary	The Masters Horse Show, Spruce Meadows
Mid-November	Edmonton	Canadian Finals Rodeo (PRCA)

BRITISH COLUMBIA

Mid-January	100 Mile House	Ski-A-Thon, Hills Health and Guest Ranch
Early February	Lac La Hache	Lac La Hache Winter Carnival
Late February	100 Mile House	Kahlua Boo Treasure Hunt on Skis
	Wells	Heritage Ski Festival
April	Kamloops	Kamloops Professional Indoor Rodeo
May	Clinton	Clinton Rodeo
	100 Mile House	Little Britches Rodeo
	Metchosin	Luxton Rodeo

	Lillooet Lake	Lillooet Lake Rodeo
	Keremeos	Elks Rodeo
	Kelowna	Black Mountain Rodeo
	Falkland	Falkland Stampede
	Princeton	Princeton Rodeo
	Ashcroft	Ashcroft Rodeo
Late May	Cloverdale	Cloverdale Rodeo
June	Riske Creek	Riske Creek Rodeo
	Prince George	Prince George Rodeo
	Doe River	Doe River Rodeo
	Smithers	Smithers Kinsmen Rodeo
Early June	Horsefly	Horsefly Rodeo
	Hudson's Hope	Hudson's Hope Rodeo
Late June	Williams Lake	Williams Lake Stampede Rodeo
July	Anaheim Lake	Anaheim Lake Stampede
	Clinton	Clinton Old Timers' Rodeo
	Summerland	Stra Rodeo
Early July	Bella Coola	Bella Coola Annual Rodeo/Dance
Mid-July	Quesnel	Annual Bill Barker Days Festival
Late July	Bridge Lake	Bridge Lake Stampede
August	Port St. John	North Peace Rodeo and Fair
	Dawson Creek	Dawson Creek Rodeo
Early August	100 Mile House	Great Cariboo Ride
Mid-August	Riske Creek	Riske Creek Rodeo
Late August	Riske Creek	Jack Palmentier Frontier Days
September	Merritt	Merritt Rodeo

WE WANT TO HEAR FROM YOU

Guidebooks are like children, constantly growing and changing. One of the joys of writing this guide has been receiving many letters from our readers. Your thoughts and ideas are important to us.

Top travel guides are great largely because of the contents and suggestions their authors receive from readers, so tell us about your favorite ranch and your not-so-favorite ranch. Tell us about new ranches that you have discovered.

We would also enjoy knowing what additional information you would like to see in future editions. We hope that you will continue to share your comments with us. You may write to us at:

Kilgore's Ranch Vacations
P.O. Box 7041
Tahoe City, Lake Tahoe
California 95730

Other Books from John Muir Publications

Asia Through the Back Door, 4th ed., 400 pp. $16.95 (available 7/93)

Belize: A Natural Destination, 336 pp. $16.95

Costa Rica: A Natural Destination, 2nd ed., 310 pp. $16.95

Elderhostels: The Students' Choice, 2nd ed., 304 pp. $15.95

Environmental Vacations: Volunteer Projects to Save the Planet, 2nd ed., 248 pp. $16.95

Europe 101: History & Art for the Traveler, 4th ed., 350 pp. $15.95

Europe Through the Back Door, 11th ed., 432 pp. $17.95

Europe Through the Back Door Phrase Book: French, 160 pp. $4.95

Europe Through the Back Door Phrase Book: German, 160 pp. $4.95

Europe Through the Back Door Phrase Book: Italian, 168 pp. $4.95

Europe Through the Back Door Phrase Book: Spanish & Portuguese, 288 pp. $4.95

A Foreign Visitor's Guide to America, 224 pp. $12.95

Great Cities of Eastern Europe, 256 pp. $16.95

Guatemala: A Natural Destination, 336 pp. $16.95

Indian America: A Traveler's Companion, 4th ed., 448 pp. $17.95 (available 7/93)

Interior Furnishings Southwest, 256 pp. $19.95

Mona Winks: Self-Guided Tours of Europe's Top Museums, 2nd ed., 448 pp. $16.95

Opera! The Guide to Western Europe's Great Houses, 296 pp. $18.95

Paintbrushes and Pistols: How the Taos Artists Sold the West, 288 pp. $17.95

The People's Guide to Mexico, 9th ed., 608 pp. $18.95

Ranch Vacations: The Complete Guide to Guest and Resort, Fly-Fishing, and Cross-Country Skiing Ranches, 2nd ed., 396 pp. $18.95

The Shopper's Guide to Art and Crafts in the Hawaiian Islands, 272 pp. $13.95

The Shopper's Guide to Mexico, 224 pp. $9.95

Understanding Europeans, 272 pp. $14.95

Undiscovered Islands of the Caribbean, 3rd ed., 288 pp. $14.95

Undiscovered Islands of the Mediterranean, 2nd ed., 224 pp. $13.95

Undiscovered Islands of the U.S. and Canadian West Coast, 288 pp. $12.95

Unique Colorado, 112 pp. $10.95 (available 6/93)

Unique Florida, 112 pp. $10.95 (available 7/93)

Unique New Mexico, 112 pp. $10.95 (available 6/93)

A Viewer's Guide to Art: A Glossary of Gods, People, and Creatures, 144 pp. $10.95

The Visitor's Guide to the Birds of the Eastern National Parks: United States and Canada, 410 pp. $15.95

2 to 22 Days Series
Each title offers 22 flexible daily itineraries useful for planning vacations of any length. Aside from valuable general information, included are "must see" attractions *and* hidden "jewels."

2 to 22 Days in the American Southwest, 1993 ed., 176 pp. $10.95

2 to 22 Days in Asia, 1993 ed., 176 pp. $9.95

2 to 22 Days in Australia, 1993 ed., 192 pp. $9.95

2 to 22 Days in California, 1993 ed., 192 pp. $9.95

2 to 22 Days in Europe, 1993 ed., 288 pp. $13.95

2 to 22 Days in Florida, 1993 ed., 192 pp. $10.95

2 to 22 Days in France, 1993 ed., 192 pp. $10.95

2 to 22 Days in Germany, Austria, & Switzerland, 1993 ed., 224 pp. $10.95

2 to 22 Days in Great Britain, 1993 ed., 192 pp. $10.95

2 to 22 Days Around the Great Lakes, 1993 ed., 192 pp. $10.95

2 to 22 Days in Hawaii, 1993 ed., 192 pp. $9.95

2 to 22 Days in Italy, 208 pp. $10.95

2 to 22 Days in New England, 1993 ed., 192 pp. $10.95

2 to 22 Days in New Zealand, 1993 ed., 192 pp. $9.95

2 to 22 Days in Norway, Sweden, & Denmark, 1993 ed., 192 pp. $10.95

2 to 22 Days in the Pacific Northwest, 1993 ed., 192 pp. $10.95

2 to 22 Days in the Rockies, 1993 ed., 192 pp. $10.95

2 to 22 Days in Spain & Portugal, 192 pp. $10.95

2 to 22 Days in Texas, 1993 ed., 192 pp. $9.95

2 to 22 Days in Thailand, 1993 ed., 180 pp. $9.95

22 Days (or More) Around the World, 1993 ed., 264 pp. $12.95

Automotive Titles

How to Keep Your VW Alive, 15th ed., 464 pp. $21.95

How to Keep Your Subaru Alive 480 pp. $21.95

How to Keep Your Toyota Pickup Alive 392 pp. $21.95

How to Keep Your Datsun/ Nissan Alive 544 pp. $21.95

The Greaseless Guide to Car Care Confidence, 224 pp. $14.95

Off-Road Emergency Repair & Survival, 160 pp. $9.95

TITLES FOR YOUNG READERS AGES 8 AND UP

"Kidding Around" Travel Guides for Young Readers

All the "Kidding Around" Travel guides are 64 pages and $9.95 paper, except for **Kidding Around Spain** and **Kidding Around the National Parks of the Southwest,** which are 108 pages and $12.95 paper.

Kidding Around Atlanta

Kidding Around Boston, 2nd ed.

Kidding Around Chicago, 2nd ed.

Kidding Around the Hawaiian Islands

Kidding Around London

Kidding Around Los Angeles

Kidding Around the National Parks of the Southwest

Kidding Around New York City, 2nd ed.

Kidding Around Paris

Kidding Around Philadelphia

Kidding Around San Diego

Kidding Around San Francisco

Kidding Around Santa Fe

Kidding Around Seattle

Kidding Around Spain

Kidding Around Washington, D.C., 2nd ed.

"Extremely Weird" Series for Young Readers. Written by Sarah Lovett, each is 48 pages and $9.95 paper.

Extremely Weird Bats

Extremely Weird Birds

Extremely Weird Endangered Species

Extremely Weird Fishes

Extremely Weird Frogs

Extremely Weird Insects

Extremely Weird Mammals (available 8/93)

Extremely Weird Micro Monsters (available 8/93)

Extremely Weird Primates

Extremely Weird Reptiles

Extremely Weird Sea Creatures

Extremely Weird Snakes (available 8/93)

Extremely Weird Spiders

"Masters of Motion" Series for Young Readers. Each title is 48 pages and $9.95 paper.

How to Drive an Indy Race Car

How to Fly a 747

How to Fly the Space Shuttle

"X-ray Vision" Series for Young Readers. Each title is 48 pages and $9.95 paper.

Looking Inside Cartoon Animation

Looking Inside Sports Aerodynamics
Looking Inside the Brain
Looking Inside Sunken Treasure
Looking Inside Telescopes and the Night Sky

Multicultural Titles for Young Readers
Native Artists of North America, 48 pp. $14.95 hardcover
The Indian Way: Learning to Communicate with Mother Earth, 114 pp. $9.95
The Kids' Environment Book: What's Awry and Why, 192 pp. $13.95
Kids Explore America's African-American Heritage, 112 pp. $8.95
Kids Explore America's Hispanic Heritage, 112 pp. $7.95

Environmental Titles for Young Readers
Rads, Ergs, and Cheeseburgers: The Kids' Guide to Energy and the Environment, 108 pp. $12.95
Habitats: Where the Wild Things Live, 48 pp. $9.95
The Kids' Environment Book: What's Awry and Why, 192 pp. $13.95

Ordering Information
Please check your local bookstore for our books, or call 1-800-888-7504 to order direct from us. All orders are shipped via UPS; see chart below to calculate your shipping charge to U.S. destinations. **No P.O. Boxes please; we must have a street address to ensure delivery.** If the book you request is not available, we will hold your check until we can ship it. Foreign orders will be shipped surface rate unless otherwise requested; please enclose $3.00 for the first item and $1.00 for each additional item.

For U.S. Orders

Totaling	Add
Up to $15.00	$4.25
$15.01 to $45.00	$5.25
$45.01 to $75.00	$6.25
$75.01 or more	$7.25

Methods of Payment
Check, money order, American Express, MasterCard, or Visa. We cannot be responsible for cash sent through the mail. For credit card orders, include your card number, expiration date, and your signature, or call (800) 888-7504. American Express card orders can be shipped only to billing address of cardholder. Sorry, no C.O.D.'s. Residents of sunny New Mexico, add 6.125% tax to total.

Address all orders and inquiries to:
John Muir Publications
P.O. Box 613
Santa Fe, NM 87504
(505) 982-4078
(800) 888-7504